Frommer's™

Paris
Free &
dirt cheap

by Anna Brooke

WILEY

A John Wiley and Sons, Ltd, Publication

UK Publisher: Sally Smith
Executive Project Editor: Daniel Mersey
Commissioning Editor: Mark Henshall
Development Editor: Rhonda Carrier
Project Editor: Hannah Clement
Photo Research: David Cottingham
Cartography: Tim Lohnes

Photos on p. xiv © Claude Thibault/Alamy; p. 4 © Dan Barka/Alamy; p. 14 ©
Directphoto/Alamy; p. 52 © Peter Forsberg/Alamy; p. 90 © Kader Meguedad/
Alamy; p. 110 © David Frazier/Alamy; p. 142 © Michael Jenner/Alamy; p. 176
© Oliver Knight/Alamy; p. 262 © Mark Bassett/Alamy; p. 296 © Chad Ehlers/
Alamy

Wiley also publishes its books in a variety of electronic formats. Some content
that appears in print may not be available in electronic books.
British Library Cataloguing in Publication Data
A catalogue record for this book is available from the British Library
ISBN: 978-0-470-68332-3
Typeset by Wiley Indianapolis Composition Services
Printed and bound in Great Britain by TJ International Ltd
5 4 3 2 1

CONTENTS

LIST OF MAPS

About the Author

British born and bred **Anna Brooke** is an adopted Parisian. She's been there for 11 years and spends her days in cafés in the heart of the 12th. When she's not writing for Frommer's (for whom she also wrote *Paris & Disneyland with your family*, and three other guidebooks), she freelances for *Time Out*, the *Financial Times*, *Sunday Times* travel, Dorling & Kindersley and Alastair Sawdays. She also sings and composes electro music for her band MONKEY ANNA (www.myspace.com/musicmonkeyanna), does keyboard and vocals for the electronic rock group Pet Trap (www.myspace.com/pettrap) and acts in the occasional French film. She can be contacted on annaebrooke@yahoo.fr.

Acknowledgments

Thanks to Mark Henshall, Fiona Quinn and Scott Totman for their top-notch editing and undying patience. Un Grand Merci to all of my friends—you know who you are; and to my family, who, as always, provided unconditional support. Last but not least, thanks to mon chéri Pascal Chind for putting up with the hours of research—he'd always suspected I was a cheapskate, but this book proved it!

Dedication

To Robin

How to Contact Us

In researching this book, we discovered many wonderful places—hotels, restaurants, shops, and more. We're sure you'll find others. Please tell us about them, so we can share the information with your fellow travellers in upcoming editions. If you were disappointed with a recommendation, we'd love to know that, too. Please write to:

Frommer's Paris Free & Dirt Cheap, 1st Edition
Wiley Publishing, Inc. ● 111 River St. ● Hoboken, NJ 07030-5774

An Additional Note

Please be advised that travel information is subject to change at any time—and this is especially true of prices. We therefore suggest that you write or call ahead for confirmation when making your travel plans. The authors, editors, and publisher cannot be held responsible for the experiences of readers while travelling. Your safety is important to us, however, so we encourage you to stay alert and be aware of your surroundings. Keep a close eye on cameras, purses, and wallets, all favourite targets of thieves and pickpockets.

Other Great Guides for Your Trip:

Frommer's Paris Day by Day

Frommer's Paris & Disneyland Resort With Your Family

Frommer's Paris 2010

Pauline Frommer's Paris

Free & Dirt Cheap Icons & Abbreviations

We also use **four feature icons** that point you to the great deals, in-the-know advice, and unique experiences that separate urban adventurers from tourists. Throughout the book, look for:

FREE   Events, attractions, or experiences that cost no more than your time and a swipe of your Metrocard.

FINE PRINT   The unspoken conditions or necessary preparations to experience certain free and dirt cheap events.

★   The best free and dirt cheap events, dining, shopping, living, and exploring in the city.

   Special events worth marking in your calendar.

Frommers.com

Now that you have this guidebook to help you plan a great trip, visit our website at **www.frommers.com** for additional travel information on more than 4,000 destinations. We update features regularly to give you instant access to the most current trip-planning information available. At Frommers. com, you'll find scoops on the best airfares, lodging rates, and car rental bargains. You can even book your travel online through our reliable travel booking partners. Other popular features include:

- Online updates of our most popular guidebooks
- Holiday sweepstakes and contest giveaways
- Newsletters highlighting the hottest travel trends
- Podcasts, interactive maps, and up-to-the-minute events listings
- Opinionated blog entries by Arthur Frommer himself
- Online travel message boards with featured travel discussions

Crowds enjoy a free concert near the Eiffel Tower on 14th July, Bastille Day, France's National Day.

THE BEST THINGS IN LIFE ARE FREE

Thank goodness for plastic! If money had to be carried around as coins, Paris would be cacophonous, pockets would scuff the floor and Louis Vuitton handbags would come with wheels. Many Parisians are so moneyed that they keep whole sectors of the economy alive. Smart designer shops, gilded palace-hotels, chic 'n' sparkly bars all add up to make the City of Lights one giant playground for the world's most wealthy.

But just because we don't always have the cash for the edible gold at the Crillon (although go to its restaurant, Les Ambassadeurs, for lunch and you might be pleasantly surprised, p. 71) that doesn't mean Paris leaves us high and dry. The French capital takes a lot of pride in its reputation as the world's cultural hub *par excellence* and to sustain that image it offers plenty of freebies. There's a vast choice of art, dance, music and drama that can be enjoyed for the price of showing up. That's not to mention the free annual cultural festivals—more than most capitals can muster in a lifetime—and the 40-plus museums and galleries that are *gratis* all year round.

And the fun continues at mealtimes. Parisians love food and also love nothing more than claiming a good-value eatery as their own. French cuisine takes pride of place of course, but there's also increasingly good, dirt-cheap ethnic food: Chinatown serves up the cheapest Chinese, Vietnamese and Thai food around (with meal-sized portions costing an average of 7€); rue Sainte-Anne (75002) is Japanese HQ, with canteens hawking noodle soups from 8€; the Marais is a great spot for 5€ falafel; and the Louis Blanc area of the 10th lures you with Paris's spiciest achievement, a Sri Lankan vindaloo at a bargain 8€.

In this book, I'll also show you how to increase your IQ for free (or at least look like you're trying) in some of Paris's most influential learning centres. For your strolling pleasure, there are also given dirt-cheap walking itineraries that will show you the city in a new light. And on top of that, I share my favourite free film venues and sports activities, including kayaking in the Bassin de la Villette, and list the bars and party zones that will allow you to let rip without denting your bank account.

The cost of living in Paris has risen, so taking advantage of its low-cost resources is a must. So don't hesitate to kit out your pad with giveaway goods—there's nothing more satisfying than freeing up someone's lounge by helping them offload something you need for yours. Don't think twice about shopping for glad rags in a charity or vintage shop, and don't worry about trying to beat the system—it's a priceless exercise that can rekindle the most cynical Parisian's love of the city, even when the ubiquitous dog do-do, traffic jams and snobby shop assistants are getting them down.

Few cities evoke so much promise and emotion as Paris—and few let cliché hang over them to such a degree, like mist on the Seine: To the couples lip-locked on park benches, the unfaltering beauty of the river, the exquisite cuisine, the breathtaking museums, the chi-chi boutiques and the idyllic cafés, I hope that this book will add an image equally enduring—that of affordability. For Paris is an every-man's kind of city—a place to love, cherish and squeeze the juice from at every opportunity!

The Venus de Milo glimpsed amid a moving throng in the Louvre Museum.

THE BEST OF FREE & DIRT CHEAP PARIS

Most of us are wary of fabulous bargains, convinced that some unidentified small print will leap up and bite us at any moment. But Parisians are very lucky—despite the city's reputation as a bastion of luxury, it also offers an endless supply of cheapies and freebies to get through (575 of which are in this book), from open-air film festivals and free kayaking along the Canal Saint-Martin, to budget dinners and complimentary concerts. And Paris's compact size means you don't have to go far to find a bargain. Exhausted the freebies in one *arrondissement*? Just stroll over to the next.

1 Best Entertainment Bets

● **Best Free Concerts and Cheap Booze:** Music-lovers of all sorts meet over a swift *bière* or three at **L'International** (5/7 Rue Moret, 75011; ℂ **01 49 29 76 45**), revered for its eclectic programme of live music that includes *chanson*, rock, indie, pop, electro, hip hop and folk. It's a welcome addition to the scene, with free entry and a host of exciting bands. See p. 81.

● **Best Open-Air Film Festival:** Drive-ins are logistically not possible in Paris, but picnic-ins are. Between mid-July and mid-August, just 1€ gets you into the Parc de la Villette's Cinéma en Plein Air film festival (Prairie du Triangle, 211 Ave. Jean-Jaurès, 75019), where cult movies are projected onto Europe's biggest inflatable movie screen and locals turn up in their thousands, picnic basket and blankets in hand. See p. 23.

● **Best Place for Half-Price Theatre Tickets:** Paris might not be Broadway or the West End, but it's got a thriving theatre scene that sees everything from slapstick French comedy to experimental dance, absurdist drama and classic vaudeville. **Le Kiosque Théâtre**, at Place de la Madeleine (75008), Place des Ternes (75011) and in front of the Montparnasse train station (75014) sells half-price tickets for same-night shows. See p. 36.

● **Best Free Jazz Awards Ceremony: Le Sunset-Sunside** (60 Rue des Lombards, 75001; ℂ **01 40 26 46 60**) has seen more great jazz musicians pass through its door since 1983 than most Parisians have had hot croissants. In early September a few more of them—up-and-comers, mostly—fight it out here over three free nights. See p. 30.

● **Best Free Radio Gig:** Journalist Isabelle Dhordain invites three of France's top popsters for a live radio show of mix 'n' match *chanson*, pop and rock. The **Pont des Artistes** is open to the public most Wednesdays and is a fine occasion to see the stars of French pop and *chanson* (Maison de Radio France, 116 Ave. du Président Kennedy, 75016; ℂ **32 30** (0.34€/min). See p. 28.

● **Best Free Classical Music Lunch:** Thursday lunchtimes need never be dull again thanks to the exquisite **Petit Palais** (Ave. Winston Churchill, 75008;

℮ **01 53 43 40 00**), which aside from being a top-notch fine arts museum holds free lunchtime music concerts in conjunction with the Radio France programme D'Une Rive à l'Autre (12.30–1.30pm, October–June). See p. 30.

• **Best Ballet Setting:** When in *gai* Paris, one must embrace the literati. Nowhere can you rub shoulders with more of them so enjoyably than at the gorgeous **Opéra Garnier** (Place de l'Opéra, 75009; ℮ **08 92 89 90 90**), the iconic 19th-century structure that inspired the tale of the Phantom of the Opera, the structure of which is frequently likened to a wedding cake. Whilst the upper-crust pays for the top spots (around 80–100€), cheap seats can be bought from just 5€! See p. 226.

2 Best Cheap Eats

• **Best Free Couscous:** On Friday and Saturday nights, Samir, owner of **La Choppe** (40 Rue de Clignancourt, 75018; ℮ **01 46 06 20 10**) serves lashings of scrumptious couscous to anyone who has bought a drink (from 8:30pm). See p. 55.

• **Best New York-Style Investment of 2.50€:** For cheap protein and a quick burst of "God Bless America", head to **La Mosaïque** (corner of Rue du Roi de Sicile and Rue Vieille du Temple, 75004), which sells tasty hotdogs dripping in all the right ketchup and mustard. See p. 62.

• **Best Fast-Food Alternative:** **Chibby's Diner** (9 Rue Jaucourt, 75012; ℮ **01 44 73 98 18**) is a cool, 1950s-style diner off the beaten track, with lip-smackingly good burgers at seriously affordable prices. See p. 67.

• **Best Luxury (but Cheap) Pâtisserie:** No *pain au chocolat* can top **Ladurée's** (75 Ave. des Champs-Elysées, 75008; ℮ **01 40 75 08 75**), especially their pistachio version striped with pistachio paste and rich chocolate. See p. 162.

• **Best Romantic Investment of 15€:** When *l'amour* is in *zee* air (and even when it isn't), Anne and Sébastien's wine bar **Rouge Passion** (14 Rue Jean-Baptiste Pigalle, 75009; ℮ **01 42 85 07 62**) is a perfect setting for sharing cheese and cold-meat platters (15€) over a vintage from the downstairs cellar (from 4€). See p. 78.

• **Best Throwback to *la Vieille France*:** Have you just stepped back in time, or are you in a larger-than-life comic book? Dining at **Chez Maurice** (26 Rue des Vinaigriers, 75010; ✆ **01 46 07 07 91**)—one of the last family-run, red-gingham bistros on the block—is a lesson in cheap eating (three-course menus from 9.50€ to 19€). It's also home to some of the most colourful characters you'll ever set eyes on. See p. 60.

● **Best Chinese Food Ever:** The chefs at **Les Pâtes Vivantes** (46 Rue du Faubourg Montmartre, 75009; ✆ **01 45 23 10 21**) chop off long spaghetti-like ropes of noodles in front of your eyes—a novel touch that becomes even more impressive once you've tasted the deliciously perfumed dishes. Food is dirt-cheap (around 9€ for a huge main, 11€ and 13€ *prix fixe* menus), but if you can come on your birthday, it's free! See p. 64.

● **Best Currywurst and Beer:** A funky Franco-German number off the Bastille Ledru-Rollin drag, **Café Titon** (34 Rue Titon, 75011; ✆ **09 53 17 94 10**) serves the best (okay, the only) German currywurst in Paris (5.50€), best washed down with a beer (3.50€). Its French cuisine is top too: just 10€ for the *plat du jour* and a coffee at lunchtime. See p. 56.

● **Best Cheap Oysters:** Seafood and eat it at **La Dame des Huîtres** fish-stand (86 Rue Lemercier, 75017; ✆ **01 46 27**

81 12) where a platter of 12 oysters fresh off the boat from Brittany will only set you back 16€. Perfect with a smooth glass of white. See p. 57.

● **Best Lunchtime Splurge:** A jewel-incrusted red carpet and an oversized crystal chandelier set the tone for a meal at **Baccarat's Cristal Room** (11 Place des Etats-Unis, 75116; ✆ **01 40 22 11 10**). The grandeur of the surroundings is reassuringly matched by chef Thomas L'Hérisson's top-class cuisine, which at lunchtime will set you back around 55€ for two courses—an affordable splurge that also gives you free access to the glistening Baccarat museum. See p. 71.

● **Best Honest French Bistro: Chez Prosper** (7 Ave. du Trône, 75011; ✆ **01 43 73 08 51**) heaves day and night—the sign of a good eating place. So what's the formula? Just a vibrant atmosphere, speedy service and hearty, honest food at low prices (9€–15€). See p. 57.

● **Best Pizza Experience:** Quirky pizzas (think goats' cheese and sliced duck breast or bacon and pineapple chutney) made from organic ingredients, delivered to your chosen picnic spot by the Canal Saint-Martin—two good reasons to go to the funky **Pink**

Flamingo (67 Rue Bichat, 75010; © **01 42 02 31 70**). See p. 70.

- **Best Vegetarian Restaurant:** In the all-veggie **Potager du Marais** (22 Rue Rambuteau, 75004; © **01 42 74 24 66**), unadventurous rabbit food is prohibited in favour of genuinely flavoursome vegetarian cuisine, several dishes of which are gluten-free. See p. 69.

3 Best Drinking & Partying

- **Best Cheap Bar Crawl:** The whole area is artfully decayed, but for dusk 'til dawn festivities (and drinks from just 3€), you can't do better than the shabby-chic bars, restaurants and clubs of the **Rue Oberkampf** (75011), Paris's ultimate, cheapskater's night out. See p. 75.

- **Best Left Bank Café: La Palette** (43 Rue de Seine, 75006; © **01 43 26 68 15**) encompasses everything that is stereotypically Left Bank—intellectual punters, frescoes on the walls and ceilings, good food and romance—and turns them into something wholly unique. See p. 76.

- **Best Funky Surprise Bar:** Nation is hardly party central, yet hidden on a residential street behind the Monoprix supermarket, **Les Pères Populaires** (46 Rue de Buzenval, 75020; © **01 43 48 49 22**) entertains nighthawks with generous measures of cheap alcohol (wine 2€, beer 2.40€) and hip tunes into the wee hours. See p. 77.

- **Best Wine Bar:** Wine buffs fight for one of just four tables at the **Le Baron Rouge** (1 Rue Théophile Roussel, 75012; © **01 43 43 14 32**), known for its 50-strong wine list and animated evenings, when punters spill out onto the street around the Marché Aligre. See p. 78.

- **Best Multidisciplinary Party Den:** Set inside France's first cooperative building, **La Bellevilloise** (19 Rue Boyer, 75020; © **01 46 36 07 07**) reels in more people than the surrounding bars put together, with its numerous drinking holes, restaurants, club, exhibition space and concert hall. The cherry on the cake is that many events are free. See p. 79.

- **Best Floating Party Boat:** Rocking takes on a whole different meaning on the **Batofar** (11 Quai François Mauriac, 75013; © **09 71 25 50 61**)—a converted lighthouse boat that has been making waves on Paris's night scene for the last few years, maintaining its reputation with a constant stream of top French and international DJs. See p. 79.

● **Best Live Electro Rock and Pop Venue:** For music-lovers, **Nouveau Casino** (109 Rue Oberkampf, 75011; ✆ **01 43 57 57 40**) is a cherished, albeit commercial venue with great acoustics and an A-list of acts and DJs who splice rock, dub, garage, rock and pop into the wee hours. See p. 79.

4 Best Living Wisely

● **Best Free Lectures:** You won't find a finer setting for your free lectures than the majestic **Collège de France** (11 Place Marcelin Berthelot, 75005; ✆ **01 44 27 12 11**). Neither will you find a more impressive crop of experts teaching the public subjects, including maths, astrophysics, chemistry, philosophy, and mediaeval literature. See p. 112.

● **Best Free Dance Classes:** From June to September the banks of the Seine below the Institut du Monde Arabe become an open-air dance floor for wannabe dirty-dancers who come to learn salsa, Argentinean tango and rock 'n' roll. Square Tino Rossi, 75005. http://tangoargentin-eric.site.voila.fr.

● **Best Relaxing Massage:** At **Serenity Passport** (63 Rue Victor Hugo, 92300 Levallois-Perret; ✆ **01 47 37 56 59** or **06 11 91 09 38**), Stéphane's healing hands have mastered Indian and Tibetan massaging techniques to replenish your energies and loosen your tightened muscles. The Tibetan singing bowls are a weird but wholly relaxing experience whereby the bowls resonate at frequencies that traverse your body.

● **Best Cheap Sleep Under 100€ a Night:** Who needs a mint on their pillow and a 300€ bill when you can stay at trendy **Mama Shelter** (109 Rue de Bagnolet, 75020; ✆ **01 43 48 48 48**) in the villagey Saint-Blaise *quartier* from 90€ a night per room. For your moolah, you get an iMac computer, CD and DVD player and free WiFi in the room, plus oodles of street cred.

● **Best Really Cheap Sleep Under 50€:** As far as youth hostels go, **St Christopher's Inn** (159 Rue de Crimée, 75019; ✆ **01 40 34 34 40**) rocks. Not satisfied with just cleaning up the area (on the old industrial Canal de l'Ourcq), it provides hip décor, a happening bar (in the men's loo the urinals are shaped like women's lips) and has excellent bedrooms (single-sex and mixed) for an average of 26€ per person/night.

● **Best Free Haircut:** For locks *en vogue* head to the **Académie**

Jean-Yves Bouley (156 Blvd. Saint-Germain, 75006; ℂ 01 53 10 82 31), where students cut and colour men and women's hair for free on Mondays and Tuesdays (call for an appointment).

5 Best Shopping

- **Best Vintage Clothes Hunting:** Compared to other countries, France caught onto the vintage bandwagon late in the day. But **Vertiges et Rag** (83/85 Rue Saint-Martin, 75004; ℂ 01 48 87 34 64) makes up for lost time with some of the best and cheapest selections of vintage-wear Paris has to offer.

- **Best Funky Second-Hand Furniture:** The **Depôt-vente Rue de Lagny** (81 Rue de Lagny, 75020; ℂ 01 43 48 86 64) brings the price of desirable antique furniture down to levels real people can afford.

- **Best English-Language Bookshop:** For book signings, poetry readings, hours flicking through second-hand books and an annual literature festival that attracts more than 5,000 visitors, there's only one address: **Shakespeare & Co** (37 Rue de la Bûcherie, 75005; ℂ 01 43 25 40 93).

- **Best Affordable Award-Winning Chocolatier:** The best-quality chocolate in Paris is sold by **François Pralus** (35 Rue Rambuteau, 75004; ℂ 01 48 04 05 05)—voted best *chocolatier* by Gault & Millau—who supplies his shop with cacao from his own organic plantation in north Madagascar.

- **Best Department Store for Tightwads:** Mention **Tati** (4 Blvd. de Rochechouart, 75018; ℂ 01 55 29 52 20) to Parisians and you'll get mixed reactions. Some shopping snobs (no matter how frugal) won't set foot there, others swear by it. Whatever your opinion, its ranges and prices are unbeatable.

6 Best Exploring

- **Best Free Bike Tour:** The City of Lights is an adventure in itself, but especially at night, when its lights sparkle. Every Friday night at 9.30pm, around 300 nighthawks gather in front of the Mairie de Paris (Hôtel de Ville, 75004) on their bicycles for a 3-hour nocturnal sightseeing tour. (www.parisrandovelo.com.) See p. 131.

Paris's Top Five Best-Kept Free Secrets

① At the beginning of the 20th century the Théâtre de la Ville went by a whole other name: Le Théâtre Sarah Bernhardt, named after its beautiful actress owner. What very few people realise is that **Sarah's dressing room** (Théâtre de la Ville, 2 Place du Châtelet, 75004; ✆ **01 48 87 54 42**) has been meticulously preserved and can be visited for free, by appointment only, during the *entr'acte* of a performance. Despite works done on the theatre in 1968, which robbed us of her lounge, anteroom and bathroom, you'll find the remaining parts (wooden panels, Empire-style mouldings, a sofa decorated with a sphinx, a bathtub and a mercury cast mirror) wonderfully intriguing.

② Marie Curie's contribution to science and research into radioactivity earned her a posthumous place in Paris's prestigious Panthéon, and her museum, the **Musée Curie** (1 Rue Pierre et Marie Curie, 75005; ✆ **01 56 24 55 31**), is where all of her Nobel prize-winning research took place. Today it makes for a short but fascinating visit—a safe one too, apparently, since the place was decontaminated.

③ At first glance the **Musée de la Préfecture de Police** (Hôtel de Police du 5ème arr., 4 Rue de la Montagne-Ste-Geneviève, 75005

● **Best Peaceful Museum with a Tearoom:** All municipal museums in Paris are free, but for an unrivalled setting, hidden from the rest of the world, the **Musée de la Vie Romantique** (16 Rue Chaptal, 75009; ✆ **01 55 31 95 67**) takes the biscuit. A charming 18th-century mansion that once housed Rossini, Chopin, George Sand and Delacroix, it has a rose garden and a summer tearoom where decadence is yours for the price of a cuppa. See p. 182.

● **Best Romantic Garden for Canoodling:** You're in the thick of touristy Paris near Les Invalides, but an oasis of calm is at your disposal, with tree-lined alleys and pristine lawns freckled with some of Rodin's most famous sculptures. The **Musée Rodin**'s gardens (79 Rue de Varenne, 75007; ✆ **01 44 18 61 10**), which can be accessed for just 1€, are arguably the most romantic spot in the city. See p. 196.

(2nd floor); ℂ **01 44 41 52 50**) looks a little old and musty, but you'll soon realise that it all adds to the intrigue of the objects on show: Old arrest warrants, nooses, murderous machines and gruesome-looking weapons—all part of our city's violent under-belly from the 19th century to today.

④ The **Serres d'Auteuil** greenhouses (1 Ave. Gordon Bennett, 75016; ℂ **01 40 71 74 00**) are almost the spitting image of the Grand Pal-ais's glass roof—a fabulous example of 19th-century ingenuity worthy of a visit in their own right. Plant-lovers should also come along to see the 5,000 species of tropical and sub-tropical plants.

⑤ Paris's underbelly is a veritable Swiss cheese that has been used over the years for mining, mushroom farming and the metro. Under the Hôpital Cochin, you can visit part of that network at the **Ecomusée des Anciennes Carrières des Capucins** (Hôpital Cochin, Rue du Faubourg Saint-Jacques, 75014; ℂ **01 43 89 78 03**)—a 1.2km section lovingly attended to by the SEADACC, an association of devotees who take you past wells, fountains and interesting graffiti by appointment.

- **Best Bohemian Afternoon Walk:** The old Canal Saint-Martin (75010) ran through central Paris, lined with empty warehouses, dishevelled cafés and masses of housing potential. This was too much for any self-respecting bohemian to refuse, and nowadays the waterway bustles with shabby-chic bars, restaurants, bistros and boutiques, making it the ultimate haunt for anyone looking to study the Parisian race of *bobos* (Bourgeois-Bohemians) and perhaps become one for the evening. See p. 272.

- **Best Free Hidden Museum:** Rodin's star pupil Antoine Bour-delle is the subject of the **Musée Bourdelle** (16–18 Rue Antoine Bourdelle, 75015; ℂ **01 49 54 73 73**), a treasure-trove that contains the artist's old work-shop and some spectacular larger-than-life statues which feel like mythological giants about to awake from a 1,000-year slumber. See p. 180.

Free jazz; performers by the Seine during the summer festival.

ENTERTAINMENT

Compared to what's on offer in other capitals, entertainment in Paris has always been relatively low-cost—a throwback from the time when *théâtre du boulevard* and *café-théâtre* were the people's entertainment. That doesn't mean you won't get stung with a 100€ ticket to see your favourite band at the Stade de France, but it does mean that when you know where to look, it's easy to find top-tier drama, comedy, dance, theatre, concerts and film for little more than the price of your metro ticket. Even high-brow haunts such as the Opéra Garnier and the Théâtre de la Ville (p. 35), known for their world-class musical and dance productions, offer a range of prices, some low enough to attract impoverished students and the unemployed. You might be up in the gods or behind a pillar, but at least you'll hear what's going on!

Another fine way to stay entertained is to attend TV and radio recordings. TV game shows in particular always need lively audiences. Then there's the music: Paris is awash with jazz, classical, electro, pop and rock sounds, and a startling amount can be listened to for free.

In short, lack of money won't stop you from experiencing fabulous Paris entertainment; the problem will be choosing where to start.

Free & Dirt Cheap Calendar of Events

Paris is an all-year-round kind of town: Not a month goes by without various citywide or district-orientated events, many of them free of charge. In addition to the listings below, Paris's Tourist Office (℃ 08 92 68 30 00; www.parisinfo.com) and the Paris Ile-de-France tourist board (CRT pidf; www.nouveau-paris-ile-de-france.fr) have the lowdown on most events.

The CRT pidf also joins forces with trendy radio station NOVA to edit an annual summer festivals magazine, Enjoy, which lists (in English and French) all the top free and dirt-cheap festivals (music, film, dance, circus and art) between June and September. The guide can be downloaded from the CRT's website.

JANUARY

Fête des Rois   The Epiphany (6th January) is France's sweet 'n' sticky post-Christmas celebration—the last chance to overeat before Easter and a means of organising a quick get-together between friends, family or colleagues before the year really kicks in. On the menu are Galettes des Rois—delicious puff-pastry pies filled with almond paste, sold in bakeries throughout the month. Watch out for the *fève* (a porcelain figurine)—whoever gets it in their slice is king for the day and has to wear a paper crown.

Mobile Film Festival `FREE`   Keeping the creative juices flowing in Paris is a year-round affair that starts with this 'virtual', two-week public film festival (usually first two weeks of January). Hopefuls enrol in October, and then have until early January to produce a short film shot entirely on their mobile phone. If you're short on cash, it's your chance to win 1,500€. There's no festival venue or award ceremony as such—just a website, and the chance to have your work seen by millions, including Nouvelle Vague director Claude Lelouche, who's on the jury. (http://fr.mobilefilm festival.com.)

Paris New Year—Grande Parade de Paris `FREE` There's no district rivalry in Paris at New Year: After a night of jubilant crowds, bangers let off willy-nilly and fireworks over the Eiffel Tower, this showy affair on New Year's Day keeps everyone happy by taking its processions of choirs, marching bands, decorated floats and performers elsewhere. The location moves each year (previous locations have included the Grands Boulevards, Montmartre and the Trocadéro) so check with the tourist office (see above) or the Mairie de Paris (www.paris.fr).

FEBRUARY

Carnaval de Paris `FREE` Homemade razzmatazz (floats, costumes, papier-mâché monsters and anything gaudy or noisy, or preferably both) hits the streets during Paris's annual carnival, which will be into its 14th year in 2011. Joyous throngs follow, and there are plenty of snack joints. The fun usually kicks off at 3pm; the starting point changes each year, but it usually finishes off by the Hôtel de Ville. (www.carnaval-paris.org.)

Chinese New Year `FREE` Come February (and sometimes January), the Chinatown south of the Latin Quarter has lions and dragon parades and live martial arts demonstrations in honour of the lunar new year. The colourful chaos fills the streets around Avenue d'Ivry and Avenue de Choisy (75013) all day. Metro: Tolbiac.

★ **Salon de l'Agriculture** A must for any animal- and food-lover, this two-week festival brings the countryside to Paris, with prize-winning bulls, cows, horses, sheep, rabbits, dogs, pigs, and billy goats gruff to pet. Tickets aren't cheap (around 14€), but once you're inside, cheese- and foie gras-makers join wine-makers and bakers for one giant celebration of France's *terroir*, and they usually give free tasters away. Almost 700,000 people attend, so get here early in the morning to avoid the crush. The President also traditionally pays an annual visit; it was here, in 2008, that Nicolas Sarkozy famously said "Casse-toi pauve con" ("Piss off idiot") when a visitor refused to shake his hand. Mid-February–early March, Porte de Versailles exhibition centre (Paris Expo), 75015. Daily 9am–7pm. Metro: Porte de Versailles. (www.salon-agriculture.com.)

MARCH

Festival Chorus FREE   Over the years, this two-week music festival has gathered great momentum, attracting big names and emerging talent to concerts across the 92 *département* (Paris's western suburb). The centre stage is La Défense's Magic Mirror concert hall (a former big top from Belgium), where free lunchtime (midday–2pm) and evening concerts drag the suits out of their corporate, high-rise hidey holes to listen to funky sounds by names such as French favourites Mickey 3D. Usually last two weeks of March. Parvis de la Défense, 92000. Metro/RER: La Défense. (www.chorus92.fr.)

National Cheese Day

We all know how attached the French are to their cheeses—especially the really smelly ones, made from *lait cru* (unpasteurised milk) freshly squeezed from Daisy's udders and left to mature for years under piles of straw. Mould in this parallel universe is the sign of quality, not indigestibility.

In celebration of these facts, the Association des Fromages de Terroir have set up **La Journée National du Fromage** (National Cheese Day, usually around 28th March), when participating *fromagers* across the capital (and France in general) will let you taste their favourite *lait cru* cheese in the hope that you too will fall in love and take some home. For a full list of participants, see www.fromages-de-terroirs.com.

Foire du Trône   A mammoth amusement park that its fans call France's largest country fair, the Foire originated in 957AD, when merchants met with farmers to exchange grain and wine. This hi-tech continuation of that tradition, held on the lawns of the Pelouse de Reuilly, lasts for two months and has a ferris wheel, carousels, acrobats, fire-eaters, and other fun (if tacky) diversions. Admission is free, but you'll need tickets for the rides (a 30€ pass gives access to 22 rides). Bois de Vincennes, 75012. Free shuttle buses from Nation (75012) and Cour St-Emilion (75012). End of March–end of May, midday to midnight. Metro: Porte Dorée or Porte de Charenton. (www.foiredutrone.com.)

★ **Le Printemps du Cinéma**   This three-day film extravaganza attracts crowds of film buffs to participating cinemas across the city, with entry costing just 3.50€ (as opposed to 9€). (www.printemps ducinema.com.)

Semi-Marathon de Paris `FREE`   There's nothing wimpy about opting for this half marathon rather than the full one (held a fortnight later)—everyone still gives their bodies a good pounding and gets manhole-sized blisters. The Esplanade du Château de Vincennes acts as both the start and the finishing line. Athletes cover 21km, starting at 10am and finishing (or at least some of them) just over an hour later, which equates to running at the speed of a bicycle. Sign up or get info at www.semideparis.com. Usually, second or third weekend of March. Metro: Château de Vincennes.

APRIL

Les Dimanches au Galop `FREE`   Pony rides, candy floss and outdoor games attract kids to this famous horseracing event; parents come for the thrill of having a flutter followed by a family picnic. See p. 101 for more details. End April–early May. ℂ **08 21 21 32 13.** (www.dimanchesaugalop.com.) **Hippodrome d'Auteil**, Bois de Boulogne, Route des Lacs, 75016. Metro: Porte d'Auteuil. **Hippodrome de Longchamp**, Bois de Boulogne, Route des Tribunes, 75016. Metro: Porte Maillot then bus 244 to Carrefour de Longchamp. **Hippodrome de St-Cloud,** 1 Rue du Camp Canadien, 92210 Saint-Cloud. Metro: Porte Maillot then bus 244 to Val d'Or.

★ **Free Cone Day de Ben & Jerry's** `FREE`   Get a scoop (or three or four) of your favourite Chunky Monkey, Phish Food, Strawberry Cheesecake or other flavours by the ice-cream giant for free one day in April (loosely corresponding to B&J's birthday). Porkers should head to the Odéon, Mabillon, Saint-Paul and Bastille branches at 7pm, when 500ml pots are also distributed for free. For exact details, join the Twitter site http://twitter.com/benjerryfr. One sure-fire participating address is 44 Rue de Rivoli, 75004. Metro: Hôtel de Ville (usually 1–7pm).

International Marathon of Paris `FREE`   If you thought the half-marathon runners looked exhausted, that's nothing compared to the state of these athletes at the end of their 42.195km jaunt around town. The torture begins on the Champs-Elysées at 9am, then the cortège passes through Bastille, Nation and Vincennes before finishing on avenue Foch. Depending on their speed and endurance, participants arrive at the finishing point 3–4 hours later. If you're feeling sporty, sign up online as early as possible (around 15th September), as prices increase the longer you leave it—the first 16,000 runners pay 58€, the last 5,000 places 90€. Early April. (www.parismarathon.com.)

Musique Côté Jardins FREE   From April to October, free concerts are performed in bandstands in the city's parks (including the Buttes Chaumont in the 19th and the Jardin du Luxembourg; p. 246 and p. 229). ✆ **39 75** (special number). (www.paris.fr.)

MAY

Festival Jazz Saint-Germain-des-Prés FREE   If it's the headliners you're after, you'll have to fork out (tickets are sold on the website for about 30€). However, there's a free, funky, unofficial 'off' programme that includes readings in **Les Editeurs** literary café (4 Carrefour de l'Odéon, 75006; ✆ **01 43 26 67 76**; www.lesediteurs.fr), concerts in the **Sorbonne** and in **Starbucks**, and a 1950s open-top bus (starting at the Place Saint-Sulpice), which skids round town with live music blasting out of its open-top deck. First two weeks in May. ✆ **01 56 24 35 50**. www.festivaljazzsaintgermainparis.com. Saint-Germain-des-Prés, 75006. Metro: Saint-Germain-des-Prés.

Foire de Saint-Germain FREE   Saint-Germain-des-Prés likes to flaunt its cultural prowess during this chic six-week festival (end May–July), marking the beginning of summer in the capital. On the cards are music concerts in the Eglise Saint-Sulpice, the Marché de la Poésie (poetry fair), the Salon des Jeux et de la Culture Mathématiques (a mathematical games fair, for those overflowing with grey matter), the Foire aux Antiquaires (antiques fair), and, for closeted thespians, the Salon du Théâtre on Place Saint-Sulpice. For exact dates, see www.foiresaintgermain.org.

Nuit des Musées FREE   This is Paris's free cultural event par excellence: more than 40 museums stay open from sundown to midnight, often offering visits by torchlight. The Grande Galerie de l'Evolution in the Muséum d'Histoire Naturelle (p. 216), the Musée Rodin (p. 196) and the Grand Palais (p. 228) are particularly impressive. One night in mid-May. (www.nuitdesmusees.culture.fr.)

★ **Le Printemps des Rues** FREE   For two days, all along the Canal Saint-Martin, innovative street-theatre performances create a buzzing atmosphere that will replenish any waning love you might have for the city. Late May or early June. (www.leprintempsdesrues.com.)

JUNE

Fête de la Danse `FREE`   Where does one start when there are more than 30 free dance shows to get through in one day in Paris's annual dance festival? Bercy Village (75012) is a good place, with a cool selection of experimental contemporary dance performed in the street between the shops and restaurants. Alternatively, the parks and gardens of the 1st, 4th, 13th, 19th and 20th become makeshift stages and several dance schools open their doors so you can try out the moves. 7th June. ✆ **01 44 73 93 24**. (www.entrezdansladanse.fr.)

Fête de la Musique `FREE`   Fancy drumming out of your 6th-floor apartment window, or singing opera in a bus shelter? This celebration at the summer solstice is the only day that noise laws don't apply in Paris, so take advantage. Musicians and wannabes pour into the streets to both make and listen to music. Musical parties pop up in virtually all open spaces, with more organised concerts at Place de la Bastille and Place de la République, and in La Villette and the Latin Quarter. 21st June. (www.fetedelamusique.culture.fr.)

Fête du Vélo `FREE`   Ah, Paris and its ubiquitous bicycles! Where would we be without you? To keep the cliché alive, and have tremendous fun at the same time, sign up for a weekend of collective *balades pittoresques* ('scenic rides') across the city. It's free if you bring your own bike—otherwise they can be hired for 1€–3€ (you'll have to leave a cheque as a deposit and show ID). For a list of meeting points, consult www.tousavelo.com. Usually, first weekend in June.

Gay Pride `FREE`   Free entertainment today starts in the metro, where larger-than-life drag queens catch everybody's eye. Then there's the parade—a rainbow swirl of loud music, costumes, seminaked bodies and awareness campaigns such as the fight for tolerance and AIDS education. Usually, last weekend in June.

Les Pestacles   A 'pestacle' is a child-like nickname for a 'spectacle' (show), and fittingly this summer festival in the Parc Floral near the Château de Vincennes and Vincennes Zoo (p. 222) entertains children every Wednesday from early June to late September (from 10:30am), with theatre, music, puppet shows, clowns and games. Entry to the parc is 5€ (free for under-7s); after that, everything is *gratis*, especially if you pack your own picnic. Parc Floral de Paris, Esplanade du Château de Vincennes, Vincennes. RER: A Vincennes.

Ⓒ **39 75**. Metro: Château de Vincennes. (www.lespestacles.fr and www.paris.fr.)

JULY

Bastille Day `FREE`   This celebration of the 1789 storming of the Bastille and birth date of modern France sees street fairs, pageants, fireworks, an air show over the centre and feasts. The day begins with a parade down the Champs-Elysées and ends with fireworks over the Eiffel Tower. The night before (on the 13th) raucous *Bals du Pompiers*—Firemen's Balls (in fire stations across town)—let you whoop it up with the city's firefighters. There are discos, concerts and even the occasional fireman's striptease. 14th July. See for more info www.pompiersparis.fr.

Paris Quartier d'Eté   For four weeks, several venues around the capital (including the Arènes de Lutèce, 75018 and the Sorbonne's Cour d'Honneur, 75006) host pop and orchestral concerts. On the fringes you can catch films, plays, jazz and parades in the Jardin de Tuileries (75001) and the futurist Parc André Citroën (75015). Mid-July–early August. Various locations. Admission varies (usually from 5€ to 30€, depending upon the performance) but under-26s get reduced rates. Ⓒ **01 44 94 98 00** or see www.quartierdete.com.

Paris Slide `FREE`   If you're into skateboards and rollerblading (or you have kids who are), don't miss this annual 'sliding' extrava-ganza, where you can get free lessons and watch experts show off their skills. Mid-July–early September. Pelouse de Reuilly, 75012. Monday to Friday 1:30–7pm; Saturday 2:30–7pm; Sunday 2:30–6pm. Metro: Porte Dorée. (http://mairie12.paris.fr.)

Paris Plages `FREE`   On the initiative of Paris's mayor, Bertrand Delanoë, the quays along the Right Bank of the river Seine (between Quai du Louvre and the Pont du Sully), together with the Bassin de la Villette in the 19th (Metro Jaurès or Stalingrad), are turned into beaches where we can stroll, relax, sunbathe and play water games. Mid-July to mid-August, 7am–midnight. Ⓒ **39 75** (special number). (www.paris.fr.)

★ **Paris Jazz Festival**   A sunny afternoon in a flower-clad park, you, some friends, a picnic and musicians lulling you into a pleas-antly hot stupor… The stunning Parc Floral in Vincennes is the setting for this annual jazz jamboree where names big and small adorn the stage on weekend afternoons. Tickets cost 5€ (2.50€

under-18s, free under-7s), or if you plan to go regularly, splash out on the 20€ pass. Early June–end July. Concerts Saturday and Sunday (3pm and 4:30pm), musical parades 1pm and 3pm. Bois de Vincennes, Esplanade du Château. Metro: Châteaude Vincennes. (http://parisjazzfestival2010.net and www.paris.fr.)

Tour de France `FREE`   The most overabundantly televised bicycle race in the world is decided at a finish line drawn across the Champs-Elysées, 75008. If you can stand the crowds, it's free fun for sports fans. ℰ **01 41 33 14 00**; www.letour.fr. July.

August

★ **Cinéma en Plein Air**   Every August, the Parc de la Villette (p. 246) becomes a giant open-air cinema with the biggest inflatable screen in the world, showing everything from cartoons for kids, old classics and recent releases. Deckchairs can be hired; don't forget your blanket and a picnic. Parc de la Villette, 75019. Metro: Porte de Pantin or Porte de la Villette. Entry 1€. (www.villette.com.)

Le Classique au Vert   For three weeks in August, the Parc Floral buzzes with more than just honeybees: Thousands of Parisians pile into its green expanses for live performances by the city's best classical musicians. Each year has a theme—revolutionary music, *chanson*, the *Années Folles*—and every year just seems to get better. Bring a picnic. Parc Floral, Esplanade du Château de Vincennes, 75012. Metro: Château de Vincennes. ℰ **01 49 57 24 84**; www.classiqueauvert2010.com or www.paris.fr. Saturday and Sunday 4pm (concerts). Admission 5€.

★ **Rock en Seine**   This toned-down Woodstock is a must-see for rock lovers, who can listen to musicians and bands such as Björk, The Offspring, The Prodigy, and The Hives in a huge park that forms part of the Domaine National de Saint-Cloud. End August. Parc Saint-Cloud. Tickets from www.fnac.com or www.rocken seine.com. Metro: Pont de Saint-Cloud. Tramway: 2 Parc de Saint-Cloud. Admission 1 day 46€ or 3-day pass 100€.

September

★ **Festival d'Automne**   Paris welcomes folk home from their August holidays with this fabulous, eclectic autumn festival of modern music, ballet, theatre and modern art in various venues. ℰ **01 53 45 17 00**; www.festival-automne.com. Admission varies (some events free). Mid-September to late December.

Festival Opéra des Rues `FREE`   Make the summer hols last just a wee bit longer by heading for the 12th and 13th *arrondissements*, where the streets become the stage for live opera featuring tenors in wigs, baritones in DJs and pianos on the lawn. Summer ain't over 'til the Fat Lady sings! 75012 and 75013. First weekend in September (usually). (www.festival-automne.com.)

Jazz à la Villette `FREE`   This homage to jazz incorporates dozens of concerts in the Parc de la Villette's Cité de la Musique (p. 101) as well as other venues around town. Past festivals have welcomed Herbie Hancock, Shirley Horn, Michel Portal and other international artists. La Villette, 75019. ℂ **01 44 84 44 84**; www.villette. com and www.cite-musique.fr. Early September. Metro: Porte de Pantin or Porte de la Villette.

Journées du Patrimoine `FREE`   Ever wondered what happened to Paris's old Roman aqueduct? Or what the Hôtel de Ville looks like from the inside? For two days only, various national heritage buildings and private institutions open their doors to the public so nosy parkers can have a good old gander at some of the hidden parts of town. Third weekend in September. (www.journeesdupatrimoine. culture.fr.)

Techno Parade `FREE`   On one day in mid- to late September, you can strut to the rhythm of hard-core electronic sound in streets that look fit to burst at this international techno parade. Meeting point is usually midday at Place Denfert-Rochereau, 75014. Metro/RER: Denfert-Rochereau. (www.technoparade.fr.)

OCTOBER

Les Coulisses du Bâtiment `FREE`   We watch our cities change before our very eyes, yet few of us get the chance to see what's actually happening on the building site—until now. The first weekend in October, the Fédération Française du Bâtiment organises public open days when you can don a hard hat and traipse through the city's most interesting *chantiers* (building sites). Central Paris doesn't always have a site to visit, so tours often take place in nearby suburbs, where urban renewal is rife. (www.ffbatiment.fr.)

★ **Fête des Vendanges de Montmartre** `FREE`   Free your inner country bumpkin at Montmartre's grape-harvest festival, a boozy excuse for a get-together and a chance to taste the Clos de Montmartre (the last wine produced in the city)—if you can afford it (bottles are auctioned off for charity). If not, there's bacchanalian fun to be had in tastings, folk-music blasts through the streets and everyone parties in good, old-fashioned *guinguettes* (dance halls). Eat your heart out, Amélie. Corner of Rue des Saules and Rue Saint-Vincent, 75018. ✆ **01 46 06 00 32/01 42 62 21 21**; www.fetedesvendanges demontmartre.com. 4–5 days in early October. Metro: Lamarck—Caulaincourt or Abbesses.

★ **Nuit Blanche** `FREE` During this all-night sightseeing event, Paris's museums and some otherwise private buildings stay open until dawn. Some cafés offer food throughout the evening, others open early to serve breakfast. The metro stays open late too, and a party vibe reigns on the night-buses. First weekend in October, all over the city. (www.paris.fr.)

NOVEMBER

★ **Beaujolais Nouveau** Parisians eagerly await the yearly release of the first new Beaujolais, that fruity wine from Burgundy. Signs are posted in bistros, wine bars and cafés, which see more customers than at any other time of the year. Third Thursday in November.

★ **Fête de la Science** `FREE` Unravel the mysteries of the universe, electricity, evolution and a myriad of other scientific subjects during the annual, national science festival. The events are centred around Le Village des Sciences, which changes location every year, so check the website for exact details. There are always excellent spin-off, family-orientated events too in affiliated museums. `FINE PRINT` Avoid the crowds by getting here early in the morning or coming at the end of the day. Usually the third weekend in November. (www.fetedelascience.education.gouv.fr.)

Journée Sans Achat `FREE` Set up as a campaign against society's excessive consumerism, the national No Purchasing Day is a godsend for frugal folk. One day at the end of November or early December. (www.casseursdepub.org.)

DECEMBER

Concerts et Chants de Noël Throughout December the city's churches throng with organ concerts, classical religious music and carols. There's a full list at www.paris.fr and most churches advertise in the street. Entry is free but donations are welcome.

Fête de Saint-Sylvestre (New Year's Eve) `FREE`   At midnight, the city explodes: strangers kiss strangers, and the boulevard Saint-Michel, the Champs-Elysées, Montmartre and the Champs de Mars by the Eiffel Tower become virtual pedestrian malls. Nightclubs, theatres and restaurants also offer New Year's entertainment, but unless you fancy splurging for the occasion, they're best avoided. 31st December.

Songes d'une Nuit DV   The city's last film festival of the year promotes documentaries and fictions that have been filmed with a digital camera. Directors from France, Belgium, parts of Africa and other French-speaking countries come over for the festivities and several cinemas host special showings. Prices are no higher than usual—around 9€. Usually the first week in December. Various venues. ✆ **01 42 43 10 30**. (www.altermedia.org.)

1 Music Uncovered

As CD sales drop and the potential of the Internet fails to be fully harnessed, music labels are dropping off like flies. Mainstream sure-fire hits often leave France's most talented pool of artists to swim on against the current, in the hope that times will change.

The silver lining of that cloud, at least for skint music-lovers, is that Paris has a blooming underground scene where, for the time being at least, you can see some of the city's hottest up-and-coming rock and pop bands for little cash. It's not just band-orientated, either. A slew of young musicians have rekindled the flame of *la chanson française* (helped along by First Lady Carla Bruni Sarkozy), in a throwback to the days of Piaf and later pigeon-voiced beauties such as Bardot and Birkin warbling (off-key) to texts by Gainsbourg, and Jacques Brel taking us all into Les Ports d'Amsterdam. Such musicians perform it, guitar in hand, in dives across the city.

Classical, jazz and world music are all up for grabs too, helped along by philanthropic patrons who open their cellars in exchange for the promise of drawing in extra punters. For bars with live music and DJs, see p. 79.

GOOD CHEAP VENUES (CHANSON, ROCK & POP)

Le Bataclan   This former 19th-century Chinese Pagoda (of which only the façade remains, now repainted in its original pastel colours) books some of the hottest jazz, rock, world music and hip hop acts in Paris and from abroad. Prices vary according to the acts (around 18€–50€), but it's often possible to get a deal by booking via www.billet reduc.com.

50 Blvd. de Voltaire, 75011. ✆ **01 43 14 00 39.** www.le-bataclan.com. Metro: Oberkampf.

La Boule Noire   The Black Ball is one of those intimate, divey Parisian haunts that attracts biggies such as the Dandy Warhols, Metallica, Cat Power, Franz Ferdinand and Jamie Cullum. Despite the star-studded line-up, prices tend to hover around the 20€ mark, making this one of the cheapest venues around.

120 Blvd. Rochechouart, 75018. ✆ **01 49 25 81 75.** www.laboule-noire.fr. Concerts vary. Adm varies. Metro: Anvers or Pigalle.

La Flèche d'Or   This former train station, one of the hippest concert halls in Paris, has changed owners more times than Parisians have had hot baguettes. Rumour has it that the newest set (the Mama Shelter hotel opposite (p. 128) and the Le Bataclan (above)) has gutted its innards but will keep the winning formula—dirt-cheap concerts by both up-and-coming French bands and international names, drinks at the gigantic bar and food in the section

Getting Info

There's so much going on, it's hard to keep abreast. Stay in the loop with the help of www.info concert.com and www.gogo paris.com, which select the funkiest venues and offer critiques in both English and French. The new *Paris Magazine* (from newsstands and English-language bookshops) also has good concert listings for mainstream events. Alternatively, the Fnac and Virgin Megastore ticket offices are a wealth of information (p. 29 and p. 165), and French radio stations FIP (105.1FM), NOVA (101.5FM), Le Mouv' (92.1FM) and OuiFM (102.3FM) give handy tip-offs.

For classical-music information try the listings magazines *L'Official des Spectacles* and *Pariscope*, monthy mags *Le Monde de la Musique* and *Diapason* (sold at news-stands). *Cadences* and *La Terrasse* are two free monthlies you can pick up in most concert venues.

overlooking the railway. Either way, the 'golden arrow' looks set to hit the bull's-eye yet again.

102 Bis Rue de Bagnolet, 75020. No telephone. www.flechedor.fr. Metro: Alexandre Dumas, Porte de Bagnolet or Gambetta.

Les Trois Baudets Between 1947 and 1966 this small theatre launched more musical careers than anywhere else (Gainsbourg, Brel, Henri Salvador and Brigitte Fontaine to name but a few), but that didn't stop it from becoming an erotic cabaret, before falling into total disrepair in 1996. After much lobbying by song-master Charles Aznavour, it was finally decided that Paris lacked a theatre for francophone music, and that the cradle of *chanson* should be brought back to launch up-and-coming artists. Today, thanks to an enviable sound system, two bars, a restaurant overlooking Pigalle and a jam-packed programme of rock, electro, folk, *chanson* and slam, it draws us in by the coachload.

64 Blvd. de Clichy, 75018. ℂ **01 42 62 33 33.** www.lestroisbaudets.com. Adm varies (usually 6€–15€). Tues–Sat 6pm–1:30am; Sun 10:30am–5pm. Metro: Pigalle.

FREE RADIO CONCERTS

★ **Concerts FIP—105.1** `FREE` Once or twice a month, Paris's funkiest radio station needs a live audience for some of the most memorable concerts in town, held in the mythical Maison de la Radio. Expect international stars and a homegrown crop along the lines of Emilie Loiseau and Thomas Dutronc, and start queuing at least an hour and a half beforehand to make sure you get in. To keep informed, listen to FIP or see the website.

Maison de Radio France, 116 Ave. du Président Kennedy, 75016. ℂ **01 42 20 12 34** or **32 30** (0.34€/min). www.radiofrance.fr. RER: Kennedy – Radio France.

★ **Le Pont des Artistes sur France Inter** `FREE` A-listers of French *chanson* pass over 'the artists' bridge'—a popular music show on the France Inter channel that has involved names such as Zazie, Sanseverino and Keren Ann. What you don't pay in money, you pay in time—recordings are on Wednesdays at 7:30pm and you have to get there early (before 6:30pm) to get a ticket, then hang around the lobby until the show begins.

Maison de Radio France, 116 Ave. du Président Kennedy, 75016. ℂ **32 30** (0.34€/ min). www.radiofrance.fr. RER: Kennedy – Radio France.

SHOWCASES

Fnac & Virgin Megastore `FREE`   Music megastore competitors Fnac and Virgin also fight it out with their showcases, when (in between the aisles of CDs) the public can watch free 'discovery concerts' of stars that have previously included Marianne Faithfull, Natalie Imbruglia and Johnny Hallyday's son, David. They usually last between 30min and an hour and are followed by a signing. (Find information online at www.fnac.com and www.virginmegastore.fr.)

Jam Session/Carte Blanche—Ecole ATLA `FREE`   Every Wednesday and Thursday from 7–10pm, this modern music school's Woodstock room hosts improvised jam sessions involving its students. The standards vary, but there are always a few pearls.

12 Villa de Guelma, 75018. ℰ **01 44 92 96 36.** www.atla.fr. Metro: Pigalle.

CLASSICAL MUSIC

Ecole Normale de Musique `FREE`   On Tuesday and Thursday lunchtimes (12:30pm) during term time, this music school's final-year students give free classical concerts inside one of Paris's hidden gems, the Salle Cortot, a wood-panelled Art Déco theatre renowned for its stunning design by Auguste Perret (architect of the Théâtre des Champs-Elysées) and its fine acoustics.

114 Blvd. Malesherbes, 75017. ℰ **01 47 63 85 72.** www.ecolenormalecortot.com. Metro: Malesherbes.

★ **Eglise Saint-Eustache** `FREE`   Get here early if you want a seat during the famed Sunday-evening organ concerts (5:30–6pm), frequently performed by the industry's biggest names.

2 Impasse Saint-Eustache, 75001. ℰ **01 42 36 31 05.** www.saint-eustache.org. Metro: Les Halles. RER: Châtelet—Les Halles.

Eglise Saint-Germain l'Auxerrois `FREE`   If I want to treat myself, or my visitors, to a truly Parisian moment, I head to this gorgeous church opposite the Louvre, to listen to the sound of its 40-bell carillon in the tower between the church and the Mairie next door (Wednesday 1:30–2pm). Bell-puller Renaud Gagneux adapted 18th-century harpsichord music for the affair, and it creates a beautiful, delicate sound unlike any of Paris's other chimes. There are benches opposite—perfect for the 30min showdown.

4 Place du Louvre, 75001. ℰ **01 44 50 75 01.** Metro: Louvre Rivoli.

★ **Petit Palais** FREE Every Thursday lunchtime (12:30–1.30pm October–June) there's a free classical concert inside the auditorium of Paris's *très bijou* Petit Palais, in conjunction with Radio France's *D'une Rive à l'Autre* programme. This is one of my favourite lunchtime activities—I make sure I have food I can eat in the outside queue, get to the Palais at 11:30am for a ticket, then head back outside (following the sign for Radio France) to wait for the doors to open.

Ave. Winston Churchill, 75008. ℂ **01 53 43 40 00.** www.petitpalais.paris.fr. Metro: Champs-Elysées—Clémenceau.

Trophées du Sunside FREE

Ever wondered what it's like to attend a jazz awards ceremony? Find out in early September for three nights when winners of the legendary Sunside venue's *soirées découvertes* ('discovery evenings') fight it out for the winning title. Entry is free. Drinks cost around 5€. This is a fine chance to rub shoulders with jazz old-timers checking out the up-and-coming competition. Sunset & Sunside, 60 Rue des Lombards, 75001. ℂ **01 40 26 84 41.** www.sunset-sunside.com. Metro: Châtelet.

JAZZ

Atelier Charonne You can opt for dinner (French cuisine) and a show at this funky new jazz bar (35€), but most people come for the dirt-cheap jazz concerts and reasonably-priced drinks. Gypsy jazz (*Manouche*) acts are the favourites.

21 Rue de Charonne, 75011. ℂ **01 40 21 83 35.** www.ateliercharonne.com. Tues–Sat 7pm–late. Metro: Bastille.

Autour de Midi FREE This jazz club is free on Tuesday nights for its Boeuf du Mardi jam session (9:30pm). Expect big names from the jazz scene to attend: Laurent Epstein, Yoni Zelnik and Bruno Casties… If hunger bites beforehand, you can calm the pangs cheaply in the upstairs restaurant.

11 Rue Lepic, 75018. ℂ **01 55 79 16 48.** www.autourdemidi.fr. Tues–Sun midday–2:30pm, 7pm–late. Metro: Blanche.

2 The Reel Cheap World

Paris loves the cinema. It was invented here, thanks to the Lumière brothers, Louis and Auguste, who are credited with the world's first public movie screening in 1895 on the Boulevard des Capucines. And *le cinéma* loves Paris too—no matter where you put the camera, you get a result, which is why so many production companies merrily ignore the traffic jams and corner off whole roads for days at a time. Perhaps it's this attachment to the seventh art that explains why more tickets are bought here than anywhere else in Europe. It certainly explains the relatively cheap prices (10€ a showing) and the numerous film festivals that either hawk free seats or offer them cheaply.

Paris's cinemas are often as much of an event as the films themselves. The city is packed with quaint *Art et Essai* picture houses and, at the other end of the scale, multiplexes that create an exciting, popcorn-perfumed 'all under one roof' experience.

Carte MK2–UGC

Cinema giants MK2 and UGC have joined forces to offer a monthly pass giving unlimited access to most cinemas across the city (558 in France and more than 700 in the rest of Europe too) for just 19.80€ a month (plus a 30€ joining fee).

With standard tickets costing around 10€, you only have to go to the flicks twice a month or more to get your money's worth—an easy task when there are more than 350 films to see in the city at any one time.

You can sign up for the card online at www.mk2.com/cartes cinema.html.

BEST CINEMA EXPERIENCES

Tickets cost the same practically everywhere you go, so the question is not 'how much?' but 'where?' Whether you're looking for charm or modernity, these are my winners.

★ **Le Grand Rex**   From the outside this place looks like an Art Déco wedding cake, while inside it's like a fairytale theatre, with three tiers and a starlit ceiling (it frequently doubles as a concert hall). The blockbuster programming usually includes big French films and Hollywood action movies that let rip on the (very) big screen.

1 Blvd. Poissonnière, 75002. ℰ **08 92 68 05 96**. www.legrandrex.com. Tickets 9€. Metro: Bonne Nouvelle.

La Géode   The novelty factor here is the shape—a giant silver ball, inside which you'll find an IMAX screen that lets you experience 3D

Meeting the Next Generation of Film-Makers

With Paris and film having such an affinity, it's not surprising that would-be directors swarm here like flies. There's a lot of mediocrity out there (although we all have to start somewhere, right?). But there are also a handful of passionate, talented film-makers bent on carving a name for themselves. Most can be found screening their short films with the Collectif Prod—a young, dynamic association that organises once-or twice-monthly projections in the Café de Paris on Rue Oberkampf (75011). Aside from the films, the room is worth the trip alone: through a door at the back of a nondescript, modern bar you find yourself inside an authentic 1920s back room (rather like an Années Folles bingo hall), kitted out with a stage and a screen.

To find out when the Collectif are screening, sign up for the newsletter at www.collectifprod.fr.

vision via animal and space documentaries, and animated adventures.

26 Ave. Corentin-Cariou, 75019. ☎ **08 92 68 45 40.** www.lageode.fr. Adm: 9€ (12.50€ for 3D films). Metro: Porte de la Villette.

★ **La Pagode** My absolute favourite: a glorious 19th-century replica of a pagoda with a silk-clad ballroom (all its tapestries have an oriental theme) that has been turned into one of the world's most beautiful screening rooms. Films tend to be arthouse, but the occasional mainstreamer inches its way in too.

57 Bis Rue de Babylone, 75007. ☎ **01 45 55 48 48.** Adm: 9€. Metro: Saint-François-Xavier.

UGC Ciné Cité Bercy Plenty of mainstream fodder finds its way onto the 18-screen Bercy, but so does the occasional arty movie. The surrounding Bercy Village is packed with shops, bars and restaurants, so before or after the showing, there's plenty to keep you entertained.

2 Cour Saint-Emilion, 75012. ☎ **08 92 70 00 00.** www.ugc.fr. Adm: 9.90€. Metro: Cour Saint-Emilion.

3 Theatre & Dance

France holds *l'art dramatique* in high regard, and Paris in particular is filled with theatres and *café-théâtres* for all budgets and tastes. As a general rule, théâtre as performed in swanky national establishments is more expensive than *café-théâtre*, which means comedies usually written by lesser-known authors and played by emerging troupes in small private theatres. But that isn't always the case. Most large theatres have cheap seats, available on a first-come first-served basis, plus reductions for the unemployed and students. So if you're hankering for a headliner, try to book well in advance.

That said, Paris has ways of giving savings to last-minuters! Several ticket *kiosques* sell half-price tickets to the evening's performances (box below), and booking via numerous discount websites can considerably ease the pain (Cheap 'n' Chirpy Tickets, p. 36). If these measures aren't enough, try the free theatre offered up by schools and institutions listed below.

When it comes to dance, Paris is avant-garde. Movers and shakers come up with futuristic moves at the drop of a hat and don't hesitate to use them during the numerous cheap festivals that freckle the year. If you're looking for free dance, you'll have to seek out the (high-quality) student presentations in the city's Conservatoires.

FREE THEATRE

Conservatoire National Supérieur d'Art Dramatique `FREE` Tomorrow's talent is here, and three or four times a year (usually before the Christmas holidays, at the end of February, April, and September), they'll show you what they're made of. Performances range from improvisation and Comeddia dell'arte to classic interpretation and dance.

2 Bis Rue du Conservatoire, 75009. ℭ **01 53 24 90 16.** www.cnsad.fr. Metro: Grands Boulevards.

Improvisation at l'Entrepôt `FREE` This cultural centre can do no wrong: known for its top-class music concerts, delicious cuisine, interesting debates and literary evenings, it also serves up lashings of free improvised theatre on the 1st (6:30pm) and 3rd (7:30pm) Sunday of the month. Get here at least 30min beforehand.

7 Rue François de Pressensé, 75014. ℭ **01 45 40 07 50.** www.lentrepot.fr. Metro: Pernety.

CHEAP MAINSTREAM THEATRE

Comédie Française Watching some of Jean-Baptiste Poquelin's (Molière's) greatest works can, on the right night, leave you change from a tenner (prices range from 8€ to 37€)—a little-known fact among Parisians, who misinterpret the pomp and circumstance surrounding the Comédie Française as a sign of high prices. Under-28s should head

Film Festival Lowdown

Paris has a film festival for almost every month of the year, so opportunities to see dirt-cheap movies come summer, winter, spring and autumn.

Winter

January: Salon du Cinéma

Every year this 'behind the scenes' fair attracts cinephiles with the promise of film-set reconstructions and the chance to watch make-up artists, cameramen, stunt-people and even famous directors at work. Usually held in the Grande Halle de la Villette, 75019. ✆ **01 40 03 75 29.** www.salonducinema.com/www.villette.com. Metro: Porte de Pantin.

Spring

March: Festival International de Films de Femmes

This retrospective gives pride of place to shorts, features and documentaries by female directors. Maison des Arts, Place Salvador Allende, 94000 Créteil. ✆ **01 49 80 38 98.** www.filmsdefemmes.com. Metro: Créteil—Préfecture.

March: ★ Printemps du Cinéma

This three-day festival gives you tickets for just 3.50€ all over the city. (www.printempsducinema.com.)

Summer

June: Côté Court

Cross the péripherique (2 stops from metro Porte de Pantin) to Pantin's 104 cinema for 10 days of new and old short films from across the

to the *petit bureau* under the arcades of the Rue Richelieu one hour before the show, where 65 tickets can be purchased for just 5€ (or head for free on the 1st Monday of the month). Visibility won't be great, but you can switch to any free places during the *entr'acte*.

2 Rue Richelieu, 75001. ✆ **08 25 10 16 80.** www.comedie-francaise.fr. Metro: Palais Royal—Musée du Louvre.

Odéon Théâtre de l'Europe   More than a theatre, the Odéon hosts debates on literature, philosophy and European politics—a Euro-enthusiasm that is translated on stage with quality plays in different European languages (including English). As it's one of France's five

world. 104 Ave. Jean Lolive, 93500 Pantin. ℂ **01 48 91 24 91.** www.
cotecourt.org. Metro: Eglise de Pantin.

July: Paris Cinéma

Paris's Mairie-de-Paris-sponsored main film festival covers both fea-
ture-length and short creations. Films are shown in cinemas across the
city (entry is 5€, or buy a 20€ pass which gets you in everywhere).
www.pariscinema.org. ℂ **01 55 25 55 25.**

August: ★ Cinéma au Clair de Lune

A party atmosphere reigns during the annual outdoor Moonlight Cinema festival—the nearest you'll come to a drive-in movie in Paris.
Giant inflatable screens pop up in squares and gardens all over the city
and the programme is always very eclectic. (www.forumdesimages.fr.)

August: 3 jours/3 euros

In this coveted film festival, every cinema in town abides by the three-
day, 3€-a-film rule, aimed at getting families into the cinema at the
end of the summer before term starts again. www.paris.fr.

Autumn

September: L'Etrange Festival

If you're into the weird this should be your first port of call, where you
might just discover that people even stranger than you have made films.
Expect explicit sex, gore and anything unconventional. Forum des Images,
75001. www.etrangefestival.com. Metro/RER Châtelet—Les Halles.

national theatres, prices start as low as 10€ a seat (rising to 32€), with
reductions for students and job-seekers.

Place de l'Odéon, 75006. ℂ **01 44 85 40 00.** www.theatre-odeon.fr. Metro: Odéon.

★ **Théâtre de la Ville**   The stuff churned out of this theatre (two sites)
is consistently inventive and often ground-breaking, with avant-garde
spectacles by both French and international directors. Full-price tickets vary according to the production, but rarely exceed 25€ for the
top seats and 17€ for the lower category.

2 Place du Châtelet, 75004. ℂ **01 42 74 22 77.** www.theatredelaville-paris.com.
Metro: Châtelet.

Cheap 'n' Chirpy Tickets

Seldom do we have to pay full price for tickets if we're not picky about what we see. When I fancy a last-minute show, my first port of call is the half-price Kiosque Théâtre in either **Madeleine** (Place de la Madeleine, 75008; left of the church. Metro: Madeleine), **Ternes** (Place des Ternes, 75017. Metro: Ternes) or **Montparnasse**, in front of the station (Metro: Montparnasse), all open 12:30–8pm Tuesday–Saturday (until 4pm Sunday), www.kiosquetheatre.com. Most Parisian theatres and *café-théâtres* give them unsold tickets for the top seats, which average about 20€ a ticket. *Tip:* Buy a *Pariscope* beforehand and single out four or five plays that tickle your fancy.

If you're lucky enough to be under 30 and can prove it, try one of the **Kiosques Jeunes**, which receive a set of reduced-price tickets for all types of theatre (addresses below). All are open Monday and Thursday 10am–1pm, Monday–Friday 2–7pm. (www.jeunes.paris.fr.)

Marais: 14 Rue François Miron, 75004. ℂ **01 42 71 38 76.** Metro: Hôtel de Ville/Saint-Paul.

Champs de Mars: 101 Quai Branly, 75015. ℂ **01 43 06 15 38.** Metro: Bir Hakeim. Mon–Fri.

Goutte d'Or: Hall du Centre Musical Fleury Goutte d'Or–Barbara, 1 Rue Fleury, 75018. ℂ **01 42 62 47 38.** Metro: Barbès-Rochechouart. Tues–Fri 11am–7pm.

The best cut-rate ticket websites are www.billetreduc.com, www.billetnet.fr, www.mesbillets.com, and http://plateforme.promo-sorties.com.

THEATRE & POETRY IN ENGLISH

★ **Bouffes du Nord**   The stronghold of all things English in Paris (and we're not just talking Shakespeare), Peter Brook's theatre has been providing us with consistently excellent, cutting-edge stuff (with French subtitles) for more than 30 years. Tickets at 12€–26€ are *très correct*!

37 Bis Blvd. de la Chapelle, 75010. ℂ **01 46 07 34 50.** www.bouffesdunord.com. Metro: La Chapelle.

Spoken Word A chance to watch excellent live poetry in English, spoken by expats passionate about the Bard's tongue (perhaps even more so now they're in France). Venues change but many events take place at Culture Rapide.

103 Rue Julien Lacroix, 75020. ℂ **01 46 36 08 04.** www.culturerapide.com. Metro: Belleville or Pyrénées. Evenings usually cost no more than the price of your drink. (http://spokenwordparis.blogspot.com.)

CAFE-THEATRE & COMEDY

When I'm in need of a Gallic giggle, I head to our city's bastion of French comedy, the *café-théâtre*—the *théâtre du peuple*—which really is affordable at less than 20€, especially if you buy a last-minute ticket online or from a *kiosque*. For roughly the same price, *le stand-up* (a French take on British and American stand-up comedy) lets belly-laugh-deprived city-dwellers have a chuckle on the cheap at numerous intimate venues across town.

★ **Café de la Gare** This *café-théâtre* has been putting on wonderfully silly and satirical plays since the 1968 student revolution.

41 Rue du Temple, 75004. ℂ **01 42 78 52 51.** www.cdlg.org. Tickets 10€–25€. Metro: Hôtel de Ville.

Les Blanc Manteaux This Marais institution has been providing top comedy pickings for almost 40 years. There are two shows a night, so if you're up for seeing both, save money by buying a dual ticket beforehand (34€).

15 Rue des Blancs Manteaux, 75004. ℂ **01 48 87 15 84.** www.blancsmanteaux.fr. Tickets 17€ (under-25s and students) and 20€. Metro: Hôtel de Ville.

Le Bout This theatre school has made it its business to prove to the French-speaking world that comedy is as noble an art-form as 'serious' drama. It's not an easy task, but it pulls it off with a quality spread of one-man-show artists, who perform more than 30 funny shows a week. FINE PRINT Seeing two shows in the same night costs just 4€ extra if you buy a dual ticket when you arrive.

62 Rue de Pigalle, 75009. ℂ **01 42 85 11 88.** www.lebout.com. Tickets: 16€, 20€ (2 shows); 8€ and 10€ reduced.

Le Comedy Club Started by comedian Jamel Debbouze as a spin-off of his successful TV show, Le Comedy Club is a career launcher for stand-up acts lucky enough to have made Jamel laugh. If you like

On the Fringe

In Paris, the world's a stage—quite literally, if you're an artist with no theatre to play in. Hence the thriving fringe scene, with enterprising thespians turning everything from factories and multidisciplinary arts squats to old washhouses and train stations into venues for some of the city's (and its suburbs') most creative and probing drama. And the good news is they're dirt-cheap.

The upholder of alternative theatre in northern Paris is the **Lavoir Moderne Parisien** (35 Rue Léon, 75018. ✆ **01 42 52 09 14.** www.rue leon.net. Metro: Château Rouge/Marcadet—Poissonniers). Housed in an old washhouse (*lavoir*) in the Goutte d'Or district, it hosts performances that frequently touch upon the themes of immigration and identity in modern society.

Moving eastwards, **Confluences** (190 Blvd. de Charonne, 75020. ✆ **01 40 24 16 34.** www.confluences.net. Metro: Alexandre Dumas) is a cultural laboratory in an old warehouse, bringing together artists from several disciplines and promoting the works of little-known authors. **La Générale** (10–14 Rue du Général Lasalle, 75019. ✆ **06 24 98 30 51.** www.lagenerale.org. Metro: Belleville or Pyrénées) is also an all-in-one cultural centre in an old factory, with a café, film studios and a theatre.

Across the Périphérique, inside a former metal factory, **Les Laboratoires d'Aubervilliers** (41 Rue Lécuyer, 93300 Aubervilliers. ✆ **01 53 56 15 90.** www.leslaboratoires.org. Metro: Pantin—Quatre Chemins) offers conceptualist productions that frequently mix drama with the disciplines of other resident artists (video, sound, dance, and so on). And lastly, the **Gare au Théâtre** (13 Rue Pierre Sémard, 94400 Vitry-sur-Seine. ✆ **01 55 53 22 22.** www.gareautheatre.com. RER: C Gare de Vitry) is a funky arts centre and theatre in Vitry-sur-Seine's former train station, promoting multidisciplinary and experimental theatre. (www.actesif.com.)

French mockery, a modern take on vaudeville and the glamour of watching folk from the telly, the acts might just make you giggle too.

42 Blvd. de Bonne Nouvelle, 75010. ✆ **08 11 94 09 40.** www.lecomedyclub.com. Show days vary. Tickets vary but usually hover around 20€. Metro: Bonne Nouvelle.

...& IN ENGLISH

★ **La Java**   There comes a time when a little humour from the home-land soothes the soul. For those moments, head to promoter Karel Beer's Laughing Matters nights at the Java, where mirth-merchants from the UK, US and Australia cross the seas to play to needy Anglo-phone audiences.

105 Rue du Faubourg du Temple, 75010. ℰ **01 53 19 98 88.** www.anythingmatters. com. Tickets vary but are usually around 17€. Check website for show dates, which tend to be confirmed at last minute. Metro: République.

LET'S DANCE

★ **Palais Garnier**   Whether you're looking for a traditional ballet along the lines of *Swan Lake* or *The Nutcracker*, or something wholly more modern, the Ballet de l'Opéra National de Paris succeeds in producing both, often with startling stage sets. While seats can set you back as much as 172€, there are always a few available for just 5€–10€—an absolute bargain, even if you do have a pillar to contend with. Seating rules slacken after the *entr'acte* so if you've spotted a free one elsewhere, you can usually claim it for the second act.

Place de l'Opéra, 75009. ℰ **08 92 89 90 90.** www.operadeparis.fr. Metro: Opéra. RER: Auber.

Théâtre National de Chaillot   Few other stages in Paris dare to show such radical modern dance performances as the Chaillot, making it a must for fans *du mouvement*. The price for such a hotbed of experi-mentation is a mere 17.50€–27.50€ for full-price places and 9€–15€ with reductions for under-25s, job-seekers and so on.

1 Place du Trocadéro, 75016. ℰ **01 53 65 30 00.** www.theatre-chaillot.fr. Metro: Tro-cadéro.

FREEBIE DANCE

Conservatoire National de Région de Paris `FREE` The national Conservatoire serves us no less than 300 free shows a year—that's almost one a day (for limited numbers). In December, there are also open days in the Théâtre des Abbesses or Théâtre de la Ville (p. 35).

14 Rue de Madrid, 75008. ℰ **01 44 70 64 08.** www.cnr-paris.com. Metro: Europe.

Conservatoire National Supérieur de Musique et de Danse de Paris `FREE` Come December, the National Ballet students are ready to perform three free shows a week until Christmas, for our pleasure. It's

Free & Dirt Cheap Dance Festivals

Start the year with the experimental **Faits d'Hiver** festival (*℮* **01 42 74 46 00**. www.faitsdhiver.com) and the hip-hop offerings of **Suresnes Cités Danse** (*℮* **01 46 97 98 10**. www.suresnescitesdanse.com), both in January.

May and June bring **Les Rencontres Chorégraphiques de Seine-Saint-Denis** (*℮* **01 55 82 08 10**. www.rencontreschoregraphiques. com)—a meeting point between classical and modern dance; the 'transdisciplinary' **IRCAM Agora festival** (*℮* **01 44 78 12 40**. www. ircam.fr); and **Onze Bouge** (*℮* **01 53 27 13 68**. www.festivalonze.org), which investigates the crossroads between dance, theatre, cinema, street art and music.

Finally, October marks the beginning of the **Rencontres de la Villette** (*℮* **01 40 03 75 75**. www.rencontresvillette.com), a multi-location dancefest that emphasises street dance and urban culture.

a fine way to see both classical and contemporary ballet. Reservation is vital, as every man and his dancing monkey wants a glimpse of Paris's future *étoiles*.

209 Ave. Jean-Jaurès, 75019. *℮* **01 40 40 46 46**. www.cnsmdp.fr. Metro: Porte de Pantin.

4 Cabaret & Circus

Think entertainment in Paris, and nine times out of ten you'll think glitzy cabaret. But be warned—this is Paris's most expensive distraction, especially if you have dinner. But all things circus can be lapped up in Paris—from lions and tigers and bears (oh my!) to avant-garde acrobatics—without having to fork out your savings.

CIRCUS

Académie Fratellini FREE   A quality circus extravaganza for absolutely zip—what more could we want? The resident troupes and apprentices get together for free shows directed by professionals once a month. There are also regular professional spectacles that won't break the bank.

Quartier Landy-France, Rue des Cheminots 93210, La Plaine Saint-Denis. ℂ **01 49 46 16 22.** www.academie-fratellini.com. RER: Stade de France/Saint-Denis.

Espace Chapiteaux—La Villette   The Parc de la Villette's big top hosts some of the most poetic and inventive acrobatic acts around, including Cirque Plume (www.cirqueplume.com, September–December).

Parc de la Villette, 75019. ℂ **01 40 03 75 75.** www.villette.com. Tickets: 9€–18€. Metro: Porte de la Villette.

CABARET

Roll up, roll up for the glamorous girls and perfectly synchronised dancing. The promise of such ocular delights is too much for most tourists to refuse, who arrive in droves for an evening of bare bottoms, feathers and exceedingly cheesy music. If you've never been before, a glamour cabaret is a fun Paris-meets-Las-Vegas kind of experience—one that is worth splurging out on just once. The cheapest way to see the show is to skip dinner and come just for a glass of champers—this can save you up to 100€.

Le Crazy Horse de Paris   The most risqué of them all: 18 lookalike dancers slink around the stage clad only in rainbow light and strategic strips of black tape. Their names are as provocative as their attire (Flamma Rosa and Nooka Caramel). The numbers are satisfyingly tantalising yet somehow always manage to stay on the right side of good taste.

12 Ave. George V, 75008. ℂ **01 47 23 32 32.** www.crazyhorse.fr. Shows 8:15pm, 10:45pm Mon–Fri and Sun; 7pm, 9:30pm, 11:45pm Sat. Adm: show only 100€, incl ½ bottle champagne 120€. Metro: Alma—Marceau or George V.

Lido   The largest cabaret of them all brims with hi-tech touches to optimise visibility (descending floors and lights). On stage, it's all about sequinned panache, breathtaking tableaux that include a huge gilded Aztec pyramid that spurts water, and costumes worthy of the catwalk.

116 Bis Ave. des Champs-Elysées, 75008. ℂ **01 40 76 56 10.** www.lido.fr. Adm: matinée (once or twice a month, incl champagne) 80€; 9:30pm show (incl ½ bottle champagne) 100€; 11:30pm show (incl champagne) 90€, free under-12s. Metro: Franklin D. Roosevelt or George V.

Moulin Rouge The most famous cabaret in the world has been around for more than 120 years, so it must be doing something right. The dining room (which packs you in like sardines) is filled with Toulouse-Lautrec posters, glittery lampposts and fake trees, while on stage, the stunning Doriss dancers cavort in *coquette* costumes while funny *entr'acte* performers such as a ventriloquist and a sexy dancer doing underwater gymnastics in a tank of real boa constrictors keep us amused between the costume changes.

82 Blvd. de Clichy, 75018. ℂ **01 53 09 82 82.** www.moulin-rouge.com. Adm: 9pm show (incl ½ bottle champagne) 102€; 11pm show (incl champagne) 99€; show only 9pm 90€, 11pm 80€. Metro: Blanche.

Paradis Latin The Paradis prides itself on being the most Parisian of the cabarets, and it is. Most of its clientele is French, including the occasional jet-setter, the presenter speaks mostly French, and the show is more dance-orientated than the other revues. That doesn't stop it from being insatiably kitsch, with generous doses of glitter and sugary music. The redemption is in the stunning Belle Epoque dining room and the warm welcome (it's family-run).

28 Rue Cardinal Lemoine, 75005. ℂ **01 43 25 28 28.** www.paradislatin.com. Adm: 9:30pm 85€ (incl ½ bottle champagne). Metro: Cardinal Lemoine.

5 Talk Is Cheap: TV & Radio Tapings

Of all the countries in Western Europe, France's television is an insulated world and one of the hardest to penetrate. Having said that, every studio-based TV programme needs a lively audience to create a bit of atmosphere, and that's where you can step in. The radio can also be great free fun if you understand a bit of French, with several intellectual programmes recorded in front of a live audience.

LA TELEVISION

Clap Online (www.claponline.com) lets you enrol online (or call ℂ **01 41 11 11 11**) to be a member of the live audience for TV programmes on France 2 (www.france2.fr), France 3 (www.france3.fr) and Canal + (www.canalplus.fr), so you don't have to traipse through the separate websites. Sign up early—popular shows such as the satirical *Le Grand Journal* (Canal +) and *LeZ'Amour*s (France 2) fill up very quickly.

The trashy pseudo-psychological analysis chat show *Ca Se Discute* by Jean-Luc Delarue (sign up on www.acces-public.com) is so popular you should expect to be put on a waiting list. For TFI (www.tfi.fr), call ✆ **08 25 80 98 10.**

LA RADIO

With radio, where your presence is less vital to the success of the programme, you often don't need to reserve—turning up just an hour to 30min beforehand usually suffices. Still, it's worth checking the website of France Inter, France Culture and France Musique (www. radiofrance.com; Maison de la Radio, 116 Ave. du Président Kennedy, 76016. ✆ **32 30**), RTL (www.rtl.fr; 22 Rue Bayard, 75008. ✆ **01 40 70 40 70**) and Europe 1 (www.europeinfos.com; 26 Bis Rue François 1er, 75008. ✆ **08 20 31 90 00**) for precise information on your favourite (or soon to be favourite) programmes. Good ones to look out for include:

FRANCE INTER **87.8**
C'est Lenoir   The best of pop and rock, with both French and international names presented by Bernard Lenoir (once a month, 10–11pm, Studio Charles Trenet—Radio France).

Le Masque et la Plume   Cinema, theatre and literary criticism by Jérôme Garcin (every other Thursday 8–10pm in studios 105/106—Radio France).

FRANCE CULTURE **93.5**
Equinoxe   World music presented by Caroline Bourgine (1st Thursday of every month, 8:30pm in Studio Sacha Guitry—Radio France).

FRANCE MUSIQUE **91.7**
Le Cabaret Classique   A hugely popular programme that demystifies music of all genres, presented by Jean-François Zygel and Antoine Hervé (live Sunday 6pm from Théâtre du Châtelet, 75001 or Studio 106 at Radio France; ✆ **01 56 40 32 01**).

ENTERTAINMENT RIGHT BANK EAST

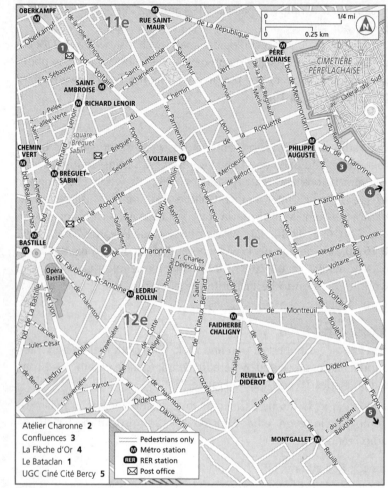

Atelier Charonne **2**
Confluences **3**
La Flèche d'Or **4**
Le Bataclan **1**
UGC Ciné Cité Bercy **5**

Pedestrians only
Ⓜ Métro station
RER RER station
✉ Post office

ENTERTAINMENT RIGHT BANK WEST

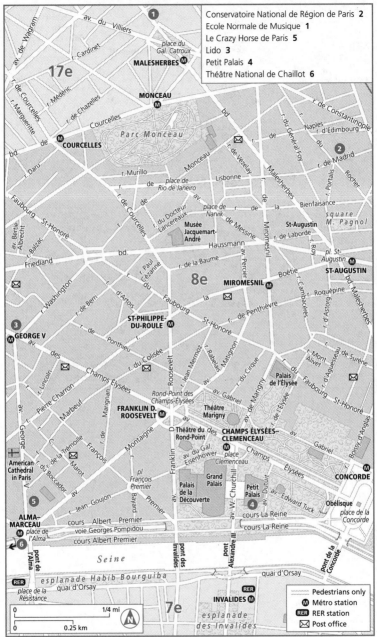

Conservatoire National de Région de Paris **2**
Ecole Normale de Musique **1**
Le Crazy Horse de Paris **5**
Lido **3**
Petit Palais **4**
Théâtre National de Chaillot **6**

Pedestrians only
Ⓜ Métro station
RER RER station
⊠ Post office

ENTERTAINMENT RIGHT BANK MARAIS

Café de la Gare **3**
Les Blanc Manteaux **2**
Paradis Latin **4**
Théâtre de la Ville **1**

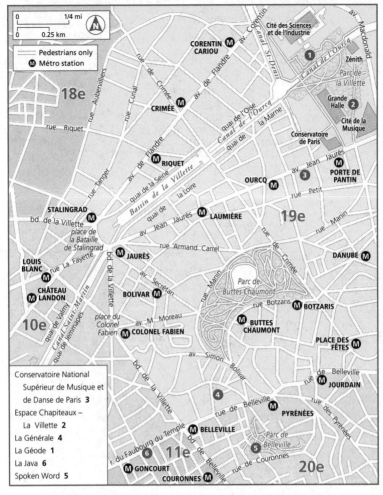

0   1/4 mi
0   0.25 km

Pedestrians only
Ⓜ Métro station

Cité des Sciences
et de l'Industrie

CORENTIN
CARIOU

Zénith

Parc de
la Villette

18e

CRIMÉE

quai de l'Oise
Canal de l'Ourcq
quai de la Marne

Grande
Halle

Cité de la
Musique

Conservatoire
de Paris

RIQUET

OURCQ

Jean Jaurès
PORTE DE
PANTIN

rue Petit

19e

STALINGRAD
bd. de la Villette

LAUMIÈRE

place de
la Bataille
de Stalingrad

rue Armand Carrel

DANUBE

LOUIS
BLANC

JAURÈS

CHÂTEAU
LANDON

BOLIVAR

Parc de
Buttes Chaumont

rue Botzaris

BOTZARIS

10e

place du
Colonel
Fabien

COLONEL FABIEN

BUTTES
CHAUMONT

PLACE DES
FÊTES

av. Simon Bolivar

rue de Belleville

JOURDAIN

Conservatoire National
   Supérieur de Musique et
   de Danse de Paris 3
Espace Chapiteaux –
   La Villette 2
La Générale 4
La Géode 1
La Java 6
Spoken Word 5

BELLEVILLE

PYRÉNÉES

Parc de
Belleville

rue de Couronnes

20e

11e

r. du Faubourg du Temple

GONCOURT

COURONNES

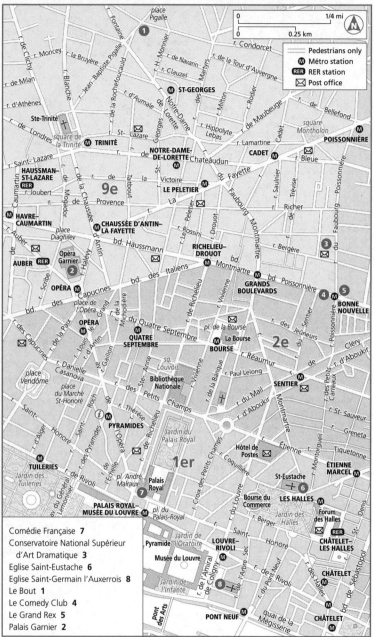

Comédie Française **7**
Conservatoire National Supérieur
  d'Art Dramatique **3**
Eglise Saint-Eustache **6**
Eglise Saint-Germain l'Auxerrois **8**
Le Bout **1**
Le Comedy Club **4**
Le Grand Rex **5**
Palais Garnier **2**

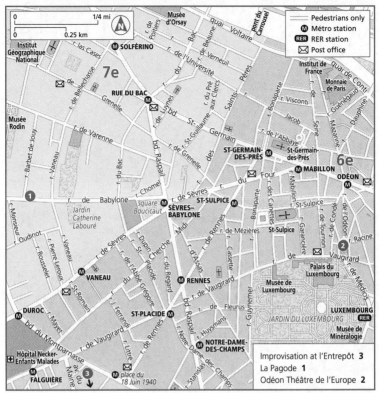

Legend:
- ~~~~ Pedestrians only
- Ⓜ Métro station
- **RER** RER station
- ✉ Post office

Improvisation at l'Entrepôt **3**
La Pagode **1**
Odéon Théâtre de l'Europe **2**

ENTERTAINMENT MONTMARTRE

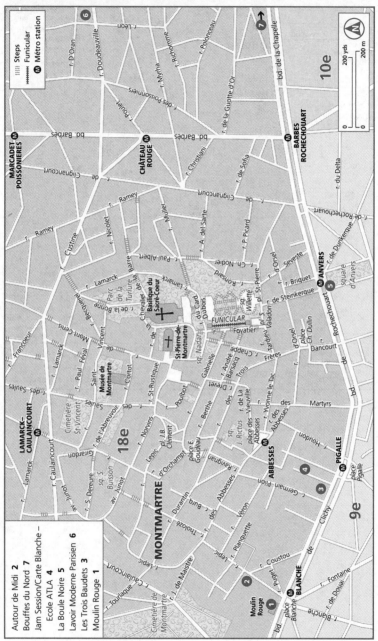

Autour de Midi **2**
Bouffes du Nord **7**
Jam Session/Carte Blanche – Ecole ATLA **4**
La Boule Noire **5**
Lavoir Moderne Parisien **6**
Les Trois Baudets **3**
Moulin Rouge **1**

The popular Le Bar Marché in rue de Seine, St-Germain-des-Pres.

EATING, DRINKING & PARTYING

P aris is a thoroughly edible city with an incredible variety of places selling good and often even great food. The snag is finding the means to pay for it all—that trusty corner bistro selling three homemade courses for 100 francs (the equivalent of 12€) practically disappeared when the euro came in, and Paris now brims with a new, more exciting and impressive type of bistro (see Worth the Splurge, p. 70)—which is wonderful news for gastronomes with at least 30€ per head to spend (that's before drinks) but not so great if you're cutting crusts. In July 2009 the government stepped in, imposing an 11.8% tax reduction on meals (i.e. the TVA or VAT on restaurant meals fell from

Key to the Eateries

Free	0€, or for the price of your drink
Dirt Cheap	less than 20€ for a fixed menu (prix fixe) or less than 13€ for a main course
Cheap	20€–30€ for a fixed menu or three courses
Do-able	30€–40€ for a fixed menu or three courses
Worth the Splurge	more than 40€

These prices are all without drink.

19.7% to 5.5%), which has lowered the cost of some dishes (restaurant owners are free to choose which dishes they decrease the price of).

Generally speaking, aside from the exceptions I've marked below, French cuisine remains the most expensive fare in the city. If you want a bargain meal, head for one of the city's international restaurants: Indian, Chinese, Japanese, Pan-Asian or North African, in many of which you can fill up for less than 15€. Some North African restaurants even offer free couscous when you buy a drink on certain nights.

A good website to join is www.lafourchette.com, which organises discounts (sometimes 50% off the price of your meal minus drinks) at restaurants across the city and will send a weekly list to you via email.

In terms of drinking and partying, Parisians (true to the café culture) enjoy starting the night in a café, usually on the terrace, before heading off to a bar (preferably one with a decent sound system or live music) or a nightclub. Compared to other capitals though, the city's club-life can be hard to fathom, even for old-timers. Big glitzy discos are easy enough to spot (anyone who's ever hung around the Champs-Elysées district can vouch for that), but finding something more underground takes a good nose, or an eye for the flyers distributed in selected bars and cafés.

Paris's cheapest soirées are often one-off events, so unless you're already part of the network, it's difficult to find information. A few good websites to try are www.flyersweb.com, www.novaplanet.com, www.lemonsound.com, and the bilingual www.gogoparis.com, which lists the city's hippest events.

Tip: One of my latest finds for discounts at more than 300 addresses is the free magazine *Pili-Pili* or the website www.pilipili.com. The magazine is distributed in bars and restaurants throughout the city (for a list of outlets see the website) and contains money-off or free-drinks vouchers that you present when you order your food or drinks, or you can print vouchers directly from the website.

Bear in mind that many restaurants close for two weeks in August.

1 Eating

FREE FOOD

La Choppe FREE *NORTH AFRICAN* MONTMARTRE   Whoever said there was no such thing as a free dinner has never been to La Choppe on Friday and Saturday nights from 8:30pm, when Samir, the honourable owner, serves lashings of flavourful Moroccan couscous (with all the trimmings) to anyone who's bought a drink (around 4€). It's immensely popular so get here at least an hour in advance.

40 Rue de Clignancourt, 75018. ✆ **01 46 06 20 10.** Metro: Château Rouge.

La Cordonnerie FREE *NORTH AFRICAN* CHATELET   A stone's throw from Les Halles (just north of the main red-light district), this is a fave with a young crowd who fight for elbow room and listen to the occasional concert while tucking into free couscous and sauces, doled out in large portions most Thursday and Saturday nights at 8:30pm. The beer is dirt-cheap too.

142 Rue Saint-Denis, 75002. ✆ **01 40 28 95 35.** Metro: Etienne Marcel.

FRENCH BISTROS & CAFÉS

A la Bière *DIRT-CHEAP* BUTTES CHAUMONT   The only thing that sets this corner brasserie apart from any other is its unbeatable 14€ fixed-price menu: Lyonnaise sausage, tender steak, hand-cut *frites* and delicious chocolate mousse. Wash it down with a beer—this *is* A la Bière.

104 Ave. Simon Bolivar, 75019. ✆ **01 42 39 83 25.** Daily midday–3pm, 7pm–1:30am. Mains from 11€; prix-fixe 14€. Metro: Colonel Fabien.

Bistro des Dames *CHEAP* PLACE DE CLICHY   The food served in the Eldorado hotel's quaint bistro, with its even quainter courtyard, is French with an international twist: think giant salads for 15€, Peking roast spare ribs for 14€, cheese platters for 7€ and ginger crème brûlée for 6€. No reservations are taken. (p. 128.)

18 Rue des Dames, 75017. ✆ **01 45 22 35 21.** www.eldoradohotel.fr. Mon–Fri midday–3pm, 7pm–2am; Sat–Sun 12:30pm–2am. Metro: Place de Clichy.

Brussels Café *DIRT-CHEAP* 16th   In a part of town where nothing else is cheap, this Belgium brasserie provides a breath of fresh air. But don't head to the area with tablecloths—head straight for the bar, where a few tables have been put aside for people to enjoy bar snacks including copious portions of *moules-frites* (mussels and fries) for 12.80€ or sauerkraut, and an excellent 19€ prix-fixe menu. There are six types of beer on tap.

71 Blvd. Exelmans, 75016. ✆ **01 46 51 24 33.** Daily 11am–11pm. Metro: Michel-Ange—Molitor.

Le Café Noir *CHEAP* ST-BLAISE   In the heart of the old village of Charonne (see Itineraries, p. 262), this hip café serves inventive French cuisine such as foie-gras speckled with speculoos biscuits, magret of duck with cardamom-vanilla, and pineapple and mango trifle. A la carte will set you back around 40€ for three courses, but there's an excellent-value 17€ prix-fixe menu and *plats du jour* at 12€. Check out the vast collection of cafetières.

15 Rue Saint-Blaise, 75020. ✆ **01 40 09 75 80.** www.cafenoirparis.com. Mon–Fri 12–2:30pm, 7–10:30pm; Sat 7–10:30pm. Metro: Alexandre Dumas or Porte de Bagnolet.

★ **Café Titon** *DIRT-CHEAP* BASTILLE–NATION   This Franco-German café has got East Berlin prices going for it—the currywurst (curry sausages and fries) at just 5.50€ won't leave you with any space for anything other than a beer at 3.50€. On the French side, the excellent dirt-cheap lunch menu (10€ for the *plat du jour* and a coffee) might include chicken Caesar salad or spare ribs with rice and stir-fried veg, and gooey chocolate *moelleux* for just 4.90€ extra.

34 Rue Titon, 75011. ✆ **09 53 17 94 10.** www.cafetiton.com. Mon–Sat 8am–2am. Metro: Faidherbe—Chaligny or Rue des Boulets.

Chamarre Montmartre *CHEAP* MONTMARTRE   This place is astoundingly good value at lunchtimes, when 17€ will buy you two courses of chef Antoine Heerah's delicious French cuisine (lots of pigeon, lamb, or perfectly cooked fish). If you want to go the whole hog, the 25€ menu is unbeatable value—especially when you know that the prices rise to between 52€ and 115€ at night!

52 Rue Lamarck, 75018. ☏ **01 42 55 05 42.** www.chamarre-montmartre.com. Daily midday–3pm, 7:30–10:30pm. Metro: Lamarck-Caulaincourt.

★ **Chez Prosper** *DIRT-CHEAP* NATION   The swarm of hopefuls hankering for a table at this hip corner bistro is a sign not to be ignored. The atmosphere is buzzing, the service quick, the food excellent—think steak 'n' fries (13€) and massive salads (12€)—and the bill never, ever unpleasant.

7 Ave. du Trône, 75011. ☏ **01 43 73 08 51.** Daily 8am–1am. Metro: Nation.

Le Dame des Huîtres *CHEAP* BROCHANT–BATIGNOLLES   Not far from the Batignolles market, this is one of my favourites when I'm in need of an oyster or seafood fix with everything arriving fresh from Brittany. There are *formules* at 16€–22€, or you may fancy a plate of sea-snails in mayonnaise (10€) or a platter of 12 oysters (16€).

86 Rue Lemercier, 75017. ☏ **01 46 27 81 12.** Wed–Sat 10am–3pm, 6–10:30pm; Sun 10am–3pm (reservations recommended). Metro: Brochant.

Les Domaines qui Montent *DIRT-CHEAP* VOLTAIRE   This is such a successful formula—a shop selling wine direct from producers (bottles 5.90€–130€) combined with a lunchtime restaurant offering a 14.50€ two-course menu, cheese fresh from the farm for 5€, wine from 2.50€ a glass and bottles sold at the same price as in the shop—that several franchises will be opening in 2010. Reservations are required for lunch.

136 Blvd. Voltaire, 75011. ☏ **01 43 56 89 15.** www.lesdomainesquimontent.com. Mon–Sat 10am–8pm (lunch midday–2.30pm). Metro: Voltaire.

L'Encrier *CHEAP* LEDRU-ROLLIN—GARE DE LYON   You'll need to book a table in this popular joint, which reels in locals with the promise of hearty *terroir* cooking (rabbit, magret of duck roasted in honey, and crunchy, garlicky potatoes), and excellent wine. Menus range from 14€ (lunch) to 20€–33€ at night. Expect to pay 15€ for a main.

55 Rue Traversière, 75012. ☏ **01 44 68 08 16.** Mon–Fri midday–2:15pm, 7:30–11pm; Sat 7:30–11pm. Metro: Ledru-Rollin or Gare de Lyon.

L'Epigramme *CHEAP* ODEON   For bourgeois style and French classics with the occasional twist, head to this lovely Left Bank dining room, where dining is a true experience but won't leave you penniless. Fixed-price menus at 22€–30€ (daytime and evening) include delicacies such as jarret of pork with lentils and, when the chef's up

Cheap Eats in Tourist Central

Whether you live here or you're visiting, it's not easy to eat near a tourist attraction without being ripped off. As a general rule, avoid anywhere that has its menus translated into English, but sometimes even that isn't enough. Here are a few of my insider's addresses—all dirt-cheap, with a pleasant atmosphere:

Arc de Triomphe

Monte Carlo   This excellent self-service canteen offers three courses at 10.20€–12.50€. The food (think boeuf bourgignon, coq au vin, salads, tarts, cakes, and fromage frais desserts) is just as good as in surrounding cafés but costs half the price. 9 Ave. de Wagram, 75017. ☎ **01 43 80 02 20.** www.monte-carlo.fr. Daily 11am–11pm. Metro/RER: Charles de Gaulle—Etoile.

Cathédrale de Notre Dame

La Fourmi Ailée   The 'flying ant' is an all-day tearoom with a 'local' feel. Serving tea, salads (11€), quiches (7.50€), a hot dish (9.50€–15€) and desserts including scrumptious ice-cream and apple crumble (5.50€). 8 Rue du Fouarre, 75005. ☎ **01 43 29 40 99.** Daily midday–midnight. Metro: Saint-Michel. RER: St-Michel—Notre-Dame.

Eiffel Tower

Le Café du Marché   A few minutes' walk away sits this hub of neighbourhood activity, with cheap plonk and decent grub (copious salads,

for it, hare 'Royale' (with lardons, truffles, and red wine). Desserts are of the highest order: the likes of Breton butter biscuits with caramelised apples, or rippled chocolate mousse.

9 Rue l'Eperon, 75006. ☎ **01 44 41 00 09.** Tues–Sat midday–2pm, 7:30pm–11:30pm; Sun midday–2pm. Metro: Odéon.

★ **La Frèsque** *CHEAP* LES HALLES   A fire gutted this place in 2009, and though it's been restored, it lacks the frescos that lent it its name. This is one of my favourite lunch spots; partly because it's central (in Châtelet), partly because it's such good value (13.50€ for two courses at lunchtime, wine for 2€). Food-wise, expect dishes with a south-west influence, like duck with olives and Toulouse sausage salad.

meaty brasserie fare with garlicky, fried potatoes) from 12€. 38 Rue Cler, 75007. © **01 47 05 51 27.** Monday–Saturday 7am–midnight, Sunday 7am–5pm. Metro: Ecole Militaire.

Opéra and Louvre

Memère Paulette   By the stock exchange (just a few minutes walk from both Opéra and the Louvre), this rustic French dining room with a fabulous wine list will bust your gut for just 16€–19€ for three courses. Nowhere else in town serves portions quite this big. 3 Rue Paul Lelong, 75002. © **01 40 26 12 36.** Monday–Friday midday–2:30pm, 8–10pm. Metro: Bourse.

Le Panthéon

Le Rostand   This is a classy literary café with a cool terrace frequented by the local bourgeoisie and, from time to time, me, when I'm hankering after a cheese and ham omelette and a glass of wine for 11€. 6 Place Edmond Rostand, 75006. © **01 43 54 61 58.** Daily 8am–11pm. RER: Luxembourg.

Sacré Coeur

Un Zèbre à Montmartre   A *bobo* café with a cosy interior, a tiny terrace to watch the world go by on, giant salads and fixed-price menus from 15€ (lunch) and 17€ (dinner) and three courses for 23€. 38 Rue Lepic, 75018. © **01 42 23 97 80.** www.unzebreamontmartre.com. Daily 9am–2am. Metro: Blanche.

Service is also with a smile (and usually a cheeky jibe too). In the evening a full meal is around 25€ per head.

100 Rue Rambuteau, 75001. © **01 40 26 35 51.** Daily midday–3pm, 7pm–midnight (closed Sun lunch). Metro: Les Halles. RER: Châtelet—Les Halles.

Pétrelle *DO-ABLE* ANVERS   Rabbit roasted with thyme and rosemary, tournedos Rossini and desserts so scrumptious you'll wish you saved room for a second one will set you back 25€ a main or 29€ for a bargain prix-fixe. All food is from local producers, so you needn't worry about your carbon footprint either.

34 Rue Pétrelle, 75009. © **01 42 82 11 02.** www.petrelle.fr. Tues–Sat 8–10pm. Metro: Anvers.

Restaurant de Bourgogne (Chez Maurice) *DIRT-CHEAP* CANAL SAINT-MARTIN   This is probably one of the last family-run *really* cheap bistros offering three-course menus from 9.50€ to 19€. The food isn't elaborate (think pâté, eggs in mayonnaise, *steak-frites*) but the *îles flottantes* (meringue on vanilla custard) are the size of a plate, and a pre-war atmosphere, reminiscent of the canal's industrial days, reigns.

26 Rue des Vinaigriers, 75010 Paris. ✆ **01 46 07 07 91.** Mon–Sat midday–2:30pm, 7–11pm. Metro: Jacques Bonsergent.

CREPES & FONDUES

Breizh Café *DIRT-CHEAP* MARAIS   You could be in Brittany at this upbeat, modern crêperie, which uses top-notch produce (mostly organic) for its unusual and delicious fillings: think potato and smoked herring, or 70% dark chocolate. There are 15 artisanal ciders.

109 Rue Vieille du Temple, 75003. ✆ **01 42 72 13 77.** www.breizhcafe.com. Wed–Sun midday–11pm. Metro: Filles du Calvaire.

Crêperie de Josselin *DIRT-CHEAP* MONTPARNASSE   For more than 15 years Madame Bénuezi has been serving her simple but delicious speciality crêpes, including *maraichère* (spinach, bacon, egg, and cheese) and Josselin (egg, ham, cheese, and mushrooms), in this

Late-Night Dining

When hunger strikes after hours, don't rush to the nearest kebab shop or McDonald's, try **Léon de Bruxelles** (p. 67), which is open until 1am on weekends; **Le Tambour** (41 Rue de Montmartre, 75002. ✆ **01 42 33 06 90.** Metro: Les Halles), which serves food along the lines of *steak-frites* from midday to 4am daily (fixed-price 20€–25€, mains 13€–16€) in a dining room filled with kitsch Paris memorabilia; or **Au Pied de Cochon** (6 Rue Coquillière, 75001. ✆ **01 42 36 02 84.** www.piedde cochon.com. Metro: Les Halles), a lovely Belle Epoque establishment open 24/7. The latter has dishes for every budget: A full-blown meal with fresh seafood or one of their famous pork dishes (practically every cut is used, including the trotters) can cost up to 60€, but there are set menus for around 20€, and the piping-hot French onion soup is legendarily restorative at 4am after a night on the town.

Eating with Kids

For decent food in an atmosphere where both you and the kids can relax, try this place:

Café du Commerce *CHEAP* MOTTE-PIQUET GRENELLE   This laid-back three-storey restaurant close to the Eiffel Tower is good fun for families with children of all ages thanks to its retractable glass roof that lets in the sunshine on a summer's day. Plenty of steak and chips, egg mayonnaise and delicious fruit tarts (mains for 14€, three courses 27€) feature on the *carte*, and there's a kiddies' menu for 10€ (chicken/burger and chips, drink and an ice-cream). 51 Rue du Commerce, 75015. ℂ **01 45 75 03 27.** www.lecafeducommerce.com. Open midday–3pm, 7pm–midnight daily. Metro: La Motte-Piquet Grenelle.

wonderful panelled, Breton-style dining room. Expect to spend around 15€ per person.

64 Rue de Montparnasse, 75014. ℂ **01 43 20 93 50.** Mon–Sat midday–11pm. Metro: Montparnasse.

Saveurs de Savoie *DIRT-CHEAP* MOUFFETARD   With menus from 10€ at lunchtime and 14€ at night, you can't go wrong in this rustic, rather romantic fondue and *raclette* restaurant, where the cheese—like the wine—goes down almost too well.

83 Rue Mouffetard, 75005. ℂ **01 45 87 90 29.** Daily midday–2pm, 7–10pm. Metro: Censier—Daubenton.

BAKERIES & SNACK STOPS

Boulangeries have always provided tasty, filling grub (the ubiquitous croissants and *jambon-beurre* baguettes are as loved today as they ever were), but as the time taken for lunch breaks decreases, snack bars are also on the rise in Paris, selling salads, sarnies, soups and fruit to those on the go.

Le Bar à Soupes *DIRT-CHEAP* BASTILLE   What a deal: a fresh market soup (six to choose from), cheese, bread and a glass of wine for 9.90€! You can also buy soup to take out.

33 Rue de Charonne, 75011. ℂ **01 43 57 53 79.** www.lebarasoupes.com. Mon–Sat midday–3pm, 6:30–11pm. Metro: Bastille.

Bread & Roses *CHEAP* SAINT-GERMAIN-DES-PRES   As far as baker-ies go, this one's expensive, but when taken in the context of Paris's food spectrum, it's highly affordable—and the food is so delicious you'll be eating every last crumb. A distinct Anglo influence can be seen in the array of cheesecakes, British fruit cakes, and puff-pastry tarts. If you fancy something more elaborate, try a plate of oysters, a Parma ham platter with fresh figs, or a tapas plate of smoked fish and calamari (about 18€ a main).

7 Rue de Fleurus, 75006. ℂ **01 42 22 06 06.** www.breadandroses.fr. Mon–Sat 8am–8pm. Metro: Saint-Placide or Rennes.

Cojean *DIRT-CHEAP* MADELEINE   Healthy ingredients go into Cojean's soups, salads, quiches, lasagnes and desserts, all of which can be bought to take out or eat at one of the counters. See the web for other branches.

64 Rue des Mathurins, 75008. ℂ **01 49 24 09 24.** www.cojean.fr. Mon–Fri 10am–4pm. Metro: Saint-Augustin.

Legay Choc *DIRT-CHEAP* MARAIS   Whether you're gay or straight, if you have a sense of humour pop into this Marais bakery with its bread that is both wholesome and unwholesome at the same time—yes, you've got it, they sell penis-shaped baguettes! The cakes are delicious, too. In case you're wondering, Legay really is the family surname: the bakery is run by two brothers but only one of them is actually gay.

45 Rue Sainte-Croix de la Bretonnerie, 75004. ℂ **01 48 87 56 88.** www.legaychoc.fr. Thurs–Tues 8am–8pm. Metro: Saint-Paul.

La Mosaïque *DIRT-CHEAP* MARAIS   A tiny corner of New York in the Marais, La Mosaïque sells hotdogs for 2.50€ day and night.

Corner of Rue du Roi de Sicile and Rue Vieille du Temple, 75004. Metro: Saint-Paul.

Le Paradis du Fruit *CHEAP* BASTILLE   After years of dismissing this chain as a tourist trap, I was forced to take a table on the small terrace here due to the cravings of a pregnant girlfriend. What a pleasant sur-prise: the huge list of fruit cocktails, freshly squeezed and served in gigantic glasses, the gargantuan fruit and chantilly-cream-clad ice-creams and the genuinely decent salad menu make it perfect for a quick snack and vitamin C boost. It's one of several branches (see the website for others).

1 Rue des Tournelles, 75004. ℰ **01 40 27 94 79.** www.leparadisdufruit.fr. Daily midday–2am. Metro: Bastille.

Rose-Bakery *CHEAP* NOTRE DAME DE LORETTE   Paris's flagship organic English bakery (with a restaurant at the back) is far too cool for its own good, offering naught but a frosty welcome. So why do I go? Because the food is so damned tasty. Never in Paris have I devoured a ham and asparagus tart like theirs (4.50€), nor have I enjoyed soup or salad more. I usually crumble for the cakes too— light, fluffy and squidgy. FINE PRINT The salads at the take-out counter are sold according to weight, so keep prices down by having a small spoonful of everything.

46 Rue des Martyrs, 75009. ℰ **01 42 82 12 80.** Tues–Sun 11am–4pm. Metro: Anvers. Second address: 30 Rue Debelleyme, 75003. ℰ **01 49 96 54 01.** Tues–Sun 9am–7pm. Metro: Filles du Calavaire or Temple.

PAN-ASIAN: CHINESE, VIETNAMESE, JAPANESE, LAOTIAN & THAI

Cheap 'n' cheerful, Paris's Asian restaurants offer some of the best deals in town. (Beware of the many *traiteurs asiatiques* who microwave food that has stood about all day.)

Dong Huong *DIRT-CHEAP* BELLEVILLE   Some of the best food in Belleville's Chinese quarter is actually Vietnamese—like this value noodle joint. I love its *bành cuôn*—delicate steamed ravioli stuffed with meat and Asian veg and spices, perfect for a shared starter—and the copious *bo-buns*—noodles topped with beef, spring rolls, veg, and crushed peanuts, a meal in itself. Mains cost around 7€, starters 4€–5€.

14 Rue Louis Bonnet, 75011. ℰ **01 43 57 18 88.** Wed–Mon midday–10:30pm. Metro: Belleville.

★ **Higuma** *DIRT-CHEAP* OPERA   This no-frills Japanese canteen is always full, so get here early if you don't want to queue in the street. Its quirky open kitchen fills the air with delicious-smelling steam, while the prices—around 11€–13€ for a starter, drink and giant bowl of soup, rice, or noodles, piled high with meat, seafood or stir-fried veg—are more than tempting.

32 Bis Rue Sainte-Anne, 75001. ℰ **01 47 03 38 59.** Daily 11:30am–10pm. Metro: Pyramides.

★ **Les Pâtes Vivantes** *DIRT-CHEAP* GRANDS BOULEVARDS   This is my absolute favourite, not only because you can watch the Chinese noodle chefs chop off long spaghetti-like ropes of noodles and throw them dramatically into the pans of boiling stock, but because it's inexpensive (around 9€ for a stomach-busting main, 11€ and 13€ for prix-fixe), and the Chinese cuisine is some of the best in Paris—fresh, tasty and worthier of a higher price-tag. Plus, if it's your birthday (and you can prove it), you can eat for free.

46 Rue du Faubourg Montmartre, 75009. ✆ **01 45 23 10 21.** www.lespatesvivantes. com. Tues–Sat midday–2pm, 7–10:30pm. Metro: Le Peletier.

Rouammit & Huong Lan *DIRT-CHEAP* CHINATOWN   Tantalising Laotian delights such as *lap nap neua* (a beef, tripe, and chilli salad) and sweet 'n' sour prawns with Thai basil and perfect sticky rice explain the queues outside this door.

103 Ave. d'Ivry, 75013. ✆ **01 45 85 19 23.** Tues–Fri midday–3pm, 7–11pm; Sat–Sun midday–4pm. Metro: Corvisart.

★ **Le Rouleau de Printemps** *DIRT-CHEAP* BELLEVILLE   When the chips are really down (and even when they aren't), The Spring Roll saves the day with its rock-bottom prices for decent no-frills Vietnamese food. The fried prawn ravioli starter (3€) is neither too oily nor too dry, the chicken fried rice is copious and tasty (3€), and the garlicky prawns stick nicely to your fingers (7€). Wash it all down with a green tea (0.50€). ⌐FINE PRINT⌐ This has become somewhat of a locals' institution, so get here bang on opening time if you don't want to wait for a table.

42 Rue de Tourtille, 75020. ✆ **01 46 36 98 95.** Daily 11:30am–3:30pm, 7–11pm. Metro: Belleville.

★ **Thai Konda** *DIRT-CHEAP* NATION   The best *bo-buns* in town for just 7.50€ and the lip-smacking lemongrass chicken and prawn soups (6€) served here come highly recommended. The take-outs are decent but blasphemously microwaved, so eat in and make sure to sample the Thai wine.

10 Rue de Picpus, 75012. ✆ **01 44 67 03 27.** Daily midday–10pm. Metro: Nation.

MOROCCAN

Au P'tit Cahoua *DO-ABLE* AUSTERLITZ   Raquel and Thierry's bright-yellow dining room, decorated with oriental fabrics and furniture, draws a happy crowd—happy because the tajines, couscous and

pastillas are so tasty, and happy because the bill won't give them pal-
pitations.

39 Blvd. Saint-Marcel, 75013. ℂ **01 47 07 24 42.** Daily 12:30–2pm, 7:30–10:30pm.
Metro: Saint-Marcel.

Mosquée de Paris *CHEAP* JARDIN DES PLANTES   It's been on the
tourist track for years, but the Paris Mosque's restaurant does have a
pretty blue and white tiled courtyard, as well as couscous and tagine
dishes at honest prices (from 9€ for vegetarian couscous to 25€ for
couscous *Royal* with brochette, merguez sausage, chicken, and kefta).

39 Rue Geoffroy-Saint-Hilaire, 75005. ℂ **01 43 31 38 20.** www.la-mosquee.com.
Daily midday–2:30pm, 7pm–midnight. Metro: Censier—Daubenton.

LEBANESE
Beyrouth Vin & Mets *CHEAP* VOLTAIRE   From the outside this looks
like nothing at all, but inside it is a low-key den of kitsch (probably
not intentional) where those in the know tuck into flavoursome Lebanese specialties such as *kellege* (Lebanese bread studded with cheese,
6.50€), hummus (5€), and *kafta neyeh* (tartare of lamb 6.50€). The
Menu Beyrouthin (23€) is excellent value, with a selection of four
starters, followed by grilled meat and salad, and a sweet white coffee.

16 Rue de la Vacquerie, 75011. ℂ **01 43 79 27 46.** www.beyrouth-vm.com. Mon–Fri
midday–2:30pm, 7–10pm. Metro: Voltaire.

ETHIOPIAN
Godjo *CHEAP* PANTHEON   In the shadow of the Ecole Polytechnique, this is a popular student haunt, but it's also where locals come
for spicy finger food—the *ye feseg*, which is a huge pancake dotted
with portions of fiery meat and stewed veg (13€). The wine is pricey,
so stick with beer (4€). Prix-fixe from 23€. Reservations are recommended.

8 Rue de l'Ecole Polytechnique, 75005. ℂ **01 40 46 82 21.** www.godjo.com. Daily
midday–2am. Metro: Maubert-Mutualité.

INDIAN & SRI LANKAN
For the cuisine that Paris's Indian and Sri Lankan populations tuck
into, go north to La Chapelle and Louis Blanc (75010), where dirt-
cheap rhymes with quality. Don't be put off by the stark interiors—
what comes out of the kitchens makes up for any shortcomings in the
décor.

If you can't make it that far, try the gaudy Passage Brady (75010. Metro: Strasbourg-St-Denis), but be prepared for higher prices and lesser quality.

Café Bharath *DIRT-CHEAP* LA CHAPELLE   Unless you don't mind reheated fried food (on display in the window when you go in), skip the starters here and opt for a copious main such as a vindaloo (it's spiced for Sri Lankan taste buds, which are far hardier than most Parisians', but Brits might find it just right). Mains start at 7€, and there's Kingfisher beer to wash away the fire.

67 Rue Louis Blanc, 75010. ✆ **01 58 20 06 20.** Metro: La Chapelle.

Krishna Bhavan *DIRT-CHEAP* LA CHAPELLE   Carnivores might shy from this vegetarian Indian restaurant at first, but the food is so tasty and textured that you soon forget it has all grown on a plant. Appetising starters include *idili,* a spicy battered vegetable ball, or, what I always come for, the 8€ *thali*—a plate of basmati rice with seven types of curry flavoured with southern Indian spices such as fenugreek (plus there's no alcohol, just delicious *lassis*—milkshakes).

24 Rue Cail, 75010. ✆ **01 42 05 78 43.** Metro: La Chapelle.

FAST-FOOD ALTERNATIVES

By the time you've bought a menu (plus an extra cheeseburger, not to mention a dessert), the tab in fast-food joints such as McDonald's and its French equivalent Quick can easily rise to 12€—not so cheap, especially when you know that for the same price you can sit in funkier surroundings and be waited on. Plus, some of the addresses below offer a take-out service when you phone ahead.

Breakfast in America *DIRT-CHEAP* MARAIS   Paris's most famous American diner offers bona fide diner surroundings, all-day breakfasts, pancakes and excellent burgers that start at just 8.50€. Fries are crunchy and the pecan pie (4.95€) a dream, while it's hard to beat the lunchtime menu, which gets you a burger and fries, Coke and coffee for just 9.95€ (7.95€ if you have a student card). There's a second branch on the Left Bank.

4 Rue Mahler, 75004. ✆ **01 42 72 40 21.** Metro: Saint-Paul. www.breakfast-in-america. com. Daily 8:30am–11pm. 17 Rue des Ecoles, 75005. ✆ **01 43 54 50 28.** Metro: Cardinal Lemoine.

Chibby's Diner *DIRT-CHEAP* NATION   The burgers at this 1950s-style diner outshine even Breakfast in America's excellent offerings, yet its hidden location down a side street stops it from being as packed. The 'Three in One' (cheese, bacon, onion, and mushrooms) is particularly comforting, at 12.60€. There are also breakfasts, brunches, excellent cheesecake and, if you don't fancy burgers, pasta and omelettes (from 10€).

9 Rue Jaucourt, 75012. ℂ **01 44 73 98 18.** www.restaurant-chibbysdiner-paris.com. Mon 8:30am–6pm; Tues–Fri 8:30am–11pm; Sat 10am–midnight. Metro: Nation.

Happy Days Diner *DIRT-CHEAP* SAINT-MICHEL   Turquoise banquettes, pink walls, black-and-white chequered floors—Paris's newest diner really does remind you of the *Happy Days* TV show. The Fonz unfortunately isn't here, but plenty of other cool dudes are, from students to professionals and groups of friends. If you haven't time to eat in, opt for Lily's Take-Out menu (which at 10€ beats McDonald's hands down). Otherwise, burger menus await you from 11.90€, and there are hotdogs if you're more *chien-chaud* than *steak-haché*!

25 Rue Francisque Gay, 75006. ℂ **01 43 29 67 07.** www.happydaysdiner.fr. Daily midday–midnight (until 1am Sat). Metro: Saint-Michel.

Léon de Bruxelles *DIRT-CHEAP* OPERA   If burgers aren't your forte, a more Continental style of fast food awaits you at Léon: mussels and chips. The chain has been stuffing Parisians with molluscs (served in dozens of different sauces) for years, and frequently entices even more of them in with special offers such as 'as many *frites* as you can eat' or 'two mains for the price of one'. Offers aside, the price of mussels (*frites* included) hovers at an affordable 14€ (except in the Champs-Elysées branch, which is always more expensive). There are several branches across the city (see the website for details).

30 Blvd. des Italiens, 75009. ℂ **01 42 46 36 15.** www.leon-de-bruxelles.fr. Daily 11:45am–midnight (1am Fri, 2am Sat). Metro: Opéra or Quatre-Septembre. RER: Auber.

FALAFEL
Chez Hanna *DIRT-CHEAP* MARAIS   For a scrumptious snack on the go (and garlicky sauce dripping down your chin), the Jewish take-outs on Rue des Rosiers in the Marais can't be beaten. L'As du Falafel is the most famous, but in my eyes this place down the road is the best of the

bunch, with sizzling *chawarmas* and lip-smacking falafels wrapped in doughy bread, salad, fried eggplant, hummus and chilli sauce.

54 Rue des Rosiers, 75004. ✆ **01 42 74 74 99.** Daily midday–midnight. Metro: Saint-Paul.

TEAROOM

★ **Fleur de Thé** *DIRT-CHEAP* BASTILLE   In the heart of the Aligre market (p. 165), this adorable multi-coloured tearoom-cum-boutique gets lots of TLC from friendly owner Marlène, who also enjoys spoiling her customers with homemade jams, biscuits, and sweets. The teas and herbal teas are all delicious—a pot will set you back just 3.50€), and you can buy your favourite for just 4.50€ per 100g.

10 Place d'Aligre, 75012. ✆ **01 44 75 04 06.** Tues–Sat 10:30am–2pm, 4–7pm; Sun 10:30am–2pm. Metro: Ledru-Rollin.

VEGETARIAN & ORGANIC

Bioboa *DIRT-CHEAP* OPERA TUILERIES   This 'food spa' with its all-white décor and giant bird fresco offers all-organic creamy smoothies, attractive take-away salads and eat-in dishes such as tofu burger with ketchup. The prix-fixe menus are good value at 13€.

3 Rue Danielle Casanova, 75001. ✆ **01 42 61 17 67.** Mon–Sat 10am–6pm. Metro: Pyramides.

Le Pain Quotidien *DIRT-CHEAP* MARAIS   This rustic international chain with four branches in Paris is perfect for both the health-conscious and vegetarians, with its scrumptious organic soups, sandwiches and salads (some of which contain meat and fish, others soya substitutes) served on communal wooden tables.

18–20 Rue des Archives, 75004. ✆ **01 44 54 03 07.** www.lepainquotidien.com. Daily 8am–10pm. Metro: Saint-Paul.

GLUTEN-FREE

As more and more people suffer from gluten intolerances, a handful of Paris's restaurants are filling a hole in the market by offering gluten-free dishes. As with all food allergies, it's best to explain the problem when you reserve a table and ask the waiter to check that the chef can cook a dish you won't be affected by. In the case of gluten, a simple fish or meat dish with vegetables is easy enough to come by, wherever you choose to dine.

Ice-cream Cravings: The Places We Go

Parisians have their pick of ice-cream joints. My favourite is the Italian **Amorino**, which serves petal-shaped scoops. Even the smallest cone (3.50€) lets you pick up to three flavours (18 Rue Mouffetard, 75005 plus another 10 branches throughout Paris. www.amorino.fr). The pistachio, speculoos (biscotti) and nutella (*L'inimitable*) are to die for.

The most famous is **Berthillon,** for those who don't mind spending half their monthly salary on a double-scoop (29–31 Rue Saint-Louis-en-l'Ile, 75004. www.berthillon.fr), or there's also **Haagen Dazs** for familiar flavours (49 Ave. des Champs-Elysées, 75008. www.haagendazs.fr) and **Ben & Jerry's** (44 Rue de Rivoli, 75004. www.benjerry.fr) for guilt-free indulgence (they guarantee their ice-cream is as environmentally friendly as possible). Ben & Jerry's offer free ice-cream once a year (p. 21).

★ **Des Si et des Mets** *CHEAP* MONTMARTRE   Traditional seafood blanquette, lemon and ginger lamb, and beef bourguignon with macaroni gratin are just some of the mouth-watering dishes (prix-fixe 26€, brunch 22€) prepared for you in this smart Montmartre restaurant dedicated to gluten-free cuisine. A group of non-gluten-intolerant friends who ate here rated it as one of the best restaurants they'd been to in the whole of the city.

63 Rue Lepic, 75018. ℂ **01 42 55 19 61.** www.dessietdesmets.com. Tues–Fri 7–10:30pm; Sat midday–2.30pm, 7–10:30pm; Sun midday–3pm, 7–10:30pm. Metro: Abbesses or Blanche.

Potager du Marais *DOABLE* MARAIS   This tiny restaurant serves vegetarian dishes (such as vegetable *croustillant* in a mushroom sauce on a bed of rice and pulses) so tasty that meat-eaters won't complain, plus several equally delicious gluten-free options. Expect to pay around 29€ per head.

22 Rue Rambuteau, 75004. ℂ **01 42 74 24 66.** Daily midday–midnight. Metro: Rambuteau.

ITALIAN & PIZZA

Il Campionissimo *CHEAP* SENTIER   Pizza chef Arlette is French, but that hasn't stopped her winning second place in the 'world pizza championships' in Italy. You can taste the triumphant pizza, the Arlecchino (fig chutney, fresh pears, foie gras, Parma ham and parmesan), for a hefty 26€. But don't worry—while every pizza is a gastronomic delight, not all are so expensive. Traditional flavours (such as margherita) start at 9€.

98 Rue Montmartre, 75002. 𝒞 **01 42 36 40 28.** www.ilcampionissimo.fr. Mon–Fri midday–2:30pm, 7–11pm; Sat 8–11pm. Metro: Sentier.

La Madonnina *CHEAP* REPUBLIQUE   Unintentionally kitsch yet strangely cool, this bright-yellow Italian restaurant has an air of romance. Menus change monthly but are always filled with home-made pasta options such as Parma ham and fig, or artichoke and ricotta ravioli. Mains linger around the 15€ mark and three courses will set you back 25€–35€, but the prix-fixe lunch menu is excellent value at 12€.

10 Rue Marie et Louise, 75010. 𝒞 **01 42 01 25 26.** Mon–Fri midday–2:30pm, 8–10:30pm (until 11pm Fri); Sat 8–11pm. Metro: Goncourt or Jacques Bonsergent.

★ **Pink Flamingo** *DIRT-CHEAP* CANAL SAINT-MARTIN   Not only are the Pink's recipes quirky (try the Poulidor: goats' cheese and sliced duck breast, at 15.50€; or the bacon-and-pineapple chutney Obama, at 16€)—they're put together with some of the best, freshest ingredients around, and the bases are baked with organic flour. Prices start at 10.50€. If you choose to picnic by the river, take a pink helium balloon with you and wait for the delivery boy to locate you (pizzas cost 1€ less this way, too). There's a second branch at 105 Rue Vieille du Temple, 75003.

67 Rue Bichat, 75010. 𝒞 **01 42 02 31 70.** www.pinkflamingopizza.com. Tues–Sat midday–3pm, 7–11:30pm (until 11pm for deliveries); Sun 1–11pm. Metro: Jacques Bonsergent.

WORTH THE SPLURGE

Life's too short to be frugal all the time—within the limits of what your wallet will let you get away with, of course. When the moment comes, Paris awaits with some of the finest restaurants in the world.

But before you run away with euro signs flashing red in your eyes, remember that choosing when to eat is just as important as where. Most restaurants offer cheaper lunch menus, and while you may not have as much choice as you do in the evening, the ingredients the dishes are prepared with are the same. This is especially true on the high end of the scale—haute cuisine in the evening can cost hundreds, but grab a table at lunchtime and you'll find menus at 70€ or 80€. That's still a lot of money, but you'll be treated to an incomparable dining experience, with a ballet of waiters bowing to your every need and plying you with *amuse-bouches* and *mignardises* (savoury and sweet nibbles) both before and after your meal.

The following addresses cost less than 90€ per person at lunchtime (and sometimes in the evening too), and are well worth putting aside a few euros for.

Les Ambassadeurs *HAUTE CUISINE* CONCORDE   Dining at the Crillon's Michelin-starred restaurant, run by chef Jean-François Piège, is like eating in a fairytale castle. The walls are marble, the chandeliers sparkle like diamonds, and gilded cherubs keep watch over the doorways. The food is quite simply outstanding—foie gras, lobster, duck and caviar, reworked with modern flair—while the wine list reads like it has come from Bacchus's personal wine cellar. If you come at night, expect to fork out more than 200€, but the lunch menu is a fabulous 80€ and the never-ending Sunday brunch is 66€–72€. Reservations are recommended.

Hôtel Crillon, 10 Place de la Concorde, 75008. ✆ **01 44 71 16 17.** www.crillon.com. Tues–Sat midday–2pm, 7:30–10pm. Metro: Concorde.

★ **Baccarat Cristal Room** *HAUTE CUISINE* CHAMPS-ELYSEES   Chef Guy Martin made a fine choice when he put Thomas L'Hérisson in charge of the Baccarat restaurant, which sparkles with crystal from the moment you step in (even the stately red carpet that mounts the stone staircase is encrusted) and wows interior design fans with its dining room kitted out by Philippe Starck. L'Hérisson's cuisine is both anchored in the old school and refreshingly light and contemporary: think fillets of red mullet in a chickpea and coriander crust, or the most delicious pan-fried veal cutlet you'll ever taste, with tandoori gnocchi, fine broccoli purée and slices of hazelnuts. Lunch is a steal at 29€–36€ for two courses, or 55€ for the whole hog. At night expect to pay 30€–40€ for a main course. FINE PRINT A meal here includes a trip around the tiny but stunningly beautiful Baccarat museum.

11 Place des Etats-Unis, 75116. ✆ **01 40 22 11 10.** www.baccarat.fr. Mon–Sat 12:15–2:15pm, 7:15–10:30pm. Metro/RER: Charles de Gaulle—Etoile.

★ **1 Place Vendôme** OPERA   There is something distinctly Chanel about this den of chic gastronomy within the Hôtel de Vendôme (p. 129) with its pink cushions on black-and-white chequered chairs.

Impress Your Date—Impressionism & Gastronomy at the Orsay

When love is in the air, a fine way to keep the flame kindled is to make a date for a Thursday evening and take your loved one to the gilded Belle Epoque restaurant in the Musée d'Orsay (p. 102). It's a splurge at 42€ a head, but by jove is it worth it, especially as it gives you free access to the whole of the museum's permanent collections (that's a 16€ saving straightaway—tickets usually cost 8€ each), which are open for late-night viewing on Thursdays until 9:45pm. The cuisine is typically French with an exotic twist; and the pleasure you get from meandering past Impressionist treasures on your way into such a stunning dining room is priceless. Musée d'Orsay, 75007. *©* **01 45 49 47 03.** www.musee-orsay.fr. RER: Musée d'Orsay.

As for the menu, you can't go wrong with exemplary dishes such as foie gras with watermelon and *Baume de Venise* chutney, Scottish langoustines roasted in salted butter, mushrooms and leeks, served with a cappuccino of cardamom, and roasted figs with thyme sorbet. Nor can you go wrong with the prices: a wholly respectable 49€ for two courses and a glass of wine at lunchtime, 72€ at night.

1 Place Vendôme, 75001. *©* **01 55 04 55 55.** www.hoteldevendome.com. Metro: Concorde or Opéra.

2 Liquid Assets: Drinking

In a city where alcohol traditionally costs less than a soft drink, an entire month's salary isn't needed for a night on the town—even more so since *La Crise* (the global financial crisis) kicked in. The silver lining to that particular cloud is the increase in the number of places hosting Happy Hours, and in the number of cheap 'n' chirpy drinking holes too.

Some of the best can be found on shabby-chic Rue d'Oberkampf in the 11th. Even sweeter deals are to be had in the student haunts of the 5th and around the Butte aux Cailles in the 13th. For the current week's *soirée* agenda, check out www.planeteparis.fr and (in English) www.gogoparis.com. And for a tip-off on where to find cheap beer, try the home-made Happy Hour website http://hhparis.free.fr, tried and tested by a handful of beer-loving blokes and their mates.

COCKTAILS & HAPPY HOURS

Charlie Birdy CHAMPS-ELYSEES   Trendy Birdy reels in the punters with a jam-packed agenda of live jazz, soul and pop, and, Monday to Friday, half-price drinks between 4pm and 8pm. That means cocktails such as Tequila Sunrises for 4.50€ and a half litre of Kronenbourg for 3.75€.

124 Rue de la Boétie, 75008. ℂ **01 42 25 18 06.** www.charliebirdy.com. Daily 11am–5am. Metro: Franklin D. Roosevelt.

★ **Dédé La Frite** BOURSE   Suits from the surrounding banks head here after work, when the cocktails are just 7€ and the beer 3.50€. When the alcohol has flowed for an hour or two, most punters give in to the aroma of juicy burgers and frites (9€) wafting from the kitchen.

135 Rue de Montmartre, 75002. ℂ **01 40 41 99 90.** Daily 8am–2am. Metro: Bourse.

Drouant OPERA   Think that this chic restaurant with its bar for a moneyed bunch doesn't suit your wallet? Think again: Every day from 5:30pm to 7:30pm drinks are just 5€, which is great news if you want to hobnob with the glitterati but not break the bank.

16–18 Place Gaillon, 75002. ℂ **01 42 65 15 16.** www.drouant.com. Daily 5:30pm–midnight. Metro: Quatre-Septembre.

Hideout Bar CHATELET   This 'untraditional' Irish pub is a scream, and with pints of beer for just 2.50€ during the extra-long Happy Hour (3–9pm daily and all night on Thursdays!), it should be made illegal! There are great Mojitos too, from 4€.

46 Rue des Lombards, 75001. ℂ **01 40 28 04 05.** www.hideout-bar.com. Daily 3pm–5am. Metro: Châtelet.

Lizard Lounge MARAIS   This expat central draws a lively crew with its long cocktail list and not one but two Happy Hours a night. The first (upstairs) kicks off at 5pm to 8pm, with Mojitos and Screaming Orgasms from 5€; the second takes over from 8pm to 10pm in the downstairs cellar with its tiny dance floor.

18 Rue du Bourg Tibourg, 75004. ℂ **01 42 72 81 34.** www.cheapblonde.com. Daily midday–2am. Metro: Hôtel de Ville.

N'Importe Quoi Bar CHATELET   Specialising in cocktails (there are more than 95) and flaming shooters, this wild party joint has several cheap drinking offers throughout the week. Thursday has a token Happy Hour for nighthawks from midnight to 1am, the rest of the week there's a Happy Hour from 6pm to 8pm, with a pint for the price of a half 4€ and cocktails for 5€, and Monday to Wednesday pints are 5€ day or night.

16 Rue Roule, 75001. ℂ **01 40 26 29 71.** www.nimportequoi.fr. Mon–Wed 6pm–4:30am, Thurs–Sat 6pm–5:30am. Metro: Louvre—Rivoli.

FUNKY BARS & COOL CAFES

Le Bar ODEON   You may well have been here before. Who knows? You won't remember. Le Bar is the sort of place you end up in at 3am, ordering yet another glass of exceedingly strong stuff and striking up slurred conversations with *inconnus*. When it gets too much, the comfy banquettes are perfect for falling asleep on. If you're looking for a strange trip into the belly of nocturnal Paris, Le Bar is waiting…

27 Rue de Condé, 75006. ℂ **01 43 29 06 61.** Mon–Sat 8pm until late. Metro: Odéon.

Café Tournesol MONTPARNASSE   Rue de la Gaïté is like a mini Soho, and the Tournesol is the best (and cheapest) bar on it. A young crowd gathers for the Stella at 2.90€ and *croque-monsieurs* at 6€, and funky soundtracks play into the wee hours.

9 Rue de la Gaïté, 75014. ℂ **01 43 27 65 72.** Daily 8:30am–1:30am (from 9:30am on Sun). Metro: Gaïté.

★ **Chez Jeanette** STRASBOURG—SAINT-DENIS   When Chez Jeanette was taken over by a young hip crowd, everyone thought it would incite the surrounding bars to clean themselves up. But Jeanette remains a lone-rider in this part of town, which makes it all the more attractive. Crowds of trendy thirtysomethings lap up the cheap wine and concentrate on being cool, while the occasional old regular sweeps in (Jack Russell in tow), seemingly oblivious to the change of clientele.

47 Rue du Faubourg Saint-Denis, 75010. ℂ **01 47 70 30 89.** www.myspace.com/chezjeannette. Daily 8am–2am. Metro: Château d'Eau.

Le Crocodile LATIN QUARTER   More than 300 cocktails are on offer in this narrow bar, drawing a young crowd from the surrounding Latin Quarter universities. The Happy Hour finishes at midnight (it starts at

The Oberkampf Bar Crawl

Still hip after all these years, Rue Oberkampf and neighbouring Rue Saint-Maur and Rue Jean-Pierre Timbaud, the main drags of the 11th *arrondissement*, are home to some of the cheapest Happy Hours in Paris and the ultimate destination for a flirt with the debaucheries of French nightlife (AKA a bar crawl). Follow this list and you should collapse in a happy heap at around 6.30am.

Note that most Happy Hours run from 6pm to 9pm and that the nearest metro stations are Parmentier, Ménilmontant and Couronnes.

Café Cannibale (93 Rue Jean-Pierre Timbaud, ✆ **01 49 29 95 59**). An intellectual atmosphere lingers around the zinc bar and red-topped tables at this fine spot for drink number 1, while you still have full control over your speech…

Café Charbon (109 Rue Oberkampf, ✆ **01 43 57 55 13**). This is easily the hippest hangout in Oberkampf. Squeeze through the *bobo* crowds to admire the former Belle Epoque dancehall, slurp on some lush margaritas and decide whether to brace the queues for a concert at the Nouveau Casino next door (p. 79).

Le Chat Noir (76 Rue Jean-Pierre Timbaud, ✆ **01 48 06 98 22**). This is a favourite for weekend jazz and Monday-night chess tournaments. Live concerts also draw the crowds in during the week.

Les Couleurs (117 Rue Saint-Maur, ✆ **01 43 57 95 61**). This is where locals chill in comfy chairs and pontificate about why beer in France costs less than bottled water.

La Mercerie (98 Rue Oberkampf, ✆ **01 43 38 81 30**). This grungy-chic haunt serves Paris's best Mojitos to loud groups of friends.

Oxyd'Bar (corner of Rue Oberkampf and 26 Avenue Jean Aicard, ✆ **01 48 06 21 81**) This newest kid on the block feels more like a sitting room than a bar. Music dudes hang out here for the chilled flow of live jazz and cheap martinis.

Place Verte (105 Rue Oberkampf, ✆ **01 43 57 34 10**). This vast 1970s-inspired space has a library, a coveted terrace and lip-smacking cocktails.

10pm when the joint opens) and generously lets you have almost anything you fancy from the cocktail list (even the champagne ones) for 6€. Don't be put off by the bar's closed shutters—it's almost invariably open.

6 Rue Royer Collard, 75005. ✆ **01 43 54 32 37.** http://lecrocodile.fr. Mon–Sat 10pm– early hours. RER: Luxembourg.

L'Entr'acte PALAIS ROYAL   If you didn't know this tiny bar was here (down a hidden 18th-century staircase behind the Palais Royal theatre), you'd never find it. It's a fine spot for a pre-dinner/pre-theatre glass of *vin*, and if hunger strikes, just 10€ will buy you a platter of cheese or charcuterie.

47 Rue de Montpensier, 75001. ✆ **01 42 97 57 76.** Daily midday–midnight. Metro: Pyramides or Palais Royal—Musée du Louvre.

Les Furieux BASTILLE   Padded red walls, fake leather banquettes, photography exhibitions, a Happy Hour from 6pm to 8pm (everything half-price) and a vigorous dose of rock and metal are all reasons to come to this cool rockers' bar.

74 Rue de la Roquette, 75011. ✆ **01 47 00 78 44.** www.lesfurieux.fr. Tues–Thurs 4pm–2am; Fri–Sat 4pm–5am; Sun 7pm–2am. Metro: Bastille.

Le Houla Oups! VOLTAIRE   This is a cool joint for rock fans: Old LP sleeves fight for wall space with ever-changing art displays; regular live-music and cinema (usually horror) nights reel in a lively crowd; and the beer is always cheap (3€).

4 Rue Basfroi, 75011. ✆ **01 40 24 18 80.** www.myspace.com/lehoulaoups. Daily 9am–2am. Metro: Voltaire.

Le Merle Moqueur BUTTE AUX CAILLES   This student institution is so well loved and still draws nostalgic thirtysomethings looking for frivolous fun just like in the old days. Its main appeal is the rum (more than 20 types) and the long list of cheap cocktails. For real fun, get here after 10pm, when the crowds get animated.

11 Rue de la Butte aux Cailles, 75013. No phone. Daily 5pm–2am. Metro: Place d'Italie.

★ **La Palette** SAINT-GERMAIN-DES-PRES   For a hint of sophistication in surroundings that are part of the Left Bank's artistic history (Jim Morrisson, Hemingway, and Picasso all drank here), choose La Palette. The leafy terrace is a godsend on a hot day, but for true romance

Le Petit Bar – The Place Time Forgot

Run by seventy- or eightysomething Madame Polo (one never asks a lady her age), who has installed her fluffy cat and canaries here, and collected enough junk for a thousand *vide-greniers*, this is possibly the most extraordinary place in Paris. But a warning: don't go to the loo or drink out of the glasses—Madame Polo doesn't enjoy cleaning, and there is dust everywhere.

So why come? Because this is a bastion of old Paris—the last living link to a district that was once filled with factories and *ateliers* (Madame Polo remembers them), and proof that in this age of over-sterilisation there are still places that (thank goodness) slip through the nets of Health & Safety.

I challenge you to find anywhere else in today's city where the local twentysomethings drink alongside immigrant Cubans, Guatemalans, Brits, retired war veterans who volunteer for the Red Cross, and trendy lawyers who have just bought a loft on Rue de Charonne. Everyone pops in to keep Madame Polo's joint afloat (even if they only stay for one beer 3€ and turn a blind eye to the dirt), because everyone knows that she and her tiny bar are anchors to the city's past, a precious link that will disappear when Madame Polo retires. 7 Rue Richard Lenoir, 75011. No phone. Daily 5pm–2am. Metro: Voltaire.

head to the fresco-clad back room where you can steal a kiss undisturbed.

43 Rue de Seine, 75006. ✆ **01 43 26 68 15.** Mon–Sat 9am–2am. Metro: Odéon.

★ **Les Pères Populaires** NATION Off the beaten track, on the far side of Nation, could this den of cool be the cheapest bar in Paris? The quaffable wine is just 2€ a glass, beer is 2.40€ (4.50€ a pint), flavoured rums fall in at 4€, and there are plates of cheese and charcuterie for just 5€. If that's not enough, perhaps the décor will be—a retro cross between a 1970s canteen and a classroom.

46 Rue de Buzenval, 75020. ✆ **01 43 48 49 22.** www.myspace.com/perespopulaires. Daily 8am–2:25am (until 1:45am weekends). Metro: Buzenval or Avron.

WINE BARS

★ **Le Baron Rouge** LEDRU-ROLLIN   This immensely popular bac-chanalian temple only has four tables, so get here before the pre-din-ner crowds sweep in if you want to sit. If not, be prepared to slurp any one of its 50 or so labels standing, or resting on a giant wine barrel outside. Snacks of cheese, charcuterie, and (when in season) oysters add to the attraction. Being slap bang in the middle of the Marché Aligre, it's also a coveted bar with the Sunday-market crowds.

1 Rue Théophile Roussel, 75012. ✆ **01 43 43 14 32.** Tues–Thurs 10am–3pm, 5–10pm; Fri–Sat 10am–10pm; Sun 10am–3pm. Metro: Ledru-Rollin.

La Belle Hortense MARAIS   No other wine bar I know maintains a bookstore in the back, and certainly no others seem so self-con-sciously aware of their role as an ersatz literary salon. Come for a glass of wine, a kiss in the corner, or to participate in a discussion within what's defined as a 'literary bar'—named after a pulpy 19th-century romance set within the neighbourhood (*La Belle Hortense*). Wine costs 3€ to 7€ a glass.

31 Rue Vieille du Temple, 75004. ✆ **01 48 04 71 60.** Daily 6pm–2am. Metro: Hôtel de Ville.

Les Caves Populaires PLACE DE CLICHY   The name says it all: this is a hugely popular wine bar with friendly waiters, rustic decor, cheap cheese and meat platters, and even cheaper wine, starting at just 2.50€ a glass. A real local's joint.

22 Rue des Dames, 75017. ✆ **01 53 04 08 32.** Mon–Sat 8am–2am; Sun 11am–2am. Metro: Place de Clichy.

La Rota NATION   This great, relatively stark, wine bar has bottles and boxes lining the walls and jazz playing on the hi-fi until 2am. Glasses start at 3€.

54/56 Rue Montreuil, 75011. ✆ **01 43 70 49 82.** Daily 11am–2am. Closed Sun in Aug. Metro: Rue des Boulets, Nation or Faidherbe—Chaligny.

★ **Rouge Passion** PIGALLE   Anne and Sébastien's wine bar is a hip, romantic joint where lovers and wine-lovers alike share giant cheese and cold meat platters (15€) over a glass of Bacchus's finest from the downstairs cellar (from 4€). Lunch is also a steal, at 15€ for two con-sistently excellent courses of French cuisine, and in the evening the place doubles as an excellent French bistro.

14 Rue Jean-Baptiste Pigalle, 75009. ℂ **01 42 85 07 62.** www.rouge-passion.fr. Wine bar: Tues–Sat 7pm–midnight; restaurant: Mon–Fri midday–2:30pm, 7–10:30pm; Sat 7–10:30pm. Metro: Pigalle.

3 Partying

CHEAP CLUBS & LIVE MUSIC

Batofar BIBLIOTHEQUE   Hip Batofar, occupying a converted light-house barge on the Seine, sometimes attracts hundreds of gyrating dancers, most of them twenty- and thirtysomething followers of the invited DJs. Come here for an insight into late-night Paris at its most raffish and countercultural, and don't even try to categorise the patrons.

11 Quai François Mauriac, 75013. ℂ **09 71 25 50 61.** www.batofar.org. Adm: free–12€ depending on which DJs are playing. Mon–Sat 11pm–6am. Metro: Quai de la Gare.

La Bellevilloise MENILMONTANT   This multidisciplinary venue (set inside France's first cooperative building) has several bars, two restau-rants, a club, an exhibition space and a concert hall where some of Paris's most exciting bands have been launched.

19 Rue Boyer, 75020. ℂ **01 46 36 07 07.** www.labellevilloise.com. Wed–Fri 5:30pm–2am; Sat–Sun 11am–2am. Adm varies and is sometimes free. Metro: Gambetta or Ménilmontant.

Nouveau Casino OBERKAMPF   Some Paris-watchers consider this the epitome of the city's hyper-hip countercultural scene. Adjacent to Café Charbon (p. 75), it's a medium-sized space crafted around an enormous industrial bar that is always heaving. Live concerts take place nightly between 8pm and 1am; on Friday and Saturday, the party continues from midnight 'til dawn with a DJ who spins some of the most avant-garde dance music in Paris. Celebrity-spotters have picked out Prince Albert of Monaco and Jarvis Cocker (although not together!).

109 Rue Oberkampf, 75011. ℂ **01 43 57 57 40.** www.nouveaucasino.net. Wed–Sat midnight–5am (earlier for concerts). Adm varies (free–30€ depending on the band). Metro: Saint-Maur, Parmentier or Ménilmontant.

Social Club GRAND BOULEVARDS   If you're the type who likes to say "I saw him/her before he/she was really famous", take a trip to the oh-so-alternative Social Club, where many trend-setting DJs and bands

Absolutely Fabulous Gay Bars

Gay life in Paris is centred around **Les Halles** and the **Marais**, with the greatest concentration of gay and lesbian clubs, restaurants, bars and shops between the Hôtel de Ville and Rambuteau metro stations. **Café Cox** (15 Rue des Archives, 75004. ✆ **01 42 72 08 00.** www.cox.fr) gets so busy in the early evening that the crowd spills out onto the pavement. This is where you'll find the most mixed gay crowd in Paris, from hunky American tourists to sexy Parisian men.

A hot, fun place in Les Halles is **Le Tropic Café** (66 Rue des Lombards, 75001. ✆ **01 40 13 92 62**), where the trendy, good-looking crowd parties until dawn. A restaurant with a bar popular with women is **Le Troisième Lieu** (62 Rue Quincampoix, 75004. ✆ **01 48 04 85 64**), where trendy lesbians (and some straights) enjoy a tasty *tartine* and a glass of something strong.

The **Banana Café** (13 Rue de la Ferronnerie, 75001. ✆ **01 42 33 35 31.** www.bananacafeparis.com) is a popular all-night bar for gays visiting or doing business in Paris, and has been known to provide go-go dancers. **Les Jacasses** (5 Rue des Ecouffes, 75004. ✆ **01 42 71 15 51**) is one of Paris's newest lesbian addresses, catering to a *très cool*, lipsticked crowd. And finally there's the legendary **Le Queen** (102 Ave. des Champs-Elysées, 75008. ✆ **01 53 89 08 90.** www.queen.fr. Metro: Franklin D. Roosevelt or George V), which is mobbed most nights, primarily by gay men but also by chic women, straight and lesbian.

are tried and tested by their record labels. The crowd is *branché* ('switched on'), arriving in (well-) dressed-down gaggles to dig the live hip hop, jazz, funk, drum 'n' bass and all-night electro parties.

142 Rue de Montmartre, 75002. ✆ **01 40 28 05 55.** http://parissocialclub.com. Thurs–Sun 11pm–6am; Wed 11.30pm–3am. Adm: free–12€ (depending on who's playing). Metro: Bourse or Grands Boulevards.

DJ BARS

L'Alimentation Générale OBERKAMPF `FREE`   This ode to all things kitsch has oodles of unusual beers (Flag, Sagres, and Orval for 3€–6€)

and inventive cocktails for 8€. But that's not the only reason to visit: DJs or live bands play here practically every night, and only the biggest names tend to have a cover charge (5€).

64 Rue Jean-Pierre Timbaud, 75011. ℭ **01 43 55 42 50.** www.alimentation-generale. net. Wed, Thurs, Sun 5pm–2am; Fri–Sat 5pm–4am. Metro: Parmentier.

L'International OBERKAMPF **FREE** The already cool 11th district got a little cooler when this joint opened—a breath of fresh air for music-lovers with its free entry and a string of on-the-up bands playing to hip indie crowds. Beer is a steal at 3€, and once a month there's an after-show party 'til 4am.

5/7 Rue Moret, 75011. ℭ **01 49 29 76 45.** www.linternational.fr. Metro: Ménilmontant.

OPA BASTILLE **FREE** Industrial-chic OPA is like a live MySpace music joint: It's free, and Paris's up-and-coming bands play from 9pm until late, before DJs take over and spice away into the wee hours. Tuesday is rock or folk, Wednesday pop or French *chanson*, Thursday varies, and Friday and Saturday nights are electro rock and pop. FINE PRINT Concert days are subject to change.

9 Rue Biscornet, 75012. ℭ **01 46 28 12 90.** www.opa-paris.com. Metro: Bastille.

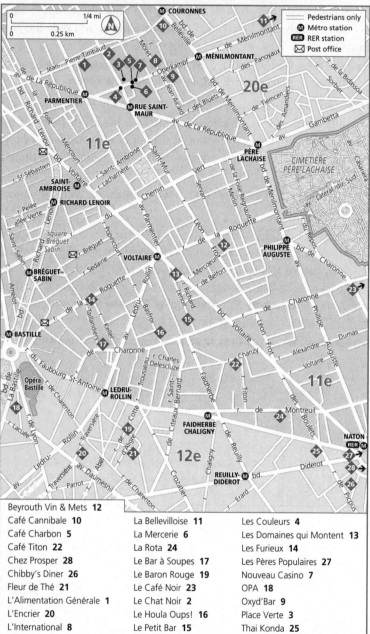

Beyrouth Vin & Mets **12**	La Bellevilloise **11**	Les Couleurs **4**
Café Cannibale **10**	La Mercerie **6**	Les Domaines qui Montent **13**
Café Charbon **5**	La Rota **24**	Les Furieux **14**
Café Titon **22**	Le Bar à Soupes **17**	Les Pères Populaires **27**
Chez Prosper **28**	Le Baron Rouge **19**	Nouveau Casino **7**
Chibby's Diner **26**	Le Café Noir **23**	OPA **18**
Fleur de Thé **21**	Le Chat Noir **2**	Oxyd'Bar **9**
L'Alimentation Générale **1**	Le Houla Oups! **16**	Place Verte **3**
L'Encrier **20**	Le Petit Bar **15**	Thai Konda **25**
L'International **8**		

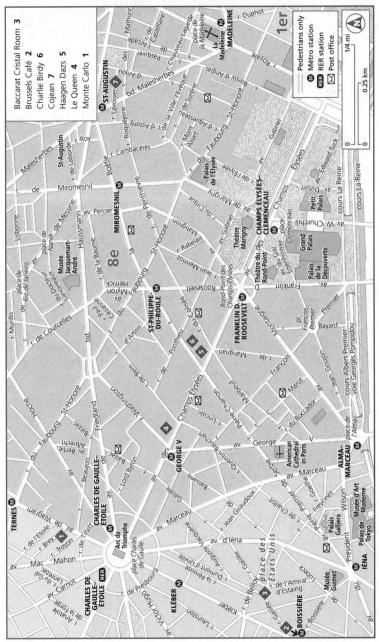

Baccarat Cristal Room **3**
Brussels Café **2**
Charlie Birdy **6**
Cojean **7**
Haagen Dazs **5**
Le Queen **4**
Monte Carlo **1**

EATING & DRINKING RIGHT BANK CENTRE

Bioboa **14**	Les Ambassadeurs **16**
Chez Jeanette **5**	Les Pâte Vivantes **4**
Dédé La Frite **7**	Memère Paulette **9**
Drouant **13**	1 Place Vendôme **15**
Higuma **12**	Pétrelle **1**
Il Campionissimo **10**	Rose-Bakery **2**
L'Entr'acte **11**	Rouge Passion **3**
Léon de Bruxelles **6**	Social Club **8**

EATING & DRINKING RIGHT BANK MARAIS

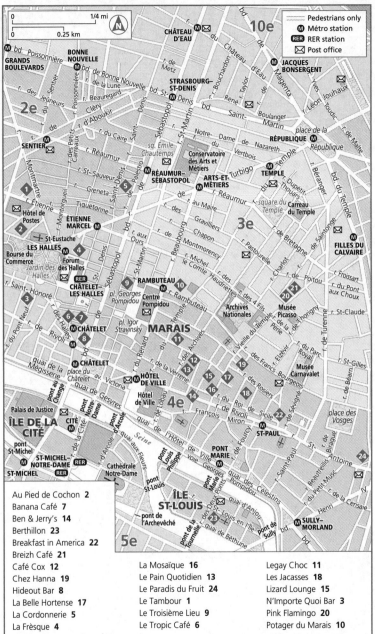

Au Pied de Cochon **2**
Banana Café **7**
Ben & Jerry's **14**
Berthillon **23**
Breakfast in America **22**
Breizh Café **21**
Café Cox **12**
Chez Hanna **19**
Hideout Bar **8**
La Belle Hortense **17**
La Cordonnerie **5**
La Frèsque **4**

La Mosaïque **16**
Le Pain Quotidien **13**
Le Paradis du Fruit **24**
Le Tambour **1**
Le Troisième Lieu **9**
Le Tropic Café **6**

Legay Choc **11**
Les Jacasses **18**
Lizard Lounge **15**
N'Importe Quoi Bar **3**
Pink Flamingo **20**
Potager du Marais **10**

EATING & DRINKING RIGHT BANK NORTH EAST

Legend:
- Pedestrians only
- Ⓜ Métro station

0 — 1/4 mi
0 — 0.25 km

19e

STALINGRAD Ⓜ
bd. de la Villette
place de la Bataille de Stalingrad
av. de Flandre
quai de la Seine
Bassin de la Villette
quai de la Loire
av. Jean Jaurès
Ⓜ LAUMIÈRE
rue Armand Carrel
rue du Rhin
rue de Crimée
rue Manin

Ⓜ JAURÈS
rue La Fayette
LOUIS BLANC Ⓜ
CHÂTEAU LANDON Ⓜ
av. Secrétan
BOLIVAR Ⓜ
Parc de Buttes Chaumont
rue Manin
rue Botzaris
Ⓜ BOTZARIS

10e
bd. de la Villette
quai de Valmy
quai de Jemmapes
rue Saint-Martin
place du Colonel Fabien
av. M. Moreau
Ⓜ 6
COLONEL FABIEN Ⓜ
BUTTES CHAUMONT Ⓜ
rue Fessart
av. Simon Bolivar

Canal Saint-Martin
rue de la Grange aux Belles
Hôpital St-Louis
quai de Jemmapes
Canal Saint-Martin
quai de Valmy
bd. de la Villette
rue Rébeval
rue de Belleville
rue des Pyrénées
Ⓜ JOURDAIN
Ⓜ PYRÉNÉES

rue Saint-Maur
rue Bichat
r. du Faubourg du Temple
av. de Parmentier
rue de la Parmentier
Ⓜ GONCOURT
COURONNES Ⓜ
Fontaine au Roi
BELLEVILLE
bd. de Belleville

place de la République
Ⓜ RÉPUBLIQUE
rue Jean-Pierre Timbaud
11e

A la Bière **6**
Café Bharath **2**
Dong Huong **7**
Krishna Bhavan **1**
La Madonnina **5**
Le Rouleau de Printemps **8**
Pink Flamingo **4**
Restaurant de Bourgogne
  (Chez Maurice) **3**

EATING & DRINKING LEFT BANK EAST

Amorino **8**
Au P'tit Cahoua **12**
Batofar **11**
Breakfast in America **7**
Godjo **6**
Happy Days Diner **2**
L'Epigramme **1**
La Fourmi Ailée **3**
Le Crocodile **5**
Le Merle Moqueur **14**
Le Rostand **4**
Mosquée de Paris **10**
Rouammit & Huong Lan **13**
Saveurs de Savoie **9**

Pedestrians only
Ⓜ Métro station
RER RER station
✉ Post office

0 ———— 1/4 mi
0 ———— 0.25 km

EATING & DRINKING LEFT BANK CENTRE

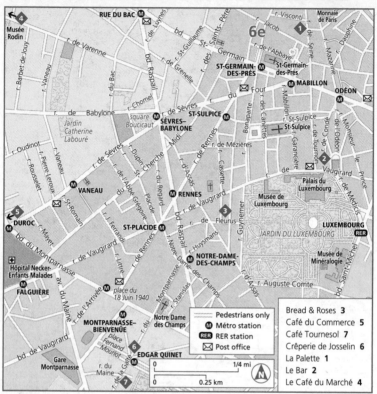

Bread & Roses **3**
Café du Commerce **5**
Café Tournesol **7**
Crêperie de Josselin **6**
La Palette **1**
Le Bar **2**
Le Café du Marché **4**

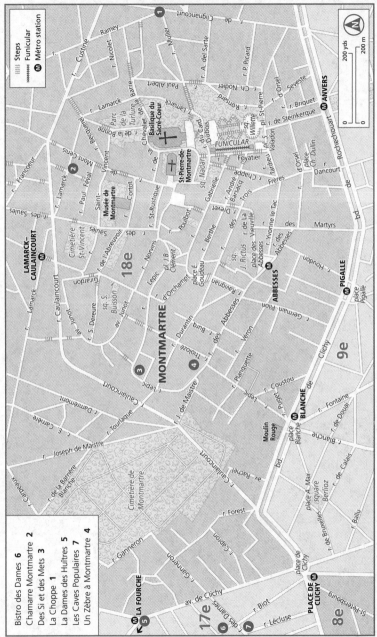

Steps
Funicular
Ⓜ Métro station

200 yds
200 m

r. de Clignancourt

Ramey

r. Custine

r. Nicolet

r. Muller

r. A. del Sarte

r. P. Picard

Paul Albert

r. Ronsard

Ch. Nodier

d'Orsel

Seveste

r. St-Pierre

r. Briquet

pl. St-Pierre

Ⓜ ANVERS

r. Lamarck

r. Turlure

Chevalier de la Barre

r. Lamarck

r. du Card. Dubois

pl. de Steinkerque

Parc de la Turlure

Willette

Basilique du Sacré-Coeur

r. Becquerel

Mont Cenis

r. de la Bonne

FUNICULAR

r. Foyatier

r. Tardieu

Valadon

d'Orsel

place Ch. Dullin

r. Francoeur

r. Lamarck

r. Paul Féval

St-Pierre-de-Montmartre

r. Gabrielle

r. André Barsacq

r. Chappe

r. des Trois Frères

Dancourt

Mont Cenis

r. Saint-Vincent

Cortot

Musée de Montmartre

r. St-Rustique

r. Poulbot

r. Drevet

r. Yvonne le Tac

des

Martyrs

LAMARCK-CAULAINCOURT Ⓜ

Cimetière St-Vincent

r. des Saules

sep

r. de l'Abreuvoir

r. Norvins

r. Berthe

sq. J. Rictus

place des Abbesses

r. des Abbesses

r. Houdon

PIGALLE Ⓜ

18e

r. Caulaincourt

r. Girardon

sq. S. Buisson

r. S. Dereure

av. Junot

Lepic

pl. J. B. Clément

place E. Goudeau

r. d'Orchampt

r. Ravignan

place Émile Goudeau

ABBESSES Ⓜ

place Pigalle

9e

r. Lepic

MONTMARTRE

r. Tholozé

r. Durantin

r. des Abbesses

r. Germain Pilon

r. Caulaincourt

r. E. Carrière

r. Damrémont

r. Tourlaque

r. de Maistre

r. Veron

r. Lepic

r. Coustou

place Blanche

BLANCHE Ⓜ

r. Fontaine

r. de Douai

Moulin Rouge

r. Puget

r. Coustou

r. Joseph de Maistre

r. de la Barrière Blanche

r. Rachel

av. Rachel

r. Cavé

Cimetière de Montmartre

bd. de Clichy

r. Blanche

r. de Calais

place A. Max

square Berlioz

r. Capron

r. Forest

r. de Bruxelles

r. Ballu

Ⓜ LA FOURCHE

r. Ganneron

r. Ganneron

place de Clichy

St-Pétersbourg

17e

av. de Clichy

r. des Dames

r. Biot

r. Lécluse

PLACE DE CLICHY Ⓜ

8e

Bistro des Dames **6**
Chamarre Montmartre **2**
Des Si et des Mets **3**
La Choppe **1**
La Dames des Huîtres **5**
Les Caves Populaires **7**
Un Zèbre à Montmartre **4**

House of wax; Lara Croft ready for action at the Musée Grevin.

FOR THE KIDS

4

Parisians love making babies: perhaps living in the world's most romantic city makes people broody? Or perhaps French State incentives make parenting a *famille nombreuse* (large family) an attractive option (you get tax cuts)? Either way, as a result the city offers a myriad of cheap ways to keep kids occupied. Indeed, many of the free and dirt-cheap museums listed in Chapter 7 are great for children—the best are highlighted in the table—and several run free children's activity days (usually Wednesdays, Saturdays, and during school holidays).

But central Paris is also well endowed with cheap merry-go-rounds and free play areas (for a full list of parks, see **www.paris.fr**.) *Guignol* puppet shows (p. 94) also provide inexpensive fun for all the family. See **www.bubblemag.fr** and **www.lamuse.net** for monthly listings for ages 0–16, and *Paris Mômes*, a bi-monthly listings magazine for 0–12s, sold with *Libération* newspaper or online at **www.parismomes.fr**.

Museums

Price	Museum	The Kids' Bit
FREE	**Mémorial de la Shoah**, p. 179	Educational and moving Jewish war memorial
FREE	**Musée Carnavalet**, p. 180	The excellent section on the Revolution
FREE	**Musée Curie**, p. 184	The actual lab where Marie Curie discovered radiation
FREE 1st Sunday of Month	**Centre Pompidou**, p. 190	The colourful modern art and the free children's workshops. See *Free & Dirt Cheap Activities*, p. 99
FREE 1st Sunday of Month	**Louvre**, p. 193	The mummies, the mediaeval vestiges and the free children's trails
FREE 1st Sunday of Month	**Musée Rodin**, p. 196	The garden to run around in, the sandpits, the statues you can touch and the cheap family activities (p. 99)
DIRT CHEAP (€4.30, €3.50 6-16s and students, free under-5s)	**Musée des Egouts**, p. 206	The whole smelly trip through Paris's sewer system
€6, €3 students	**Musée de Minéralogie de l'Ecole des Mines**, p. 205	The unrivalled rock collections for budding geologists
€5	**Musée de la Monnaie**, p. 203	Learning how coins are minted then buying some rare ones in the shop
Worth the Splurge (€7, €3.50 14–25s, free for under-13s	**Catacombes**, p. 212	The endless, spooky tunnels of skulls and bones
€6, €4 under-26s	**Musée de l'Air et de l'Espace**, p. 214	The aeroplanes, flight simulators and rockets
€8, €5 4–13s **Galerie de Minéralogie**; €7, free under-26s **Galerie de Paléontologie**; €9, free under-26s, **Galerie de l'Evolution**; €8, €5 4–13s Menagerie	**Musée d'Histoire Naturelle**, p. 216	The dinosaur bones, the gallery of evolution and the surrounding botanical garden with its menagerie and wonderful carousel featuring extinct species like the Dodo

Price	Museum	The Kids' Bit
€10, €7.50 7–17s, free under-7s	**Musée Jacquemart-André**, p. 218	The beautiful stately home and the summer workshops with face-painting and dressing up (p. 99)
€7, €5 18-25s from outside the EU, free under-26s from the EU, free under-18s from outside the EU	**Musée de la Marine**, p. 215	The models of old royal fleets
€7, €5 12-25s and over-65s; €3 3-11s, free under-3s	**Musée de la Poupée**, p. 102	The doll museum and hospital

1 Value-for-Money Kids' Attractions

Cité des Sciences ★ A hit with kids of all ages, this hi-tech, hands-on science museum looks at communication (sound and images) on cars, energy, aeronautics, and space (including a planetarium). It also houses the Cité des Enfants—a museum designed for 2–7s and 5–12s, with science-themed interactive installations—and the Géode Imax cinema showing family-friendly films, frequently in 3D.

30 Ave. Corentin-Cariou, 75019. ✆ **01 40 05 70 00.** www.cite-sciences.fr. Adm: 10€, 7€ (under-25s) Explora (the space section); 15.50€, 14€ (under-25s) Cité des Enfants and Géode; 11€, 8€ (under-25s), 6€ (under-7s) Cité des Enfants and Explora; 17.50€, 14€ (under-25s), 9€ (under-7s) Explora and Géode; 11€, 8€ (under-25s), free (under-7s) Explora and Planetarium. Tues–Sat 10am–6pm, Sun 10am–7pm. Metro: Porte de la Villette.

Les Etoiles du Rex The Grand Rex Cinema, one of Europe's last remaining Art Deco picture houses (and the biggest, seating 2,800 people), witnessed the golden age of cinema: From the 1920s to the 1950s, 'going to the Rex' was synonymous with seeing an all-round showstopper, with live music, dancers and on-stage fountains. The cinema museum, Les Etoiles, is a hit with families, taking you backstage into the projection room, behind the giant screen, into the film-director's office and into a special-effects room where you become Hollywood actors and remake scenes from famous movies, such as *King Kong*. It's cheesy but fun.

Le Grand Rex, 1 Blvd. Poissonière, 75002. ✆ **01 45 08 93 58.** www.legrandrex.com. Adm: 15.50€, 13.50€ (under-16s). Wed–Sun (and public holidays) 10am–7pm. Metro: Bonne Nouvelle.

Cheap 'n' Chirpy: Guignols

Guignols are the French equivalent of Punch and Judy shows, and our wee ones love them as much today as when they were first invented in Lyon in 1808 (by public tooth-puller Laurent Mourget, who attracted the crowds and hid the screaming with his puppet shows). Paris still has no less than eight *Guignols* (fortunately minus the tooth-pullers), all of which keep the kids quiet, in French, for a mere 3/3.50€ (most run from March to Christmas). The Mairie's website (**www.paris.fr**) has a full list, but these are my favourites:

Théâtre Guignol   On the Champs-Elysées, this is the oldest puppet show in the capital, dating from 1818 and handed down from father to son. Rond-Point des Champs-Elysées, 75008, corner of Avenues Matignon and Gabriel. ✆ **01 42 45 38 30.** www.theatreguignol.fr. Wednesday, Saturday–Sunday and school holidays 3pm, 4pm and 5pm. Metro: Champs-Elysées Clemenceau.

Le Théâtre Guignol Anatole   In the Parc des Buttes Chaumont, this one keeps the kids giggling with strings of sausages, Napoleonic *gendarmes* and a ponytailed Mr Guignol. Parc des Buttes Chaumont, entrance opposite the Mairie, 75019. ✆ **01 40 30 97 60.** Wednesday, Saturday–Sunday and school holidays 3:30pm and 4:30pm. www. petits-bouffons.com. Metro: Laumière.

Le Théâtre du Guignol du Parc Floral   In southeastern Paris, there is a bright, sophisticated set and reams of shows with names (The Witch in the Bois de Vincennes, Holidays in the North Pole, and What will Happen to Madame Michel's Cat?) that leave the imagination whirring. Parc Floral, entrance off the Esplanade du Château de Vincennes, Vincennes. ✆ **01 49 23 94 37.** www.guignol-parcfloral.com. Wednesday, Saturday–Sunday 3pm, 4pm and 5pm term time; daily 3pm and 4pm school holidays (plus 5pm spring and summer. Closed Monday July–August). Metro: Château de Vincennes.

Grévin   France's kitsch version of Madame Tussaud's lets children get up-close and personal with more than 300 wax figures of international stars, artists, sporting greats and historical figures, from Einstein to Barack Obama, from Michael Jackson to Charles de Gaulle, and from Mozart to Britney Spears. Don't miss the Palais des Mirages—an eerie hall of mirrors built for the 1900 World Fair and saved by the museum in 1906—and 'Tout Paris', a sumptuous Belle Époque theatre (one of the best preserved in Paris) full of waxwork stars such as Céline Dion, Monica Bellucci and Elton John. Perhaps most educational is 'Snapshots of the 20th century', where historical moments such as Armstrong walking on the moon and the fall of the Berlin Wall are recreated. FINE PRINT To avoid queuing, buy tickets on the website or in Fnac and Virgin stores.

10 Blvd. de Montmartre, 75009. ✆ **01 47 70 85 05.** www.grevin.com. Adm: 19.50€; 16.50€ (adult with 3 or more children, students, over-60s); 11.50€ (6–14s or 10€ per child when there are 3 or more); free (under-6s). Mon–Fri 10am–6:30pm, Sat–Sun 10am–7pm (last entry 1hr before closing). From 9am during school holidays. Metro: Grands Boulevards or Richelieu-Drouot.

★ **Jardin d'Acclimatation** On a warm day this is kiddywinkle heaven, with farm animals to pet, bears, an aviary, two free playgrounds, a paddling area (*pataugeoire* with sprinklers), a fun-park with small rollercoasters and merry-go-rounds, a small lake for radio-controlled boats and the *Rivière Enchantée*, a narrow man-made river taking you past ducks, squirrels and weeping willows, puppet shows and distorting mirrors.

Bois de Boulogne, 75016. ✆ **01 40 67 90 82.** www.jardindacclimatation.fr. Adm: 2.90€; prices vary for each attraction. Metro: Porte Maillot, Porte de la Muette or Porte d'Auteuil.

★ **Musée des Arts et Métiers** Founded in the 18th century by the Abbot Grégoire as "a store for useful, new inventions", this is one of Paris's best kids' attractions, with something for budding scientists, mechanics, astronomers, and pilots, or in fact anyone curious about the world around them. Highlights include Foucault's original pendulum, used by physician Léon Foucault in 1851 to make the rotation of the earth visible to the human eye, Clément Ader's Avion III, the world's first working airplane (1897), with just three wheels, two steam motors and two rotors, and Henry Ford's model 'T', which brought cars to the masses. Audio guides are available for all ages; the *Junior* guide for kids 7–12 is presented by a little robot who helps them find a hidden key in the museum via 34 different objects and solve the enigma of what the key was made for. FINE PRINT Free for under-26s year round, and for everyone on the 1st Sunday of the month and after 6pm on Thursday.

Ten Ways to Save at Disneyland Resort Paris

If the whippersnappers cry "I want to go to Disneyland!", and nowhere else will do, follow this money-saving guide.

1. Always check Disney's own website, which often offers 20–30% off tickets and date-specific and last-minute package deals.

2. Set yourself a souvenir budget and resist buying ice-cream, soft drinks and extortionate mouse-ears!

3. Pack a picnic to be eaten in the designated area outside the park entrance (food and drink inside the park is unrelentingly expensive, and you aren't allowed to enter with anything other than water and baby food—although in my experience, no checks are made so you could risk it). If you don't bring a picnic, self-service restaurants are cheaper than those with waiter service.

4. If you're staying in an onsite hotel with half-board, find out if your deal includes 15% off selected restaurants inside the parks (that said, the quality of the food is almost unremittingly poor).

5. Don't let your brood so much as glimpse the money-swallowing games arcades.

6. If you're making a two-day trip, you can save a few euros by buying two separate one-day tickets and spending a day in each park.

60 Rue Réamur, 75003. ℂ **01 53 01 82 00.** www.arts-et-metiers.net. Adm: 6.50€. Audio guides 5€. Tues–Sun 10am–6pm, Thurs until 9:30pm. Metro: Arts et Métiers or Réaumur-Sébastopol.

Musée de la Magie   Magic wands, vanishing chairs, magic mirrors and live shows unite to make this a captivating family experience. The main museum is in atmospheric vaults that contain all sorts of curiosities from a time when Paris was a world centre for illusionists, including an early box used to saw a woman in half and a 'Secret Objects Cabinets' with wands, old toys, and 'spirit objects' used in the 19th century to simulate ghost-writing and the paranormal

⑦ If you know you'll be coming back within a year, buy a three-day hopper for free movement between the parks for one or two days, then use it again on your next trip.

⑧ Don't forget raincoats and/or umbrellas so you don't have to buy any if it rains.

⑨ Compare prices of package deals from Disneyland and tour operators, as well as the price of individually reserved entry tickets, hotel rooms and travel—it can be cheaper to book everything yourself separately.

⑩ If you're a local and plan to frequent Disney often (more than three times a year), contemplate buying an annual pass, which gets you all sorts of money off at sites around the resort. The Fantasy pass (129€) gives you free access to the park 335 days a year (not during special events) and the Dream pass (189€) buys you a free reign year round.

Disneyland Resort® Paris, Marne-la-Vallée, 77705. ℂ **08 25 30 60 30.** www.disneylandparis.co.uk or www.disneylandparis.com. Adm: 1 park 51€, 43€ 3–11s; 2 parks 1 day 62€, 54€ 3–11s; 2 days 112€, 95€ 3–11s; 3 days 139€, 118€ 3–11s. RER: Marne-la-Vallée. *Tip:* Check Disney's offers in your own currency too as depending on exchange rates, it might be cheaper to book in pounds and dollars than in euros.

moving of objects. Live magic shows for kids take place in the little theatre; times vary so check beforehand. The tricks are simple to understand even if your kids' French is non-existent (most magicians speak broken English anyway), and they are usually asked to step up on stage and pick a card or hold the end of a rope. Finish your visit by admiring the charming 100-plus automated toys in the Musée des Automates.

11 Rue St-Paul, 75004. ℂ **01 42 72 13 26.** www.museedelamagie.com. Adm: 9€, 7€ under-18s. Wed, Sat–Sun 2–7pm (daily in school holidays except Jul–Aug). Metro: Saint-Paul.

Palais de la Découverte   This old-fashioned science museum covers all the basics of chemistry, physics, maths, biology, earth sciences, and astronomy in a fun and informative manner. Kids love the daily interactive demonstrations, when a presenter carries out experiments to reveal the secrets behind the exhibits; a timetable is posted in the main hall. One of the best sections is the electricity area of the physics department, where kids watch in wonder as a metal disk hovers as if by magic (thanks to alternative currents), and real fork-lightning strikes just above their heads. There's also a planetarium that recreates the night skies as seen through the ages and predicts the next total eclipse of the sun.

Ave. Franklin Roosevelt, 75008. ℂ **01 56 43 20 20 21.** www.palais-decouverte.fr. Adm: 7€, 4.50€ under-18s, free for under-5s. Planetarium 3.50€. Open Tues–Sat 9:30am–6pm, Sun (and some public hols) 10am–7pm. Planetarium Tues–Sun 11am, 2pm, 3:15pm, 4:30pm (and weekends 5:45pm). Metro: Champs-Elysées Clemenceau or Franklin Roosevelt.

★ **Parc Astérix**   Just 30km north of Paris, France's home-grown Astérix the Gaul theme-park is lesser known than Disneyland Paris and *much* cheaper. It's also much more charming, defining its attractions with true *Gaulois* spirit, down to the last Wild Boar burger. Thrill-seekers will find bigger stomach-churning rides here than at Disney, including the gravity-defying **Tonnère de Zeus**, the biggest wooden rollercoaster in Europe with a vertical 30m drop. Younger kids squirm to get wet on **Le Grand Splatch** log-flume, and a jamboree of quality shows add to the experience, including wonderful dancing dolphins in the **Théâtre de Poséidon** and amusing acrobatics and antics inside the **Roman Circus**. Food is reassuringly French— look out for the **Rélais Gaullois** canteen, where you can 'get-ya-fix' on three 'coursixs' for around 15€. FINE PRINT Entry is frequently cheaper (at around 25€) if you book online at least a week in advance.

Plailly, 60128. ℂ **08 26 30 10 40.** www.parcasterix.fr. Adm: 39€; 29€ 3–11s; under-3s free. Apr–Jun daily 10am–6pm, Jul–Aug 9:30am–7pm, Sept Sat–Sun 10am–6pm. Parking 8€. Oct and Nov school hols (usually last week Oct, first week Nov) and Sat–Sun 10am–6pm. Closed Nov–Mar; call or check website for extra closure dates. RER: Roissy-CDG T1, then shuttle (platform A3 at Charles de Gaulle airport bus station; info ℂ **01 48 62 38 33;** 9am–7pm every 30min, 7.50€, 5.50€ 3–11s; or direct shuttle from Louvre (M° Palais Royal, ℂ **08 26 30 10 40;** access via staircase in Hall Charles V, on shop-level, 8:45am to park and 6:30pm back to Louvre, 20€, 16€. By car: A1 (dir. Lille), exit Parc Astérix between junctions 7 and 8.

2 Free & Dirt Cheap Activities

★ **Ateliers Impromptus du Centre Pompidou** `FREE` Not only do under-26s get into Paris's flagship modern art museum (p. 181) for free, but on the first Sunday of every month, its *Ateliers Impromptus* (3–6pm) invite families to discover an artist, a work of art or part of an exhibition in a fun, hands-on workshop. The rest of the week, the *Galerie des Enfants* (Children's Gallery) on the ground floor, conceived by top artists, introduces kids to modern art and design, usually with interactive sections about the current exhibitions; this is also free for under-18s (accompanying adults need a standard 12€ ticket). Also, when school's out on Wednesday afternoons, and at weekends, over-2s can participate in 'contemporary creation workshops' (prices average 10€ per child and accompanying adult, see website for details). FINE PRINT These activities are understandably popular so reserve at least 30 days in advance, preferably online (http://billetterie.centrepompidou.fr).

Place Georges Pompidou, 75004. ℂ **01 44 78 12 33.** www.centrepompidou.fr. Wed–Mon 11am–9pm (11pm for temporary exhibitions). Metro: Rambuteau or Hôtel de Ville. RER: Châtelet–Les Halles.

★ **Ateliers Rodin** The Musée Rodin (p. 196) is surprisingly family-friendly, even if you just want access to its lovely statue-dotted gardens (just 1€ for adults, free to kids), which have plenty of room for your kids to run around in, plus sandpits and a café selling ice-cream. Otherwise, there are numerous workshops throughout

---

`FREE` **Playing Dress-Up at the Musée Jacquemart-André**

In summer this stately home par excellence runs '**Le Family-Fun Program**' (Jul–Aug, 2:30–5:30pm daily) for kids 4–6 and 7–12, who can dress up in period costumes and participate in activities such as fan-making and belt-decorating. During the visit they also learn the history of some of the paintings on show and about the artists behind them. The rest of the year, pick up a free treasure-hunt leaflet for 7–12s, which challenges them to solve an enigma and teaches them about the history of the building.
158 Blvd. Haussmann, 75008. ℂ **01 45 62 11 59.** www.musee-jacquemart-andre.com. Adm: 10€, 7.50€ 7–17s, free under-7s. Daily 10am–6pm. Metro: Miromesnil or Saint-Philippe du Roule.

the year: School holidays are particularly busy, with themed visits that might include the stories behind works such as *The Gates of Hell* and *The Kiss* (6€), while on Wednesdays (3–4.30pm) there are family tours (for 6–12-year-olds; first child 6€, others 4.50€, adults free) organised around such themes as Rodin's portrayal of the body. FINE PRINT Reservation at least a month in advance is highly recommended.

79 Rue de Varenne, 75007. ℂ **01 44 18 61 10.** www.musee-rodin.fr. Adm: 6€ museum only; 10€ museum and temporary exhibits; 5€ 18–25s from outside EU; free under-26s EU. Free 1st Sun of month. Open 9:30am–5:45pm Tues–Sun (garden until 6:45pm). Metro: Varennes, Invalides or Saint-François-Xavier. RER: Invalides.

★ **Bercy Village Treasure Hunts** FREE One Wednesday a month (March–October) parents can bring kids 6–11 on a free *chasse au trésor* (treasure hunt) around Bercy 'village' just beyond Bastille and the Gare de Lyon. Clues are strewn all around Cour Saint-Emilion; if they get all the questions right, your kids might be one of 10 prize-winners. Free *pains au chocolat* and croissants are provided by Paris's baking school (the Ecole de Boulangerie de Paris) at 4:30pm. A wonderful, wholly Parisian family experience. FINE PRINT Check the website for exact dates.

1 Cour Saint-Emilion, 75012. ℂ **08 25 16 60 75.** www.bercyvillage.com. Metro: Cour St-Emillion.

Cafézoïde Games, readings, story-telling, *goûters* (afternoon get-togethers where snacks are provided) in English, concerts for babies, and a host of unusual activities (such as body-painting) for families with children under 16 are offered by this unique 'children's cultural café' by the Basin de la Villette (and handy for the Cité des Sciences, p. 93, the Cité de la Musique, p. 101, and the Parc des Buttes Chaumont, p. 246)—a wonderful place to while away an afternoon and meet other families. Children 9 and up can come alone. FINE PRINT Extra donations are welcome.

92 Bis Quai de la Loire, 75019. ℂ **01 42 38 26 37.** www.cafezoide.asso.fr. Membership 2.50€, then 1.50€ per child per day, including drinks and a snack. Wed–Sun 10am–7pm. Metro: Crimée.

★ **Centre de la Mer** Don't be put off by the old-fashioned look of Prince Albert of Monaco's Institut Océanographique (it's a surprising, excellent-value-for-money place organising fun, marine-themed educational workshops for children of all ages on Wednesdays). Subjects might include 'Shells and Crustaceans', where kids 3–8 learn about and handle small sealife, or 'Sea Detectives', where 8–12-year-olds look for clues to find the name of a sea creature. During the school holidays there are also regular screenings of animal and marine documentaries in a wonderful panelled amphitheatre.

195 Rue St-Jacques, 75005. ℭ **01 44 32 10 70.** www.oceano.org. Adm: 5€, 3.50€, 2.50€. Mon–Fri 10am–12:30pm, 1:30pm–5:30pm. Metro: RER Port-Royal.

Cité de la Musique FREE Once a month (excluding months with school holidays), this music museum (in the Parc de la Villette) runs free *conférences participatives* (active workshops) for children over 8, who can try their hand at singing, conducting an orchestra and testing a musical instrument in the company of a musicologist; places are limited so reserve well in advance. Monthly educational concerts also take place in the Cité itself or in the affiliated Salle Pleyel and Conservatoire de Paris, with families with kids over 8 attending for just 8€ per person. Beforehand, the *Ateliers de Préparation en Famille* are excellent workshops that introduce kids to percussion instruments and some of the musicians who'll be playing them on stage, costing just 2€ extra for kids and 4€ more for adults.

Parc de la Villette, 221 Ave. Jean-Jaurès, 75019. ℭ **01 44 84 45 00.** www.cite-musique.fr. Adm: concerts 8€ (10€ or 12€ with *atelier*). Tues–Sat 12–6pm, Sun 10am–6pm. Metro: Porte de Pantin.

FREE Free Horse-Racing: Les Dimanches au Galop

During the *Dimanches au Galop* racing festival in May, Sundays at the Longchamp, Auteuil and St-Cloud horseracing tracks become a picnicker's Eldorado, with pony rides, candy floss stalls and outdoor games as well as top-notch horse-racing for free (excluding your flutter and certain rides). End April–early May. ℭ **08 21 21 32 13.** www.dimanchesaugalop.com.

Hippodrome d'Auteil, Bois de Boulogne, Route des Lacs, 75016. Metro: Porte d'Auteuil.

Hippodrome de Longchamp, Bois de Boulogne, Route des Tribunes, 75016. Metro: Porte Maillot then bus 244 to Carrefour de Longchamp.

Hippodrome de St-Cloud, 1 Rue du Camp Canadien, Saint-Cloud, 92210. Metro: Porte Maillot then bus 244 to Val d'Or.

★ **Musée d'Orsay** FREE Reserve well in advance to get one of only 12 tickets to the Musée d'Orsay's (p. 193) free family tours (for ages 5–7 and 8–12) on the first Sunday of each month. The tours last 2 hours and are linked to either the permanent or temporary collections. Free music concerts or films are also held on the first Sunday of the month in the Auditorium (level2) at 11am.

62 Rue de Lille, 75007. ✆ **01 40 49 48 14.** Free to everyone 1st Sun of month. Tues–Sun 9:30am–6pm (until 9:45 Thurs). Metro: Solférino/RER Musée d'Orsay.

STORY-TIME

★ **Librairie des Orgues** FREE On Wednesdays at 3.30pm (except in school holidays), you can bring your brood (ages 4–6) to this vast library near the Bassin de la Villette in northeast Paris for an animated story-telling session, followed by a painting or reading workshop and *le goûter* (free snacks). FINE PRINT Booking required; phone or email librairiedesorgues@wanadoo.fr.

82 Ave. de Flandres, 75019. ✆ **01 40 37 16 80.** Metro: Crimée.

La Maison des Contes et des Histoires This fairy-story themed centre a few steps from the Centre Pompidou is free to visit, with a mini gallery whose story-themed art changes every two months and with books and games at kids' disposal. The story-telling afternoons are also sure-fire hits (6€–10€, depending on story and age group), whether for babies (Friday 5pm), toddlers (Wednesday and Saturday 11am) or primary-school kids (Wednesday 3:30pm and 4:30pm; Saturday 4:30pm; Sunday 11am and 4:30pm).

7 Rue Pecquay, 75004. ✆ **01 48 87 04 01.** www.contes-histoires.net. Metro: Rambuteau or Hôtel de Ville.

Musée de la Poupée Wednesday at this doll museum is a busy day: 10am marks the start of a guided visit for kids 5 and up, which begins with handling of dolls from different eras. At 11am workshops for 5–12-year-olds might include making toys' clothes, patchwork teddy bears or masks. Lastly, 2.30pm is story-time for 3–10-year-olds. Prices range from 7€ to 10€ but include entry to the museum, so activities really are a steal.

Impasse Berthaud, 75003. ✆ **01 42 72 73 11.** www.museedelapoupeeparis.com. Tues–Sun 10am–6pm. Metro: Rambuteau.

DISCOVERING NATURE & ANIMALS

Le Clos des Blancs-Manteaux `FREE` Run by the Mairie, this environmental centre near the Centre Pompidou teaches youngsters how to become responsible eco-citizens in their everyday lives, with a garden for observing plant life, a workshop for experimenting, and an exhibition that highlights ways to preserve the environment (recycling and so on).

21 Rue des Blancs Manteaux, 75004. ℂ **01 71 28 50 56.** www.paris.fr. Sat 1.30–6:30pm (until 5:30pm in winter); Sun 10:30am–12:30pm and 1:30–6pm (until 5:30pm in winter). Metro: Hôtel de Ville.

Deyrolle `FREE` This taxidermist haven has displays of crocs, bears, wolves and just about anything else that ever had fur, plus creepy crawlies by the dozen.

46 Rue du Bac, 75006. ℂ **01 42 22 30 07.** www.deyrolle.fr. Mon 10am–1pm, 2–7pm, Tues–Sat 10am–7pm. Metro: Rue du Bac.

La Ferme de Paris `FREE` Paris's very own farmyard in the Bois de Vincennes in the southeast is a sure hit with kids, with friendly cows, sheep, rabbits, and hens. See p. 248.

1 Route du Pesage, 75012. ℂ **01 43 28 47 63** or **08 92 68 30 00.** www.paris.fr. Sat–Sun 1:30–5pm (until 5:30pm Oct and Mar, 6:30pm Apr–Sept and 6pm during Easter and Summer holidays). Metro: Château de Vincennes, then bus 112 and 15min walk. RER: Joinville le Pont, then 20min walk.

Les Jardins Passagers de la Villette `FREE` Though most people have heard of the Parc de la Villette in northeastern Paris, few know its small, secluded gardens (*jardins passagers*), where flowerbeds, veggie patches and honeybees provide a bucolic backdrop for guided tours suitable for all the family. The gardens are open weekends 3–7pm (May–Sept, with guided visits starting at 5pm). Workshops for ages 3–6 and 4–8 (7€) are also hosted to teach kids the importance of insects, and about how flowers are pollinated. Book on the website.

Parc de la Villette, 75019. ℂ **01 40 03 75 75.** www.villette.com. Metro: Porte de Pantin or Porte de la Villette.

★ **SPA Jeunes** `FREE` At 'Chihuahuas', the French Society for the Protection of Animals in the suburb of Gennevilliers, youngsters (11–17) not only learn how to care for our furry and feathered friends, they get to spoil them. The *Jeune* voluntary programmes offer a complete package for animal-lovers, who can walk and fuss the dogs, attend veterinary workshops, learn about animal rights and the environment, and even spend the school holidays in animal parks FINE PRINT To become a young SPA, you have to pay a yearly membership fee of 8€.

30 Ave. du Général de Gaulle, 92230 Gennevilliers. ℂ **01 47 98 71 53.** http://jeune spa.spa.asso.fr. RER: Gennevilliers.

SPORTS

Base Nautique de Choisy-le-Roi FREE During the school holidays, canoeing, kayaking, and windsailing are the coveted watersports on offer for 12–17s on the lake at Choisy-le-Roi 16km southeast of Paris. FINE PRINT To enroll, you need 2 passport photos and written proof that you can swim 50m. Week-long lessons can also be reserved on ℂ **01 42 76 30 00.**

Parc Interdépartemental de Choisy-le-Roi, chemin des Boeufs. ℂ **01 48 52 56 31.** www.paris.fr. RER: Villeneuve-Prairies.

Base Nautique de la Villette FREE Teenagers (12–17) can kayak for free in northeast Paris's Bassin de la Villette on Wednesdays in term time (9am–midday and 2–5pm) or Monday–Friday during the school holidays. They need written proof that they can swim 25m, your signature on the enrolment form and a change of clothes.

41 Bis Quai de la Loire, 75019. ℂ **01 42 40 29 90.** www.paris.fr. Metro: Riquet.

★ **Circus Arts with the Chapiteau d'Adrienne** If you live in the 18th, your kids can learn tightrope walking, juggling, dressing up as clowns, and numerous other skills of the circus trade for free on Wednesdays April–September and daily in the spring and summer holidays. If you live elsewhere, it's 5€ a session—well worth the splurge.

62 Rue René-Binet, 75018. ℂ **01 43 31 80 69.** www.chapiteau-adrienne.fr. Metro: Porte de Clignancourt.

Sports Fun With the Mairie

If you're a resident, ask at the Mairie of your *arrondissement* about free sports activities. All year round, but especially during the school holidays, lessons in sports such as table tennis, swimming, badminton, fencing, judo, rugby, karate and gymnastics are given free of charge to local kids of all ages. ℂ **39 75** (special number for the Mairie). www.sport.paris.fr.

★ **Ice Skating at the Palais Omnisports** The grassy knoll in Bercy (AKA the Omnisports arena), open Wednesdays and weekends for skaters of all levels, is incredibly cheap for families: Just 4€ for adults and 3€ for under-26s. Teenagers can also skate 'til late on Fridays and Saturdays. FINE PRINT Skate hire costs 3€, helmets, knee and elbow pads 1€.

8 Blvd. de Bercy, 75012. ℂ **01 40 02 60 60.** www.paris.fr. Wed and Sat 3–8pm; Sun 10am–midday and 3–6pm; Fri–Sat 9:30pm–12:30am. Metro: Bercy.

RIGHT BANK WEST FOR KIDS

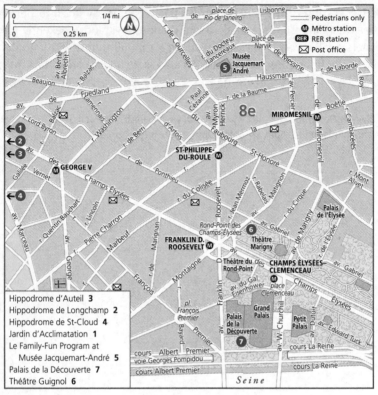

Hippodrome d'Auteil **3**
Hippodrome de Longchamp **2**
Hippodrome de St-Cloud **4**
Jardin d'Acclimatation **1**
Le Family-Fun Program at
    Musée Jacquemart-André **5**
Palais de la Découverte **7**
Théâtre Guignol **6**

RIGHT BANK MARAIS FOR KIDS

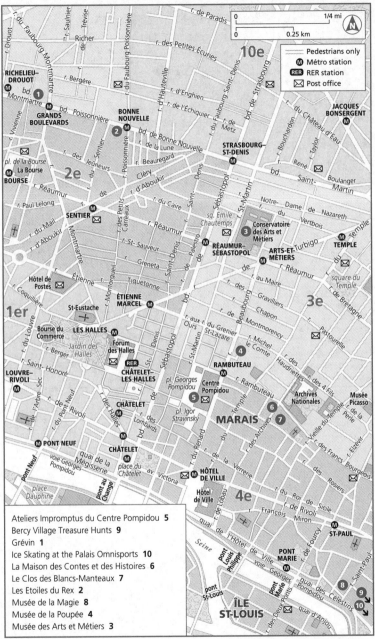

Ateliers Impromptus du Centre Pompidou **5**
Bercy Village Treasure Hunts **9**
Grévin **1**
Ice Skating at the Palais Omnisports **10**
La Maison des Contes et des Histoires **6**
Le Clos des Blancs-Manteaux **7**
Les Etoiles du Rex **2**
Musée de la Magie **8**
Musée de la Poupée **4**
Musée des Arts et Métiers **3**

RIGHT BANK NORTH EAST FOR KIDS

Base Nautique de la Villette **5**
Cafézoïde **6**
Cité de la Musique **3**
Cité des Sciences **1**
Le Théâtre Guignol Anatole **7**
Les Jardins Passagers de la Villette **2**
Librairie des Orgues **4**

LEFT BANK CENTRE FOR KIDS

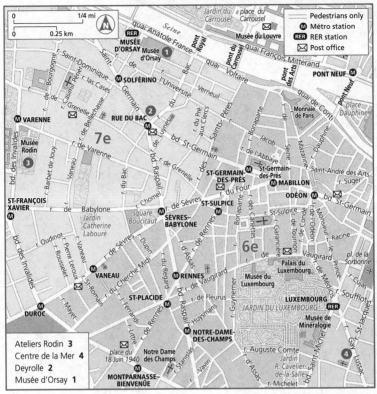

Ateliers Rodin **3**
Centre de la Mer **4**
Deyrolle **2**
Musée d'Orsay **1**

A rack of rental bicycles form part of the Velib bike transit system.

5 LIVING

Let's face facts: It's not easy to live in Paris without a sinfully huge wad of cash. There's the rent, for a start: At least 450€ a month for a 10m2, loo-less stamp (in older top-floor flats, toilets are often on the shared landing), rising to 1,300€ for a decent 1–2-bed-roomed pad and even more for a family-sized space. This might seem cheaper than NYC or London, but French salaries are usually lower, so unless you're here on ex-pat wages, putting a roof over your head (let alone buying one) is a costly business.

Then there are the overheads: Transport, keeping fit, education, entertainment—just about everything often comes with a heinous price tag. At least there's the healthcare (almost entirely reimbursed by the government)—France's saving grace. And this book, of course!

In any case, things can't be *that* bad if 3 million people choose to stay within the walls. The experience of being a Parisian is too inspiring to drag residents down for long. If the flat's too small, spend the day in a café. If you can't afford the Club Med gym, head to the park.

When you know where to go, Paris offers plenty of free and cheap opportunities for improving your quality of life, from classes and lectures, to sports and pampering. So once the rent is out of the way, everyone can live like a king on a pauper's budget. Hurrah!

1 Sense for Centimes: Education

LECTURES, SEMINARS & CLASSES

Just queuing for a baguette can be a learning experience in Paris, but most of us crave edification at another level. Luckily, Parisians are a philosophical lot and there are free classes and lectures on every subject under the sun. Here's the pick of the bunch, in French—giving you the chance to improve your language skills if your *français* is under par. Alternatively, the Shakespeare & Co bookshop (p. 161) is Paris's flagship English-language events organiser, offering debates and literary evenings. Also check out the Expat Living section (p. 121).

GENERAL KNOWLEDGE

★ **Collège de France** `FREE`   You'll be hard pushed to find a more beautiful location for lessons than François I's establishment, founded in 1530. Term starts in October, with the general public invited to listen to world experts in subjects such as maths, astrophysics, chemistry, philosophy and mediæval literature. Pick up a programme at the college or check the website for dates and subjects; there's no need to reserve.

11 Place Marcelin Berthelot, 75005. ℗ **01 44 27 12 11**. www.college-de-france.fr. Metro: Cluny—La Sorbonne or Maubert-Mutualité.

Conférence Berryer au Palais de Justice `FREE`   Once a month at 9pm, France's law courts open to the general public for live debates with French celebrities. The origins of this 'rhetorical happening' go back to the Revolution, but the subjects addressed are wholly modern and often flippant: "Does confidence reign?", for instance, or "Will super-poets save the Earth?". Such philosophical frivolity is hard to come by these days, so the conferences are very popular—get here at least an hour beforehand to get a seat. (See also Palais de Justice, p. 220).

4 Blvd. du Palais, 75004. ✆ **01 45 49 67 60** or **01 45 02 19 19.** http://laconference. typepad.fr. Once a month 9pm. Metro: Cité.

Institut de France `FREE`   Three of the five departments that make up Paris's iconic 'parliament of the wise' share their knowledge with mere mortals. Most Mondays at 3pm, the **Académie des Sciences Morales et Politiques** (✆ **01 44 41 43 26.** www.asmp.fr) holds conferences on subjects such as the communication tactics of prominent personalities. On some Tuesdays, the **Académie des Sciences** (✆ **01 44 41 44 60.** www.academie-sciences.fr) invites a scientific big-wig to lecture on his or her specialised subject (not for novices), and most Fridays at 3:30pm the **Académie des Inscriptions et Belles-Lettres** (✆ **01 44 41 43 10.** www.aibl.fr) hosts lectures on subjects such as archaeology, philology and history. For exact information and schedules, check the websites or give them a call.

23 Quai Condi, 75006. ✆ **01 44 41 44 01.** www.actualites.institut-de-france.fr. Metro: Pont Neuf or Louvre—Rivoli.

★ **Université de Tous les Savoirs** `FREE`   Don't worry if you miss any of these prestigious conferences (50min followed by a 20min debate with the public)—they are all re-broadcast on the Net (www.canal-u. education.fr, www.lemonde.fr/utls, http://mediatheque.parisdecartes. fr), or on France Culture radio the following morning (93.5). Subject areas are wide and may include 'Israel, today and tomorrow' or 'Sustainable development'.

Université René Descartes, 75006. ✆ **01 42 86 20 62.** www.canal-u.fr.

The Arts

★ **Centre National d'Art et de Culture Georges Pompidou** `FREE` Philosophers, writers, and artists get together most Mondays at 7pm in the Petite Salle of the Pompidou Centre's library (BPI), to debate subjects such as 'Why Write?' and 'The Role of Cartoons in Society'. Meetings are consistently stimulating.

BPI, Rue du Renard entrance, 75004. ✆ **01 44 78 12 33.** www.bpi.fr. Metro: Rambuteau or Hôtel de Ville.

Cité de l'Architecture et du Patrimoine `FREE`   One Monday a month, at 7pm, an architect is invited here to present his projects. At other times throughout the year, free live debates are organised

Beekeeping Classes

Learn to be a fully fledged beekeeper with the **Société Centrale d'Apiculture** (www.la-sca.net, ℂ **01 45 42 29 08**), which offers lessons in the Jardin du Luxembourg (6th) and the Parc Georges Brassens (15th) for just 185€ a year (payable in installments). This is a wonderful way for city folk to keep in touch with nature and spread something they helped to make on their toast in the mornings.

Despite car pollution, the Ile de France has more bee colonies than anywhere else in the country (around 300), attracting them with the promise of flower-filled window boxes, and parks and avenues lined with acacia, chestnut and linden trees. The bee school hopes to raise awareness of this fact and ensure that Parisian bees remain well cared for.

Check the website for enrolment dates (usually the end of September for the new school year) then make a beeline for the parks!

around the museum's current temporary exhibitions, with topical themes including environmentally friendly lodgings and buildings in Greater Paris. See the website (under 'Auditorium') for details and subjects.

1 Place du Trocadéro, 75016. ℂ **01 58 51 52 00.** www.citechaillot.fr. Metro: Trocadéro.

Forum des Images FREE   End the week on a cinematographic note with the Forum's 'Cours de Cinéma' on Fridays at 6.30pm. Each meeting brings a cinema critic or a historian who dissects and analyses a film by a famous (usually French) director. You can even watch previous lessons online. (See also Forum des Images, p. 201).

2 Rue du Cinéma, Forum des Halles, 75001 (Porte Saint-Eustache). ℂ **01 44 76 63 00.** www.forumdesimages.fr. Metro: Les Halles. RER: Châtelet—Les-Halles.

Musée du Louvre FREE   Underneath the Pyramide, in the Louvre's auditorium, top-notch conferences and exchanges on art and archaeology take place most Mondays and Fridays. Speakers are always of the highest calibre; Umberto Eco was a guest last year. Check the website under 'Auditorium' for exact dates.

Enter via main Pyramide, Cour Napoléon, 75001. ℂ **01 40 20 55 55.** www.louvre.fr. Metro: Palais-Royal.

THE EARTH & ENVIRONMENT

Centre de la Mer et des Eaux—Institut Océanographique `FREE` Most Wednesdays at 7:30pm, specialists present interesting sea-themed conferences on subjects such as climatology, marine biology and navigation in the Oceanic Institute's Grand *Amphithéâtre.*

195 Rue Saint-Jacques, 75005. ✆ **01 44 32 10 92.** www.oceano.org. RER: Luxembourg.

Société de Geographie `FREE`   If subjects such as 'Looking for worlds beyond our solar system', 'Palestine—geopolitical issues', and 'Will agriculture feed 9 billion mouths in 2050?' tickle your fancy, Friday nights (6pm) at the Geographical Society are for you. See the website for topics and dates.

184 Blvd. Saint-Germain, 76006. ✆ **01 45 48 54 62.** www.socgeo.org. Metro: Saint-Germain-des-Près or Mabillon.

HISTORY

Hôtel Cail—Mairie du 8ème `FREE`   Once a month (usually Friday 6–8pm), inside the 8th *arrondissement*'s prestigious Hôtel Cail (one of Paris's most beautiful Second Empire buildings), you can listen to experts give wonderful, historic talks such as 'The Mysteries, Myths and Legends surrounding Napoléon's Death', or 'The Renaissance of vines in Greater Paris'. Also look out for the free music concerts most Thursday lunchtimes (1–1:45pm).

3 Rue de Lisbonne, 75008. ✆ **01 44 90 76 43.** www.mairie8.paris.fr. Metro: Villiers.

Société Historique et Archéologique du 15ème Arrondissement de Paris `FREE` (almost)   Once a month, join fans of the 15th in its Mairie's Salle Lambert, where you can watch a series of projections commentated by a local historian. The society also organises interesting free walks around the district and guided visits of buildings usually closed to the public. `FINE PRINT` There is a 22€ joining fee, valid for the whole year.

Mairie du 15ème, 31 Rue Péclet, 75015. www.paris15histoire.com. Metro: Vaugirard.

SCIENCES

Cité des Sciences et de l'Industrie `FREE`   Throughout the year (Tuesday, Wednesday, Thursday at 6:30pm; Saturday at 10:30am), the Villette's gigantic science museum (p. 93) offers fascinating conference-debates on current affairs and the sciences. Previous subjects have included 'Adolescence', 'The Scientific Police', and 'Natural Resources'. You can also listen to any conferences you've missed on the website (under 'Conferences').

30 Ave. Corentin Cariou, 75019. 📞 **01 40 05 80 80.** www.cite-sciences.fr. Metro: Porte de la Villette.

Espace des Sciences de Paris `FREE`   If you need to brush up on your science, Paris's Ecole Supérieure de Physique et de Chimie Industrielles simplifies physics and chemistry for the masses at the Espace Pierre-Gilles de Gennes. Hold onto your hat during the 'experimental' demonstrations (one Monday a month at 6:30pm, except in summer).

Ecole Supérieure de Physique et de Chimie Industrielles de la Ville de Paris, 10 Rue Vauquelin, 75005. 📞 **01 40 79 58 15.** www.espci.fr/esp. Metro: Monge or Censier-Daubenton.

PHILOSOPHY

Collège International de Philosophie `FREE`   Daily seminars here (6:30pm, 8pm or 9pm) target those who enjoy questioning the world around them. Saturdays are for literature fans, with debates on books (that you have hopefully read), usually accompanied by a guest speaker.

1 Rue Descartes, 75005. 📞 **01 44 41 46 80.** www.ciph.org. Metro: Cardinal Lemoine.

DANCE CLASSES

Maybe it's their Latin blood, but I am always amazed at how easily the French (especially the blokes) get up and dance without worrying about what they look like. While we Anglo-Saxons move like wooden blocks, questioning whether our 'Big Fish, Little Fish, Cardboard Box' mimicry fits the rhythm, the French are rockin 'n' rolling like 1950s kids in 21st-century clothing.

   To forget your stiff upper lip and get the moves *à la Parisienne*, try one of several free and cheap dance classes, whether you're looking to swing someone over your hips (or be swung over someone else's), tango in the moonlight, or salsa 'til you drop.

L'ENSAM `FREE`   During term time the Cité Universitaire is the place to be on Tuesday nights, when the Ecole Nationale Supérieure des Arts et Métiers holds free classes on beginner's rock 'n' roll, advanced rock 'n' roll, and basic salsa, followed by a chance to test out your new moves on the open dance floor. It's a popular night (more than 200 people usually turn up), so get there at 7pm to make sure of a slot. A map of the vast Cité Universitaire can be found online.

Résidence du ENSAM, Cité Universitaire, 27 Blvd. Jourdan, 75014. © **01 44 24 62 99.** http://rock.ueensam.org. RER: Cité Universitaire.

Paris Danse en Seine FREE Paris's most famous free dance lessons are also the most visible, taking place on the river's edge, a stone's throw from Notre Dame. When the weather's good (between June and September), join the hoards to learn Argentinian tango every night (plus the occasional rock and swing on Tuesdays, rock 'n' roll on Friday nights, salsa Wednesday to Sunday, and even traditional Breton folk dancing). Initiation classes take place at 7–8pm (3pm Saturday and Sunday), then the evening's dancing starts at 9pm. Pack a picnic if you plan to stay 'til late. FINE PRINT Donations are appreciated. The programme might change at the last minute, so check the website or head to the river for an update.

Becoming a Star: Castings

You might not be destined for Cannes' red carpet, but if you fancy starring in short films, being an extra (easy money), or finding out if your self-refined acting skills are good enough to land you a role in an ad, check out these casting websites.

As a general rule, any other sites that ask you for a monthly fee or sting you for a one-off joining charge are just after your money. For everything other than extra-ing, you need a CV (of am-dram, semi-professional or professional stuff) and two or three photos (two head-shots and at least one full-length).

www.cast-prod.com FREE Good for music, theatre, dance and cinema.

www.paris-casting.com FREE Good for theatre, ads and cinema.

http://cineaste.org/ FREE A must for short films, features, extra-ing or voice-overs (sign up for the weekly newsletter).

www.maison-du-film-court.org This costs 65€ to join but is money well spent, giving both student-filmmakers and industry professionals the chance to consult your file and hopefully call you for a casting. Training is a plus but is not necessary, and there is always a need for English-speaking actors and extras.

Free Summer School

Acting FREE

The **Ecole de Théâtre l'Eponyme** is one of the only schools in Paris to offer free lessons to the over-16s in summer (30 June–1 October). Not surprisingly, there's a lot of demand, so each actor is limited to one 3-hour lesson (stage) a week: Learning to embrace one's fear (basic training) or improvisation. Sign up at http://leponyme.free.fr or call ✆ **01 43 43 05 51.** 2 Passage Ruelle, 75018. Metro: La Chapelle.

Square Tino Rossi, 75005. http://tango argentin-eric.site.voila.fr. Metro: Jussieu or Gare d'Austerlitz.

Télécom Danse Rock The telecommunications school's dance club is open to all; but only students get in for free—others have to pay an affordable 3€. The soirées are open to both rock 'n' roll beginners and experts, with music that ranges from grandparent era 'rock' to 1980s neo-rock 'n' roll. Lessons start at 8pm on Tuesday; from 9pm it's 'strut your stuff time' on the dance floor (until 11pm).

Ecole Nationale Supérieure des Télécommunications, 53 Rue Vergniaud, 75013. www.telecom.soiree-rock.org. Metro: Corvisart.

THEATRE CLASSES

"There are few places on Earth where we don't have to worry about what others think: but the theatre is one of them, so make the most of it."

Stéphanie Grosjean, from the Ecole Charles Dullin (p. 118).

Whether you're an exhibitionist in need of some limelight, a wallflower in search of self-confidence or a budding thespian with a career in sight, Paris has dozens of schools in which to free your inner beast. The problem is that they are all, almost without exception, expensive—full-time courses can reach 300€ a month without extra options. Amateur courses aren't much better.

For a list of theatre schools in Paris, see www.cours-theatre.fr. Meanwhile, here are my personal, cheap(ish) favourites.

In French

Ecole Charles Dullin Although specialising in professional training, this excellent school offers 4-hour theatre classes (Monday and Friday from 6pm) to amateurs aged 16 to 116. Improvisation and ultra-classic text analysis are on the cards—perfect for an all-round introduction to the art form. Enrolment is by appointment only, 1 April–31 July

For Budding Professionals: *Classes Libres* at the Cours Florent

France's most famous acting school has through-the-ceiling prices (minimum 300€/month), but that doesn't mean you can't try and win two years' worth of free lessons. Every year, 900 hopefuls put themselves through three gruelling rounds of tests (which include reciting from a newspaper, presenting a scene from a play of their choice and for non-French nationals, presenting a piece in your mother tongue) in the hope of winning a place in the school and following in the footsteps of Classe Libre winners Audrey Tautou and José Garcia (the school covers acting in English).

If you're up to it, download the enrolment form from www.cours florent.fr (under 'Classe Libre') and send your application in before 10th January of the year you wish to start the full-time course.

37/39 Ave. Jean-Jaurès, 40 Rue Mathis and 44 Rue Archereau 75019. ℭ **01 40 40 04 44.** www.coursflorent.fr. Metro: Crimée.

or 1 September–1 October. Numbers are restricted to 20 people per class so sign up early.

5 Rue de l'Hôpital Saint-Louis. ℭ **01 42 39 29 80.** www.ecolecharlesdullin.com. Adm: 40€ joining fee, then 85€/month. Classes run 15 Oct–30 Jun (closed school hols). Metro: Jacques Bonsergent or Colonel Fabien.

★ **Lumen Théâtre**   Xavier Brière is part of the Claude Mathieu clan—a prestigious theatre school in the 18th (www.ecoleclaudema-thieu.com). Lumen Theatre, however, is his own set-up—a night school for those who take acting but not themselves seriously. Most people here are either professionals (in the private or public sectors) who want to blow off steam, or wannabe actors who can't devote the time or the money to full-time lessons. If you enjoy working towards an end-of-year show, Lumen is for you; it usually bags a well-known theatre for the event. FINE PRINT Enrol as early as possible—September at the latest for the new school year.

Contact by phone only ℭ **06 75 96 45 91.** http://lumentheatre.com. Adm: 40€ yearly, then 85€/month.

Music Lessons

Learning to sing or play a musical instrument cheaply in Paris can be difficult. You have two choices: Private lessons, for which prices vary, or the Conservatoires de la Ville de Paris— national subsidised music schools that cover music theory and practice. The latter are by far the cheapest option but are not suitable for everybody, with age restrictions.

For private lessons:

http://cours-de-musique.annonceetudiant.com lists ads by independent teachers.

www.acadomia-musique.com and www.fasiladom.fr offer music lessons in your own home.

FUSAC, Paris's free Anglo-orientated ad magazine (distributed in pubs and cafés and online at www.fusac.fr), sometimes includes ads from music teachers.

The ARIAM association (9 Rue La Bruyère, 75009. ✆ **01 42 85 45 28.** www.ariam-idf.com) is full of resources for singers and musicians, and while it targets professionals, there is a section for amateurs, so they should be able to point you in the right direction.

Conservatoires:

Most professional musicians started their musical education in a Conservatoire (Paris has one for every *arrondissement*), whose aim is to push their students into higher musical education. As a result, they like students to start young. But the Conservatoires in the 10th and 20th *arrondissements* accept adults for some amateur music lessons. For a full list of Conservatoires, check out www.paris.fr. Prices tend to depend upon your income, and lessons follow the school year.

10th: Conservatoire Municipal Hector Berlioz, 6 Rue Pierre Bullet 75010. ✆ **01 42 38 33 77.** Metro: Jacques Bonsergent.

20th: Conservatoire Municipal Georges Bizet, 54 Rue des Cendriers, 75020. ✆ **01 40 33 50 05.** Metro: Père Lachaise.

Bilingual Acting

Ateliers Théâtre Thierry Hamon   Wednesday night is bilingual night at the Thierry Hamon acting school (8:30–11pm), which runs a comprehensive programme of lessons for am-dram lovers of all ages.

8 Rue Vital, 75016. ℓ **01 45 04 24 26.** www.atth.net. Metro: Trocadéro or La Muette. Prices on request.

2 Expat Living: English Only Please (Meetings & Conversation Exchanges)

★ **Centre Culturel Irlandais** `FREE`   The Irish Cultural centre is a hub of English-language activities, from free commentated art exhibitions and poetry readings to storytelling for the wee ones, free films by Irish directors (or about Ireland) and cheap music concerts by Irish groups (7€). There's even a *bibliothèque patrimoniale* (heritage library). The website has a comprehensive list of dates and activities.

5 Rue des Irlandais, 75005. www.centreculturelirlandais.com. Metro: Place Monge. RER: Luxembourg.

Paris Soirées   Founded by the American Patricia Laplante-Collins, Paris Soirées brings together expats of all nationalities and a hip French crowd for Sunday dinner-parties and Wednesday networking cocktails. There's great food (think spicy Thai beef and Caribbean fish), wine on tap, plenty of English conversation, and the chance to make the right connections, and, with a bit of luck, lasting friendships. The evenings feature themes such as literature, art, business, African-American and Black Paris, and after dinner there is usually a guest speaker. To sign up, email parissoirees@ gmail.com.

Evenings start at 6.30pm. Details on how to get there once you've applied. ℓ **06 43 79 35 18.** www.parissoirees.com.

Expat websites

Looking for information on life, love, culture and generally anything relevant to being an expat? Check out the following or contact your country's embassy (see list, p. 303).

http://france.angloinfo.com/
www.paris-anglo.com
www.craigslist.com
www.easyexpat.com
www.paris-expat.com

★ **Shakespeare & Co**   There comes a time in every expat's life when, no matter how good their French is, they long to hear the mother tongue. When such moments arise, Shakespeare & Co awaits with regular readings and workshops, usually in the atmospheric upstairs library surrounded by owner George Whitman's personal book collection (although his daughter Sylvia runs everything nowadays). Readings (usually free) range from poetry to fiction, plus the occasional autobiography read by the authors. Workshop-wise, **The Big Ben Club** offers free weekly conversation-exchange classes in English and French; the **Evening Writing Workshop** is a 7-week writing course for budding authors of all genres; the British **Faber Academy** also holds regular writing courses (extortionate at 505€ for just two days); and the **Other Writer's Club** works as a forum where you can bring along your own prose and poetry for constructive criticism. Good to know is that aspiring writers can stay in the upstairs rooms for free in exchange for some part-time work in the shop.

37 Rue de la Bûcherie, 75005. ℂ **01 43 25 40 93.** www.shakespeareandcompany. com. Daily 10am–11pm (from 11am Sun). Metro: Saint-Michel or Cité.

3 Wellbeing, Beauty & Pampering

Anyone who's lived in Paris for any length of time can attest to the fact that Parisians know how to spoil themselves. Luxuries such as massages, facials and a cut 'n' blow-dry every Friday aren't splurges, they're necessities. But French-style grooming doesn't come cheap. The pampering market has been assailed by luxury spa and hair institutes to sell us delicious-sounding gunk ('chocolate mud', 'heavenly organic orange oil'), knead away our aches and pains, and taper our locks to perfection, but also to systematically whack us where it hurts when the bill arrives.

To ensure that all that relaxation doesn't go to waste, I've sniffed out some addresses that won't break the bank and won't make you feel like you're settling for second-best either. And guess what?—some of them are even free.

BODY TALK

Centre Européen d'Enseignement Supérieur de l'Ostéopathie   Pop over the *Périphérique* to the A Mains Nues clinic in Saint-Denis, where final-year osteo students (under the watchful eye of a qualified doctor) will give you a check-up and a massage and click anything untoward back into place for a mere 25€ for non-members; 10€ if you're a student, under-18, unemployed or pregnant; and 15€ if you've already joined (membership is 35€ a year). Also, if you don't mind stripping down in front of a panel of judges, you can get free treatment during the exam periods (just leave your details at the welcome desk).

175 Blvd. Anatole France, 93200 Saint-Denis. ℭ **01 48 09 47 49.** www.amainsnues. com. Metro: Carrefour Pleyel.

Ecole Supérieure de Masseurs-Kinésithérapeutes et Pédicures FREE
Phone plenty of time in advance if you want a free pedicure from a final-year student at the physio and massage school—it's hugely popular. It all takes place under the watchful eye of the professors, but that doesn't take any of the pleasure away. FINE PRINT Students here pay for their schooling, so a 5€ contribution is appreciated.

17 Rue de Liège, 75009. ℭ **01 46 74 62 87.** www.ecoledanhierdekinesitherapie.fr. Metro: Liège.

MASSAGE & HAMMAM
Health & Safety regulations aren't as strict in France as in the English-speaking world, so when it comes to hammams in particular, don't go in if you can't see where you're going. (It sounds ridiculously obvious, but I'm speaking with the experience of someone who sat on hot coals in a hammam where a light bulb was broken.)

Les Bains du Marais There are several formulas at this smart spa, which mixes the modern and traditional (mint tea and lounging beds). The cheapest are a soothing two hours in the hammam and sauna (35€), an exfoliating massage (*gommage*) at 35€, a relaxing or invigorating massage with essential oils (70€ for 50min), or a manicure or a pedicure for 30€–41€.

For the hammam and sauna there are both mixed and single-sex days (women Monday–Wednesday, men Thursday–Friday, mixed Wednesday 7–11pm and Saturday–Sunday). FINE PRINT It's open by appointment only.

Hug me Stranger!
If being hugged by a stranger doesn't leave you rushing for your antiseptic wipes, check out www.calins-gratuits.com to find where and when the next round of free hugs will be given. This 'social happening' (originally from Australia) tries to discourage individualism and break down social inhibitions by offering a random squeeze to passers-by. And in Paris, it's turning out to be quite a success. Guess we all need a little TLC, even from a perfect *inconnu*.

Freebie Massages FREE

When you're desperate for a massage but don't have a centime to your name (or are just feeling thrifty), don't despair. For more than six years, the L'Association de Décontraction à la Française has been practising 'street massage' at the Place de la Contrescarpe in the 5th (Metro: Monge), and sometimes on the bridges around Notre Dame, for absolutely zip. It couldn't be simpler: on warm evenings, find them (they're usually there after 7pm), pull up a chair and spend 10min in bliss, before walking away less stressed than when you arrived. Tipping is appreciated. ℰ **06 69 91 86 35.**

31-33 Rue des Blancs Manteaux, 75004. ℰ **01 44 61 02 02.** www.lesbainsdu marais.fr. Mon, Fri–Sat 10am–8pm; Tues–Thurs, Sun 10am–11pm. Metro: Hôtel de Ville or Rambuteau.

Mosquée de Paris Clean, despite the volume of visitors (avoid weekends, when the numbers make it less relaxing than it should be), and excellent value for money, the mosque's 1920s hammam (tiled in Moorish design from floor to ceiling) is one of the best in town. Start off with a steam session, then let one of the muscled team of exfoliators strip your skin with a rough mitten, before relaxing with a 10min massage and finishing it all off with a mint tea—all for just 38€ (48€ for a 20min massage; 58€ for 30min). FINE PRINT The Mosque is a working, religious edifice, so men and women are always separate in the hammam (women Monday, Wednesday–Thursday, Saturday 10am–9pm; Friday 4–9pm; Men: Tuesday 2–9pm, Sunday 10am–9pm).

The Mosque's restaurant is also excellent value, with sticky oriental pastries at 2€ a pop and couscous at 12€–19€ (p. 65.)

39 Rue Geoffroy-Saint-Hilaire, 75005. ℰ **01 43 31 38 20.** www.la-mosquee.com. Metro: Jussieu or Censier—Daubenton.

★ **Serenity** My absolute favourite: Ex-computer expert Stéphane discovered massage by chance in India and then Tibet—a life-changing experience for him, and also for you once you've tested his healing handiwork. He is a master of both Indian and Tibetan massaging techniques. The former is softer and more relaxing, the latter is more toning although still soothing. It can be accompanied by Tibetan singing bowls (an absolute must), which resonate at frequencies that vibrate the water in your body, performing a kind of internal massage. Prices are wholly reasonable considering what you get, starting at 60€ for an anti-stress *Ayurvédique* (Indian) or Tibetan massage (1hr) and rising to 100€ for a four-handed massage (utter bliss). You can also buy a monthly pass for 120€ or 180€, or book massage lessons for families or couples. FINE PRINT Stéphane's practice is in his front room but it's a totally wholesome and peaceful place in which to be pampered—plus he'll bring you a cup of tea.

63 Rue Victor Hugo, 92300 Levallois-Perret. ℂ **01 47 37 56 59** or **06 11 91 09 38.** http://serenitypassport.free.fr/. Metro: Louise Michel.

MAKE-UP & BEAUTY

If you can't afford to pay for a make-over, make-up schools are just as good at giving you a new look and are always free. If you don't like what you get, you can wash it off when you get home.

Also, check out the make-up counters at department stores Galeries Lafayette (p. 157) and Printemps (p. 157), as well as the cosmetics specialist Sephora (www.sephora.fr, several branches), where the sales folk are trained in make-up demonstrations (they don't have to know you have no intention of spending).

Atelier International de Maquillage FREE Call beforehand to check that they need models (classes are usually Monday–Friday 1.30pm), then await your new look. Although lessons are planned in advance so you can't always get what you want, it's a fun experience.

13 Rue de le Pierre Levée, 75011. ℂ **01 48 05 16 40.** www.ateliermaquillage.com. Metro: République.

Make-up Art Academy FREE Training here only takes place at certain periods of the year, but if you get the timing right, the students will do whatever you fancy: evening make-up, a day look, or something theatrical. Drop them a line to find out the dates. FINE PRINT It's by appointment only.

269 Rue de Charenton, 75012. ℂ **01 48 06 38 88.** www.makeupartacademyparis. com. Metro: Dugommier.

HAIR

What a hairdresser does can have a direct impact on our self-confidence (especially in Paris where looks count so much)—bear that in mind if you sign up as a hair model (the only way to get a free or dirt-cheap haircut in

Paris unless your hairdresser is your best friend). On the plus side, a lot of the students that will be let loose on your locks are very talented. Just ask lots of questions before you go (what styles they're working on, whether you'll get a say in the cut, etc.) to make sure that it's the right hair academy for you.

Académie Jean-Yves Bouley `FREE` This place specialises in trendy, up-to-the minute looks and colours for men and women of all ages. Call to make an appointment; teaching days are usually Mondays and Tuesdays, and they're always looking for models.

156 Blvd. Saint-Germain, 75006. ℂ **01 53 10 82 31.** www.academiejeanyvesbouley. com. Metro: Mabillon.

Ecole Dessange You need to fit specific criteria to get a cheap haircut at the famous Dessange school: You have to be a girl over 16, have straight hair, be available for at least two hours and be willing to have a radical cut (you should expect to lose at least 6cm) and possibly even a colour change. Sittings are usually on Mondays, Tuesdays, and Wednesdays, by reservation only (by telephone Monday–Friday 10am–5pm).

51 Rue Rocher, 75008. ℂ **01 44 70 08 08.** www.jacques-dessange.com. Adm: 5€ for under-25s, 10€ for everyone else. Metro: Europe or Saint-Lazare.

ISEC If a hairdresser's credentials matter to you, this could be the school for you: Most students are already professionals, looking to perfect their techniques. The school's salon is open September–June (closed during school holidays), Tuesday–Friday, and you don't need to reserve—just turn up at 9:30am for the morning session or 1:30pm for the afternoon. Cuts are on a first-come, first-served basis.

28 Rue de Trévise, 75009. ℂ **01 47 70 83 49.** www.ecole-isec.com. Adm: 6€ for men; 11€ for women. Metro: Cadet.

4 Cheap Sleeps

Whether you're travelling to Paris or, like me, you're a resident who is constantly bombarded by the question "Do you know anywhere cheap we could stay?", it's handy to have a few addresses up your sleeve. Here are a few of mine, plus a few tips on finding a flat to rent if you plan to live here for a while.

One important thing to bear in mind when reserving a hotel room is that the 'official' prices (rack rates, not website offers) displayed are mere benchmarks and that almost every establishment will sell you a room for less. If you order over the phone or by email, always try to barter, or at least convince them to include breakfast in the price. Also, as a general rule, Internet rates are lower than rates quoted over the telephone.

DIRT-CHEAP HOSTELS

Centre International BVJ Paris-Louvre   This 207-bed hostel with modern amenities is run by the Bureau des Voyages de la Jeunesse. Rooms are far and away cleaner than in the average hostel, and you can't beat the location close to the Louvre. Plus, it's open 24/7, so the management won't kick you out during cleaning. If you're in a Left Bank state of mind, there's a sister hostel on 44 Rue des Bernardins, 5th, with individual rooms for 45€ per person. FINE PRINT Bedclothes are provided but not towels.

20 Rue Jean-Jacques Rousseau, 75001. ✆ **01 53 00 90 90.** www.bvjhotel.com. 31€ double; 29€ dorms (4–10 beds). Rates include breakfast. Metro: Louvre—Rivoli.

★ **St Christopher's Inn**   This British youth-hostel chain has helped gentrify a stretch of the Canal de l'Ourcq, sprucing up an old hangar with funky décor and offering unbeatable prices in its bar. Rooms-wise it offers excellent marine-themed bedrooms and dorms for an average of 26€ per person, making it one of the cheapest kids on the block. FINE PRINT There are single-sex and mixed dorms so stipulate when you book.

159 Rue de Crimée, 75019. ✆ **01 40 34 34 40.** www.st-christophers.co.uk. 12€–28€ (occasional special offers) dorm; 37.50€–50€ double. Metro: Crimée.

Le Village Hostel   The Village is in a great location on the hip side of Montmartre, and some rooms have amazing views over the Sacré Coeur. It lets you choose between standard dorms, bedrooms (doubles to quads), and studios with their own kitchen area.

20 Rue d'Orsel, 75018. ✆ **01 42 64 22 02.** www.villagehostel.fr. 28€–35€ dorm for 3–8; 35€–45€ double; 32€–38€ triple; 28€–30€ quad; 35€ studio. Metro: Anvers.

DIRT-CHEAP HOTELS & B&BS

Unlike hostels, which charge per person, hotels and B&Bs in Paris always charge per room. The following all cost less than 100€/night for a double.

Alcôve & Agapes   This popular B&B booking service has more than 100 addresses throughout central Paris, with a wide variety of hosts, from bohemian artists and housewives to super-grannies and business folk who are away a lot. Apartments are all regularly inspected and all top-notch.

℘ **01 44 85 06 05.** www.bed-and-breakfast-in-paris.com. Doubles start at 79€.

Hôtel Eldorado   Eccentric and kitted out with flea market finds, this funky hotel is also a coveted address among locals, who come for the cheap Bistro des Dames (p. 55) and pretty, sheltered courtyard. FINE PRINT The cheapest rooms share bathrooms and loos.

18 Rue des Dames, 75017. ℘ **01 45 22 35 21.** www.eldoradohotel.fr. 70€–80€ double. Metro: Place de Clichy.

★ **Mama Shelter**   The founders of Club Med opened this place in 2008—an übër-trendy, low-priced address with décor by design guru Philippe Starck and a hip location in the up-and-coming St-Blaise *quartier* in the 20th. Each room has an iMac computer, CD and DVD player, and free WiFi. Book a saver rate online—non-exchangeable and non-refundable, but guarantees a low price.

109 Rue de Bagnolet, 75020. ℘ **01 43 48 48 48.** www.mamashelter.com. Doubles from 90€. Metro: Alexandre Dumas or Porte de Bagnolet.

VALUE-FOR-MONEY HOTELS

The following all cost less than 180€/night for a double.

★ **Aviatic**   This gem of a hotel is family-run, which is why so much attention goes into every element of your stay here. It's definitely one for historians—the building is on the site of the house where Louis XIV's illegitimate children were brought up, away from the prying eyes of the court, and it was frequented by pilots during both World Wars (hence the name Aviatic). The hotel is plushly decorated in raspberry, chocolate, and coffee tones, and most rooms have parquet floors. The breakfast salon, covered in old bistro posters, feels like a Left Bank institution.

105 Rue de Vaugirard, 75006. ℘ **01 53 63 25 50.** www.aviatic.fr. Doubles from 169€. Parking 27€. Metro: Montparnasse or Saint-Placide.

Hôtel Amour   It's the height of cool to stay at this Pigalle hotel with its 20 rooms designed in a retro style by designers and artists such as

Worth the Splurge

Sometimes, after saving money for a week or two, you want to treat yourself to somewhere special for a night—this is the capital of chic, after all. When that happens, you could do worse than the three below:

The Bohemian-Chic One: Banke   Gorgeous, with true Belle Epoque style and a touch of Spanish-style grandeur, Banke (owned by a Spanish group) is a wonderful choice for a night of luxury, with sleek rooms, views over Paris's rooftops, and a mini art gallery on every floor.

20 Rue La Fayette, 75009. ℂ **01 55 33 22 22.** www.derbyhotels.com. Doubles from 330€. Metro: Chaussée d'Antin.

The Classical One: Hôtel de Vendôme   Smack bang in the middle of the most expensive square in the world (Place Vendôme, dripping in designer jewellers' shops), this place is surprisingly discreet and understatedly palatial, with a fabulous restaurant, N° 1 Place Vendôme (p. 71) and a unique whisky bar that sells some rare malts.

1 Place Vendôme, 75001. ℂ **01 55 04 55 00.** www.hoteldevendome. com. Doubles from 535€. Metro: Tuileries.

The Ultra-Modern One: Hôtel Five   *Bijou* in every sense of the word, this Left Bank boutique hotel drips in Chinese lacquer, LED lighting—embedded in the walls to look like starry skies—and velvet fabrics. If you can afford the suite, it's worth every centime, with its own wee garden and a Jacuzzi.

3 Rue Flatters, 75005. ℂ **01 43 31 74 21.** www.thefivehotel.com. Doubles from 180€. Metro: Les Gobelins.

Marc Newson, M/M, and Sophie Calle. Some bathrooms are not separate from the sleeping area, which is fine if you're in a couple—if you're sharing with friends you might like more intimacy. The look carries on through to the sweet 1950s courtyard where you can have a natter, eat, drink, look pretty (if you want to fit in), and watch the goldfish.

8 Rue Navarin, 75009. ℂ **01 48 78 31 80.** www.hotelamourparis.fr. Doubles from 140€. Metro: Anvers, Pigalle or Saint-Georges.

Renting a Flat

As Parisians all know, finding a flat can be hell, because (a) They're expensive (b) You have to have a list of credentials as long as your arm (proof of income, guarantors, etc.) (c) There's fierce competition and (d) You often have to put down a deposit worth up to two months' rent.

Whether you're looking for a short- or long-term rent, some of the cheapest *arrondissements* are the 19th, 20th, 11th, 10th, 13th, 14th, 18th (except Montmartre) and 17th (north of Les Batignolles). Also, flat-shares (*collocations*; a relatively new concept in Paris) are increasingly popular these days.

Here are some must-see websites:

Apartments:
www.fusac.fr
http://paris.kijiji.fr (and flat-shares)
www.acheter-louer.fr
www.avendrealouer.fr
www.seloger.com (and flat-shares)
Flat-shares:
www.recherche-colocation.com
www.appartager.com

5 Free & Dirt Cheap Recreation

When hauling groceries and laundry up six flights of steps to your top-floor pad is no longer exercise enough, you know it's time to get physical. Paris is awash with gyms, swimming pools and (since the Council introduced the self-service bike-hire system, Vélibs) bicycles, so there really is no excuse. Whether you're looking to run, hop, skip, jump, pedal, or even chuck a boomerang around, something low-cost awaits your discovery.

What follows are the cheapest addresses. There are dozens more (I could have written an entire book on just gyms and sports centres alone). For more information on what's out there, visit www.paris.fr (under 'Sports'). See also Green Peace: Gardens in the chapter Exploring Paris (p. 243). Note that certain free activities are seasonal, so it's worth making a note in your diary.

BIKING

Parisians on bicycles may be an age-old cliché but the stereotype still rings true—and not always minus the baguette, although berets are—pun intended—old hat at the moment! Perhaps it's because Paris has plenty of road-ways that can easily be turned into recreational opportunities. There are an increasing number of cycle paths across town too. The Ville de Paris's website, www.paris.fr (under 'Déplace-ments'), has a map you can download. But be careful: that other cliché about Parisians driv-ing like maniacs is *complètement* true!

Custombrigade Night Cruise FREE The second Friday of every month, at 10pm, the own-ers of custom-designed bicycles get together for a night cruise around town. As the wheels of the Beach Cruisers, Low-riders, Choppers, and other funky con-traptions turn, so do passers-by's heads. You can join in, of course, but only if you've got a custom bike.

Meeting point: in front of Notre Dame, 75004. www.custombrigad.com.

Paris Rando Vélo FREE One of the best ways to take advantage of Paris's hard surfaces (and stunning scenery) is to band up with fellow riders. Most Friday nights at 9:30pm, wheeled crews turn up in front of the Hôtel de Ville in the 4th to reclaim the roads (and cause traffic jams as drivers wait for hundreds of bikes to pass) and do a spot of sightseeing. It also takes place on the third Sunday of every month at 10:30am.

www.parisrandovelo.com.

Vélo Hire

If you need to hire a bike for more than a short journey (in which case, take a Vélib—see p. 132), then try **Vélo et Choco-lat** (75 Quai de la Seine, 75019. ✆ **01 46 07 07 87.** Metro Riquet), which doubles as a café (specialising in hot chocolate). There's also **Cyclo Pouce** (38 Quai de la Marne, 75019. ✆ **01 42 41 76 98.** Metro Ourcq), which can provide baby and tod-dler seats. **Allo Vélo** (44 Rue des Petits Carreaux, 75002. ✆ **01 40 35 36 36.** www.allovelo.com) and **Paris à Vélo C'est Sympa** (22 Rue Alphonse Baudin, 75011. ✆ **01 48 87 60 01.** www.paris velosympa.com. Metro: Saint-Sébastien—Froissart) are both in handy, central locations. All charge around 8€ for two hours or 25€ a day.

Vélibs `FREE` (almost) Kitting Paris out with self-service bikes was a jolly good idea—so good that two years on, they're ridden all over the city, and a similar scheme with cars, the Autolib, is being introduced in 2010 or 2011. It works like this: You buy a one-day pass with your credit card at an access terminal (there's one every 300m). The fee is just 1€ for the day, plus a 150€ deposit, which is retained only if the bike gets stolen or damaged. The ticket gives unlimited access to the bikes for 24 hours. There is no additional charge for every journey that doesn't last more than 30min. For every extra half-hour you spend on the bike (after the first 30min), you will be charged 1€. You can return your bike to any stand in the city, but will have to take a bike from a different stand if you want to continue your journey for another 30min. Alternatively, spend a euro and go from A to B without stopping.

There are also weekly cards (7€) or an annual pass (29€); apply online). The latter saves you oodles of time as you just need to swipe it on the stand corresponding to the bike you decide to take, rather than input the code on your ticket. Popular stands at train stations and favourite Parisian meeting points (like Bastille and St Michel) often run out of bikes, but you can check online for up-to-the-minute numbers of bikes in every stand across Paris and adjust your journey accordingly. `FINE PRINT` The website has up-to-the-minute info on the number of bikes available at the stands, which are next to access terminals.

www.velib.paris.fr/.

> ### Paris Respire—Paris Breathes
>
> On Sundays and public holidays during the warmer months certain Paris roads (mostly those along the river) are closed to traffic in favour of cyclists, rollerbladers and strollers.

CHEAP SKATES

Zee French love zhere rollers, so there are opportunities for collective outings galore. Rollerblades are also tolerated on the pavement, so you can don your wheels whenever you fancy. Whilst helmets and other protection aren't obligatory for adults, they are highly recommended, and outings organisers insist that children are protected.

Pari Roller `FREE` "It's 9:30pm on a Friday night and a few skaters are pulling on their wheels at the base of the Montparnasse tower. Half an hour later, around 15,000 of them whizz off for a 30km sprint around Paris that lasts until 1am." Thus goes the online introduction to Pari Roller—and it's true down to a T (I watch them out of my lounge window!).

Meeting point: Place Raoul Dautry, 75014. www.pari-roller.com. Metro: Montparnasse.

Rollers & Coquillages   **FREE**
These rollerblading excursions around Paris every Sunday (2:30–5:30pm, from Bastille) are great for families or anyone who can keep up. Parents with toddlers can bring their children along in a sturdy pushchair and youngsters can join in as long as they know how to change direction and brake. The route covers 17–23km in 3 hours, police and ambulances provide security, and you can hire reasonably priced equipment from **Nomades** (37 Blvd. Bourdon, 4th; www.nomadeshop.com) near the departure point.

www.rollers-coquillages.org.

Gathering Speed FREE

If you're fed up of stopping at traffic lights and slowing down for traffic, the Bois de Boulogne has 3.6km trail cycling around the Hippodrome de Longchamp (horse-racing track), while in the Bois de Vincennes, 4.9km of roads (route de Bourbon, route Royale de Beauté and route Dauphine) create a triangle that is perfect for speeding. Tour de France, here we come!

GYM GEMS & JOGGING

Joining a gym in Paris can cost up to 1,000€ a year—a big investment, meaning you'd better stick with it if you want to get your money's worth. The biggie (and possibly the most expensive) is **Club Med** (www.clubmedgym.fr), with gyms all over town, followed closely by **Vit'Halles** (www.vithalles.fr).

For a cheaper gym check out the **Gym Suédoise** (www.gymsuedoise.com), which promotes Swedish gym techniques and has classes (at several sites across the city) that start at 255€ a year. Or try some of thefollowing:

★ **Attractive FREE**   Attractive is France's first sports shop dedicated to women, but that doesn't mean that men can't take advantage of the free hour-long mixed stretching, muscle-toning and running lessons held every Saturday (meet at 10.45am in the boutique) in the Jardin du Luxembourg. (Single gentlemen: between you and me, it's a fine way to meet the ladies.)

Rules of the Roller Game

1 Bring enough to drink—even in winter—and an energising snack for the pause.

2 Bring an extra pair of shoes and a metro ticket in case you get tired, your skates break or you need to leave early.

3 Make sure you're insured.

4 Note that the event will be called off if it's raining.

123 Rue de Rennes, 75006. ℂ **01 42 22 11 49.** www.attractive.fr. Sat 10:45am. Metro: Saint-Placide or Rennes.

Cours de Gym Eléctro Tonic `FREE` Every Monday at 7:20pm, keep-fitters on a shoestring meet for free open-air cardiovascular sessions (muscle-building, breathing, and relaxation) in the Parc des Buttes Chaumont (at the corner of Rues Botzaris and Bolivar); if it rains, lessons sometimes take place in a gallery in Rue Jean-Pierre Timbaud, 75011. www.collectif-surprise-party.com.

Qi Gong `FREE` At 9am almost every day come rain or come shine Master Thoï Tin Cau gives free, hour-long Qi Gong lessons (gym for your organs, where slow, harmonious movements create a sense of well-being and give your innards a workout) in the Parc des Buttes Chaumont, next to the Café Weber (south of Rue Botzaris. Metro: Botzaris), or a sheltered square elsewhere in the park if it's raining. If the Master thinks you're good enough, you can stay on until 11am and practise tai chi.

PAUPERS' POOLS

Swimming in Paris is dirt-cheap. There are 38 municipal pools (piscines de la Ville de Paris) to choose from, all charging just 3€ a ticket (2.40€ if you buy a card of 10, valid in any municipal swimming pool). If it's a retro feel you're after, the **Piscine de Pontoise** (17 Rue de Pontoise, 75005. ℂ **01 55 42 77 88**) is a gorgeous 1930s offering with three levels and old-fashioned cabins. Alternatively, the **Piscine de la Butte aux Cailles** (5 Place Paul Verlaine, 75013. ℂ **01 45 89 60 05**) is a red-brick Art Nouveau edifice with imposing arches, built on a natural source.

For a complete list of addresses and opening times, see www.paris.fr.

MEDITATION

Centre Kalachakra `FREE` Dress comfortably to join around 30 devotees each week for an hour and a half of sweet vacuity. `FINE PRINT` A donation of around 5€ is much appreciated.

Passage Delessert, 75010. ℭ **01 40 05 02 22.** www.centre-kalachakra.com. Metro: Château-Landon.

WATERSPORTS

Base Nautique de Choisy-le-Roi `FREE` Just 10min from Paris by RER lies this slice of country life: A huge lake where you can learn canoeing, kayaking and windsailing. `FINE PRINT` You'll need two passport photos and proof that you can swim 50m to enrol. No reservations are taken, so turn up at least 20min beforehand. Children can also partake on certain days and during school holidays (p. 104.)

Parc Interdépartemental de Choisy-le-Roi, Chemin des Boeufs. ℭ **01 48 52 56 31.** www.paris.fr. Sat 9am–midday, 2–5pm; Sun 9am–midday mid-March to end July and mid-Sept to mid-Dec (closed public hols). RER: Villeneuve-Prairies.

Base Nautique de la Villette `FREE` Rowing and kayaking in central Paris are absolutely free at the Bassin de la Villette on Saturdays (weather permitting). They're popular so reserve at least a week in advance. `FINE PRINT` Bring ID, proof of address (you'll need a Paris address, folks), two passport photos and proof you can swim 25m (un brevet). A change of clothes is handy too.

41 Bis Quai de la Loire, 75019. ℭ **01 42 40 29 90.** www.paris.fr. Metro: Riquet.

BOOMERANG

Art Boomerang Club `FREE` You don't need to take a trip Down Under to learn the Aboriginal art of boomerang throwing, nor do you even have to own one—there are plenty to borrow at Art Boomerang Club, which welcomes novices and experienced throwers on the first Sunday of the month (and on other dates during warm weather) at the Parc de Sceaux (RER: B Croix de Berry) and, when the nights get longer, most Friday nights at the Parc de Bagatelle in the Bois de Boulogne (Metro: Porte Maillot, then bus 244 to Carrefour de Longchamp and walk to the *terrain d'entrainement*, as it is called on certain maps).

http://artboomerangclub.free.fr.

RIGHT BANK WEST LIVING

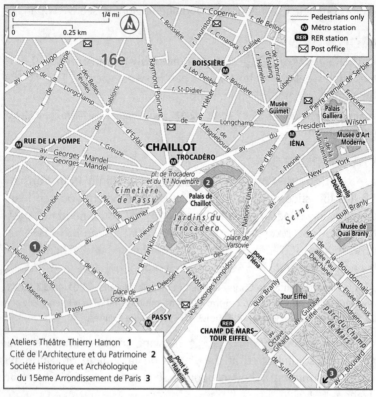

Ateliers Théâtre Thierry Hamon **1**
Cité de l'Architecture et du Patrimoine **2**
Société Historique et Archéologique
   du 15ème Arrondissement de Paris **3**

Centre International BVJ Paris-Louvre **1**

Centre National d'Art et de Culture Georges Pompidou **3**

Conférence Berryer au Palais de Justice **6**

Custombrigade Night Cruise **7**

Forum des Images **2**

Les Bains du Marais **4**

Make-up Art Academy **8**

Paris Rando Vélo **5**

RIGHT BANK CENTRE LIVING

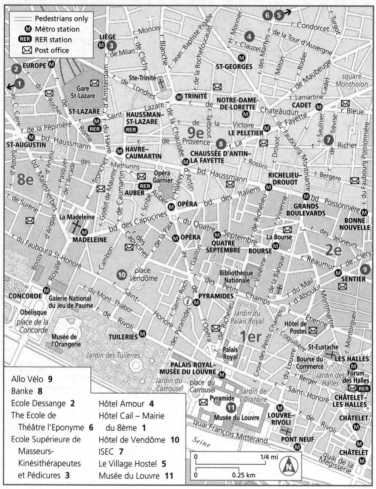

- Pedestrians only
- Ⓜ Métro station
- RER RER station
- ✉ Post office

Legend / List:

Allo Vélo **9**
Banke **8**
Ecole Dessange **2**
The Ecole de
  Théâtre l'Eponyme **6**
Ecole Supérieure de
  Masseurs-
  Kinésithérapeutes
  et Pédicures **3**

Hôtel Amour **4**
Hôtel Cail – Mairie
  du 8ème **1**
Hôtel de Vendôme **10**
ISEC **7**
Le Village Hostel **5**
Musée du Louvre **11**

0 ———— 1/4 mi
0 ———— 0.25 km

RIGHT BANK NORTH EAST LIVING

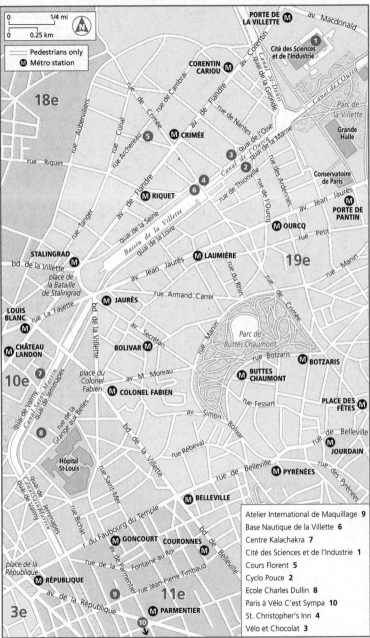

Atelier International de Maquillage **9**
Base Nautique de la Villette **6**
Centre Kalachakra **7**
Cité des Sciences et de l'Industrie **1**
Cours Florent **5**
Cyclo Pouce **2**
Ecole Charles Dullin **8**
Paris à Vélo C'est Sympa **10**
St. Christopher's Inn **4**
Vélo et Chocolat **3**

LEFT BANK CENTRE LIVING

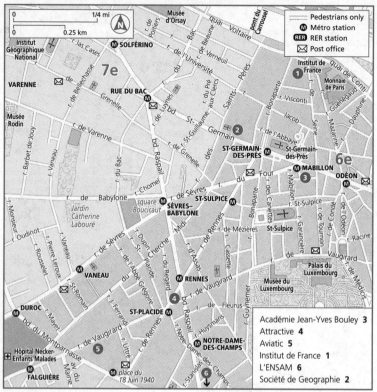

0   1/4 mi
0   0.25 km

Musée d'Orsay
quai Voltaire
pont du Carrousel

Pedestrians only
Ⓜ Métro station
ⓇⒺⓇ RER station
✉ Post office

Institut
Géographique
National

r. las Cases   Ⓜ SOLFÉRINO

r. de Poitiers
r. du Bac
r. de Beaune
r. de l'Université
r. de Verneuil

Institut de
France ①

Monnaie
de Paris

quai de Conti

7e

VARENNE ✉ de Bellechasse

RUE DU BAC

r. du Pré-
aux Clercs
Saints-Pères

r. de Luynes

r. de Bonaparte
r. Visconti
Jacob
Seine

Guénébaud

Dauphine

Grenelle

Ⓜ

bd. St-Germain

r. de l'Abbaye

r. de St-Guillaume

Mazarine

de

Musée
Rodin

r. de Barbet-de-Jouy
r. Vaneau

r. de Varenne

bd. Raspail

r. de Grenelle

② ✝

ST-GERMAIN-
DES-PRÉS

Ⓜ St-Germain-
des-Prés

6e

Ⓜ MABILLON
③

ODÉON
Ⓜ

r. Chomel

r. de Sèvres

du Four

r. des-Canettes

Bonaparte

r. Mabillon

de l'Odéon

de Babylone

square
Boucicaut

Ⓜ
SÈVRES–
BABYLONE

r. de Sèvres
Midi

ST-SULPICE
Ⓜ

St-Sulpice

r. de Mézières   St-Sulpice

r. de Tournon

St-Sulpice

r. Garancière

r. Racine

r. Monsieur
r. Oudinot

Jardin
Catherine
Labouré

r. Dupin
r. du Cherche

r. de Rennes

Cassette

✉

de Vaugirard

r. de Médicis

r. Pierre Leroux
r. Rousselet

Ⓜ r. de l'Abbé Grégoire

d'Assas

Palais du
Luxembourg

VANEAU
Ⓜ

r. Dupin
St-placide
r. du Regard

Ⓜ RENNES
④

r. de Vaugirard

r. Guynemer

Musée du
Luxembourg

DUROC
Ⓜ

✉ r. St-Romain

bd. Raspail

de Fleurus

Académie Jean-Yves Bouley ③

r. Mayet

r. Ferrandi

ST-PLACIDE
Ⓜ

r. Notre-Dame-des-Champs

r. Huysmans

Attractive ④

Aviatic ⑤

bd. du Montparnasse

r. de Vaugirard
r. Littré

r. de Rennes

NOTRE-DAME-
DES-CHAMPS

Institut de France ①

L'ENSAM ⑥

Hôpital Necker-
Enfants Malades

⑤

av. du Maine

place du
18 Juin 1940

r. Stanislas

⑥
↓

Société de Geographie ②

FALGUIÈRE
Ⓜ

LEFT BANK EAST LIVING

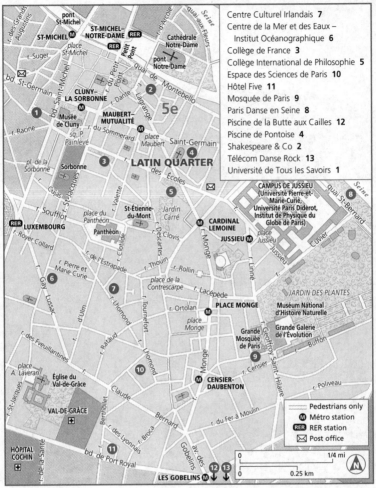

Centre Culturel Irlandais **7**
Centre de la Mer et des Eaux –
Institut Océanographique **6**
Collège de France **3**
Collège International de Philosophie **5**
Espace des Sciences de Paris **10**
Hôtel Five **11**
Mosquée de Paris **9**
Paris Danse en Seine **8**
Piscine de la Butte aux Cailles **12**
Piscine de Pontoise **4**
Shakespeare & Co **2**
Télécom Danse Rock **13**
Université de Tous les Savoirs **1**

Pedestrians only
Ⓜ Métro station
ᴿᴱᴿ RER station
✉ Post office

0 ————— 1/4 mi
0 ————— 0.25 km

The well known retailer Tati on the Boulevard Rochechouart.

SHOPPING

Parisians love 'window-licking' or *lèche-vitrine*—'window-shopping', as we describe it. This is a city that positively drips with haute-couture boutiques, luxury markets, exclusive *chocolatiers*, expensive department stores, lavish antique-dealers and *cavistes* selling one-off vintage wines—things that make you salivate even when you're all too aware that your purse-strings won't stretch that far.

To avoid overworking your tongue (and reduce window-cleaning bills), follow my **Six Shopper's Commandments**:

① Thou shalt avoid the designer shops around the Champs-Elysées, Madeleine and Avenue Montaigne, and in the 1st and 6th *arrondissements*, where, generally speaking, everything is expensive.

② Thou shalt only visit department stores during the sales.

③ Thou shalt never be tempted to take on a store credit card, which will undoubtedly end up costing you more in the long run.

④ Thou shalt check out cheap 'n' chirpy chain stores and vintage shops.

⑤ If thou art really hankering after a designer outfit, thou shalt head to a luxury *dépôt-vente* (second-hand shop), where prices are usually halved.

⑥ Thou shalt not be afraid of heading off the beaten track.

Unlike some cities, such as New York, where stores of a similar price-range pack themselves into the same neighbourhood, Paris doesn't have specific dirt-cheap shopping areas—just a sprinkling of low-price shops on seemingly random streets. This makes bargain shopping an emotional rollercoaster ride: Annoying when you can't find what you're looking for, but joyous when you snatch that deal in an affordable boutique on a hitherto unexplored street.

1 Shopping Zones Quick List

Where the city does help us out is in the fact that stores of a similar stripe tend to cluster in the same area. Antiques shops, for instance, are rife in the 7th *arrondissement*, while you'll find numerous second-hand bookshops in the 5th.

Although not all of the shops within them are cheap, I find these clusters as good a place to start as any. What follows is a list of the main shopping zones and their specialities (for specific affordable addresses, see the shopping A–Z).

- **Street-chic and lifestyle outlets:** The Marais and around the Rue Etienne Marcel in the 2nd.

- **Vintage clothing:** The Marais.

- **Antiques shops:** Around Rue Saint-Paul in the Marais and the 7th *arrondissement*.

- **Curiosities:** The covered passages in the 2nd and 9th (see the walk on p. 279).

- **Books:** The 5th, including the riverside *bouquinistes*, especially on the Quai de Montebello and Quai Saint-Michel (p. 160).

- **Shoes:** The 6th, around Rue du Cherche-Midi and Rue de Grenelle.

- **Department stores and high-street fashion:** Opéra, around the Boulevard Haussmann.

- **Porcelain:** The Rue du Paradis in the 10th.

- **Bikes and cameras:** The boulevard de Beaumarchais, 11th.

- **Furniture and children's clothes:** Rue du Faubourg Saint- Antoine. 11th/12th.

Opening hours

Generally speaking (and unless otherwise specified here), shops open Monday to Saturday 10am–7pm, with a few specialist boutiques closing for an hour at lunch. Late-night shopping is Thursday, when department stores and most shops stay open until 8pm. President Sarko is pushing for widespread Sunday trading, but until then your options are limited to the Marais (75004. Metro: Saint-Paul), Bercy Village (75012. Metro: Cour Saint-Emilion), Champs-Elysées (75008. Metro: Franklin D. Roosevelt) and the Carrousel du Louvre, underneath the museum (99 Rue de Rivoli, 75001. Metro: Palais Royal) to spend on the 'Holy' day.

- **Flea markets:** Porte de Clignancourt (18th) and Porte de Vanves (14th).

- **Shopping mall:** Châtelet—Les Halles.

- **Quirky fashion:** The Canal Saint-Martin, 10th and Abbesses, 18th.

- **Window-licking designer-wear:** The 8th, 1st and 6th.

2 Dirt Cheap Threads

Dirt-cheap clothing in Paris falls into four categories: Charity, vintage, *dépôt-vente* (bring and buy luxury second-hand stores) or high-street.

In the charity shops, you'll have to sift through piles of junk to find that perfect jacket, but it won't set you back more than a few euros. For vintage clothes, there are two types of store to look out for: *Fripperies*, which tend to concentrate on attire from the 1970s to the 1990s and *boutiques vintages*, which concentrate on older items from 1900 onwards (they also usually clean the clothes before they sell them).

For luxury bargains at 30%–70% of their usual retail price, I always head to a *dépôt-vente*. This is where locals go to sell their unwanted designer-wear, and more often than not the clothes there have never been worn (although if it's a Chanel suit you're after, it's still a several hundred euro commitment).

Finally, Paris's high street is jam-packed with affordable brands (albeit those you'll find everywhere else in the western world) so you can kit yourself out without denting the old bank balance.

DIRT-CHIC VINTAGE

France caught onto the vintage bandwagon relatively late in the day. Fortunately for us tightwads, they've made up for lost time and vintage clothes are now a permanent part of the shopping scene. What follows are my favourites. Most are open 2–7pm, including Sundays.

Come On Eileen   At first glance this boutique is tiny, but head downstairs and you'll find a vast area packed to the gunnels with everything from 1960s shift dresses to 1970s suits and 1980s rock and punk gear. There's also a good designer section, but watch the prices (or haggle). Budget items sit next to the more expensive stuff, so whilst you'll find bargains at 20€, you'll also come across price tags as high as 300€–400€.

6–18 Rue des Taillandiers, 75011. ℂ **01 43 38 12 11.** Metro: Bastille.

Culotte   Run by a Japanese Parisian, Minako Ito, this is where you come for funky jewellery made from vintage beads. For the price (just 5€–40€), the effect is rather cutting-edge. There's a small selection of clothes too, but there aren't any changing rooms, so only buy if you're sure.

7 Rue Malher, 75004. Metro: Saint-Paul.

Freep'star   Loud music and the whiff of second-hand clothes permeate this tiny Marais HQ of funky 1970s and 1980s wear for men and women, costing from 10€ upwards. There's a particularly wild selection of party dresses (around 20€) in the corner, above the rickety staircase, which leads down to the furs and coats section, and if you have the patience to rummage through the boxes, you can find trendy bags and belts for both sexes from 5€. There's a second branch at 61 Rue de la Verrerie (75004).

8 Rue Sainte Croix de la Bretonnerie. © **01 42 76 03 72.** www.freepstar.com. Metro: Hôtel de Ville.

★ **Guerrisol** Undoubtedly the cheapest *fripperie* in town, with items as low as 1.50€, this is also the biggest and the smelliest, so hold your nose as you rifle through the rows of skirts, trousers, jackets, coats, shoes, shirts, and anything else that can be worn. It's usually worth it. If you don't find what you're looking for, there are three other Guerrisol shops.

17 Bis Blvd. Rochechouart, 75009. No phone. Metro: Barbès-Rochechouart.

Also: 29–31 Ave. de Clichy (75017. Metro: Place de Clichy), 22 Blvd. Poissonnière (75009. Metro: Grands Boulevards) and 21 Blvd. Barbès (75018. Metro: Château Rouge).

King of Frip A hip crowd can be found combing through the 'King's' myriad hangers dangling with gaudy 1970s fabrics, lace, lycra, cotton and denim. This is the cheapest *fripperie* in the Marais, hence the crowds, especially at weekends. If you're looking for leather, check out the back room, where you can pick up cool jackets for 20€ upwards and kitsch cowboy boots.

33 Rue du Roi de Sicile, 75004. © **01 42 78 33 72.** Metro: Saint-Paul.

Kiliwatch Somewhat of a vintage trailblazer, this funky urban boutique dares to mix new clothes (mainly streetwear by Pepe Jeans and Diesel) with second-hand attire. It's not the cheapest *fripperie* on the block, but it's one of the best, especially for shoes and accessories that won't break the bank.

64 Rue Tiquetonne, 75002. © **01 42 21 17 37.** http://espacekiliwatch.fr. Metro: Etienne Marcel.

Noir Kennedy If Pete Doherty and Buffy the Vampire Slayer went shopping together, this is where they'd come. Modish T-shirts, chequered shirts and semi-risqué heavy rock garb by brands such as Cheap Monday and April 77 sit among boots and 1980s shoes with attitude, costing from 5€ upwards.

12 and 22 Rue du Roi de Sicile, 75004. © **01 42 74 55 58.** www.noirkennedy.fr. Metro: Saint-Paul.

★ **Rags and Vertige**   This Ali-Baba's cave of retro fashion contains some of the best and cheapest selections of vintage wear that Paris has to offer, with oodles of original 1960s shift dresses for 10€, tuxedo jackets for 20€, skinny 1980s jeans for 8€ and lots more bargains. The next-door shoe shop (part of the same company) sells rows of cool vintage Converse sneakers and cowboy boots, while a third address (81 Rue Saint-Honoré, 75001) provides interesting designer offerings at a wide range of prices (5€ to 500€, depending on the brand and the quality).

83/85 Rue Saint Martin, 75004. ℂ **01 48 87 34 64.** Metro: Hôtel de Ville.

ALMOST-NEW LUXURY: DEPOT-VENTES

Fashionistas delight in Paris's well-stocked *dépôt-ventes*—temples of second-hand luxury fashion at a sliver of the price. That doesn't mean dirt-cheap, however—think value for money.

Nor does it always mean cutting-edge fashion. The stock depends on what locals bring in to sell, so there's no guarantee you'll find this season's Jean Paul Gaultier bustier, or that 'must-have' YSL suit and tie. That said, the fickle nature of Paris's designer clientele is reliable (those who can afford to buy can also afford to change their minds), so chances are you'll find something hot off the catwalk whether you're a boy or a girl.

★ **Chercheminippes**   A sure-fire hit with everyone thanks to its vast range of fashion items for women, men and children, plus oodles of accessories and home decorations, this store (actually several shops) occupies a chunk of the Rue du Cherche-Midi (6th), so it's easy to hop between sections. In the women's boutique, items are classed by brand (think Agnès B and Vanessa Bruno) or colour. I recently picked up a Maje dress for 20€ (150€ when new) and, in the designer section, a slinky YSL skirt for just 70€. Menswear, just as affordable, might include Issey Miyake shirts (40€) and reasonable bits and bobs by brands such as Dior and Pierre Cardin.

102, 109, 111, 112, 114 and 124 Rue du Cherche-Midi, 75006. ℂ **01 45 44 97 96** (womenswear), **01 42 22 53 76** (menswear), **01 42 22 33 89** (childrenswear). Metro: Falguière.

Les Ginettes   Scoring 10/10 for atmosphere, wares and prices but only 5/10 for service (staff are slightly standoffish and you have to stand in the middle of the shop to see what you're trying on in the mirror), Les Ginettes has an excellent range of womenswear by French high-street brands (high and low end) such as Maje, Sandro, Les Petites, Claudie Pierlot, and all-rounder H&M.

4 Rue du Sabot, 75006. ℭ **01 42 22 45 14.** www.lesginettes.net. Metro: Saint-Germain-des-Près.

J'y Troque   If it's basics you're after, and service with a smile (a rarity in Paris), J'y Troque is for you. French brands such as Isabel Marant, Madame à Paris, and See by Chloé adorn the rails, swimwear and simple tops and T-shirts are nestled in one corner, bags by Marni and Fendi hang on the other side, and there's the occasional designer bargain to be found—perhaps a Burberry trench coat at 400€ instead of 950€ when new. Certain items (and their prices) can be consulted on the website. *Tip:* Don't be afraid to haggle.

7 Rue Villedo, 75001. http://jytroque. com. Metro: Pyramides.

★ **Réciproque**   Another fashion institution, Réciproque takes up several boutiques on Rue de la Pompe. If you're looking for a Chanel suit at a third of the price, a vintage Dior dress or any other old designer-wear and accessories, this should be your first port of call. Budget-wise, you're still looking at hundreds, but that's better than the thousands you would pay if it was new. N° 93 is for women's eveningwear, with a flurry of cocktail dresses. N° 92 is for gentlemen, offering a large range of ties, suits, sportswear,

★ **Je Loue du Luxe (if you can't afford it, hire it)**

If buying a brand-new Prada evening dress, or a limited-edition Chanel jacket is out of the question, don't despair. **Je Loue du Luxe** ('I Hire Luxury') lets you do what it says on the packet—play at being the proud (but temporary) owner of items worthy of Cannes' red carpet for just 150€ for three days for dresses and jackets or 65€ for designer handbags (then 25€ per extra day). The boutique opened in 2009, so the only brands available at the time of writing are Chanel, Lanvin and Jay Ahr (plus YSL and Louis Vuitton handbags), but that's enough to make a serious impact, and you can have immense fun trying the clothes on. FINE PRINT By appointment only.

31 Rue Etienne Marcel, 75001. ℭ **06 28 42 03 89** or **06 25 48 77 18.** www.jelouedeluxe.com. Metro: Etienne Marcel.

Top Secret: An Insider's Address for the Girlies

I would have preferred not to share this address with you, but all's fair in love and shopping! Six times a year, the **Tiennette la Belette** Parisian *créateurs* (fashion and accessory designers) get together for an open-atelier sale day (usually Tuesday after work). It works like this: You scale the rails for that 'must-have' item, then accessorise at the hand-crafted jewellery stands before heading off to the underwear section (matching knickers and bras please!) and on to the till for a pleasant 30%–70% discount (off normal retail price, not necessarily off what's on the label). This is insider's stuff, so you'll have to sign up to the newsletter on the website to get an invitation to the sales.

49 Rue de Bagnolet, 75020. ℂ **01 44 64 77 67.** www.tiennettela belette.com. Metro: Alexandre Dumas.

shirts and cufflinks. N° 89 is for knick-knack lovers, N° 101 has endless supplies of bags, fantasy jewellery and leather, and N° 95 has two floors of women's streetwear, fur, hats and shoes.

89, 92, 93, 95 and 101 Rue de la Pompe, 75016. ℂ **01 47 04 30 28** (womenswear), **01 47 04 30 28** (menswear), **01 47 27 93 52** (accessories). Metro: Rue de la Pompe.

★ **Violette et Léonie** The trendiest of all the *dépôt-ventes*, this is where you'll find *très parisienne* brands at half the retail price. Men should look out for Burberry shirts at 67€, Viktor & Rolf gear from 30€, and Celio linen suits for 50€. Ladies, check out the Vanessa Bruno silk dresses at 112€, Helmut Lang skirts for 80€, and even H&M items (although H&M's own sales are cheaper than here). There's also a good jewellery and accessories collection. The website allows you to search for items and consult prices from the comfort of your home.

27 Rue de Poitou, 75003. ℂ **01 44 59 87 35.** www.violetteleonie.com. Metro: Saint-Sébastien—Froissart.

CHARITY CHARITY

Parisians are a snobby lot. Unlike in Britain, where Oxfam and Help the Aged have been dressing the nation for decades (especially students and hipsters looking for extra-cheap vintage gear), the French have always considered charity shops unfashionable places where the needy are forced to shop. Only now are Parisians cottoning on to their full potential: Cheap prices, helping the environment by reusing items that would otherwise be thrown to waste, raising money for charities and, of course, sourcing that one-off bargain that no-one else will have.

Emmaüs (the charity founded by the great Abbé Pierre in 1953 to help the homeless) is the only real charity shop to have made any headway in France, so it's not surprising that it was, until 2009 (when Merci opened; p. 152), the only one with clothes shops in central Paris. In conjunction with the Paris Council, Emmaüs also plans to open a dozen or so bric-à-brac stores in the centre between now and 2013 (one is already open in the 14th; p. 158) so keep your eyes peeled.

Emmaüs Charonne and Beaumarchais The key to good Emmaüs shopping is to choose your neighbourhood well. Most stuff is brought in by the locals, so if you visit a branch in a trendy area, you're more likely to find decent clothing. The stores on hip Rue de Charonne and nearby boulevard de Beaumarchais are my favourite rummaging haunts. I don't always find what I want, but turnover is quite fast and every now and again I get lucky.

54 Rue de Charonne, 75011. ℂ **01 48 07 02 28.** Metro: Charonne or Ledru-Rollin and 22 Blvd. Beaumarchais, 75004. ℂ **01 47 00 70 44.** Metro: Bastille or Chemin Vert. Other addresses: 105 Blvd. Davout (ℂ **01 46 59 13 06**) and 340 Rue des Pyrénées (ℂ **01 40 33 69 07**), both 75020. www.emmaus-france.org.

Salon Emmaüs

Fancy some one-off, cheap vintage wear and a clean conscience? The Salon Emmaüs (usually held in June at the Porte de Versailles exhibition) is a 27,000m² hunting ground for charity items (clothes, shoes, belts, buckles, beads, buttons, scarves, hats…). Last year, fashion designers Christian Lacroix, Stella Cadente, and the Elle Foundation chipped in with some unique rags, and upcoming editions promise more shopping fun, with bric-à-brac and household stuff. The money raised all goes to charity, of course.

Salon Emmaüs, Porte de Versailles, 75015. www.emmausfrance.org. Adm: 3€, free under-15s and unemployed. Metro: Porte de Versailles.

La Fripperie Solidaire This is the first of a new sort of charity shop (also owned by Emmaüs) that gives work to the unemployed and the occasional homeless person. Prices are seriously low (you can pick up most clothes items for less than 8€) and there's an excellent kids area at the back of the shop, selling clothes and toys in good condition.

17 Rue de Chaligny, 75012. ✆ **01 46 28 83 57.** www.lafriperiesolidaire.com. Metro: Reuilly-Diderot.

Merci Just down the road from Emmaüs on boulevard Beaumarchais is Paris's first charity concept store, created by Marie-France and Bernard Cohen, founders of the French children's brand Bonpoint. Items aren't always second-hand (some clothes, objects and furniture ranges have been created for the shop) and prices aren't always low, but there are bargains to be had. Profits go to humanitarian organisations in Madagascar (where one baby dies of malnutrition every five minutes). There's also a funky café, a florist and an Annick Goutal perfume section.

111 Blvd. Beaumarchais, 75003. ✆ **01 42 77 01 90.** Metro: Saint-Sébastien—Froissart.

TRES CHEAP HIGH-STREET FASHIONS

C&A It's not *très* à la mode (has it ever been?), but for basics such as underwear, nightwear, simple shirts and bottoms, you can't beat C&A's prices. Whereas all branches in Britain closed several years ago, C&A is still alive and kicking on the continent, selling its own toned-down copies of trendy clothes to everyone from grannies to young parents and students (although most of the latter would swear they'd never set foot there). There are three stores in Paris.

49 Blvd. Haussmann, 75009. ✆ **01 53 30 89 33.** Metro: Chaussée d'Antin—La Fayette or Opéra. RER: Auber.

Maine Montparnasse shopping centre, 3 Rue de l'Arrivée, 75014. ✆ **01 43 21 49 20.** Metro: Montparnasse.

126 Rue de Rivoli, 75001. ✆ **01 53 40 93 23.** Metro: Châtelet. www.c-et-a.fr.

★ **H&M** Swedish discounter Hennes & Mauritz knocks out the latest cool fashions for men, women and children at low prices, yet you don't feel you're buying tat. In fact, they're such a hit across the board that shops are cropping up like mushrooms. The newest (and biggest) branch is next door to Galeries Lafayette, in the old Bouchara building (1 Rue Lafayette, 75009). Other good ones are at 135–9 Rue de Rennes (75006), 88 Rue de Rivoli (75004) and 54 boulevard Haussmann.

Main address: 54 Blvd. Haussmann, 75009. ✆ **01 55 31 92 50.** www.hm.com. Metro: Chaussée d'Antin—La Fayette or Opéra. RER: Auber.

SHOES INS & OUTS

All the kilometres that Parisians log as pedestrians explain their obsession with shoes. Practically every *quartier* has a few boutiques dedicated to precious Parisian pegs, but my favourite clusters are the 6th—where the Rues de Rennes, du Cherche-Midi and Grenelle form the backbone of the Left Bank's fashionable shoe-shop offerings (a great place for inspiration, even if you don't buy)—and Châtelet, both inside and around the outside of the Forum des Halles (p. 154), where you can find everything from cheap 'n' cheerful tat to quality high-street offerings. The Rue de Rivoli and its eastern continuation, Rue Saint-Antoine, between Châtelet and Bastille, are also shoe-shop hotspots known for their reasonable prices. Here are some reasonably priced high-street brands to look out for along the way.

Eram   The latest trends (usually in bright colours) in shoes, sandals, pumps, sneakers and boots are gathered here under one roof, or you can buy online.

12 Rue de Rivoli, 75004. ℭ **01 40 27 01 37.** Metro: Saint-Paul.

130 Rue de Rennes, 75006. ℭ **01 45 48 60 47.** Metro: Rennes. www.eram.fr.

La Halle aux Chaussures   This warehouse-style megastore is where you come for dirt-cheap up-to-the-minute fashions for all the family. I'm not promising that what you buy will last more than a season, but at least you won't have broken the bank.

12 Rue Brantôme, 75003. ℭ **01 42 74 35 32.** www.lahalleauxchaussures.com. Metro: Rambuteau.

★ **Jonak Stock**   Jonak is slightly chicer than Eram, slightly cooler than Minelli (below) and much better quality than the Halle aux Chaussures, with most models made from real leather. This is also one of the only high-street brands to have a discount shop (on last season's models)—this place, Jonak Stock, where you'll get up to 50% off retail prices. But sorry, boys—it's only for the ladies.

44 Blvd. de Sébastopol, 75003. ℭ **01 40 27 07 09.** www.jonak.fr. Metro: Châtelet.

★ **Minelli**   Minelli makes up for its shortcomings in terms of its displays (stacks of waist-high boxes) with its original footwear for men, women, and children at reasonable prices.

96 Rue de Rivoli, 75004. ℭ **01 42 72 25 75.** www.minelli.fr. Metro: Châtelet.

LOW-COST SHOPPING MALLS

Forum des Halles   Rabbits would have done a better job on this three-floor, underground shopping warren—Paris's least enjoyable mall, although a facelift should be completed by 2013. However, Les Halles is a must if you're looking for cheap shops and high-street favourites all under one roof (including Mango, Zara, H&M, Habitat, and a massive Fnac). There are also two multi-screen cinemas, a cinema museum (Le Forum des Images; p. 201), fast-food restaurants and a swimming pool.

Rue Pierre Lescot and Rue Rambuteau, 75001. ☎ **01 44 76 96 56.** www.forumdes halles.com. Metro: Les Halles. RER: Châtelet—Les Halles.

Cashback?

If you hold a non-EU passport and live outside France (for more than six months a year), you can claim a 12% VAT refund (*détaxe*) when you spend more than 175.01€ in one boutique. Just ask for a *formulaire de détaxe* (tax-back form) when you pay, fill it in, then when you leave the EU present your purchases to the customs officer, who will validate your form, and next to a reimbursement counter (*comptoir de remboursement*) to get the tax refunded to your card (or ask for cash).

For more info, check out www.globalrefund.com and www.premiertaxfree.com. *Détaxe* doesn't cover food, drink, antiques, art, or services.

La Vallée Village   Agnès B, Cacharel, Celine, Cerruti, Burberry, Apostrophe, Ralph Lauren, and dozens more are all in force at La Vallée Village luxury outlet, at a minimum of 33% off normal retail prices. All you have to do is get here (it's close to Disneyland Paris in Marne La Vallée). Once you've made the effort, it's a discount heaven (especially if you qualify for tax back; see the box, left). If you're not a local, there are now direct links to the Village by Eurostar (direct from London, same train for Disneyland). For Parisians, the best bet is to get the RER A towards Marne La Vallée and get off at Val d'Europe. (The Cityrama shuttle-bus from central Paris is a ripoff at 22€, 11€ for kids.)

3 Cours de la Garonne, 77700 Serris. ☎ **01 60 42 35 00.** www.lavalleevillage. com. Eurostar/TGV: Marne-la-Vallée—Chessy. RER: Val d'Europe. Open daily 10am–7pm (from 11am Sun).

3 Flea Paris

When looking for free weekend stimuli, Parisians love nothing more than flea markets—veritable touchable museums, where the dealers are often as curious as the items they're flogging. Prices are certainly not as low as they should be (this is the lair of the strong-headed professional who can tell his Louis XVI sideboard from his elbow and spot a tourist in the dark), but there are ways to tip the scales in your favour.

Try haggling as closing time approaches or, in the outside sections, use bad weather to your advantage (no-one wants to buy a sodden leather coat for full price). Here, perhaps more than elsewhere, it's all about attitude: Seem disinterested from the start and you'll get a better price than the guy who dribbles longingly over that chipped Ming vase.

Marché Aligre The cheapest market in Paris (p. 165) also has a flea-market section, although you'll have to sift though a lot of junk. Recently, immigrants have nestled in on the outer edges too, peddling their own belongings in a bid to make some cash. Don't be put off—if you come on the right day, there are bargains to be found. You just have to be patient and keep moseying around when you do your food shopping.

Street Stalking

Spring and autumn in Paris are synonymous with *vide-greniers* (literally, attic emptying—the French equivalent of car-boot sales) and *brocantes* (antiques fairs). Each *arrondissement* organises its own street sales—wonderful opportunities to examine old art, loose photos, and other oddball junk that has lingered in someone's basement.

Price-wise, *brocantes* are more expensive as they're run by professionals. *Vide-greniers* are run by locals, so it's easy to get a good price. To find out when and where to go, see www.info-brocantes.com and http://vide-greniers.org, or ask at your local Mairie.

Place d'Aligre, 75012. Tues–Sun 7:30am–1:30pm. Metro: Ledru—Rollin.

★ **Marché aux Puces de la Porte de Vanves** The early bird catches the worm at this fun, human-scope flea market—the only one within Paris's boundaries. In Vanves' case, the worm is the very best in vintage rags, dolls and teddies, jewellery, and knick-knacks at better prices than at Clignancourt.

Ave. Georges Lafenestre and Ave. Marc Sangnier, 75014. http://pucesdevanves.type
pad.com. Sun 7am–7.30pm. Metro: Porte de Vanves.

★ **Les Puces de Saint-Ouen—Porte de Clignancourt**   There's a knack
to this flea-market emporium, the biggest in Europe, which is to head
straight to the Rue des Rosiers, the central artery, then work out where
you want to go. There are around 2,500 antiques stands, shared over 20
sections each specialising in specific eras and objects, covering everything from 18th-century chairs to Art Deco commodes and retro lighting.

Ave. de la Porte de Clignancourt, 75018. ℭ **08 92 70 57 65** (0.34€/min). www.
marchesauxpuces.fr. Sat–Mon 7am–7:30pm. Metro: Porte de Clignancourt.

4 Shekels & Chains: Department Stores

Not only do department stores thrive in the capital of fashion, they
even define the skyline. Galeries Lafayette and Printemps, for instance,
are architectural attractions in their own right—Art Nouveau masterpieces with breathtaking views from their rooftops. Department stores
also come into their own at Christmas, when their bright window displays reel in the crowds.

Unfortunately, with the exception of Tati (Paris's discount super-
store *extraordinaire*), none of them gives enough bang for your buck,
so the only real time to visit is during the sales (p. 157). What's for
non-French nationals to know is that with a foreign passport (presented *before* you pay for your goods), Galeries Lafayette and Printemps will both give you a 10% discount. It's also worth knowing that
the maps given out by Paris's Tourist Office also contain a 10% discount card, although you can't use both at the same time of course.

BHV   The Bazar de l'Hôtel de Ville lives up to its name, with a mish-
mash of goods ranging from DIY and pet equipment (some DIY equipment can be hired) to men and women's fashion and bed linen.

52–64 Rue de Rivoli, 75004. ℭ **01 42 74 90 00.** www.bhv.fr. Metro: Hôtel de Ville.

Le Bon Marché   Though it's not as 'bon marché' (cheap) as its name
implies, the city's oldest department store (opened in 1848) is user-
friendly and a fave with fashionistas, who flock for its fine selection of
global designer labels. You can also tantalise your taste buds in its
fabulous next-door food hall, La Grande Epicerie (www.lagrandepic-
erie.com). You'll find it hard not to crack, despite the high prices.

24 Rue de Sèvres, 75007. ℭ **01 44 39 80 00.** www.bonmarche.fr. Metro: Sèvres-Babylone.

Galeries Lafayette Lafayette fights with Printemps for pole position, putting most of its eggs in the luxury basket. A few upper-end high-street brands creep in, but otherwise this is 'sales only' territory whether you're looking for clothes, houseware or food.

40 Blvd. Haussmann, 75009. ℂ **01 42 82 34 56.** www.galerieslafayette.com. Metro: Chausée d'Antin. RER: Auber.

Printemps Shoes and beauty products are where Printemps excels. The usual designer suspects intermingle with high-street brands on the upper floors. Having a cup of tea under the Art Nouveau cupola is a civilised way to end a shopping trip.

64 Blvd. Haussmann, 75009. ℂ **01 42 82 50 00.** www.printemps.com. Metro: Chaussée d'Antin. RER: Auber.

★ **Tati** If you think a euro won't get you far in Paris, you've never been to Tati, the cheapest of all the department stores (and possibly the cheapest shop in town). Unfortunately, the phonetics ring true—Tati is rather tatty (and the security guards look frosty enough to sink the Titanic). But the stores bustle all day with bargain hunters stocking up on low-cost clothes, household items and gifts. There's even an inexpensive bridal section.

4 Blvd. de Rochechouart, 75018. ℂ **01 55 29 52 20.** www.tati.fr. Metro: Barbès-Rochechouart.

Come Sale Away

Oh la la, c'est compliqué! At the time of writing the government has just changed shopping regulations to the effect that legally there can only be three sales periods a year: Six weeks in winter and six weeks in summer, the dates of which are decided by the government (usually January and June), plus a third two-week sale, held at any moment during the year as long as it starts more than four weeks before summer or winter sales. The rest of the year, reasonable discounts are tolerated. Got it?

This should be good news for us as it means that, in theory, we can get money off all year round. In reality, unless you happen to walk past the shop during its random two-week sales period, the only sure-fire moments are in summer and winter, when stores trumpet their markdowns on windows, in magazines, and even on the Metro, offering between 30% and 70% off. However, every man, woman, and dog will hit the shops at the same time, so try to go mid-week in the morning, and avoid weekends and lunchtimes.

The best web source for current sales is www.shoppingbyparis.com.

5 Dirt Cheap Shopping A–Z

ANTIQUES

Also see Flea Paris, p. 155.

★ **Emmaüs Défi** This charity depot is filled to the brim with unwanted treasures: Quality retro furniture, abandoned antiques (victims of Parisian fickleness), old books, toys, and a thousand other things you probably never knew existed. Plus, it's cheap! Note that you can only actually buy on Saturdays (10am–6pm; to give items to Emmaüs, or pick up what you've bought, the shop is open Tuesday–Friday 3–6pm, Saturday 10am–6pm).

80 Blvd. Jourdan, 75014. www.emmaus-defi.org. Metro: Porte d'Orléans.

Village Saint-Paul You just never know what you'll find in this mini antiques village housed in small, linking courtyards, with boutiques selling everything from retro furniture to clocks, kitchenware, and knick knacks. Always try to haggle.

Rue Saint-Paul, Rue Charlemagne and Quai des Célestins, 75004. Metro: Saint-Paul.

ART STUFF

★ **Passage Clouté** Budding Picassos and those who've already made a name for themselves flock to this art provisions shop—one of

---

Antique *Dépôt-Ventes*

A whole host of funky antique paraphernalia (chairs, tables, vases, chessboards, cabinets, and sofas) await their second, third or fourth lives in the city's several vast *dépôts-ventes* (second-hand stores) for antiques and furniture. The best quality for money ratio can be found at the following:

- ★ **Le Dépôt-vente Rue de Lagny** 81 Rue de Lagny, 75020. ✆ **01 43 48 86 64.** http://le-grand-depot-vente-de-paris.fr. Metro: Porte de Vincennes.

- **Dépôt-vente Quai de Seine** 63 Quai de Seine, 75019. ✆ **01 40 35 40 29.** www.lasalledesventes.fr. Metro: Riquet.

- **Dépôt-vente Alésia** 117 Rue d'Alésia, 75014. ✆ **01 45 42 42 42.** www.lasalledesventes.fr. Metro: Alésia.

the cheapest and best in town. Everything you could need is here: paints, pastels, brushes, clay, tools, paper, and so on. On the other side of the courtyard is a vast canvas section and just over the road you can get your work framed.

5–7 Rue des Boulets, 75011. ℰ **01 43 73 10 43.** Metro: Nation.

BABY-CARE

Bébé Cash A must for young parents on a budget, Bébé Cash sells perfect-condition baby-everythings (bottles, cots, dummies, covers, thermometers, nappies, and so on) at unbeatable prices, with regular special offers.

27 Rue de Picpus, 75012. ℰ **01 43 43 32 14.** www.bebecash.com. Metro: Nation.

Sauval Natal Just when you think you'll never be able to afford a brand-new pushchair, or to kit out baby's bedroom, let alone dress and feed him, Sauval saves the day with its discounts (around 30%) on practically everything baby could need. Brands include Bébé Confort, Eguizier (furniture), Babybjörn, Tomy, and Maxi-Cosy.

25 Rue Desnouettes, 75015. ℰ **01 42 50 47 47.** www.sauvel.com. Metro: Convention.

BEAUTY-CARE & PERFUME

Monoprix For straightforward make-up by brands such as L'Oréal, shampoos, razors, and anything else we use to enhance our looks, you can't beat the cosmetics sections in bog-standard Monoprix supermarkets, which tend to be cheaper than beauty shops such as

★ **A Free Ethical Make-over—and a Quick Cuppa**

Fancy a cup of coffee and a make-over, girls? The natural make-up brand, Couleur Caramel has opened two Maquillage Cafés (make-up cafés) in Paris. The concept is simple: You indulge in Fair Trade caffeine while one of the beauticians paints your face for absolutely free.

The idea, of course, is that you like what you see and buy a product, but even that won't break the bank. In addition, by 2010, Couleur Caramel should have obtained Ecocert and Cosmébio certifications for all its organic formulas (some 300 or so products in all), so it's no-guilt, low-cost pampering all round.

8 Rue Nicolas Flamel, 75004. ℰ **01 48 04 02 94.** Metro: Châtelet or Hôtel de Ville. 10 Rue Jean du Bellay, 75004. ℰ **01 40 46 05 74.** Metro: Hôtel de Ville or Pont Marie. www.couleur-caramel.com.

Séphora (www.sephora.fr). There's one in each neighbourhood but the Champs-Elysées branch is handily open from 9am to midnight (closed Sunday).

52 Ave. des Champs-Elysées, 75008. *(C)* **01 53 77 65 65.** www.monoprix.fr. Metro: Franklin D. Roosevelt.

Raoul & Curly   It's rare to get a discount on perfumes in Paris, but at R&C you get roughly 25% off most luxury brands. You can also ask for a fidelity card and have it stamped, with even more money off after a certain number of purchases.

47 Ave. de l'Opéra, 75002. *(C)* **01 47 42 50 10.** Metro: Opéra.

BIKES

The sports emporia Go Sport and Decathlon also sell new bikes for all budgets (look under Sports; p. 166).

Bicloune   An alley of used and new bicycles draws you into this grotto of cycling opportunities. All second-hand bikes are tested, repaired and guaranteed for three months after purchase. New models include funky retro-looking Monty F19s from Spain and Holland's Batavus 'Oma'. Price-wise, you'll pick up a good-quality used bicycle from 150€—a great deal on wheels! Note that it's closed 1–2pm.

93 Blvd. Beaumarchais, 75003. *(C)* **01 42 77 58 06.** www.bicloune.fr. Metro Saint-Sébastien—Froissard.

BOOKS

Paris's literary history makes it a book-hunter's paradise. Wander around the 5th and you'll find plenty of dusty bookshops filled with Hemingway wannabes and local *intellectuels*. Then there are the *bouquinistes* with their iconic green metal containers that line the riverbanks (mainly in the 4th and 5th) to form the largest open-air bookshop in the world. Here are a few other favourites:

★ **Book-Off**   Hardly anyone had heard of this second-hand, Japanese-owned bookshop until last year; now there are three of them. Their success is probably down to the fact that you can pick up second-hand fiction from 1€ plus a whole host of other tomes, including glossy coffee-table books for just a few euros more. Two branches have an English section too, plus DVDs and CDs.

Book-Off Opéra (books in Japanese): 29–31 Rue Saint Augustin, 75002. *(C)* **01 42 60 04 77.** Metro: Opéra.

Book-Off Quatre-Septembre (English and French): 11 Rue Monsigny, 75002. ℭ **01 42 60 00 66.** Metro: Quatre-Septembre.

Book-Off Saint-Antoine (English and French): 90 Rue du Faubourg Saint-Antoine, 75012. ℭ **01 58 51 21 72.** Metro: Ledru-Rollin. www.bookoff.co.jp.

Gibert Joseph   Gibert is actually a row of bookshops that are particularly frequented by Sorbonne and Sciences Po students, with everything from textbooks on politics, history, psychology and veterinary practice to art books, religious theory and CDs. Prices are always low and some books are second-hand. FINE PRINT Other branches are at 30, 32 and 34 of the same boulevard.

26 Blvd. Saint-Michel, 75006. ℭ **01 44 41 88 88.** www.gibertjoseph.com.

Mona Lisait   If you're looking for a rare or beautifully illustrated hardback, an end-of-series cookbook, cartoons, or a coffee-table edition on anything from fine arts to outer space, Mona's is legendary, with heavy discounts (often 50%) and the facility to buy online. Seven stores await, the main one in Châtelet—Les Halles.

Place Joachim du Bellay, 75001. ℭ **01 40 26 83 66.** www.monalisait.fr. Metro: Châtelet (exit Place Sainte-Opportune).

★ **Shakespeare & Co**   Under Sylvia Whitman (daughter of the famous 90-something owner George Whitman), 'S&Co' has gone from famous second-hand bookstore to literary institution, holding regular readings, signings and even an annual literature festival that attracts more than 5,000 visitors. Despite the attention, the shop continues to focus on second-hand American and European literature at competitive prices. FINE PRINT The shop is open to 11pm every night.

37 Rue de la Bûcherie, 75005. ℭ **01 43 25 40 93.** www.shakespeareandcompany. com. Metro: Saint-Michel.

ELECTRONIC EQUIPMENT

In the Rue Montgallet (75012. Metro: Montgallet), a score of computer and electronic boutiques, run by shopkeepers of Chinese origin, await those who know what they're looking for and aren't afraid to haggle. The prices can vary throughout the day but are nearly always lower than at institutions such as Fnac (www.fnac.com; see also p. 165) and Darty (www.darty.com). If you prefer somewhere more conventional, try the following (or Fnac and Darty during the sales).

Gros Bill   Part of Auchan supermarkets, Gros Bill has the leverage to offer hefty discounts throughout the year. This includes everything from computers and cameras to fridges and washing machines. If you've already decided what you want, you can order online or at one of the ordering posts at the entrance.

60 Blvd. de l'Hôpital, 75013. ℂ **08 92 02 21 21** (0.34€/min). www.grosbill.com. Metro: Gare d'Austerlitz. RER: Gare d'Austerlitz.

Surcouf   With 6,000m^2 of space dedicated to computers and soft- ware and 10–15,000 visitors a day, Surcouf's statistics speak for them- selves. But size alone isn't the attraction—items are all sold at web prices, a cut below normal retail price, and there are frequent deals.

139 Ave. Daumesnil, 75012. ℂ **08 92 70 76 20** (0.34€/min). Metro: Reuilly—Diderot or Gare de Lyon.

FANCY DRESS

Au Fou Rire   If you're looking for wigs, false moustaches, vampire teeth, or other sillies, this is one of the cheapest party places in town. For those who want to go the whole hog, more than 3,000 costumes await upstairs. Passage Brady and the boulevard de Strasbourg in the 10th (between metro stations Château d'Eau and Strasbourg Saint- Denis) also have a few addresses worth checking out.

22 Bis Rue du Faubourg Montmartre, 75009. ℂ **01 48 24 75 82.** www.aufourire.com. Metro: Grands Boulevards.

FOOD STUFF

Cooking at home is the obvious way to cut costs, but it's a shame to do it every day when you're in the capital of gastronomy. *Chocolat- iers-patissiers*, *fromagiers,* and *pâtisseries* await you on every corner, and a surprising number of them won't break the bank.

L'Autre Boulange   Michel Cousin's delicious organic bread and bis- cuits are baked in a wood-fired oven. His 20-plus breads (some of which are used in the sandwiches sold at lunchtime) include the yummy flutiot (rye bread with dried fruit, walnuts, and hazelnuts)—a meal in itself, heavenly with salted butter.

43 Rue de Montreuil, 75011. ℂ **01 43 72 86 04.** www.lautreboulange.com. Metro: Faidherbe—Chaligny or Nation.

Ladurée   Sweet, soft pistachio paste marbled with rich chocolate, enveloped in fluffy, sugary pastry: As far as luxury pastries go, the *pains au chocolat à la pistache* at Ladurée's take-out counter are not only superlatively delicious, they're surprisingly affordable at 2.70€.

75 Ave. des Champs-Elysées, 75008. ✆ **01 40 75 08 75.** Metro: George V.

16 Rue Royale, 75008. ✆ **01 42 60 21 79.** Metro: Madeleine or Concorde.

21 Rue Bonaparte, 75006. ✆ **01 44 07 64 87.** Metro: Saint-Germain-des-Près. www.laduree.fr.

★ **François Pralus** Pralus is so concerned about what goes into his chocolate, he bought an organic cacao plantation in northern Madagascar. Despite credentials as long as his wooden spoon (in 2009 he was voted best *chocolatier* by Gault & Millau), this is his only Parisian boutique. It's a place in which to meditate, salivate and overindulge in organic frivolities such as heart-shaped chocolate lollipops (2.45€) or divine praline-filled brioches (pralulines).

35 Rue Rambuteau, 75004. ✆ **01 48 04 05 05.** www.chocolats-pralus.com. Metro: Rambuteau.

Pascal Trotté If it's a quick cheese fix you're after, Trotté has a few ripe ones fresh from the farm. The shop's not big, but neither is it touristy (despite its Marais location), which means that oozing Camemberts and 48-month-matured Comtés are wholly do-able.

97 Rue Saint Antoine, 75004. ✆ **01 48 87 17 10.** Metro: Saint-Paul.

GIFTS & OTHER CURIOSITIES

Potiron For trendy, wholly useful gifts (or treats for yourself) this goldmine of cheap but funky tea-sets, candle-holders, tableware, bathroom stuff, and innovative gift ideas (such as bright pink telephones shaped

---

Online Prezzies with Pivoine & Tapioca

Ebay (www.ebay.fr) isn't the only online present provider. When I'm looking for a low-cost/high-impact gift, my first port of call is **Pivoine & Tapioca** (www.pivoine-et-tapioca.com), a melting pot of gift ideas that organises items by price, colour, trends, purpose and designers. Categories include household, children, fashion accessories, furniture, stationery and lighting. Preference is always given to emerging *créateurs* and hand-made items. There's even a handy 'Idées Cadeaux' section (gift ideas) if you're short on inspiration. Presents start at 5€ and delivery is free if you spend 100€.

like lips) turns over its stock roughly every two weeks, so there's nearly always something new to find. The sales (often 70% off) are unbeatable.

57 Rue des Petits Champs, 75001. ℂ **01 40 15 00 38.** www.potiron.com. Metro: Pyramides.

HOUSEHOLD

GIGA Store   If you want to replace your shower curtain, need school pads and pens, shampoo, clothes, DVDs or bits and bobs for the kitchen, Giga rivals Tati (p. 157) for its low prices. It won't win any awards for quality, but it'll get you out of a tight spot until the cash flows in.

106 Blvd. Diderot, 75012. ℂ **01 53 02 41 41.** www.gigastore.fr. Metro: Reuilly—Diderot.

★ **IKEA**   There's no escaping this Swedish-born, affordable style sanctuary, now with six locations on the outskirts of the city, all open seven days a week. It's the same the world over: Sleek, no-risk simulations of living rooms, lounges, bathrooms, and kitchens in a labyrinthine floor plan that forces you to go past every section of the shop so that you can remember you need an incredibly cheap pack of 50 tealights and extra hooks to hang your new mugs on. But then no-one else on Earth seems able to compete with the decent-looking designs, and no other in-store cafeteria can combine flavour with such damned low prices (4.90€ for a plate of Swedish meatballs, 2.50€ for organic pasta and tomato sauce). Merci, IKEA! The easiest IKEA to get to using public transport is Paris Nord 2.

Roissy Paris Nord 2, 95000, Parc des Expositions. ℂ **08 92 30 01 00** (0.34€/min). www.ikea.fr. RER: B to Parc des Expositions, then bus 640 or 23.

MARKETS

Paris wouldn't be Paris without its bright, bustling markets (both covered and open-air), but most are so expensive you can't afford a sack of *pommes de terre* let alone fresh meat or fish. The city council's website, www.paris.fr, has a full list of details for each *arrondissement* (remember that covered markets are systematically more expensive); if you want your euro to stretch a wee bit further, these two will oblige:

★ **Marché Aligre** This markets winds its way round Place d'Aligre almost every day. Inside the covered market, you'll find top-notch meat, fish, cheese, and charcuterie at the usual Parisian prices, but outside awaits a sea of cheap stalls, a wine bar, Le Baron Rouge (great for a sneaky slurp before lunch; p. 78), cafés and a *brocante* (p. 155). If organic fruit and veg are *prioritié* for you, there are two decent stalls at opposite ends of Rue d'Aligre, both of which give you a plastic container to fill with whatever greens and fruits you fancy for 2.80€ a kilo (the stand nearest the covered market tends to be fresher).

Rue d'Aligre, 75012. Tues–Sun 7am–2pm. Metro: Ledru-Rollin.

Marché de Joinville On Thursdays and Sundays, Place de Joinville (just beyond Place de Bitche—it still makes me laugh) on the Canal de l'Ourcq turns into a heaving mess of market stalls and crowds. It's not a relaxing market, but it is dirt cheap; and the butcher in the right-hand corner (with the canal behind you; look for the queue and you'll find it) does the most delicious roasted Portuguese chicken for 9€ a pop.

Place de Joinville and opposite 1 Rue de Joinville, 75019. Thurs 7am–2:30pm, Sun 7am–3pm. Metro: Crimée.

MUSIC

Fnac Despite closing its Bastille branch (dedicated to music) in 2009, Fnac drags us in with its promise of new releases and discounts on old CDs, as well as electronic equipment and books. Competition from the Internet is causing the firm to rethink its music strategy, the Champs-Elysées address keeps on the ball with regular free music showcases that coincide with album releases, sometimes by big names, while the annual Fnac Indétendances is a popular free music festival held during Paris Plages (p. 22), featuring acts of the calibre of Neneh Cherry and Damon Albarn. FINE PRINT This branch is open until 11:45pm daily (from midday on Sundays).

74 Ave. des Champs-Elysées, 75008. ☎ **08 25 02 00 20.** www.fnac.com. Metro: Franklin D. Roosevelt.

Monster Melodies Whether you're looking for treasured tracks on CD or rare vinyls, Monster will help, with more than 10,000 items (vinyls are upstairs), knowledgeable staff and reasonable prices. Plus, if you buy in bulk staff sometimes give a discount.

9 Rue des Déchargeurs, 75001. ☎ **01 40 28 09 39.** Metro: Les Halles.

Heading for Rome: Musical Instruments & Sheet Music

Behind Saint-Lazare station, the Rue de Rome in the 8th is paradise for musicians of all talents, with strings of specialised music shops. While bargains are to be found in all, some of the cheapest and most comprehensive supplies of sheet music are to be had in **Flûte de Pan** (www.laflutedepan.com). Flûte has three branches: N° 49 (② **01 42 93 65 05**) is for strings, woodwind, chamber music and orchestral scores; N° 53 (② **01 43 87 01 81**) covers sax, brass, percussion, jazz and pop (including vocals); N° 59 (② **01 42 93 47 82**) is for piano and organ.

If it's musical instruments you're after, **Rome Instruments** (N° 54. ② **01 42 93 23 62.** www.romeinstruments.com) puts a good price on an array of string instruments (both for sale and hire); **Pianos International** (N° 48. ② **01 42 93 75 78.** www.pianos-international.com) has a wide selection of grand, upright, and electric pianos and will lighten the burden by allowing you to pay in several instalments; and **Feeling Musique** (N°61. ② **01 45 22 30 80.** www.feelingmusique.com) is the Paris HQ for wind instruments.

Music shops are usually closed 1–2pm. In addition to standard hours, Pianos International is open Sundays 2–5pm. Metro: Rome.

Virgin Megastore   If you visit Virgin's Champs-Elysées branch, you can sample CDs on the listening posts (by scanning the bar code) until midnight every day of the week. As with Virgins across the board, new releases hover around the 16€–20€ mark, but there are regular discounts on old albums and singles. FINE PRINT It opens at midday on Sundays.

52–60 Ave. des Champs-Elysées, 75008. ② **01 49 53 50 00.** www.virginmega.fr. Metro: Franklin D. Roosevelt.

SPORTS

Decathlon   In the same vein as Go Sport (below), Decathlon is where the masses go for reasonably priced sportswear that doesn't fall apart. In fact, there are even maintenance ateliers where you can bring your bikes, kits, skis, and fishing rods (all bought at Decathlon, of course) for a quick once-over.

113 Ave. de France, 75012. ✆ **01 44 06 82 00.** www.decathlon.fr. Metro: Bibliothèque François Mitterrand (for other addresses, see website).

First Boutique   Philippe Houillez, former European land-yacht champion, set up this sports-shoe boutique as an extra to his successful website, www.firstboutique.net. You'll find more than 300 models (professional and streetwear) at discount prices, including a quite impressive collection of roller-shoes.

223 Rue de Charenton, 75012. ✆ **01 43 40 77 14.** Metro: Dugommier.

Go Sport   This sportswear megastore sells everything from football boots and leotards to sports towels, bags, golf clubs, horse-riding helmets, and bicycles, at highly competitive prices.

135 Ave. Daumesnil, 75012. ✆ **08 25 10 60 60** (0.15€/min). www.go-sport.com. Metro: Montgallet.

UNDERWEAR
C&A and H&M (p. 152) both have excellent, dirt-cheap underwear for men and women.

Say "Fromage" on Rue de la Photo

Between Bastille and République, the boulevard Beaumarchais (75011) is where most of Paris's photo shops congregate, earning it the nickname *Rue de la Photo* ('photo street'). The effect of this single-product density is that the shops are all in competition, which gives you bargaining power galore—you don't like the price, just head up the road.

Whether you're looking for second-hand or new materials, Leica, Nikon, Hasselblad or Mamiya, here are a few to look out for: **ABDON PhotoRent** (N° 6. ✆ **01 47 00 66 77.** www.photorent.fr) and **Photo 40** (N° 24. ✆ **01 43 55 89 06**) for good-priced material hire; **Moyen Format** (N° 50. ✆ **01 48 07 13 18.** www.lemoyenformat.com) updates its second-hand stock on the website daily so you can check out a model before you get to the shop, while the **Maison du Leica** (N° 52. ✆ **01 43 55 24 36.** www.lamaisonduleica.com) is excellent for new and used Leica lenses and cameras. Most are closed on Mondays and for lunch.

WINES & SPIRITS

Caves Michel Renaud A local personality, Michel Renaud, stocks hand-picked quality wines and spirits at a range of prices. If you're eating *coq au vin* and don't want to spend more than 6€–8€, *pas de problème*—Renaud and his staff will find your poison at the right price. For connoisseurs there are also (more expensive) Armagnacs, Cognacs, rums, and other French specialities.

12 Place Nation, 75012. ✆ **01 43 07 98 93.** Metro: Nation.

Cru & Découvertes The passionate owners of this small boutique promote their favourite producers (many organic) and organise regular wine-tasting afternoons, usually on Saturdays.

7 Rue Paul Bert, 75011. ✆ **01 43 71 56 79.** Metro: Faidherbe – Chaligny.

Nicolas This chain fills a niche in the drinks market by selling alcohol of all sorts and strengths for every budget. Its Petite Récolte range of wine starting at 2.95€ is surprisingly quaffable, while if you want to splash out on champagne, Nicolas's own range starts at 19€ or there are frequent offers on brands such as Moët & Chandon, Mumm and Demoiselle. Every *arrondissement* has a Nicolas or two (see the website for a list).

31 Place de la Madeleine, 75008. ✆ **01 42 68 00 16.** Metro: Madeleine. www.nicolas.com.

6 Totally Free

My apartment would be an ode to minimalism had it not been for the laziness of fellow Parisians who, rather than call the street cleaners to pick up their unwanted *objets encombrants* (over-sized items), leave them near a bin for passers-by. My Henri II-style chairs, a chandelier, an under-sink unit and a 1920s etching of an 18th-century boating scene in Fontainebleau are all *trottoir* (pavement) takeaways. The only problem is that you never know when and where you'll find something worth nabbing.

Fortunately, there are more reliable ways of kitting yourself out for free. Whether you're in need of a new look or furniture, several websites can put you in touch with those giving things away and those looking to swap.

Consoglobe FREE This environmentally friendly collective tries to limit consumerism and the waste that takes place in France by linking to websites that encourage us to give things away or swap. Consorecup is where you find the freebies—usually local treasures such as couches, tables, fishbowls, and grandma's old sideboard. Digitroc is where people swap items such as DVDs, computer games, wives (just kidding), and books. For access to both, sign up on www.consoglobe.com then surf away.

Craigslist Paris FREE Started in San Francisco, these small ads have become a global phenomenon. Propelled mainly by British and American expats in Paris, this is where you'll find giveaway furniture, pet-sitters, turtles, old clocks and even karma! Just log on to http://paris.fr.craigslist.org and look for the 'gratuit' section under 'A Vendre'.

Freecycle Paris FREE In a similar vein to Consorecup (above), Freecycle is part of a global association of freebie-givers, with more than 8,000 members in Paris alone at the time of writing. If you want to be on the receiving end, you just sign up by joining http://groups.yahoo.com/group/freecycleparis/. There's no cost to join: You just have to pledge that you will one day give something away for free (no trading is allowed). Your email box will inevitably be overrun with ads, most of which won't interest you, but it's worth holding out for something you need.

Getting Reimbursed

How many of us buy a specific brand of rice or crème fraîche just because it says 'satisfaction or your money back' on the packet, or even 'absolutely free', but never do anything about getting our money back? Two sites, www.madstef.com and www.achatgratuit.com, provide weekly listings of all the latest supermarket offers and explanations of how to claim your money back. Apparently, we could all save 100€–200€ a month per person by following their guides to the letter.

SHOPPING RIGHT BANK WEST

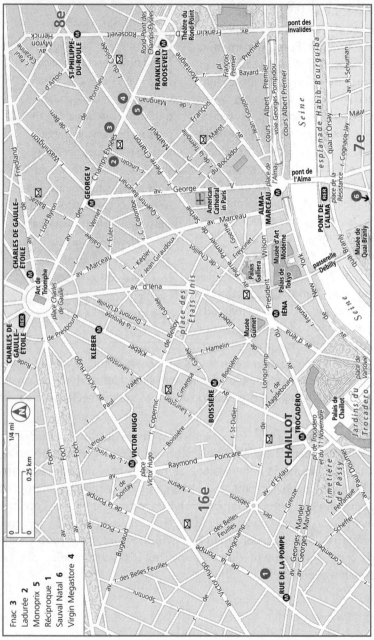

Fnac **3**
Ladurée **2**
Monoprix **5**
Réciproque **1**
Sauval Natal **6**
Virgin Megastore **4**

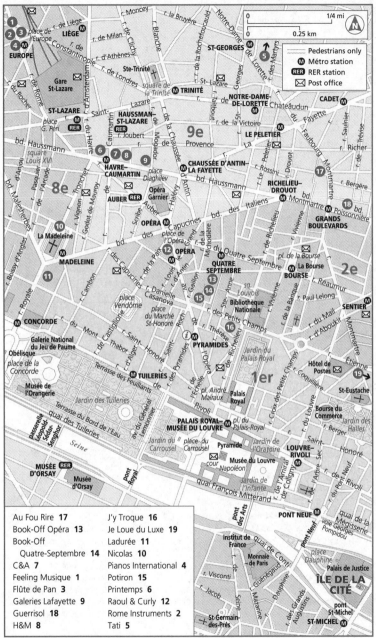

| 0 | | 1/4 mi |
| 0 | 0.25 km | |

- Pedestrians only
- Ⓜ Métro station
- RER RER station
- ✉ Post office

9e

8e

2e

1er

Au Fou Rire **17**	J'y Troque **16**
Book-Off Opéra **13**	Je Loue du Luxe **19**
Book-Off	Ladurée **11**
Quatre-Septembre **14**	Nicolas **10**
C&A **7**	Pianos International **4**
Feeling Musique **1**	Potiron **15**
Flûte de Pan **3**	Printemps **6**
Galeries Lafayette **9**	Raoul & Curly **12**
Guerrisol **18**	Rome Instruments **2**
H&M **8**	Tati **5**

SHOPPING RIGHT BANK MARAIS

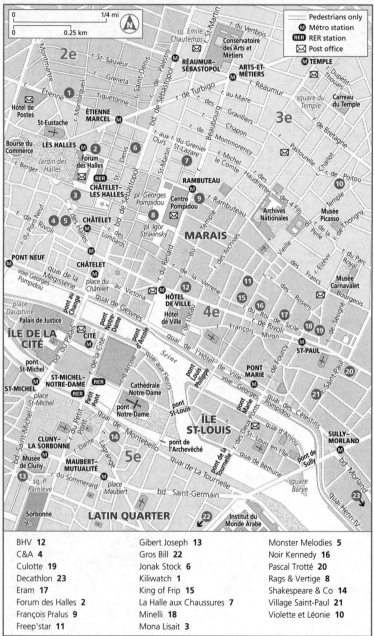

BHV **12**	Gibert Joseph **13**	Monster Melodies **5**
C&A **4**	Gros Bill **22**	Noir Kennedy **16**
Culotte **19**	Jonak Stock **6**	Pascal Trotté **20**
Decathlon **23**	Kiliwatch **1**	Rags & Vertige **8**
Eram **17**	King of Frip **15**	Shakespeare & Co **14**
Forum des Halles **2**	La Halle aux Chaussures **7**	Village Saint-Paul **21**
François Pralus **9**	Minelli **18**	Violette et Léonie **10**
Freep'star **11**	Mona Lisait **3**	

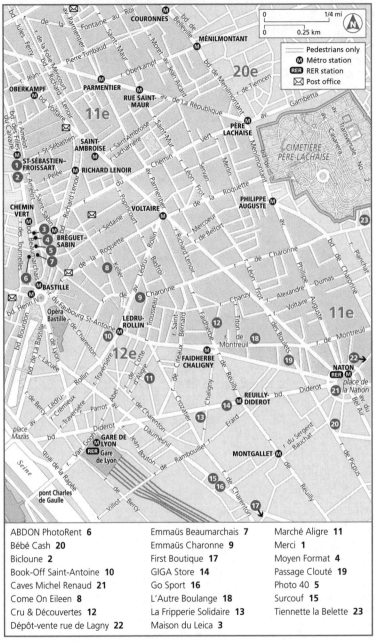

0		1/4 mi
0	0.25 km	

Pedestrians only
Ⓜ Métro station
RER RER station
☒ Post office

ABDON PhotoRent **6**	Emmaüs Beaumarchais **7**	Marché Aligre **11**
Bébé Cash **20**	Emmaüs Charonne **9**	Merci **1**
Bicloune **2**	First Boutique **17**	Moyen Format **4**
Book-Off Saint-Antoine **10**	GIGA Store **14**	Passage Clouté **19**
Caves Michel Renaud **21**	Go Sport **16**	Photo 40 **5**
Come On Eileen **8**	L'Autre Boulange **18**	Surcouf **15**
Cru & Découvertes **12**	La Fripperie Solidaire **13**	Tiennette la Belette **23**
Dépôt-vente rue de Lagny **22**	Maison du Leica **3**	

SHOPPING RIGHT BANK NORTH EAST

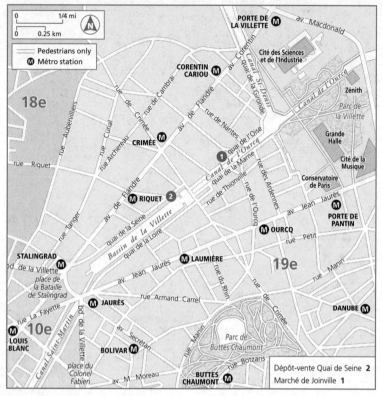

——	Pedestrians only
Ⓜ	Métro station
RER	RER station
✉	Post office

C&A **5**
Chercheminippes **4**
Dépôt-vente Alésia **7**
Emmaüs Défi **8**
Ladurée **1**
Le Bon Marché **3**
Les Ginettes **2**
Marché aux Puces
   de la Porte de Vanves **6**

The Musée Bourdelle, hidden away in a quiet corner of Montparnasse.

EXPLORING PARIS

When it comes to culture, Parisians are spoilt: Not only does the city boast some of the world's greatest cultural attractions, but most of them can be visited for free. Entry to the permanent collections of 14 municipal museums is totally gratis, 18 others (plus numerous monuments) are free on the first Sunday of the month (some all year round, others November to March) and a handful of little-known private museums allow *entrée libre* (complimentary entry) to their eccentric collections on specific days or by appointment (see Free Curiosities; p. 183). But that's just the tip of the iceberg: Add churches, art galleries, free tours and parks, and you'll find that accessing Paris's treasures on the cheap is a veritable piece of *gâteau*.

1 Museum Peace

Even when you do have to pay, standard museum prices in Paris are surprisingly reasonable: 9€–12€ seems to be the going rate for big institutions such as the Louvre and the Centre Pompidou. Additionally, buying a ticket at some venues can get you money off at others: At the Louvre, for instance, a 9€ ticket gives you free access to the Musée National Eugène Delacroix. Lastly, under-18s (and usually under-26s from the European Union), students and over-60s get in for nothing, or very little, almost everywhere.

Below, you'll find alphabetical listings of places that either (a) never charge for permanent collections, (b) are free on specific days, or (c) are dirt cheap, plus a list of venues that are not to be missed despite the entry charge. So go on, have your croissant and eat it!

Note that last entry to the following is usually 45min before the indicated closing time and that some smaller museums (especially the curiosities) are closed during August.

ALWAYS FREE

Fondation Jean Rustin Few Parisians know about this small museum-gallery devoted to the works of French painter Jean Rustin (born 1928), though it recently moved to the Marais to rub shoulders with the Centre Pompidou and to take advantage of the lovely new Jardin d'Anne Frank. Rustin's abstract art had a wide following until the late 1960s, but declined after he decided to concentrate on figurative work. Today, however, he is viewed by many as one of Europe's most important 20th-century figurative artists for his disturbing paintings beset with melancholic, tortured characters. FINE PRINT The museum is closed in summer (late July to beginning of September).

1 Impasse Berthaud, 75003. ℭ **01 42 84 46 35.** www.rustin.be. Thurs–Sat 3–7pm (and by appt). Metro: Rambuteau.

Maison de Balzac The 19th-century French novelist Honoré de Balzac lived in this *maison bourgeoise* under a false name (Brugnol, that of his housekeeper mistress) to dodge his many creditors. It was here that he finished his most prominent work, *La Comédie Humaine* (between 1840 and 1847), and things have changed very little since then: The back entrance he used to flee during emergencies remains, and memorabilia on display includes drawings and paintings of his family and friends, among them Madame Hanska, the Russian pen-friend he married just 5 months before his death, after 18 years of correspondence. FINE PRINT There is usually a 3€ or 4€ charge for temporary exhibitions.

47 Rue Raynouard, 75016. ℂ **01 55 74 41 80.** www.balzac.paris.fr. Tues–Sun 10am–6pm (closed public hols). Metro: Passy or La Muette. RER: C Boulainvilliers or Radio France.

Maison de Victor Hugo   This atmospheric family apartment on the second floor of the Hôtel de Rohan Guéménée in the Marais is where Hugo wrote some of his greatest novels between 1832 and 1848, including *Mary Tudor* and part of *Les Misérables*. Highlights are Hugo's drawings—more than 450 scenes from his own works—and mementos including handwritten documents, his inkwell and first editions of his works. If you're a big fan, visit the library—a beautiful, wood-panelled affair with more than 11,000 works linked to his life. FINE PRINT The library can be viewed by appointment Mon–Fri 10am–12:30pm and 2–5:30pm. ℂ **01 42 72 82 89.**

6 Place des Vosges, 75004. ℂ **01 42 72 10 16.** www.musee-hugo.paris.fr. Tues–Sun 10am–6pm (closed public hols). Metro: St-Paul, Bastille or Chemin-Vert.

Mémorial de la Shoah   A wall showing the names of 76,000 Jews deported from France during the Second World War is the hard-hitting centrepiece of this memorial centre. There's also a permanent exhibition retracing Jewish history during the Shoah and a gigantic contemporary archive library. FINE PRINT A booklet for 8–12-year-olds guides them through the exhibition avoiding the most shocking images.

17 Rue Geoffroy l'Asnier, 75004. ℂ **01 42 77 44 72.** www.memorialdelashoah.org. Sun–Wed, Fri 10am–6pm, Thurs 10am–10pm (closed some public and Jewish hols). Metro: Saint-Paul.

Mémorial Leclerc et de la Libération de Paris—Musée Jean Moulin   Don't let the unappealing architecture of this dual war museum set on top of the Jardin Atlantique, the modern garden over the Montparnasse train station, put you off: Telling the tales of two of France's most prominent war heroes (the Maréchal Leclerc de Hauteclocque and the Resistance figurehead Jean Moulin) since 1994, it has interesting film archives that plunge visitors into occupied, war-struck and liberated Paris. FINE PRINT There is usually a 3€ or 4€ charge for the museum's frequent war-themed temporary exhibitions.

Sarah Bernhardt's Dressing Room

Before you rush to the bar during the *entr'acte* of a performance at the Théâtre de la Ville (p. 35), consider this wholly unique option: A trip backstage, past dancers and technicians to the former dressing room of the glamorous French tragedian Sarah Bernhardt. The latter acquired the theatre in 1898, and if you make an appointment, a guide will take you to see the memorabilia (old mirrors, her bathtub, jewellery, and letters to her son) for no extra charge. Théâtre de la Ville, 2 Place du Châtelet, 75004. ℃ **01 48 87 54 42.** www.theatredelaville-paris.com. Metro: Châtelet.

23 Allée de la 2e DB75015. ℃ **01 40 64 39 44.** www.ml-leclerc-moulin.paris.fr. Tues–Sun 10am–6pm (closed public hols). Metro: Montparnasse-Bienvenue, Gaîté or Pasteur.

Mona Bismarck Foundation Created in the 1980s by the late American philanthropist Countess Mona Bismarck (who was admired by Dalí and celebrated in a song by Cole Porter), this foundation in her former townhouse overlooking the Eiffel Tower attracts expats and a handful of Parisians with its eclectic programme of exhibitions and seminars, which usually focus on Franco-American culture or reflect Bismarck's wide-ranging interests (arts, culture, fashion, horticulture, and botanical studies).

34 Ave. de New York, 75016. ℃ **01 47 23 81 73.** www.monabismarck.org. Tues–Sat 10:30am–6:30pm (closed public hols). Metro: Alma-Marceau.

★ **Musée Bourdelle**   Hidden away from the hustle and bustle of Montparnasse lies this workshop where Rodin's star pupil, Antoine Bourdelle (1861–1929), lived and worked with its array of sumptuous statues. Many were inspired by Greek mythology: Hercules metamorphosing into a bird, a dying centaur writhing in agony, Penelope, who waited 20 years for her husband Ulysses to return, and the colossal horse statue of General Alvear—part of an allegorical monument that was never finished. The visit ends in Bourdelle's workshop, which is movingly unchanged, as if the genius is about to come home. FINE PRINT During temporary exhibitions there is a 7€ charge (3.50€ for ages 14–26) for the whole museum.

16–18 Rue Antoine Bourdelle, 75015. ℃ **01 49 54 73 73.** www.bourdelle.paris.fr. Tues–Sun 10am–6pm (closed public hols). Metro: Montparnasse-Bienvenue.

★ **Musée Carnavalet—Histoire de Paris**   This 15th- and 16th-century Renaissance palace is most closely associated with the letter-writing of

Madame de Sévigné, who moved here in 1677 to be with her daughter, and poured out nearly every detail of her life in her correspondence. Nowadays it's a wonderful museum, with 100 rooms telling the story of Paris from its origins to today, with a particularly good section on the Revolution that includes a bust of Marat and the chess set that Louis XVI used to distract himself while waiting to go to the guillotine. In a second building, the Hôtel le Peletier de Saint-Fargeau across the courtyard, you'll find furniture from the Louis XIV era to the early 20th century, including a replica of Marcel Proust's cork-lined bedroom containing his actual furniture, and artefacts such as Neolithic pirogues—shallow oak boats used for fishing and transport from about 4400 to 2200bc. FINE PRINT Look out for the refined, intimate classical music concerts held in the garden some weekends; tickets are usually 10€–15€.

23 Rue de Sévigné, 75003. ℂ **01 44 59 58 58.** www.carnavalet.paris.fr. Tues–Sun 10am–6pm (closed public hols). Metro: Saint-Paul or Chemin Vert.

★ **Musée Cernuschi** One of Paris's oldest museums (inaugurated in 1898), the fabulous Cernuschi contains France's second-largest collection of Chinese art—more than 900 pieces assembled by the Italian banker Henri Cernuschi on his travels to the Far East in the 1870s. The collections cover all the Chinese dynasties, with items ranging from Neolithic terracotta and Wei dynasty funeral statues (386–534) to Sung porcelain, jade amulets and rare Liao dynasty (907-1125) gold *objets d'art*.

7 Ave. Vélasquez, 75008. ℂ **01 53 96 21 50.** www.cernuschi.paris.fr. Tues–Sun 10am–6pm (closed public hols). Metro: Villiers or Monceau.

★ **Musée Cognacq-Jay** Ernest Cognacq and his wife Louise Jay, founders of the currently closed La Samaritaine department store, amassed an exquisite collection of decorative works in the early 1900s and today the panelled rooms of the Hôtel Donon still drip with their breathtaking 18th-century ceramics, cabinets and rococo paintings by Canaletto, Fragonard, Greuze, Chardin, Boucher, and Watteau, plus a sprinkling of English works by Reynolds, Lawrence and Romney.

8 Rue Elzévir, 75003. ℂ **01 40 27 07 21.** www.cognacq-jay.paris.fr. Tues–Sun 10am–6pm (closed public hols). Metro: Chemin Vert or Saint-Paul.

★ **Musée d'Art Moderne de la Ville de Paris** Paris's modern art museum takes you on a journey through 20th-century 'isms': Fauvism, Cubism, Surrealism, Realism, Expressionism, and Neo-realism, with works by artists such as Matisse, Braque, Dufy, Picasso, and Leger presented in chronological order. Dufy's gargantuan 1937 *La Fée électricité*, which measures 60m x 10m, is one of the largest paintings in the world. FINE PRINT The museum is known for its world-class temporary exhibitions, for which there is usually a 4.50€–9€ entry fee. To avoid the queues, get here at least 10min before opening time, or opt for the late-night showing on Thursday.

11 Ave. du Président Wilson, 75016. ℂ **01 53 67 40 00.** www.mam.paris.fr. Tues–Sun 10am–6pm (until 10pm Thurs during temporary exhibitions). Metro: Alma-Marceau or Iéna. RER: Pont d'Alma.

Musée de la Vie Romantique This villa, where the great Romantic painter Ary Scheffer (1795–1858) received guests such as George Sand, Delacroix, Chopin, and Rossini, is just half of the attraction: On a warm day, there is nothing better than sitting in its rose-garden café, sipping tea and sampling homemade quiches and cakes. Within the house, a few period rooms give an inkling as to what life might have been like in the company of so many artists, but literary detectives on the trail of Baronne Aurore Dupin (George Sand) might be disappointed—the jewellery and watercolours the writer left behind reveal little about her life. FINE PRINT On a sunny day grab a table before 12:15pm if you want to eat lunch, and visit the museum afterwards.

Hôtel Scheffer-Renan, 16 Rue Chaptal, 75009. ℂ **01 55 31 95 67.** www.vie-romantique. paris.fr. Tues–Sun 10am–6pm (closed public hols). Metro: Pigalle, Saint-Georges, Blanche or Liège.

Musée Zadkine It was within this small house that the Cubist sculptor Ossip Zadkine (1890–1967) lived and worked from 1928 until his death. The 300-plus pieces in the museum and dotted about the charming garden were inspired by musical instruments and mythological or religious subjects. Eccentricities included the *têtes* (heads) carved between 1908 and 1923. Zadkine's progression from left-wing Cubist extremism to a renewed appreciation of the classic era is evident throughout. Don't miss the changing contemporary exhibitions held in the former studio. FINE PRINT Temporary exhibition admission is 4€, under-26s 2€.

100 Bis Rue d'Assas, 75006. ℂ **01 55 42 77 20.** www.zadkine.paris.fr. Tues–Sun 10am–6pm (closed public hols). Metro: Notre-Dame-des-Champs or Vavin.

Pavillon de l'Arsenal Displays at this urban resource centre show Paris through the ages, with a video focusing on edifices built between the 5th and 16th centuries, a 2/1,000 scale model of Paris, information on new and potential builds, and 120 archived films and conferences that can be watched on request. Diehards can also sign up for free guided visits (previous trips have included a tour of La Défense's First tower) and attend regular conferences given by the city's key architects and decision-making bodies.

21 Blvd. Morland, 75004. ⓒ **01 42 76 33 97.** www.pavillon-arsenal.com. Tues–Sat 10:30am–6:30pm, Sun 11am–7pm. Metro: Sully-Morland or Bastille.

★ **Le Petit Palais**   Built in 1900 for the World Fair and lit entirely by natural light, the 'Little Palace' is one of Paris's loveliest fine arts museums, with an extensive collection of works by Ingres, Delacroix, Courbet, and the Impressionists, as well as other paintings and sculptures from the Renaissance to 1900. Art Nouveau fans get more than an eyeful in the ground-floor galleries, where whole sections are devoted to Belle Époque biggies such as Hector Guimard (designer of Paris's iconic metro station entrances), whose entire dining room is reproduced, and the ceramicist Jean Carriès, whose grotesque masks and imaginary creatures add an element of fairytale fantasy. The palace is also a hotspot for world-class exhibitions: In 2010 look out for the first ever Yves Saint Laurent retrospective (11 March–29 August).

FINE PRINT Temporary exhibition prices vary but rarely exceed 7€.

Ave. Winston Churchill, 75008. ⓒ **01 53 43 40 00.** www.petitpalais.paris.fr. Open Tues–Sun 10am–6pm (closed public hols). Metro: Champs-Elysées—Clemenceau.

FREE CURIOSITIES

★ **Cabinet des Médailles et Antiques** FREE   Treasure-hunting on a grand scale was a favourite royal pastime, with every king from Philippe Auguste to Louis XIV collecting booty from around the world. Today, France's national library (BNF) displays some of those heart-stopping treasures in a gem of a museum where Charlemagne's chess set, Dogobert's bronze throne and an emerald ordered by Catherine de Medici are just par for the course.

Bibliothèque Nationale, 58 Rue Richelieu, 75002. ⓒ **01 53 79 83 32.** www.bnf.fr. Mon–Sat 1–5:45pm, Sun midday–6pm. Metro: Bourse.

★ **Ecomusée des Anciennes Carrières des Capucins** FREE   At a depth of 20m below the Hôpital Cochin lies part of Paris's 300km underground maze of tunnels created in the 12th century when Capucin monks decided to mine the limestone. A third of the stone for Notre Dame came from here, and the site is also where the world's first *champignons de Paris* (mushrooms) appeared in the early 1800s after cart drivers flushed their horses' dung into the holes. You can visit a small section of the tunnels by emailing SEADACC at the address below, experiencing a fascinating 1.2km topographical journey past wells, fountains and even a stone picnic table. FINE PRINT Bring your woollies—the temperature never exceeds 58 °F (14.5°C).

Hôpital Cochin, Rue du Faubourg Saint-Jacques, 75014. ℭ **01 43 89 78 03** or association@seadacc.com. Visit by appointment only. RER: Port-Royal.

Fragonard—Musée du Parfum and Théâtre des Capucines FREE You can cover 5,000 years of perfume history at these two intimate sister perfume museums. The Musée du Parfum is set in a typical Haussmann-style apartment built in 1860 close to the Opéra Garnier and has a small but intriguing range of perfume-related curiosities. The second, set in a former theatre, displays items such as 19th-century copper-distilling apparatus used for extracting raw materials and also has a Fragonard boutique. Neither will keep you occupied for long, but if you like perfume there are plenty of interesting facts to be picked up on the free guided tours.

Musée du Parfum, 9 Rue Scribe, 75009. ℭ **01 47 42 04 56.** www.fragonard.com. Mon–Sat 9am–6pm, Sun and public hols 9am–5pm. Metro: Opéra. RER: Auber.

Théâtre des Capucines, 39 Blvd. des Capucines, 75002. ℭ **01 42 60 37 14.** www.fragonard.com. Mon–Sat 9am–6pm. Metro: Opéra. RER: Auber.

Le Panthéon Bouddhique FREE This annexe of the wonderful Musée Guimet of Asian arts (p. 216) is entirely devoted to Buddhism, with more than 250 colourful statues pertaining to kings and divinities collected during the travels of industrialist Emile Guimet to Japan in 1876. Buddha, of course, takes pride of place, recognisable by his simple toga and meditative sitting position—usually in a lotus flower. The short visit ends in the bamboo-filled Japanese garden—a relaxing slice of oriental exoticism with a tea pavilion where tea ceremonies are occasionally held. FINE PRINT Call ahead to check it's open and to find out when the tea ceremonies (12€) will take place.

19 Ave. d'Iéna, 75016. ℭ **01 56 52 53 00.** www.guimet.fr. Wed–Mon 9:45am–5:45pm. Metro: Iéna.

Musée Curie FREE Despite dating back to a time when radium was considered harmless (in the 1920s mineral water, fertiliser, anti-wrinkle creams, and even cigarettes were infused with the stuff), Marie Curie's lab and office still look as they would have done when she won her Nobel Prize for research into radioactivity. Fear not—the space has been decontaminated (although one letter, written by Curie in 1902, has conserved its radioactivity and will do for the next 1,600 years at least!)

1 Rue Pierre-et-Marie-Curie, 75005. ℭ **01 56 24 55 31.** www.curie.fr. Tues–Fri 10am–6pm (free guided visits in English usually Fri 4pm, but call in advance to check). RER: Luxembourg.

Musée de la Préfecture de Police `FREE` Bloody tales, VIP arrest warrants, and gruesome-looking weapons are just some of the exhibits at this musty old police museum—the only place in Paris where a guillotine blade rubs shoulders with a reproduction of the home-made 24-barrel mini-canon (*machine infernale*) created by Giuseppe Fieschi to assassinate Louis-Philippe in 1835. Look out for the pulley used by mass-murderer Docteur Petiot during the Second World War to winch the bodies of his 27 victims into his cellar. `FINE PRINT` Old police archives can be consulted in the reading room Monday to Friday 9am–5pm (closed Monday and Tuesday until August 2010).

Hôtel de Police du 5ème arrondissement, 2nd floor, 4 Rue de la Montagne-Sainte-Geneviève. ℭ **01 44 41 52 50.** www.prefecture-police-paris.interieur.gouv.fr. Mon–Fri 9am–5pm, Sat 10am–5pm. Metro: Maubert-Mutualité.

★ **Musée de Matière Médicale** `FREE` If you ask Professor François Tillequin nicely, you might gain access to Paris's pharmacy faculty, where a mind-blowing 19th-century apothecary museum contains thousands of glass jars filled with more than 25,000 drugs (dried animal or plant substances) and other pharmaceutical curiosities, taking you back to a time when cocoa butter was used in suppositories (because it melts at 99°F(37°C)) and coca-cola wasn't American (one cabinet shows how Corsicans macerated cacao leaves in wine—an idea the American pharmacist John Pemberton took up in 1863, replacing wine with soda, before Coca-Cola snapped up the idea). `FINE PRINT` Ever-fewer students or professors can take time out of their studies to show you round, so ask well in advance.

Faculté de Pharmacie Paris V, 4 Ave. de l'Observatoire, 75006. ℭ **01 53 73 98 04.** www.pharmacie.univ-paris5.fr. By appointment only. RER: Luxembourg.

Musée des Compagnons Charpentiers des Devoirs du Tour de France `FREE` You have to go through a restaurant, kitchens and past the bins to get to this carpentry school museum. France's virtuoso carpenters, Les Compagnons, created all the delicate wooden treasures on display

★ A Short-Back-and-Sides with Maître Alain

Maître Alain is a barber with a difference: Not only is he skilled in 'proper' shaving (with a cut-throat razor, 28€), but he'll cut your hair (27€), trim your moustache (6€) and let you look—for free—at his one-of-a-kind collection of hair-themed objects before, during, and after the pampering. His shop—a living museum of Indonesian razors, Belle Epoque shampoos and 1950s chairs—is frequently used in films and is a fine way to stimulate your imagination whilst indulging in a new haircut (although it's hardly cheap). Salon musée de Maître Alain, 8 Rue Saint-Claude, 75003. ℭ **01 42 77 55 80.** http://maitre barbier.com. Tuesday to Saturday 9:15am–7pm. Metro: Saint-Sébastien-Froissart.

here between 1860 and 1870, which provide a veritable 3D encyclopaedia of carpentry techniques. Each model still bears the name of its creator; the structure labelled Viannay won the top prize at the 1900 World Exhibition. FINE PRINT Telephone beforehand to let them know you're coming, then reserve a table to sample manager Gigi's hearty, carpenter-sized portions of French cuisine (approx. 14€ for a meal).

161 Ave. Jean-Jaurès, 75019. ℭ **01 42 40 53 18.** Officially open daily 2:30–5:30pm but call before. Metro: Ourcq.

Musée du Compagnonnage FREE Another ode to France's famous Compagnon tradesmen (carpenters, masons, plumbers, and so on…), this museum, housed in another school, shows models perfect enough to make any geometry or engineering specialist weep with admiration. Learn how the Compagnons assisted Viollet-le-Duc in renovating Notre Dame's spire, and worked with Eiffel on his tower. A retired Compagnon is usually at hand (and happy) to talk you through the exhibits.

10 Rue Mabillon, 75006. ℭ **01 43 26 25 03.** www.compagnons.org. Mon–Fri 2–6pm. Metro: Mabillon.

Musée Edith Piaf FREE This veritable two-room shrine to *la môme* (one of the nicknames for Edith Piaf), run by an ardent fan who waited two decades to buy her former apartment, brims with memorabilia, including her handbag, one of her famous black dresses (signed Jacques Esterel), old love letters, a schoolbook, and a teddy bear. FINE PRINT A donation is appreciated.

Near the Metro Menilmontant, 75011. ☎ **01 43 55 52 72.** Mon–Wed 1–6pm, Thurs 10am–midday by appt only.

Musée Maçonnique FREE An air of mystery surrounds France's Freemasons' headquarters, built in 1894 over a brook that once ran through the crypt. This ambience continues in its museum, where more than 5,000 masonic objects from the 18th and 19th centuries are displayed, 200 at a time, in rotating, two-monthly exhibitions. You might find embroidery, medals, pottery, jewellery and manuscripts, all embellished with recurring symbols: The Sun, compasses, crosses, triangles, and beehives. Two of the building's 15 temples can also be visited: The Grand Temple and the Franklin D. Roosevelt Temple, which like the others, are awash with symbolism, face the east and are crowned with a starry ceiling (a wink to the Mason's ancient open-air lodges). There is also a wonderful library of more than 100,000 masonic works. FINE PRINT Non-Masons—male and female—can organise a visit by writing. Masons can turn up at any time providing they have their password.

8 Rue de Puteaux, 75017. ☎ **01 53 42 41 41.** www.gldf.org. Daily 2–6pm. Metro: Rome.

Musée National de la Légion d'Honneur et des Ordres de Chevalerie FREE This relatively unknown museum set in the stables of the beautiful 18th-century Hôtel de Salm beside the Musée d'Orsay does justice to those admirable enough to have received the Legion of Honour with moving displays of medals, paintings and other objects. Audioguides enrich the visit and an interactive resource room lets you consult the profiles of more than 300 men and women.

2 Rue de la Légion d'Honneur, 75007. ☎ **01 40 62 84 25.** www.musee-legiondhonneur. fr. Wed–Sun 1–6pm (except public hols). Metro: Solférino. RER: Musée d'Orsay.

Musée Puiforcat FREE Few of us will ever be wealthy enough to own a Puiforcat dinner service: The company, which has been making gold and silver services since 1820, charges nothing less than an arm and a leg. Keep your limbs intact and opt instead for a trip into the basement of the Champs-Elysées boutique, where a small museum displays more than 100 stunningly beautiful silver pieces from the 1920s and 1930s. FINE PRINT The museum can be visited by appointment only, so call ahead.

48 Rue Gabriel, 75008. ☎ **01 45 63 10 10.** www.puiforcat.com. Mon–Sat 10:15am– 6:30pm. Metro: Champs-Elysées–Clemenceau.

Musée Sainte-Anne `FREE` Aspiring doctors, nurses and psychologists, and anyone who's even remotely interested in the 'science of the brain', find this psychiatric museum fascinating. Set in one of the Hôpital Sainte-Anne's outbuildings, it retraces the history of the hospital from 1867 to today via a remarkable and sometimes frightening collection of documents, objects and medical apparatus linked to psychiatry, psychopathology, neurology, neurosurgery and anaesthetics. Think wrist-shackles, electroshock machines, chloroform masks and even an old psychometric test used to analyse RATP metro drivers' reactions. `FINE PRINT` Free guided visits are by appointment only. Ask for a map of the hospital at the welcome desk.

Hôpital Sainte-Anne, 1 Rue Cabanis (Pavillon L, 2nd floor), 75014. 🕾 **01 45 65 84 33.** Tues or Thurs by appt. Metro: Glacière.

Musée Valentin Haüy `FREE` Valentin Haüy was the 18th-century precursor to Louis Braille, creating books, globes, clocks, and other items with raised sections that blind people could identify. This small museum (a 19th-century classroom) devoted to his work shows many of the items he used in his teachings. It's a particularly enlightening experience for normal-sighted kids, who can close their eyes and see if they can understand what they are touching, or for those with sight problems, used to handling Braille.

Association Valentin Haüy, 5 Rue Duroc (1st floor). 🕾 **01 44 49 27 27.** www.avh. asso.fr. Tues–Wed 2:30–5pm. Metro: Duroc.

Musée du Thé `FREE`

Museums don't get smaller than the Mariage Frères tea museum, squeezed into a miniscule space above its fashionable Marais tearoom. If you're passing by or calling in for a cuppa, pop upstairs to see beautifully decorated tea tins and teapots in styles ranging from naturalist and post-modern to Art Deco and Art Nouveau. 30 Rue du Bourg Tibourg, 75004. 🕾 **01 42 72 28 11.** www.mariage freres.com. Daily 10:30am–7:30pm. Metro: Hôtel-de-Ville.

Salle des Martyrs d'Extrême Orient `FREE` It all started in 1843, when the decapitated body of the missionary Pierre Bory was sent back to France in a trunk from Vietnam. It was the first in a long, sad series of body repatriations from Asia—and one that inspired Paris's foreign missionaries to set up a memorial room in honour of the martyrs' sacrifices. On display are moving and surprisingly tasteful sets of artefacts (robes, shoes, letters, paintings, and engravings) that once belonged to the missionaries, hinting at how they lived their lives. FINE PRINT Access is via the church crypt.

Missions Etrangères de Paris, 128 Rue du Bac, 75007. ℭ **01 44 39 10 40.** www.mepasie.org. Tues–Sat 11am–6:30pm, Sun 1–6pm. Metro: Sèvres-Babylone.

SOMETIMES FREE

FIRST SUNDAY OF MONTH

Archives Nationales Aside from boasting a sumptuous setting within the 18th-century Rohan and Soubise mansions in the Marais, the national archives contain the French History Museum (Musée de l'Histoire de France)—for now at least (Sarkozy has declared that he'd like to develop a larger French history museum, possibly in Versailles). The current museum is dedicated to objects and documents relating to the history of France from mediaeval times to today, and parts of the interior are truly palatial, with paintings by Van Loo and Boucher together with some historic furniture. Other sections display pieces that were either confiscated in police raids (in the 18th, 19th, and 20th centuries) or donated by well-wishers. FINE PRINT Look out for Saturday-afternoon classical-music concerts (12€) and events with costumed actors. Locals can buy a 30€ membership card that gives free access to permanent and temporary exhibitions, plus 50% off concert tickets.

Free Exhibits at Libraries
FREE

Both the Bibliothèque Nationale François Mitterrand (BFM) and Bibliothèque Nationale Richelieu (BNR) hold ever-changing temporary exhibitions on anything from art and photography to rediscovered ancient manuscripts and ballet. Exhibitions are nearly always free and consistently interesting. In 2010 look out for Bettina Rheims's *C'est Paris* photography exhibition (at BNR 8 April–11 July) and a Hans Hartung (1904–1989) retrospective of abstract etchings (BFM, 8 June–15 September). Also worth seeing at the BFM is the permanent collection of Louis XIV's globes—astonishing beauties, cleverly hung to contrast with contemporary images of our universe.
BNF François Mitterrand: Quai François-Mauriac, 75013. ℭ **01 53 79 59 59.** Metro: Bibliothèque François Mitterrand.
BNF Richelieu: 58 Rue de Richelieu,75002. ℭ **01 53 79 59 59.** Metro: Bourse.

60 Rue des Francs-Bourgeois, 75003. ℭ **01 40 27 60 96.** www.archivesnationales. culture.gouv.fr. Adm: exc 1st Sun of month 3€ (2.30€ 18–26, free under-18s). Wed–Mon 10am–12:30pm, 2–5:30pm (closed public hols). Metro: Hôtel de Ville or Rambuteau.

Maison d'Auguste Comte
FREE

Auguste Comte (1798–1857) was the father of positive thinking—he coined the term 'sociology', founded the Religion of Humanity, a humanistic, non-theistic religion (the chapel of which can be visited at 5 Rue Payenne, 75003) and promoted positive thinking in new and structured ways. His Parisian apartment, barely changed since his death, only contains his library, bed and furniture—and copious amounts of positive energy—but for those who adhere to his philosophy, it's a necessary pilgrimage site. 10 Rue Monsieur-Le-Prince (1st floor, on left), 75006. ℭ **01 43 26 08 56.** www.augustecomte.org. Wednesday 2–5pm. Closed August and Christmas holidays. Metro: Odéon.

★ **Centre Pompidou** When this temple to modern art, designed by Richard Rogers and Renzo Piano, opened in 1977 it was hailed the most avant-garde building in the world for its bold, 'exoskeletal' architecture made up of brightly painted pipes, ducts, and transparent escalator tubes. Today it's a city unto itself, with a collection of modern art (nearly 5,000 artists and more than 50,000 works) that is rivalled only by that of MoMA in New York. There are six floors to cover, plus regular re-hangs and cutting-edge temporary exhibitions. Don't miss the Atelier Brancusi in an annexe opposite the Centre, a recreation of the Jazz Age studio of Romanian sculptor Brancusi painstakingly moved from his home in Montparnasse to this spot in 1997. FINE PRINT Queues are even longer than usual on the 1st Sunday of the month, so get here early or book online beforehand.

Place Georges Pompidou, 75004. ℭ **01 44 78 12 33.** www.centrepompidou.fr. Adm: exc 1st Sun of month 12€ adults, free under-26s (under-18s for temporary exhibitions). Wed–Mon 11am–9pm (11pm for temporary exhibitions). Atelier Brancusi Wed–Mon 2–6pm. Metro: Rambuteau or Hôtel de Ville. RER: Châtelet–Les Halles.

★ **Cité de l'Architecture et du Patrimoine** The City of Architecture and Heritage lives up to its name, dedicating 8km2 of space in the east wing of the Palais de Chaillot to the French architectural heritage. The

850-plus copies of French architectural treasures on show include moulded portions of churches, chateaux, and great French cathedrals such as Chartres, and there are some reconstructions of modern architecture, the centrepiece of which is an apartment by Le Corbusier. Don't miss the wall-painting gallery with its stunning reconstructed church vaults and domed ceilings and a collection of frescoes copied from mediaeval murals.

Palais de Chaillot, 1 Place du Trocadéro, 75016. $\mathbb{C}$ **01 58 51 52 00.** www.citechaillot. org. Adm: exc 1st Sun of month 8€, free under-18s and under-26s from EU, 5€ 19–25s from outside EU. Wed–Mon 11am–7pm (until 9pm Thurs). Metro: Trocadéro.

Cité Nationale de l'Histoire de l'immigration All Frenchmen descend from Astérix the Gaul, right? *Mais non*—despite what the history and comic books might imply. The government has finally decided to pay homage to the immigrants that have made the mighty Gaul what it is today with this national immigration museum, fittingly set in the eye-catching colonial palace built at the Porte Dorée in 1931 for the World Colonial Fair. The permanent collection covers 200 years of immigration through stirring images, everyday objects and artwork that symbolises the struggle immigrants faced when integrating with French society, and there are frequent immigration/integration-themed temporary exhibitions.

Before you leave, immigrants from the animal kingdom (crocodiles, turtles, and fish) await you in the downstairs aquarium (www.aquarium-portedoree.fr)—a quirky

Save Money on the Colline des Musées

With more museums per square metre than anywhere else in Paris, the Chaillot hillside dubbed Museum Hill (the Colline des Musées) bears its nickname well. Its four biggies—the **Palais de Tokyo** (p. 229), the **Musée d'Art Moderne de la Ville de Paris** (p. 181), the **Musée du Quai Branly** (p. 194) and the **Cité Chaillot** (p. 190)—make it even easier to visit their treasures by offering a downloadable voucher that saves you money (www.lacollinedesmusees.com). You pay full price at one of the museums the first time, visit any of them a second and third time at a reduced rate, and then gain free entry the fourth time. The offer is mainly for temporary exhibitions but can sometimes be extended to permanent collections (ask upon arrival).

throwback to the World Colonial Fair FINE PRINT Joint museum/aquarium tickets can be purchased for 4.50€, or 6.50€ during exhibition periods.

Palais de la Porte Dorée, 293 Ave. Daumesnil, 75012. ℭ **01 53 59 58 60.** www.histoire-immigration.fr. Adm: exc 1st Sun of month 3€, 5€ during exhibitions; 3.50€ under-18s from outside EU, free under-26s from EU. Tues–Sun 10am–5:30pm (until 7pm Sat–Sun). Metro: Porte Dorée.

★ **Musée de la Chasse et de la Nature**   After a two-year facelift, the city's hunting museum has gone from being old and musty to downright special. The setting (the 17th-century Hôtel de Mongelas and Hôtel de Guénégaud mansions) has always been lovely, but the new displays lend a pleasant, art-gallery feel and are really quite educational. The section in the Hôtel de Mongelas looks at how the relationship between humans and wild animals has evolved via a series of themed rooms. A 'naturalist's cabinet' shows how hunters tracked the animals, with drawers you can open to reveal footprint casts and droppings. On the Hôtel de Guénégaud side you feel like you've stepped into a hoarder's house, with interesting hunting-themed art from various eras.

62 Rue des Archives, 75003. ℭ **01 53 01 92 40.** www.chassenature.org. Adm: exc free 1st Sun of the month 6€; students and 18–25s 4.50€; under-18s free. Tues–Sun 11am–6pm. Metro: Hôtel de Ville or Rambuteau.

★ **Musée de l'Orangerie**   Just off Place de la Concorde, this winter garden dating from the Second Empire is where Claude Monet chose to hang his eight gigantic water-lily paintings. The fact that the museum is frequently (and unjustly) overlooked in favour of bigger, more famous Monet-related sites such as the Musée d'Orsay (p. 193), Giverny (p. 217) and the Musée Marmottan Monet (p. 218) can be good news, as you won't be fighting off as many crowds to see the Nymphéas, which Monet hung as low as possible to recreate the effect of seeing them from just above the water. The result is breathtaking. There are also works by other great Impressionist painters such as Renoir (including his self-portrait as a clown) and by Cézanne, Utrillo, and Picasso. FINE PRINT If you're going to the Musée d'Orsay on the same day, save money by buying a combined 13€ ticket which gives fast-track entry to the Orsay (except Monday, Tuesday and the first Sunday of the month).

Jardin des Tuileries, 75001. ℭ **01 44 77 80 07.** www.musee-orangerie.fr. Adm: exc 1st Sun of month 7.50€, 5.50€ 19–25s from outside EU, free under-18s from outside EU and under-26s from EU. Open Wed–Mon 9am–6pm. Closed some public hols. Metro: Tuileries or Concorde.

★ **Musée d'Orsay**   Set in the old Orsay train station and one of the world's greatest museums, the Orsay holds an astounding collection devoted to the watershed years 1848 to 1914, with a treasure-trove of works by the big names (Monet, Renoir, Manet, and more) and lesser-known groups (the Symbolists, Pointillists, Nabis, Realists and late Romantics). Throughout the 80 galleries there are also Art Nouveau furniture, photographs, *objets d'art* and architectural models. This, together with a cinema showing old classics (mostly in French) and live chamber music (p. 102), makes the museum an excellent place in which to while away an entire day. FINE PRINT Save your ticket for, within 7 days of your visit, reduced entry to the Musée Gustave Moreau (p. 195) and the Palais Garnier opera (p. 226). Or, buy a same-day passport ticket that can be combined with the Musée Rodin (12€) or Musée de l'Orangerie (13€).

1 Rue de Bellechasse or 62 Rue de Lille, 75007. ℂ **01 40 49 48 14.** www.musee-orsay. fr. Adm: exc 1st Sun of month 8€; 5.50€ 18–25s from non-EU countries, everyone after 4:15pm (except Thurs) and after 6pm Thurs; free under-18s from non-EU countries and under-26s from EU. Tues–Sun 9:30am–6pm (until 9:45pm Thurs). Metro: Solférino. RER: Musée d'Orsay.

★ **Musée du Louvre**   This former royal palace is so vast you could spend a day in each wing and still not see everything. And it's getting even bigger, with a new Islamic Art section set to open at the end of 2010. Like the palace itself, the Louvre's collections developed over the ages and now cover everything from Ancient Egypt to the 19th century. Some 35,000 art treasures are shared between eight huge departments (Oriental, Egyptian, Greek, Etruscan and Roman antiquities, European Paintings and Sculptures, the Decorative and Graphic Arts, and Islamic Arts), set in three vast wings, Sully, Denon and Richelieu. This, of couxe, is where you can see the *Venus de Milo*, *Winged Victory* and Da Vinci's smiling lady, the *Mona Lisa*. But don't just hit the biggies—it's well worth browsing the website beforehand to see which parts interest you most, and perhaps downloading one of the free thematic trails covering a range of subjects from Still Life painting in Northern Europe to the 'Da Vinci Code' (separates the fact from the fiction). FINE PRINT IM Pei's glass Pyramide makes for an iconic entrance, but it's also the museum's busiest. Cut the queues by buying a ticket in advance (from branches of Fnac or Virgin—p. 165—or on the Louvre's own website) and then enter via the

Richelieu wing (off Rue de Rivoli) or the Carrousel du Louvre (99 Rue de Rivoli), which also has automatic ticket machines.

Main entrance under Pyramide or 99 Rue de Rivoli, 75001. Ⓒ **01 40 20 50 50.** www. louvre.fr. Adm: (exc 1st Sun of month, which is free for permanent exhibitions) 14€ (temporary and permanent collections); 12€ (permanent and temporary exhibitions 6–9:45pm Wed, Fri); 11€ (temporary exhibitions); 9€ (permanent collection); 6€ (permanent collection 6–9:45pm Wed, Fri); free under-26s from EU and under-18s from outside EU. Wed–Mon 9am–6pm (late-night opening Wed and Fri until 10pm). Closed 1 Jan, 1 May, 25 Dec. Metro: Louvre-Rivoli or Palais Royal–Musée du Louvre.

★ **Musée du Quai Branly**   This Jean Nouvel-designed arts temple recognises the heritage of peoples and civilisations the western world tends to forget, via a 3,500-strong collection of anthropological and ethnological artefacts from Africa, Oceania, Asia and the Americas. Treasures include Vietnamese costumes, Aztec statues, rare Ethiopian frescoes, sculptures from the Cameroon, and the curiosity cabinets that regroup families of objects such as divinatory tools from Africa. Soak up the ambience by ambling in and out of the atmospherically lit sections, married by a central path or 'river'. Music, the universal language, is a key feature of the museum—a spectacular *tour aux instruments*, a circular glass tower, cuts through the centre of the building, showing instruments from all over the world. ⌈FINE PRINT⌉ The Quai Branly is part of the Colline des Musées money-saving scheme (p. 191).

37 Quai Branly, 75007. Ⓒ **01 56 61 70 00.** www.quaibranly.fr. Adm: exc 1st Sun of month 8.50€; 6€ 18–25s from non-EU countries; free under-18s and under-26s from EU. Joint museum and temporary exhibition 10€. Open Tues, Wed and Sun 11am–7pm Thurs–Sat 11am–9pm). Metro: Iéna or Alma-Marceau.

Musée Eugène Delacroix   The non-conformist Romantic painter lived and worked in this house on one of the Left Bank's most charming squares, known for its catalpa trees and old-fashioned streetlamps, from 1857 until his death in 1863. A large arch on a courtyard leads to Delacroix's studio with its sketches, lithographs, watercolours, and oils. The passionate and highly coloured works cover every period of his art, but highlights include *Mary Madeleine in the Wilderness*; a rare self-portrait (1821) dressed as Edgar Ravenswood, a character from Walter Scott's novel *The Bride of Lammermoor*; and *Charles V at the Monastery of Yuste*, painted for his student and friend Marie-Elisabeth Boulanger-Cavé in 1837.

Combine your visit with a trip to the nearby Saint-Sulpice church (Place Saint-Sulpice), where, inside the Chapelle des Anges, you can see the original murals that Delacroix worked on when he lived here. FINE PRINT Visit the museum after the Louvre (on the same day, with the Louvre's standard 9€ ticket or the 14€ combined temporary and permanent collection ticket) and get into the Delacroix for free.

6 Rue de Furstenberg, 75006. ℂ **01 44 41 86 50.** www.musee-delacroix.fr. Adm: exc 1st Sun of month and 14th July 5€, free for under-18s. Wed–Mon 9:30am–5pm (until 5:30pm on Sat–Sun June–Aug). Metro: Saint-Germain-des-Près.

★ **Musée Gustave Moreau**   He may have been around at the same time as the Impressionists, but Gustave Moreau (1825–98) worked against the prevailing mood, drawing inspiration from Greek mythology, Biblical stories, Leonardo da Vinci, Michelangelo, and Indian miniatures for his Symbolist art. This atmospheric museum where he lived and produced much of his work reveals Moreau's obsession with collecting family furniture, knick knacks and portraits, as well as displaying canvases with mystical beasts, fantasy worlds, writhing maidens, and visages in a trance-like state. Don't miss his masterpiece, *Jupiter et Sémélé*, the lovers Zeus struck by lightning after saving their child Dionysus, god of wine, agriculture and the theatre. FINE PRINT The museum closes at lunchtime but if you start your visit in the morning you can re-enter using the same ticket after lunch.

14 Rue de la Rochefoucauld, 75009. ℂ **01 48 74 38 50.** www.musee-moreau.fr. Adm: exc 1st Sun of month 5€; 3€ 19–26s from outside EU; free under-18s (under-26s from EU). Wed–Mon 10am–12:45pm, 2–5:15pm. Metro: Trinité.

★ **Musée National du Moyen Age (Cluny)**   If you love mediaeval history, this is a must-see, housing some rare European pieces such as the blue *Mille Fleurs* (thousand flowers) tapestry portraying noble mediaeval gentleman hunting with falcons while ladies sit around sewing, some 15th-century stained-glass windows, 21 heads dating from 1220 and corresponding to the Kings of Judah plundered from Notre Dame during the Revolution and rediscovered in 1977 during the construction of a car park, and the world-famous *Lady and the Unicorn* tapestries depicting the five senses through scenes that feature a princess and her handmaiden, mythical unicorns, lions, monkeys and house pets. Fans of the Roman era can get their fix in the downstairs baths (AD 200), one of Paris's few visible Roman ruins. FINE PRINT Audio-guides can be hired in English for just 1€.

★ Out of Town – MAC/VAL

The ode to contemporary art that is the **Musée d'art contemporain du Val-de-Marne** outside Paris in Vitry-sur-Seine (about 50min on public transport) is less swamped than its Parisian counterparts on the first Sunday of the month, despite being France's third largest contemporary art museum. It offers a fabulous snapshot of French art from the 1950s to today, including works by Gilles Barbier and Christian Boltanski.

The museum's goal is to make contemporary art accessible to people who wouldn't usually visit galleries, so prices are attractively low, and regular events are hosted during which visitors can meet the artists. You can also visit the MAC/VAL as part of the TRAM modern art tours around the Ile-de-France (p. 228). Place de la Libération, 94404 Vitry-sur-Seine. ℂ **01 43 91 64 20.** www.macval.fr. Adm: exc 1st Sun of month 4€; free under-18s. Tues–Sun midday–7pm. Metro: Porte de Choisy, then bus 183 direction Orly Terminal Sud to MAC/VAL or RER: Vitry-sur-Seine, then bus 180 direction Villejuif–Louis Aragon to MAC/VAL.

6 Place Paul Painlevé, 75005. ℂ **01 53 73 78 00.** www.musee-moyenage.fr. Adm: exc 1st Sun of month 8.50€; 18–25s from outside EU 6.50€; free under-18s from outside EU, under-26s from EU. Wed–Mon 9:15am–5:45pm. Closed 1 Jan, 1 May, 25 Dec. Metro: Cluny-La Sorbonne, Saint-Michel or Odéon.

Musée National du Sport   After 10 long years the national sports museum has reopened its doors in a brand-new building in the 13th, with a wonderful, unique collection of audiovisual, photographic and written pieces, plus more than 2,000 sports accessories that trace the history of sport in France—both as a hobby and as a competitive activity—from the 16th century to today.

93 Ave. de France, 75013. ℂ **01 45 83 15 80.** www.museedusport.fr. Adm: exc 1st Sun of month 4€; 2€ 18–25s: free under-18s. Mon–Fri 10am–6pm; every Sat, 1st Sun of month and public hols (except 25 Dec) 2–6pm. Metro/RER: Bibliothèque François-Mitterrand.

★ **Musée Rodin**   After Rodin chiselled his last, he left many of his sculptures to the State as payment for having lived and worked for free in one of Paris's most elegant mansions: The Hôtel Biron, built in 1731. The exhibits, arranged by themes and spanning Rodin's life, include the famous, Dante-inspired *The Kiss* and a moving display of works by Camille Claudel, Rodin's long-time lover. Outside, the shaded alleyways and gardens (which can be visited separately for just 1€) are dotted with great works such as *The Thinker*, *The Gates of Hell* and *Balzac*. In summer the shrubbery and leaves create screened-off sections that provide plenty of canoodling opportunities. FINE PRINT If you plan to visit the Musée d'Orsay on the same day, there's a 12€ same-day passport ticket. Those visiting the nearby Musée Maillol can show their Rodin ticket for a 2€ reduction.

79 Rue de Varenne, 75007. ℂ **01 44 18 61 10.** www.musee-rodin.fr. Adm: exc 1st Sun of month 1€ gardens only; 6€ museum only; 10€ museum and temporary exhibitions; 5€ 18–25s from outside EU; free under-26s from EU. Open 9:30am–5:45pm Tues–Sun (garden until 6:45pm). Metro: Varennes, Invalides or Saint-François-Xavier. RER: Invalides.

FREE WEDNESDAY PM

Fondation Cartier-Bresson A relaxed feel pervades this intimate gallery dedicated to the works of photographer Henri Cartier-Bresson. There are two floors of images, a small archive open to researchers, a lounge with film screenings, and Le Corbusier armchairs that cry out to be sat on. Cartier-Bresson also

The Mounted Republican Guard FREE

France's Republican Guard (Garde Républicaine) has been around for centuries and still patrols on special occasions. Most Parisians don't get more than a sniff of their headquarters—quite literally, since though the stately building's façade gives no inkling as to what lies within, the odour of stables and the city's 204 horses often fills the air. The exception is September, when an open day (usually the weekend after the Journées du Patrimoine; p. 198) gives you access to a former stable in which kitsch waxwork figures and a 1,500-strong collection of objects tell the tale of France's mounted police. The highlights of the day are the live horse shows, which demonstrate just how well trained the national cavalry has to be.

18 Blvd. Henri IV, 75004. ℂ **01 58 28 29 99.** www.garderepublicaine. gendarmerie.defense.gouv.fr. Two days near end of September (check website or Pariscope in advance) 9am–7pm. Metro: Sully-Morland or Bastille.

drew, with some of his works on display on the fourth floor, and assisted on three of Jean Renoir's films—hence the three annual

★ **Journées du Patrimoine (National Heritage Days)** FREE

Curiosity kills *le chat* but not on National Heritage days (usually the second weekend in September), when nosy-parkers can poke around a host of private buildings usually closed to the public. Embassies, ministries, universities, scientific establishments, and even corporate headquarters all chip in for a weekend of free illicit sightseeing. Buy *Le Monde* or *Le Parisien* newspapers for a full low-down. See also Calendar of Events. p. 24. www. journeesdupatrimoine.culture.fr.

shows when the foundation opens its doors to other disciplines.

2 Impasse Lebouis, 75014. 🕐 **01 56 80 27 00.** www.henricartierbresson.org. Admission 6€; 3€ under-26s; free Wed 6:30–8:30pm. Tues–Fri and Sun 1–6:30pm (until 8:30pm Wed), Sat 11am–6:45pm. Metro: Gaîté.

★ **Maison Européenne de la Photographie** Housed in a spacious Marais mansion with modern extensions, this is easily Paris's best photography exhibition space, drawing a savvy crowd to its top-notch retrospectives, which frequently include big names such as Larry Clark and Alair Gomes, plus works by up-and-coming photographers. The permanent collection covers the 1950s to today—a start date chosen thanks to photographer Robert Frank, whose 1958 book *The Americans* (acclaimed for its fresh and sceptical outsider's view of American society) marked a turning point in modern photography.

5–7 Rue Fourcy, 75004. 🕐 **01 44 78 75 00.** www.mep-fr.org. Adm: 6.50€; 3.50€ over-60s and students: free under-8s; free Wed 5–8pm. Wed–Sun 11am–8pm (closed public hols). Metro: Saint-Paul.

FREE LAST WEDNESDAY OF MONTH

Musée Dapper Taking its name from the 17th-century Dutch humanist Olfert Dapper who, despite having never left his native country, wrote the encyclopaedic *Description of Africa* first published in 1668, this private, non-profit organisation aims to raise the profile of sub-Saharan Africa's artistic heritage and contribute to its conservation by staging exhibitions and offering research bursaries. It also covers works linked to the mixed-race communities of Europe, Latin America and the Indian Ocean. For you and me, this means several Africa-themed exhibitions a year, a performance space, an excellent bookshop and a café selling tasty homemade cakes. FINE PRINT Regular films, theatre events, and music concerts (7€–12€) are hosted to familiarise audiences with culture from Africa and mixed-race societies. On show night, the café opens at 7pm.

35 Bis Rue Paul Valéry, 75016. ℂ **01 45 00 91 75.** www.dapper.fr. Adm: exc last Wed of month 6€; 3€ students and OAPs; free under-18s. Wed–Mon 11am–7pm. Metro: Victor Hugo.

DIRT CHEAP (LESS THAN 6€)

★ **Cinémathèque Française**   Frank Gehry's spacious 1992 Cubist building makes a striking setting for this excellent cinema and museum, which now has four screens, a specialist bookshop, a five-floor film library, a funky café (with an outdoor area that offers cool brunch-concerts June–August), oodles of exhibition space and the Musée du Cinéma. The latter, an ode to the Seventh Art, displays movie memorabilia such as Mrs Bates's rotting head from Hitchcock's *Psycho* (1960) and jewellery worn by silent movie star Louise Brooks (1906–85). Regular temporary exhibitions also draw the crowds; fabulous retrospectives have previously included Dennis Hopper's snapshots of 1960s Hollywood and German Expressionism. FINE PRINT The building itself is worth a visit; architectural tours take place most Sundays (11€; ask abut tours in English).

51 Rue de Bercy, 75012. ℂ **01 71 19 33 33.** www.cinematheque.fr. Adm: 5€; 2.50€ under-18s; free under-6s. Mon–Sat midday–7pm (until 10pm Thurs), Sun 10am–8pm. Metro: Bercy.

Collection de Minéralogie de Jussieu   Diamonds may be a girl's best friend, but Jussieu University's mineral collection with its glimmering gallery of malachite, turquoise fluorite, hematite, and opals is a must for anyone who is interested in semi-precious stones and a rare occasion to see such quality in France. The collection will be inside the university entrance for the next few years while a new home worthy of the sparkle is sought.

Université Pierre et Marie Curie, 4 Place Jussieu (entry on right), 75005. ℂ **01 44 27 52 88.** www.lmcp.jussieu.fr. Adm: 5€; 3€ students and under-18s. Wed–Sun 1–6pm. Metro: Jussieu.

Crypte de Notre Dame   All Parisians know that their city has more layers than a giant club sandwich but few have made the effort to visit the archaeological crypt in front of Notre Dame, where bits and

Musée Galliera

Set in the Renaissance-style palace built for the Duchesse de Galliera in 1892, this fashion museum is only open for its twice-yearly temporary exhibitions. When the doors are unbolted, fashion-lovers fight to get in to see the themed exhibitions that display part of the vast period-costume collections, comprising more than 50,000 items of clothing and 40,000 accessories (jewellery, hats, canes, gloves, and umbrellas) dating from the 18th century to the present day. Many outfits were donated by the illustrator Maurice Leloir (1851–1940), who collected costumes worn by stars such as Sarah Bernhardt, Mistinguett (the 'people's singer'), Coco Chanel and Thomas Burberry. FINE PRINT Free audio guides for children and adults are available.

10 Ave. Pierre 1er de Serbie, 75016. ⓒ **01 56 52 86 00.** www.galliera.paris.fr. Adm: 8€, 4€ 14–26s, free under-13s. Open during temporary exhibitions only, 10am–6pm Tues–Sun. Metro: Iéna or Alma-Marceau. RER: Pont d'Alma.

pieces of Roman ramparts, quay-sides, mediaeval shops, pavements, an 18th-century hospital, and part of a 19th-century sewer reveal snippets about the lives of those who preceded us. This mishmash of vestiges takes you on a journey through 2,000 years of urban history, with a temporary exhibition (until September 2010) showing you how remnants of Roman Paris (or Lutèce) still affect the city's urbanisation today.

7 Parvis Notre Dame (Place Jean Paul II), 75004. ⓒ **01 55 42 50 10.** www.carnavalet.paris.fr. Adm: 4€; 3€ students; 2€ under-18s; free under-13s. Tues–Sun 10am–6pm. Closed public hols. Metro: Cité. RER: Notre Dame or Saint-Michel.

Fondation Dubuffet   Follow the winding garden path to get to *art brut* artist Jean Dubuffet's gallery-museum, founded by the artist himself in 1985, 10 years before his death. Today it is run by a foundation that safeguards his works and makes sure that a decent handful are on show through regular changing displays. FINE PRINT The foundation also runs trips to see Dubuffet's gargantuan, 3D, black-and-white masterpiece, the Hourloupe Cycle, in Périgny-sur-Yerres, east of the city (by appointment only; 4.50€–8€).

137 Rue de Sèvres, 75006. ⓒ **01 47 34 12 63.** www.dubuffetfondation.com. Adm: 4€; free under-10s. Mon–Fri 2–6pm (closed Aug and public hols).

Fondation Pierre Bergé—Yves Saint Laurent When Yves Saint Laurent retired from designing in 2002 and needed a place to store the works from his fashion house, the solution was found to lie in this *hôtel particulier* inside the Golden Triangle of designer fashion (the roads around the Champs-Elysées and Avenue Montaigne). It holds more than 5,000 items of designer clothing and 15,000 accessories and provides exhibition space for YSL's pieces. The items are preserved at exactly 64°F (18°C) with 50% humidity (a godsend for visitors in the heat of summer) and are displayed in meaningful ways—for instance, artworks by Andy Warhol and Picasso hang beside the dresses they inspired.

3 Rue Léonce Reynaud, 75016. © **01 44 31 64 00.** www.fondation-pb-ysl.net. Adm: 5€; 3€ under-18s and students; free under-10s. Tues–Sun 11am–5:30pm. Closed Aug. Metro: Alma-Marceau. RER: Pont d'Alma.

★ **Forum des Images** After three years of programming *hors les murs*, the energetic Forum des Images finally reopened its doors at its home inside Les Halles in December 2008. The brand-new open layout makes it easier for cinephiles to move between the five cinemas, the specialised library (p. 114), the research centre and the bar where you can head to wash it all down. This goldmine of film archives frequently screens old and unknown movies, ranging from the work of the Lumière brothers freshly digitalisedto new films. It's also a centre for film festivals, hosting no less than four of them including Pocket Films, showcasing works shot on mobile phones. FINE PRINT Membership is available on request.

2 Grand Galerie, Porte Saint-Eustache, Forum des Halles, 75001. © **01 44 76 63 00.** www.forumdesimages.net. Adm: 5€ (a film and 2hrs' access to the collections); 4€ under-12s. Tues–Sun 1–9pm (closed 2 wks Aug). Metro: Les Halles. RER: Châtelet–Les Halles.

★ **Galerie–Musée Baccarat** The former mansion of arts patron Marie-Laure de Noailles, known for her extravagant parties, is like a fairytale palace with its surreal rococo décor evoking the spirits of Dalí, Lewis Carroll, and Jean Cocteau. It's an atmospheric backdrop for Baccarat's small but perfectly formed crystal collection, where opulent, over-sized chandeliers swing above crystal furniture and numerous Belle Epoque pieces (the winners of several 19th-century Universal Exhibitions), including an intricately carved red and transparent crystal chess set. FINE PRINT If you fancy a splurge with the money you've saved by visiting cheap museums, treat yourself to the 29€–55€ lunch menu (it's cheaper than dinner) in Baccarat's trendy Cristal Room restaurant.

11 Place des Etats-Unis, 75016. ℂ **01 40 22 11 00.** www.baccarat.fr. Adm: 5€; 3.50€ students and 19–25s; free under-18s. Mon and Wed–Sat 10am–6pm. Metro: Iéna.

★ **Institut du Monde Arabe**   This bastion of Arab intellect and aesthetics sheds light on the culture of countries too often overshadowed by international politics. Designed in 1987 by architect Jean Nouvel and funded by 22 different countries, the museum covers the religion, philosophy, and politics of the Arab/Islamic world as well as calligraphy, decorative arts, architecture, and photographs. Architecture buffs will appreciate the building with its shuttered windows, inspired by the forms on Moorish palaces, that open and close like camera apertures according to the amount of sunlight. Views from the roof terrace include Notre Dame and the Sacré-Coeur.

1 Rue des Fossés-Saint-Bernard, Place Mohammed V, 75005. ℂ **01 40 51 38 38.** www.imarabe.org. Adm: 5€; 4€ students; free under-12s. Temporary exhibitions vary. Roof terrace free. Tues–Sun 10am–6pm. Metro: Jussieu or Cardinal Lemoine.

Laboratoire Aérodynamique Eiffel   Gustave Eiffel's old aerodynamics laboratory is unknown to most Parisians, but it's fascinating to see the gigantic industrial fans the engineer created at the age of 70. He worked here until his death in 1923, and since then the company has specialised in ventilation and fan research in the car, plane, and building industries (with clients such as Peugeot, Citroën, and Thales Air Defense). Visits are by appointment only (ask for Martin Peter).

67 Rue Boileau, 75016. ℂ **01 42 88 47 40.** www.aerodynamiqueeiffel.fr. Adm: 5€. Guided visits only, Fri after midday and weekends. Metro: Exelmans.

★ **Musée Albert-Kahn**   Like several other museums in the *proche-banlieue* ('inner suburbs'), the Musée Albert-Kahn rarely gets packed, so on a sunny day come for a peaceful stroll through its gardens—four hectares of sumptuous greenery inspired by gardens from around the world (a Vosgienne forest, a Japanese village garden, contemporary Japanese gardens, and English and French gardens). The site belonged to the early-20th-century banker and philanthropist Albert Kahn, who spent much of his time financing 'discovery' missions across the world. Each mission brought back films and snapshots of their findings, constituting a fascinating collection that Kahn called 'Les Archives de la Planète', now on show inside the house.

10–14 Rue du Port, 92100 Boulogne-Billancourt. 🕐 **01 55 19 28 00.** www.albert-kahn.fr. Adm: 1.50€; under-12s free. Tues–Sun 11am–6pm (until 7pm May–Sept). Metro: Boulogne Pont de Saint-Cloud.

★ **Musée Clemenceau**   Georges Clemenceau (1841–1929), mayor of Montmartre, journalist, senator, French Home Secretary and President of the Council, got up at 3am, was a dab hand at duelling with a pistol (he duelled more than 50 times in the Bois de Boulogne, until it was outlawed in 1914) and somehow found the time to become a celebrated author. In the audio guide, his great-great niece (who you may well meet here) divulges all this plus a few lesser-known family secrets as you wind your way through the great man's former house, which is a lesson in 19th-century living itself, with furniture to die for and a rather splendid bathroom, complete with a 1920s toothbrush.

8 Rue Benjamin Franklin, 75016. 🕐 **01 45 20 53 41.** www.musee-clemenceau.fr. Adm: 6€; 3€ 12–25s; free under-12s. Tues–Sat 2–5:30pm (closed public hols and Aug). Metro: Trocadéro or Passy.

Musée de la Contrefaçon   This small museum set up by France's anti-counterfeiting agency carries a serious message: Buying fake goods, which now account for 5–9% of world trade, encourages global organised crime. But as each display cabinet shows, it's not always that easy to separate the brand from the bogus, allowing you to play a fun spot-the-phoney game with everyday items such as Nintendo Gameboys, Bic pens, and Barbie dolls.

16 Rue de la Faisanderie, 75016. 🕐 **01 56 26 14 00.** www.unifab.com. Adm: 4€; 3€ students; free under-12s. Tues–Sun 2–5:30pm (closed public hols and Aug). Metro: Porte Dauphine.

Musée de la Monnaie   Within the neo-classical Palais Conti (circa 1770s) on the Seine, this oft-overlooked minting museum is well worth a visit, especially with kids. Hi-tech displays trace the history of global and local coinage chronologically from pre-Roman times, with good audio guides available in English. There are also good-value guided tours; the standard guided visit (5€) explains the numismatic history and culture of France and the various techniques used for striking coins, or there are architectural tours of the building, taking in the little-visited 18th-century reception rooms (Sunday 3pm, 6€). FINE PRINT Guided tours, free for under-16s, are best reserved by email (musee@monnaiedeparis.fr).

11 Quai de Conti, 75006. ℂ **01 40 46 56 66.** www.monnaiedeparis.com. Adm: 5€. 11am–5:30pm Tues–Fri, Sat–Sun midday–5:30pm. Metro: Odéon or Pont Neuf. Metro/RER: Saint-Michel.

Musée de la Poste   Stamp-collectors rejoice: Here are floors devoted to the history of the postal service, with uniforms, carriages, letter-boxes, waxwork figures, pistols, official documents and, of course, stamps—hundreds of them documenting French and international philately. The shop sells packets of stamps from around the world.

34 Blvd. de Vaugirard, 75015. ℂ **01 42 79 24 24.** www.museedelaposte.fr. Adm: 5€; 3.50€ students; free under-26s. Mon–Sat 10am–6pm (closed public hols). Metro: Montparnasse, Pasteur, or Falguière.

Musée de l'Assistance Publique   Trace the history of sick Parisians from mediaeval times to today through paintings, drawings, a mock ward, and a pharmacy. This is a goldmine of information for dinner-party conversational gambits: Did you know that Paris's first hospital was the Hôtel Dieu in front of Notre Dame, founded by the mediae-val clergy to help the sick? Or that by the 17th century, if you were Protestant and ill, you had to renounce your religion to get treatment? (You can read the names of those unlucky enough not to be Catholic on a register in the museum.) Then there's the revolting list of prac-tices employed by Louis XIV to "clean up the city" of "undesirables" such as landless peasants, unpopular politicians, blasphemers, liber-tines, homosexuals, and magicians. Perhaps most affecting is the 'tower of abandonment'—a box in which mothers could abandon their children anonymously, safe in the knowledge that the child would be taken in by the hospice nuns.

Hôtel de Miramion, 47 Quai de la Tournelle, 75005. ℂ **01 40 27 50 05.** www.aphp.fr. Adm: 4€; 2€ 13–18s; free under-13s. Tues–Sun 10am–6pm (closed public hols and Aug). Metro: Maubert-Mutualité.

Musée de l'Eventail   Tutankhamun, Madame de Pompadour, and geishas have one thing in common: Fans. Whether used for swiping flies, as a fashion accessory or as a tool of seduction, they've been around for centuries, and this arcane museum (a fan-making *atelier* since 1805) pays homage to the fan-making art within a wood-pan-elled Henri II-style salon that displays 100 fans at a time (out of a 1,000-strong collection). Intriguing displays teach visitors historical tit-bits such as how, during the Spanish Inquisition, fan movements were used as secret codes—a fan held in the right hand posed on the face meant 'Follow me', while a fan opened and closed in the left hand meant 'We're being watched'.

Atelier Anne Hoguet, 2 Blvd. de Strasbourg, 75010. ℰ **01 42 08 90 20.** www. annehoguet.fr. Adm: 6€. Mon–Wed 2–6pm (closed public hols and Aug). Metro: Strasbourg-Saint-Denis.

Musée de l'Historie de la Médecine   Was it the doctor, in the medical museum, with the diamond-cutter's false hand? Or was it the nurse, with the false teeth made of hippopotamus bone? This entire museum looks like something out of a Sherlock Holmes story—the long panelled room is lined with glass cabinets filled with surgical implements used from antiquity to the 19th century. Look out for Dr Gachet's homeopathic case, which he probably used to treat Van Gogh, and the 'magic cup' engraved with verses from the Koran, which turns white if arsenic is poured into it (thanks to its metallic composition). FINE PRINT If you read French, the Petit Guide du Visiteur (1.50€) is full of interesting facts about the displays.

Université René Descartes, 12 Rue de l'Ecole de Médecine (2nd floor), 75006. ℰ **01 40 46 16 93.** www.bium.univ-paris5.fr/musee. Adm: 3.50€; 2.50€ students. Mon–Sat 2–5:30pm (closed Thurs in winter and Sat in summer). Metro: Odéon.

★ **Musée de Minéralogie de l'Ecole des Mines**   The world's fourth-largest mineral collection contains more than 100,000 specimens from Earth and space: Meteorites that fell to Earth in the Ardèche and the Gobi Desert, precious and semi-precious gems, and a myriad of rocks and minerals from the four corners of the world, beautifully displayed in a 70m-long gallery with its Hungarian oak cabinets.

Ecole des Mines de Paris, 60 Blvd. Saint-Michel, 75006. ℰ **01 40 51 91 39.** www. musee-ensmp.fr. Adm: 6€; 3€ students. Tues–Fri 1:30–6pm, Sat 10am–12:30pm, 2–5pm. RER: Luxembourg.

Musée des Années 30   Fans of Art Deco will be in heaven at this museum covering one of the 20th-century's most creative eras through arts and crafts (with some 1920s works creeping in). Not everything on display is high quality, but lovers of the shapes and esprit of the 1930s will enjoy the modernist sculptures by the Martel brothers, Jean Burkhalter's elegantly angular drawing 'La Parade Foraine' (1922), and a handful of paintings by artists of the Ecole de Paris. FINE PRINT Hardcore lovers of the decade can take a guided tour around Boulogne-Billancourt's 1930s buildings, followed by a guided visit around the museum in the afternoon. Call ℂ **01 55 18 54 40** or **01 55 18 46 64** (French and English) for dates and prices.

Espace Landowski, 28 Ave. André Morizet, 92100 Boulogne-Billancourt. ℂ **01 55 18 53 00.** www.annees30.com. Adm: 4.50€; 3.50€ students, families with 3 or more children, over-60s; free under-16s. Tues–Sun 11am–6pm (closed 1st two weeks Aug). Metro: Marcel Sembat.

Musée des Egouts   Getting acquainted with Parisians' bowel movements doesn't sound like the basis for a great day out, yet Paris's sewer museum tracing the history of all 2,100km of Paris's underworld offers genuinely fascinating films and exhibits and a trip through the tunnels. FINE PRINT Visiting times may change in bad weather and during 'peak times' (when a larger-than-usual percentage of the population goes to the loo or makes a drink—in half-time of big football matches, for instance!), when a sudden surge in water can make the sewers dangerous. Things can also get pretty whiffy in summer—be warned.

Pont de l'Alma (Left Bank, opposite 53 Quai d'Orsay), 76007. ℂ **01 53 68 27 81.** www.paris.fr. Adm: 4.30€; 3.50€ 6–16s and students; free under-5s. Open 11am–5pm Sat–Wed (until 4pm Oct–Apr). Metro: Alma-Marceau. RER: Pont de l'Alma.

Musée des Lettres et Manuscrits   As the world goes virtual and handwriting becomes less legible, this new and relatively unknown museum on the Left Bank flies the flag of old-fashioned letter writing, with more than 250 pieces written and signed by folk who made history, covering 700 years of correspondence in French, from Charles V to François Mitterrand. Look out for rarities including letters retrieved from *boules de Moulins*—little zinc containers that transported the post underwater in the Seine during the 1870 Prussian siege.

8 Rue de Nesle, 75006. ℂ **01 45 62 21 47.** www.museedeslettres.fr. Adm: 6€; 4.50€ students. Tues–Sun 10am–6pm. Metro: Odéon.

Musée des Moulages Dermatologiques   The dermatological mask museum remains a closely guarded secret, (a) because the Hôpital Saint-Louis doesn't want to be swarmed with visitors and (b) because the skin diseases on show (wax moulds in glass cases lining the walls from floor to ceiling) are really rather gruesome. Paris's only remaining 19th-century learning museum (galleries set up by hospitals for medical students) contains more than 5,000 mouldings, made between 1867 and 1958, of every skin disease under the sun, including leprosy, gangrene, syphilis, eczema, gout, and acne. Leave your morbid curiosity at the door (or at least pretend to) and thank modern-day science that we rarely have to face such terrible disfigurements. FINE PRINT It's open by appointment only, and you'll need to put a good story together as they'll ask why you want to come.

Hôpital Saint-Louis, 1 Ave. Claude Vellefaux, 75010. ☎ **01 42 49 99 15.** www.bium. univ-paris5.fr/sfhd. Adm: 4€; 2€ students. Metro: Colonel Fabien.

Musée du Fumeur   The cigarette-loving French gave up smoking in public places in 2007, making this miniscule smokers' museum a pilgrimage site for anyone who's ever loved tobacco. All aspects of smoking are covered (tobacco, opium, cigars, chocolate cigarettes, and pipes, plus ways to kick the habit, and there's a small 'plantarium' where all sorts of smokable plants are cultivated. FINE PRINT For aficionados there's a cave à cigares and a good specialised bookshop.

7 Rue Pache, 75011. ☎ **01 46 59 05 51.** www.museedufumeur.net. Adm: 4€; 3€ under-25s. Tues–Sat 12:30–7pm. Metro: Voltaire.

Musée du Montparnasse   Set down a pretty cobbled lane and surrounded by modern-day artists' ateliers, this museum was once the workshop of artist Marie Vassilieff, who also used it as a canteen for needy artists, including Braque, Modigliani, Léger, Picasso, Matisse, and Cocteau––as well as Trotsky and Lenin, which caused problems with the police. It keeps the old Montparnasse spirit alive via temporary exhibitions (photos, paintings, letters, and sculptures) by up-and-coming and established artists. The **Espace Krajcberg** FREE next-door (Tuesday–Sunday 2–6pm), a joint gallery venture between France and Brazil, promotes both modern art and environmental awareness.

21 Ave. du Maine, 75015. ☎ **01 42 22 91 96.** www.museedumontparnasse.net. Adm: 5€; 4€ under-18s, students and OAPs; free under-12s. Tues–Sun 12:30–7pm. Metro: Montparnasse or Edgar Quinet.

★ **Musée Dupuytren**   Not for the faint-hearted, this mind-blowing but educational museum of horrors was opened in 1835 by the successor of Guillaume Dupuytren, a famous surgeon from the Hôtel Dieu hospital (on Île de la Cité) and is full of jars containing weird and wonderful body parts gone wrong. More than 6,000 items—pustules, tumours, cysts, hermaphrodite sexual organs, and even a Cyclops foetus—from the 18th to the 20th centuries demonstrate to visitors how doctors once studied and taught medicine. FINE PRINT Call before you set out to make sure someone is manning the museum, and for information about the regular temporary exhibitions and conferences about the human body.

15 Rue de l'Ecole-de-Médecine, Centre des Cordeliers, 75006. ✆ **01 42 34 68 60.** www.upmc.fr. Adm: 5€; 3€ students. Mon–Fri 2–5pm (until 4:30pm Fri) (closed during university hols). Metro: Odéon.

Musée National de Céramiques Sèvres In the 18th century, under Louis XV, Vincennes became a centre for porcelain, and in 1756 the factory moved from the Château de Vincennes (p. 222) to Sèvres, 10km west of Paris, where it produced a creamy-white biscuit-baked porcelain known as *porcelain de Sèvres*. The museum here today is set inside the old *manufacture*—a building more akin to a palace than a factory, and a knick-knack lover's haven. The collections cover ceramics in general, through the ages, including Peruvian earthenware, faience, bone china, and rare glass.

Place de la Manufacture, 92310 Sèvres. ✆ **01 41 14 04 20.** www.musee-ceramique-sevres.fr. Adm: 4.30€; 3€ 18–25s; free under-18s. Wed–Mon 10am–5pm (closed 25 Dec, 1 Jan). Metro: Pont de Sèvres then bus 169, 171, or 179/ T2 (tramway) to Musée de Sèvres.

Musée Nissim de Camondo Coming to this museum is a bit like visiting the sumptuous townhouse of rich relatives: You feel at home, but you can't touch the furniture! Each room drips with needlepoint chairs, tapestries (many from Beauvais or Aubusson), antiques, paintings, bas-reliefs, silver, Chinese vases, crystal chandeliers, Sèvres porcelain (above), and Savonnerie carpets. Downstairs are the old kitchens, once capable of serving hundreds of dinner guests at one time and insulated with concrete to ensure the cooking smells didn't disturb them. It's a fascinating trip into the upstairs/downstairs world of 18th- and 19th-century aristocratic households. FINE PRINT A combined 10.50€ ticket can be bought for Les Arts Décoratifs (p. 211).

63 Rue de Monceau, 75008. ✆ **01 53 89 06 50.** www.lesartsdecoratifs.fr. Adm: 6€; 4.50€ 18–25s; free under-17s. Wed–Sun 10am–5:30pm (closed 1 Jan, 1 May, 14 July, and 25 Dec). Metro: Villiers.

★ **Musée Pasteur** Louis Pasteur's discoveries (notably pasteurisation) revolutionised the modern era, and this gem of a museum, where he lived and worked, takes you through his discoveries chronologically (from crystallography and rabies prophylaxis to fermentation and cures for animal illnesses) as well as leading you into his former apartments, still adorned with family portraits and *objets d'art*. The cherry on the cake is the crypt where Pasteur's body was laid to rest—a neo-Byzantine-style mausoleum covered in intricate mosaics, several of which refer to his scientific discoveries.

25 Rue du Docteur Roux, 75015. ✆ **01 45 68 82 83.** www.pasteur.fr. Adm: 3€; 1.50€ students. Mon–Fri 2–5:30pm. Metro: Pasteur.

Trésor de Notre Dame Few Parisians let alone visitors know that the relics of Christ's Crown of Thorns, part of the cross and a nail are displayed every first Friday of the month at 3pm in Notre Dame's treasure room. If you're not here at the right time, there are still plenty of religious objects on show, intricately crafted from gold and encrusted with precious stones, that formed grandiose offerings to God from the kings and Emperor of France.

Cathédrale Notre Dame de Paris, Parvis de Notre Dame (Place Jean Paul II), 75004. ✆ **01 42 34 56 10.** www.notre damedeparis.fr. Adm: 3€; 2€ students; 1€ under-18s. Daily 9:30am–6pm (closed Sun morning). Metro: Cité.

WORTH THE SPLURGE
(MORE THAN 6€)

Cité de la Musique This freshly renovated music museum does a good job of introducing visitors old and young to music with its chronological displays of instruments from Europe (from the 17th to the 20th century) and around the world. The audio guide lets you listen to the instruments in each section—a unique treat considering the rarity of some of those on show. Other

The Petit Hôtel Bourrienne: How the Other Parisians Live

If Parisian walls had ears, they'd have wonderful stories to tell—especially those of this private 18th-century home, which first belonged to Fortunée Hamelin, a wealthy aristocrat from the Antilles, known for her decadent parties and close friendship with Joséphine and Napoléon Bonaparte. Her audacity either amused or shocked society: She would wet her clothes to create a perfect drape regardless of whether the material turned transparent or not!

After Fortunée, Bonaparte's personal secretary Antoine Fauvelet de Bourrienne moved in with his wife and turned the house into the *Consulate*-style beauty we see today—a busy, fanatically symmetrical décor with fresco-clad walls, painted ceilings, intricate parquet flooring and luscious drapes. FINE PRINT This is a private home so visits are usually by appointment only.

58 Rue d'Hauteville, 75010. ✆ **01 47 70 51 14.** Adm: 6€. Open by appointment all year or without appointment daily 1–15 July and 1–30 September midday–6pm. Metro: Poissonnière.

areas of the vast building are used for concerts (p. 246), music workshops (p. 101) and conferences.

221 Ave. Jean Jaurès, 75019. ℭ **01 44 84 44 84.** www.cite-musique.fr. Adm: 8€ (10€ with guide); 6.40€ 18–25s (8€ with guide); free under-18s (6€ with guide). Tues–Sun midday–6pm (from 10am Sun). Metro: Porte de Pantin.

★ **Collection 1900 de Pierre Cardin** This is easily Paris's most expensive museum, but if you're into the Belle Epoque, Pierre Cardin's personal Art Nouveau collection will take your breath away. Some 450 pieces (some signed Tiffany, Gallé, or Marjorelle) collected over 60 years, and handpicked by the fashion designer himself, are on show in rooms mocked up to look like a courtesan's apartment above the famous restaurant Maxim's. The Marjorelle bedroom, an opulent delight, gives pride of place to Sarah Bernhardt's silver hairbrushes. FINE PRINT Visits are by guided tour only.

Maxim's, 3 Rue Royale, 75008. ℭ **01 43 41 39 03.** www.maxims-musee-artnouveau. com. Adm: 15€. By appt Wed–Sun 2pm, 3:15pm, 4:30pm. Metro: Concorde.

Espace Dalí A sofa in the form of giant pink lips, an elephant with spindly legs carrying a pyramid on its back, and melting clocks are just some of the bizarre creations that fire the imagination in this small exhibition space, the only permanent Dalí collection in France, entirely devoted to his extravagant and Surrealist works. Dalí's phantasmagorical sculptures often juxtapose the humorous and philosophical messages.

11 Rue Poulbot, 75018. ℭ **01 42 64 40 10.** www.daliparis.com. Adm: 10€; 6€ 8–26s; free under-8s; 7€ over-60s. Daily 10am–6pm. Metro: Anvers or Abbesses and then *funiculaire*.

Fondation Cartier pour l'art contemporain This glass and steel building designed by Jean Nouvel (a work of art in itself) has become a beacon for contemporary art lovers, with ever-rotating shows and exhibitions that push the boundaries of modern art. Events are wideranging and sometimes downright strange; they usually follow a theme that is combined with live evening events called Les Soirées Nomades. The permanent collections include monumental works such as *La Volière* ('The Aviary') by Jean-Pierre Raynaud and *Caterpillar* by Wim Delvoye.

261 Blvd. Raspail, 75014. ℭ **01 42 18 56 50.** http://fondation.cartier.com. Adm: 6.50€; 4.50€ under-25s; free under-10s (and under-18s 2–6pm Wed). Tues–Sun 11am–8pm (until 10pm Tues). Metro: Denfert-Rochereau or Raspail.

Halle Saint Pierre   This *Art Brut* (Outsider Art) gallery, museum, bookshop, theatre, and café draws an eclectic mob. The displays in the hall can be real eye-openers, including as they do wild temporary exhibitions by unknown artists that touch on anything from book illustration to art-therapy workshops. The museum section contains the Max Fourny collection—a permanent exhibition of the Naïve Art-works the arts journalist Fourny collected in the 1970s. The bookshop also sells some excellent reference material.

2 Rue Ronsard, 75018. ℂ **01 42 58 72 89**. www.hallesaintpierre.org. Adm: 7.50€; 6€ under-25s. 10am–6pm daily (midday–6pm Mon–Fri in Aug). Metro: Anvers.

Jeu de Paume   Set within Napoléon III's personal tennis courts and affiliated with the Hôtel de Sully exhibition space in the Marais (62 Rue Saint-Antoine, 75004. ℂ **01 42 74 47 75**), this photography and image museum draws fans of photography, film and anything avant-garde. It is more like a large art gallery than an actual museum, exploring the world of images, their uses and the issues they have raised from the 19th century to the present. FINE PRINT Entry is free for students and under-26s 5–9pm on the last Tuesday of the month.

1 Place de la Concorde, 75008. ℂ **01 47 03 12 50**. www.jeudepaume.org. Adm: 6€; 3€ under-25s and families with 3 or more children; free under-10s. Tues–Fri midday–7pm (until 9pm Tues), Sat–Sun 10am–7pm (closed 25 Dec, 1 Jan). Metro: Concorde.

La Maison Rouge – Fondation Antoine de Galbert   The place you go when you're in the know, the Red House (set inside a former print-works) promotes different facets of contemporary creation through ever-changing temporary exhibitions by independent commissioners, usually via thought-provoking international private collections (wall art, sculpture, and wacky installations) and monographic shows by today's confirmed and emerging contemporary artists.

10 Blvd. de la Bastille, 75012. ℂ **01 40 01 08 81**. www.lamaisonrouge.org. Adm: 7€; 5€ 13–18s, students, full-time artists, and over-65s; free under-13s. Wed–Sun 11am–7pm (until 9pm Thurs). Metro: Quai de la Rapée or Bastille.

★ **Les Arts Décoratifs**   One of the world's foremost collections of design and decorative art, this vast attraction shares space with the **Musée de la Mode et du Textile** with its 86,000-strong collection of clothing and accessories displayed in ever-changing temporary exhibitions, and the **Musée de la Publicité**, an advertising museum also known for its temporary exhibitions. Over nine floors, you follow a chronological trail that demonstrates how fashion and lifestyle have evolved through the ages, with exhibits ranging from mediaeval liturgical items, Art Nouveau and Art Deco furniture, gothic panelling, and Renaissance porcelain, to 1970s psychedelic carpets, chairs by Philippe Starck, and soft-furnishings from France's high-speed TGV trains. FINE PRINT Les Arts Décoratifs is linked to the Musée Nissim de Camondo (p. 208), so grab a joint ticket (8€–10.50€) and do both.

Palais du Louvre, 107 Rue de Rivoli, 75001. ⓒ **01 44 55 57 50.** www.lesartsdecoratifs. fr. Adm: 8€; 6.50€ 18–25s from outside EU; free under-18s from outside EU and under-26s from EU. Pass Arts Décoratifs (all museums and temporary exhibitions) 16.50€ (13.50€ concessions as above). Tues–Fri 11am–6pm, Sat–Sun 10am–6pm (until 9pm Thurs). Metro: Palais Royal or Tuileries.

★ **Les Catacombes**   See the dark side of the City of Lights with nearly 1km of mysterious corridors located 18m below the street and filled with ghoulishly arranged, anonymous bones and skulls and altars. In the Middle Ages, these were quarries, but by the end of the 18th century, overcrowded cemeteries became a menace to public health and city officials decided to use the space as a burial ground. As you leave, admire the two wonderful *cloches de fontis* (vaulted ceilings created during the quarrying process)—some of the finest examples open to the public. *Tip:* Bring a torch to get a good look at the bones and wear footwear that you don't mind getting dirty as the ground is often wet and chalky.

1 Place Denfert-Rochereau, 75014. ⓒ **01 43 22 47 63.** Adm: 7€; 3.50€ 14–25s; free under-13s. Tues–Sun 10am–5pm (last ticket sold 4pm). Metro/RER: Denfert-Rochereau.

★ **Les Invalides**   Napoléon's tomb takes centre stage within the gilded Dôme church, commissioned by Louis XIV in 1676, that forms the sparkling centrepiece of the Invalides military complex—an enormous *hôtel* for disabled French soldiers injured in battle. Nowadays, most of the wards have been replaced with museums. The Musée de l'Armée, one of the most comprehensive military museums in the world, has a vast armoury collection that includes Henri II's suit of armour, Viking swords, Burgundy battle-axes, 14th-century blunderbusses, American Browning machine guns, and First World War mementoes, including the Armistice Bugle that sounded the ceasefire on 7 November 1918, before the general ceasefire on 11 November. The Musée des Plans-Reliefs contains scale models of French towns and monuments, including some Vauban replicas from Louis XIV's military campaign. The Musée de l'Ordre de la Libération is dedicated to those who offered "outstanding service in the effort to procure the liberation of France and the French empire" in WW2; exhibits include drawings made in the concentration camps and clothing that belonged to Resistance figure-head Jean Moulin (p. 179). Lastly, the Historial Charles de Gaulle is an underground multi-media centre about De Gaulle's life.

129 Rue de Grenelle, 75007. (℃) **01 44 42 38 77.** www.invalides.org and www.ordrede laliberation.fr. Adm: (all museums) 8.50€; 6.50€ 18–26s; free under-18s. Open 10am–6pm daily Apr–Sept (until 5pm Oct–Mar and until 9pm Tues Apr–Sept). Closed 1st Mon of month (except July–Sept) and most public hols. Metro: La Tour-Maubourg, Varenne, or Saint-François-Xavier. Metro/RER: Invalides.

Manufacture des Gobelins   Anyone who's ever doubted the splendour of tapestry will change their tune after visiting France's national factory—an ode to the art of patience (30cm of tapestry takes six months to make) and French royal taste. They've been weaving them here for kings, queens, aristocrats, and ministerial palaces since 1443, when the Bièvre tributary ran into the Seine. The visit takes you into the heart of the *manufacture*, where you pick up tit-bits like how to guess the weight of a tapestry (bear in mind that it takes 2–8kg of wool to cover one square metre) and how to distinguish a Savonnerie tapestry from a Gobelin one. It may sound archaic, but like the thousands of bobbins used every day, you'll soon be reeled in!

42 Ave. des Gobelins, 75013. (℃) **01 44 08 52 00.** www.mobiliernational.culture.gouv. fr. Adm: 6€; 4€ under-25s; guided tours 10€; 7.50€ under-25s. Tues–Sun 12:30–6:30pm; guided tours Wed and Fri–Sat 3.30pm and 5pm. Metro: Les Gobelins.

Musée d'art et d'histoire du Judaïsme   In the 17th-century Hôtel de Saint-Aignan, this handsome, impressively installed museum of Jew-ish history traces the development of Jewish culture not only in Paris but in France and Europe as a whole. Many exhibitions are devoted to religious subjects, including menorahs, Torah ornaments and ark curtains, in both the Ashkenazi and Sephardic traditions. Some of the most interesting documents relate to the notorious Dreyfus case. Also here is a collection of illuminated manuscripts, Renaissance Torah arks. and artwork by leading Jewish painters (Soutine, Zadkine, Chagall, and Modigliani), along with Jewish gravestones from the Middle Ages.

71 Rue du Temple, 75003. www.mahj.org. (℃) **01 53 01 86 60.** Adm: 6.80€; 4.50€ 18–26s; free under-18s. Mon–Fri 11am–6pm, Sun 10am–6pm. Metro: Rambuteau or Hôtel de Ville.

Musée Branly

This is another of those hidden Parisian museums most locals don't know about, yet the stuff that went on within these walls changed history. Edouard Branly, a physics professor in the Institut Catholique, discovered that electric waves could move without wires and through objects, and as a result created the first electric telegraph. The first ever message was exchanged on 5 November 1898 between the Eiffel Tower (p. 225) and the Panthéon (p. 223), and it was because of this that the tower, which was originally designed as a temporary structure, was saved.

Dozens of Branly's hand-built instruments are on show in the laboratory, next to which lies the so-called 'Salle de Nautilus' (after Jules Verne's submarine, in *Twenty Thousand Leagues Under the Sea*), entirely covered in copper plating to avoid electric interference. The visit ends in Branly's wood-panelled office, with his writing-stand still stained with ink. FINE PRINT Visits are by appointment only; ask for Madame Charles. Institut Catholique de Paris (ground floor of Institut Supérieur d'éléctronique de Paris), 21 Rue d'Assas, 75006. ✆ **01 49 54 52 40.** http://museebranly.isep.fr. Guided tours (by appointment) 10€. Metro: Saint-Placide or Rennes.

★ **Musée de l'Air et de l'Espace**   The oldest aeronautical museum in the world, set in the former Le Bourget passenger terminal, gets very busy with families and lovers of man-made things that fly. A visit takes you past brittle-looking biplanes and the command cabin of a Zeppelin airship, then outside to see Mirage fighter-planes, Ariane launchers and a Boeing 747, the insides of which can be explored. Plenty of other planes can be visited too: A Dakota in the Second World War hall and a Concorde. Then there's a planetarium that shows how you can fly from Le Bourget to Santiago in Chile, using only the stars as guidance. Kids and parents fight to try the hour-long simulated flying lessons of the *Classe Pilote* (sign up when you arrive). Any money left over is easily spent in the shop, where books on flying machines and model aircrafts vie for shelf space. FINE PRINT Audio guides are available for 3€.

Aéroport Paris Le Bourget, 93352 Le Bourget. © **01 49 92 71 62.** www.mae.org.
Adm: 6€; 4€ under-26s main museum and planes; 5€, 3€ planetarium; 5€ *Classe Pilote.*
Tues–Sun 10am–6pm (until 5pm Oct–Mar) (closed 1 Jan, 25 Dec). Metro: Gare de l'Est
then Roissypôle 350 bus; or Metro: La Courneuve or RER to Le Bourget then 152 bus.

Musée de la Marine Dropping anchor in this fabulous marine
museum is like sailing back in time through 400 years of French naval
history. Set in the west wing of the Palais de Chaillot, it comprises one
of the oldest nautical-themed collections in the world. Most items
were donated to Louis XV (1710–74) by one of his generals, on condition they be used to instruct marine engineers. The ensemble of boats
includes an ornate *barque* that belonged to Napoléon Bonaparte and
the prow of the gondola Marie Antoinette used to sail up and down
the canal in Versailles. In the following rooms are striking sculptures
used to decorate galleons; models of the old royal fleet, including a
replica of *La Belle Poule* used to retrieve Napoléon's ashes from Saint
Helena; a quarter-sized model of *Le Velox*, France's largest schooner
(1903–7); and, in the final room, a scaled-down replica of the *Charles
de Gaulle*, France's nuclear aircraft carrier, able to house 2,000 crew
members.

Palais de Chaillot, 17 Place du Trocadéro, 75016. © **01 53 65 69 69.** www.musee-
marine.fr. Adm: 7€, 5€ 18–25s from outside EU, free under-26s from EU, under-18s
from outside EU; temporary exhibitions extra. Open Wed–Mon 10am–6pm. Metro:
Trocadéro.

Musée de la Poupée Step away from noisy Rue Rambuteau into this
old-fashioned, flower-filled alley and you're in another world—an
old-fashioned place of porcelain faces, miniature ball gowns and
golden locks preened and curled as if they belonged to real children.
Started in 1994 by two avid collectors, Guido Odin and his son Samy,
the collection includes more than 500 dolls dating from 1800 to
today, displayed chronologically. The museum also doubles as a *cli-
nique pour poupées,* so if you have a sick doll at home (from any era),
bring it along for a quote.

Impasse Berthaud, 75003. © **01 42 72 73 11.** www.museedelapoupeeparis.com.
Adm: 7€, 5€ 12–25s and over-65s, 3€ 3–11s, free under-3s. Tues–Sun 10am–6pm
(closed public hols). Metro: Rambuteau.

Musée de l'Erotisme It's not all vulgarity at the museum of eroti-
cism: If phallic chairs, sex toys, chastity belts, and 19th-century lesbian postcards aren't your thing, head upstairs to the *exotique* section,

where collections of erotic art from around the world (including oriental miniature statues and scenes from the *Kama Sutra*) raise the tone. The top floor is all about *maisons closes*, with archive documents and photos that give a rare insight into life inside bordellos, including some *Scènes de maisons closes* monotypes by Degas discovered after his death in 1917. FINE PRINT The museum stays open to 2am, making a night-time visit a fun option.

72 Blvd. de Clichy, 75018. 📞 **01 42 58 28 73.** www.musee-erotisme.com. Adm: 8€ (5€ with online booking). Daily 10am–2am. Metro: Blanche.

Musée de Montmartre   Most Parisians would kill to live in this 17th-century building, abode of Roze de Rosimond (a member of Molière's theatre company) and later the residence of artists including Renoir, Dufy, and Utrillo. Today it's a museum recapturing the atmosphere of old Montmartre, then a village separate from Paris, with vintage posters from the famous Chat Noir cabaret (now vanished), photos, etchings, porcelain, and a reconstruction of the Café de l'Abreuvoir that Utrillo frequented all too often. Spending some time in the quiet garden on a sunny day will make you feel like you've gone back in time.

12 Rue Cortot, 75018. 📞 **01 49 25 89 37.** www.museedemontmartre.fr. Adm: 8€, 6€ over-60s, 4€ 12–26s, free under-12s. Tues–Sun 11am–6pm (until 7pm Fri–Sun July–Aug). Closed 1 Jan, 25 Dec. Metro: Abbesses, Blanche, Lamarck-Caulaincourt, or Anvers (then *funiculaire*).

★ **Musée Guimet**   This magical temple to Asian and oriental arts features treasures mostly collected and donated by the 19th-century industrialist Emile Guimet, displayed chronologically over four floors that radiate out from a monumental staircase. The 45,000-plus artworks represent artistic traditions from China, Japan, Korea, Vietnam, India, and Afghanistan as well as including the most splendid collection of Cambodian (Khmer) art in the west.

The Panthéon Bouddhique (free entry; p. 184) next to the museum occasionally holds traditional tea-drinking ceremonies.

6 Place d'Iéna, 75016. 📞 **01 56 52 53 00.** www.museeguimet.fr. Adm: 6.50€; 4.50€ 18–25s; free under-18s. Open Wed–Mon 10am–6pm. Metro: Iéna.

Musée d'Histoire Naturelle   Founded in 1635 as a science and nature research centre by Guy de la Brosse, physician to Louis XIII, Paris's highly atmospheric natural history museum offers up displays on dinosaurs and endangered and vanished species within its evolution gallery

★ Giverny

When Monet moved his mistress and their combined eight children into a quaint pink-brick house in Giverny 63km northwest of Paris in 1883 to cultivate the garden and paint its flowers, he could never have guessed that after his death it would become one of the biggest attractions outside of the captial. But in spring and summer when the gardens and waterlilies on the ponds are in bloom, you can understand why it's so popular—the whole place (despite the crowds) is picture-perfect, with garden scenes that remain remarkably faithful to Monet's paintings. His house, filled with touching mementoes of his family's life, can be visited too, while further up the road, the Musée d'Art Américain de Giverny (99 Rue Claude Monet. 𝒞 **02 32 51 94 65.** www.maag.org) houses Impressionist works by Monet's American disciples (Breck, Vonnoh, Wendel). FINE PRINT Aim to get here early, before 9.30am, when the tour buses roll in, or jump the queues by buying your ticket online at www.fnac.com.

84 Rue Claude Monet, Giverny 27620. 𝒞 **02 32 51 28 21.** www.fondation-monet.com. Adm: 6€, 3.50€ 7–12s, free under-7s. Daily 9:30am–6pm August to November. Train from St-Lazare to Vernon (45min, about 13€), then 7km taxi ride or 240 bus (2€) from station. (You can also hire bikes from the station or walk along special paths.)

(Grande Galerie de l'Evolution). Within the grounds (the Jardin des Plantes; p. 245) are further galleries specialising in palaeontology and anatomy (Galeries de Paléontologie et d'Anatomie comparée) and mineralogy and geology (Galerie de Minéralogie et de Géologie). Also within the grounds are winter gardens with tropical plants and a menagerie (p. 249). FINE PRINT The Pass 2 Jours saves you money on all the galleries over a 2-day period (including the menagerie): 25€ adults, 20€ 4–13s. Also, present a full-price ticket for reduced-price entry to another part of the museum (within a 3-month period).

56 Rue Cuvier, 75005. 𝒞 **01 40 79 54 79.** www.mnhn.fr. Adm: 8€, 5€ 4–13s Galerie de Minéralogie; 7€, free under-26s Galeries de Paléontologie et d'Anatomie comparée; 9€, free under-26s Grande Galerie de l'Evolution; 8€, 5€ 4–13s Ménagerie. Open Wed–Mon 10am–5pm. Metro: Jussieu or Gare d'Austerlitz.

Tip for Tourists: Museum Pass

If you're visiting Paris and planning on cramming in as many museums and monuments as possible, the Paris Museum Pass is a good way to save dough at paying venues, offering unlimited, queue-jumping access to more than 60 of them over a 2-, 4- or 6-day period. They can be bought online, at Tourist Information points at CDG and ORLY Airports, at most participating museums and at Fnac (p. 165). They cost 32€, 48€ and 64€ respectively. www.parismuseum pass.com. FINE PRINT The pass is ony activated the first time you use it, so can be bought in advance.

Musée Jacquemart-André More a stately home than a museum, this is the treasure-trove of Edouard André, last scion of a family who made a fortune in banking and industry in the 19th century, and his wife, portraitist Nélie Jacquemart. Together they compiled a collection of rare 18th-century French paintings and furnishings, 17th-century Dutch and Flemish paintings, and Italian Renaissance works fit for a king. The salons drip with gilt and the ultimate in *fin-de-siècle* style. Works by Bellini, Carpaccio, Uccelo, Van Dyck, Rembrandt, Tiepolo, Rubens, Watteau, Boucher, Fragonard, and Mantegna complement Houdon busts, Gobelin tapestries, Della Robbia terracottas and an awesome collection of antiques. Mme Jacquemart's high-ceilinged tearoom will restore you with its delicious sticky buns and piping hot tea (11:45am–5:30pm).

158 Blvd. Haussmann, 75008. ✆ **01 45 62 11 59.** www.musee-jacquemart-andre. com. Adm: 10€; 7.50€ 7–17s; free under-7s. Daily 10am–6pm. Metro: Miromesnil or Saint-Philippe du Roule.

Musée Marmottan Monet Historian Paul Marmottan started this museum at the end of the 19th century with a collection of Renaissance, Consular, and First Empire paintings, furniture, and artefacts. Upon his death in 1932, the ensemble became the property of the Académie des Beaux-Arts, but the collection really started to draw attention in 1966, when Claude Monet's second son Michel died in a car crash, leaving a multi-million bequest of his father's art to the Académie—130-plus paintings, watercolours, pastels, and drawings that trace the evolution of Impressionism and the great man's work in a single museum. Private donors have since added treasures by Boudin, Corot, Gauguin, Renoir, and Berthe Morisot, as well as countless miniatures.

2 Rue Louis-Boilly, 75016. ✆ **01 44 96 50 33.** www.marmottan.com. Adm: 9€, 5€ 8–25s, free under-8s. Open Tues–Sun 11am–6pm (until 9pm Tues). Metro: La Muette. RER: Boulainvilliers.

Musée du Vin   This wine museum, set up by Paris's Confrérie Bacchique (a regional association of wine professionals) in 1984 inside the cellars of an old wine-producing monastery in Passy in western Paris, pays tribute to the wine of Paris and France as a whole with cheesy displays on viticulture, waxwork peasants handling old tools and bottles, and tasting sessions. You can also opt for lunch in the vaulted restaurant. The food's good if not cheap (fixed-price menus 26€, 35€ and 56€, including two glasses of wine) and you get free access to the museum.

Rue des Eaux, 75016. ✆ **01 45 25 63 26.** www.museeduvinparis.com. Adm: 11.90€ museum and 1 glass of wine (9€ students and over-60s); 17€ museum and 3 glasses of wine. 27€ museum, 3 glasses and 20min with a sommelier (cheese platters 7€); free under-14s (14s–18s get juice rather than wine). Tues–Sun 10am–6pm (restaurant midday–3pm Tues–Sat). Metro: Passy. RER: Champs de Mars—Tour Eiffel.

2 Monumental Magic

Many of the city's monuments are not only gorgeous but also visible on the outside for absolutely zip. Most are also located beside the Seine, providing copious eye-candy over an 8km stretch of the river (enough for a pleasant two-hour walk).

Getting inside them is a different matter—nearly all charge an entry fee, usually 7€–9€ (unless you're under 18 or 26). This is wavered only once a month—usually the first Sunday of the month in winter—and during annual events such as the Journées du Patrimoine (normally the third weekend in September; p. 198).

ALWAYS FREE

Assemblée Nationale FREE   The Madeleine church's architectural twin was built for the Duchesse de Bourbon, Louis XIV's daughter, in 1722 and is now the seat of the French parliament (along with the Sénat). Here you can watch live political debates by writing to a *député* (French MP) three months before your visit (if you live in Paris, apply to the *député* of your *arrondissement*); there's a list on www.assemblee-nationale.fr/infos/visiter.asp. If you're one of the lucky few, you'll receive a *billet de séance* (invitation) for a public session

Churches & Cathedrals FREE

If your bank account subsists on a wing and a prayer, a trip to the city's religious edifices could be in order. Architecturally stunning and oozing with history, they make pleasant alternatives to the museums—and won't cost you a centime. Here are ten of my favourites:

Chapelle de la Médaille Miraculeuse   (140 Rue du Bac, 75007. Metro: Sèvres-Babylone). A curiosity for many, a pilgrimage site for others, this elegant rococo chapel is where the Virgin Mary supposedly appeared to Catherine Labouré in 1830. Her 'miraculously' preserved body is on display next to the altar.

Cathédrale de Notre Dame de Paris   (Parvis de Notre Dame/Place Jean Paul II, 75004. Metro: Cité. RER: Saint-Michel). Even Parisians admit that this iconic edifice is worth a visit. Free guided tours in English Wed–Thurs 2pm, Sat 2:30pm. (For towers, see p. 222.)

Cathédrale St Alexander Nevsky   (12 Rue Daru, 75008. Metro Courcelles). This beautiful, incense-filled, neo-byzantine Russian Orthodox cathedral's golden domes and icons wouldn't look out of place in Moscow.

Sacré-Coeur   (75018. Metro: Anvers or Abbesses). The eerie beauty of this white-domed church's interior will relieve you of any breath you have left after the walk up the steps to the top of Montmartre's *Butte*.

Saint-Etienne du Mont   (Place Sainte-Geneviève, 75005. Metro: Cardinal Lemoine. RER: Luxembourg). A stunning fusion of Gothic and

(Tuesday–Thursday, passports mandatory). If not, look out for the Journées du Patrimoine (p. 198) when the Assemblée and a handful of other government buildings are usually open to the public.

33 Quai d'Orsay, 75007. ✆ **01 40 63 60 00.** www.assemblee-nationale.fr. Open by appt only. Metro: Concorde or Assemblée Nationale. RER: Invalides.

Palais de Justice FREE   Whiling away a morning or afternoon listening to the oratorical fireworks of French lawyers pleading their cases in the law courts is a fine way to experience life behind Paris's closed doors as well as glimpse the inside of this beautiful 18th-century building. Sessions start at 9.30am and 1.30pm (call in advance). Also look out for the once-monthly Berryer conferences—rhetorical

Renaissance styles (1492–1626) including a double spiral staircase—part of the only Renaissance rood screen left in Paris.

Saint-Eustache   (Rue du Jour, 75012. Metro: Les Halles. RER: Châtelet—Les Halles). Despite its prime location, this 16th-century church is frequently overlooked. Inside are impressive paintings, including Luca Giordano's haunting *Descent from the Cross*, and a magnificent organ made of 8,000 pipes.

Saint-Germain-des-Près   (3 Place St-Germain-des-Près, 75006. Metro: St-Germain-des-Près). The oldest church in Paris contains several illustrious tombs, including those of Polish King Jean Casimir (Abbot of St-Germain in 1669) and philosopher Réné Descartes.

Saint-Germain l'Auxerrois   (2 Place du Louvre, 75001. Metro Louvre—Rivoli). Above this church's intricate, Flamboyant-Gothic porch hangs Paris's prettiest sounding chimer—the bell, Marie, that famously rang during the 1572 St Bartholomew's Day Massacre.

Saint-Sulpice   (Place Saint-Sulpice, 75006. Metro: Saint-Sulpice). It took 120 years (from 1646) and six architects to get Saint-Sulpice standing as proud as it does today, with its ostentatious Italianate façade and paintings by Delacroix (p. 195).

Saint-Vincent de Paul   (Place Franz Liszt, 75010. Metro: Gare du Nord). This 19th-century neo-classical church is where Louis Braille (inventor of Braille) used to play the organ.

'happenings' with quick-witted French political figures and personalities such as Bernard Tapie (also see p. 112).

4 Blvd. du Palais, 75001. (C) **01 44 32 51 51.** www.justice.gouv.fr. Metro: Cité.

SOMETIMES FREE

FREE FIRST SUNDAY OF MONTH IN WINTER

★ **Arc de Triomphe**   Like the Eiffel Tower, the Arc de Triomphe is so familiar to Parisians that they forget to visit it. Yet the biggest triumphal arch in the world (about 49m high and 44m wide) has incredible views over much of the city. Commissioned by Napoléon in 1806 to commemorate the victories of his Grand Armée, it wasn't completed until 1836, under the reign of Louis-Philippe. Four years later, Napoléon's remains, brought from Saint Helena, passed under the arch on their journey to his tomb at the Hôtel des Invalides (p. 212), and since then it has been the focal point for state funerals. It's also the site of the tomb of the Unknown Soldier, in whose honour an eternal flame burns.

Place Charles de Gaulle—Etoile, 75008. ℂ **01 55 37 73 77.** http://arc-de-triomphe. monuments-nationaux.fr. Adm: exc 1st Sun of month Nov–Mar 9€; 5.50€ 18–25s from outside EU; free under-18s and under-26s from EU Apr–Sept daily 10am–11pm; Oct–Mar daily 10am–10:30pm. Metro/RER: Charles-de-Gaulle—Etoile.

★ **Cathédrale de Notre Dame de Paris and its towers**   Notre Dame de Paris, with its slender, Gothic columns, is the flagship of the Catholic Church in France, containing the supposed relics of the True Cross and part of Jesus' crown of thorns (p. 209). If you don't want to just mosey around by yourself, the weekly free guided tours (see website for details) are the best way of learning about its treasures. The cathedral is the realm of Victor Hugo's *Hunchback of Notre-Dame*, especially the towers, which still contain Quasimodo's famous bell, Le Bourdon. The 387 stairs take you up to a menagerie of gargoyles designed by Viollet-le-Duc and stunning panoramas over the city. FINE PRINT Avoid the queues by coming to the towers early or just before last entry.

Cathedral: Parvis de Notre Dame (Place Jean Paul II), 75004. ℂ **01 42 34 56 10.** www. notredamedeparis.fr. Adm: free. Daily 8am–6:45pm.

Towers: Rue du Cloître-Notre-Dame, 75004. ℂ **01 53 10 07 00.** http://notre-dame-de-paris.monuments-nationaux.fr. Adm: exc 1st Sun of month Nov–Mar 6€; 5€ 18–25s from non-EU countries, free under-18s and under-26s from EU countries. Daily 10am–6:30pm Apr–Sept (until 11pm Sat–Sun and June–Aug); daily 10am–5:30pm Oct–Mar. Metro: Cité. Metro/RER: Saint Michel. RER: Notre Dame.

★ **Château de Vincennes**   It's odd that the authorities haven't turned Charles V's second home (boasting the tallest mediaeval dungeon in Europe, which held famous prisoners including Fouquet, the Marquis de Sade, and Mirabeau) into something really special. The keep was recently restored to its mediaeval glory and is very impressive, but it leaves the rest looking a little forlorn. All the same, the guided tours (ℂ **01 44 54 19 30**) include lots of intriguing historical tit-bits (such as the fact that England's Henry V died here in 1422), especially in the

Sainte-Chapelle (modelled on the Sainte-Chapelle on Île de la Cité; p. 224), which sometimes serves as exhibition space, and the west portal of which is one of the masterpieces of the Flamboyant-Gothic style.

Ave. de Paris, Vincennes, 94300. ✆ **01 43 28 15 48.** www.chateau-vincennes.fr. Adm: exc 1st Sun of month Nov–Mar 8€; 5€ 18–25s from outside EU, free under-26s from EU and under-18s. Daily 10am–6pm (until 5pm Oct–Mar); closed most public hols. Metro: Château de Vincennes.

★ **Conciergerie** This haunting yet majestic monument beloved of mediaeval and Revolutionary history fans shares space with the Palais de Justice law courts (p. 220), the Sainte-Chapelle (p. 224), and police offices. Before the Revolution, it had a long regal history, and certain parts remain as they were in the Middle Ages while other sections have been forever stained by the Reign of Terror, living on as infamous symbols of the time when carts hauled off fresh victims for Dr Guillotin's grisly invention. The old prison cells (filled with musty waxwork figures) include Marie-Antoinette's room, converted into the **Chapelle Expiatoire** under Louis XVIII during the Restoration era. FINE PRINT Buy combined tickets for the Conciergerie and Sainte-Chapelle (10€), best visited together.

Mémorial de la Déportation FREE

Approached through a garden behind Notre Dame on the tip of Île de la Cité, this poignant underground memorial commemorates the French citizens (mostly Jews) deported to concentration camps and exterminated during World War II. Carved into stone are these blood-red words (in French): "Forgive, but don't forget". Monday–Friday 8:30am–nightfall (from 9am at weekends).

2 Blvd. du Palais, 75001. ✆ **01 53 40 60 80.** http://conciergerie.monuments-nationaux. fr. Adm: exc 1st Sun of month Nov–Mar 7€; 4.50€ 18–25s from outside EU, free under-18s and under-26s from EU. Daily 9:30am–6pm (until 5pm 1 Nov–Feb); closed 1 Jan, 25 Dec and 1 May. Metro: Cité. Metro/RER: Saint-Michel. RER: Notre Dame.

★ **Le Panthéon** The 18th-century Panthéon, located on the crest of the Mont Sainte-Geneviève (named after the patron saint of Paris), is the final resting place of such Republican greats as Rousseau, Souf-flot, Zola, Braille, and Pierre and Marie Curie (the latter the only woman deemed worthy of being in this 'hall of fame'). Another reason to visit is the copy of Foucault's pendulum, which hangs 67m in the air in homage to Foucault's original demonstration of the Earth's rotation to Napoléon here in 1851. In summer (by guided tour only), the viewing galleries around the dome give breathtaking 360° panoramas over the city.

Place du Panthéon, 75005. ⓒ **01 44 32 18 00.** http://pantheon.monuments-nationaux. fr. Adm: exc 1st Sun of month Nov–Mar 8€; 5€ 18–25s from outside EU, free under-18s and under-26s from EU. Daily 10am–6:30pm (until 6pm Oct–Mar). Metro: Maubert-Mutualité or Cardinal Lemoine. RER: Luxembourg.

★ **Sainte-Chapelle** This jewel-box of a mediaeval chapel is one of the most breathtaking mediaeval edifices in the world. Countless writers have tried to describe the 'light show' cast on the interior when the sun shines through the stained-glass windows. The tacky tourist boutique in the Chapelle Basse (the lower chapel, supported by flying buttresses and ornamented with *fleur-de-lis* designs, formerly used by the palace servants) brings a nasty 'we want your money' feel to the start of the visit, but upstairs in the King's Chapelle Haute (the upper chapel) the Gothic art is unblemished. On a bright day, its 15 stained-glass windows—some measuring 670m2—glow with Chartres blue and with deep reds that have inspired the saying 'wine the colour of Sainte-Chapelle's windows'. FINE PRINT Look out for regular classical music concerts in summer. If you also plan to visit the Conciergerie (p. 223), save money by buying a combined ticket for 10€.

Palais de Justice, 6 Blvd. du Palais, 75001. ⓒ **01 53 40 60 80.** http://sainte-chapelle. monuments-nationaux.fr. Adm: exc 1st Sun of month Nov–Mar 8€; 5€ 18–25s from outside EU; free under-18s and under-26s from EU. Daily 9:30am–6pm (until 5pm Nov–Feb); closed 1 Jan, 25 Dec and 1 May. Metro: Cité. Metro/RER: Saint Michel. RER: Notre Dame.

DIRT CHEAP (LESS THAN 6€)

Tour Jean Sans Peur This solitary mediaeval tower is the only remaining part of the Hôtel de Bourgogne, a sumptuous palace built by Jean Sans Peur (Fearless John; 1371–1419), Duke of Burgundy and cousin to both Charles VI and his brother Louis of Orléans. Though often overlooked (in fact, after falling into disrepair in the 15th century and being split into 13 lots by François I, it was forgotten until the Rue Etienne Marcel was built in 1868), it stands witness to some of France's most interesting mediaeval episodes. A half-hour visit will reveal a rare newel staircase copied from Charles V's stairway in the old Louvre (now disappeared), a unique vaulted ceiling on the stairwell (the only one in France with plant sculptures—oak, hawthorn, and hop, symbols of Jean Sans Peur's father Philippe le Hardi, mother Marguerite de Flandre and himself); restored chambers (including the latrines); repaired mediaeval stained-glass windows; and a small chunk of Philippe Auguste's ramparts.

20 Rue Etienne Marcel, 75002. ℭ **01 40 26 20 28.** www.tourjeansanspeur.com. Adm: 5€; 3€ under-18s and students. Wed, Sat–Sun 1:30–6pm Nov–Mar; Wed–Sun 1:30–6pm Apr–mid Nov. Metro: Etienne Marcel or Sentier. RER: A Châtelet—Les Halles.

WORTH THE SPLURGE (MORE THAN 6€)

★ **Basilique Cathédrale de Saint-Denis**   Say Saint-Denis to a Parisian, and the hairs on their neck stick up: The northern suburb has been associated with gangs for so long now, they forget that one of France's most important architectural treasures lies in its centre (don't worry: The area is quite safe during the day). The basilica, France's first monumental Gothic masterpiece (started in 1130) and a royal necropolis from the 6th century on (the crypt dates back to the 5th century), is now a museum of French funerary sculpture, with 70 sculpted recumbent statues—the only set of its kind in Europe—bathed in the multi-coloured light of the 12th- and 19th-century stained-glass windows.

1 Rue de la Légion d'Honneur, 93200 Saint-Denis. ℭ **01 48 09 83 54.** http://saint-denis.monuments-nationaux.fr. Adm: 7€; 4.50€ 18–25s from outside EU; free under-18s from outside EU and under-26s from EU. Mon–Sat 10am–6:15pm, Sun midday–6:15pm (until 5pm Oct–Mar). Metro: Basilique de Saint-Denis. RER: D and T1 Basilique de Saint-Denis.

★ **Eiffel Tower**   'Eyeful Tower' would be a more suitable name—not only is the Tour Eiffel visible from most parts of the city, but the views from the top are fabulous. Yes, it's touristy and yes, it's expensive (if you go to the top), but if you've never done it before, don't miss out on one of the most iconic towers in the world. FINE PRINT From the end of 2009, you can skip the terrifying queues by reserving online.

Champ de Mars, 75007. ℭ **01 44 11 23 23.** www.tour-eiffel.fr. Adm: Lift to 1st and 2nd floors 8€; 6.40€ (12–24s); 4€ (4–11s). Lift to top 13€; 9.90€ (12–24s); 7.50€ (4–11s). Stairs to 1st and 2nd floors 4.50€; 3.50€ (12–24s); 3€ (4–11s). Free under-4s. Daily Jan–mid June, Sept–Jan 9:30am–11:45pm (last lift to top 10:30pm, to 2nd floor 11pm, stairs 6pm); mid June–end Aug 9:30am–00:45am (last lift to top 11pm, to 2nd floor and stairs midnight). Metro: Bir Hakeim, Dupliex, or Ecole Militaire. Metro/RER: Champs de Mars—Tour Eiffel.

★ **Opéra Garnier** The city's 'giant wedding cake' and inspiration behind Leroux's *Phantom of the Opera* is a masterpiece of Napoléon III-style architecture, with a domed roof, gilt statues and Carpeaux's famous sculpture *La Danse* on the façade. The interior is like a fairytale castle, with marble staircases, imposing statues, and painted ceilings, including one, on the amphitheatre's central vaulted ceiling, by artist Marc Chagall (1962). Somewhat quirkily, the roof (like that of Le Grand Palais; p. 228) is home to thousands of bees, and after touring the building (or before a show) you can buy some of the Opéra's honey in its shop. There are also guided visits in English, 11:30am and 2:30pm Wednesday and Saturday–Sunday (in French 11:30pm and 3:30pm) for 12€ (9€ 11–25s; 6€ under 10s).

Place de l'Opéra, 75009. ✆ **01 40 01 24 93.** www.operadeparis.fr. Adm: 8€, 4€ 11s–25s, free under-10s. Daily 10am–5pm (from 1pm only on matinée performance days). Metro: Opéra. RER: Auber.

3 Gallery Scene

After museums, galleries are Paris's best low-cost cultural resource. Not only do they keep us in the loop about emerging and established art scenes (both home-grown and international), they also dole out free booze and nibbles on *vernissages* (opening nights).

Don't be shy about walking into a gallery. Snobby staff do exist, but the advent of scruffy jeans has made it harder for them to differentiate between wealthy art connoisseurs and your average *Jacques* Blogs. Most gallery owners are overjoyed when we walk in and show some interest.

Certain parts of town are better-endowed than others. Paris's big-money art scene tends to confine itself to the 8th *arrondissement*, freckling streets such as Rue du Faubourg Saint-Honoré and avenue Matignon with bankable names. The Beaubourg area and the Marais reward strollers with dozens of serendipitous, seemingly randomly placed commercial galleries beckoning you in for a spontaneous browse. Ditto Saint-Germain-des-Près (around the Rues de Seine, des Beaux-Arts, Mazarine, Guénégaud, and Visconti), which has also become a hub of new interior design galleries (p. 234). Rue Louise Weiss in the 13th has a hip vibe and some interesting exhibitions; other hotpots to look out for are in the northeast of town, in the 11th

Sources

The national papers have frequent run-downs on high-profile shows and provide extensive listing information online. *Pariscope* and *L'Officiel des Spectacles* (on sale in *kiosques* across the city) offer weekly listings; as does *A Nous Paris*, a free paper given out in the metro with entertainment guides that can also be perused online (**www.anous. fr**). Other gallery info can be found on the websites of the Fondation Entreprise Ricard (**www.fondation-entreprise-ricard.com**, p. 234), parisART (**www.paris-art.com**) and *Gogo Paris* (**www.gogoparis.com**).

If you want invitations to the *vernissages*, leave your name and address when you visit the galleries. Or for underground venues, try *Olalaparis* (**http://olalaparis.free.fr**), an email-notification platform specialising in contemporary art events across Paris and the Ile-de-France. Other sources include **www.galerie-art-paris.com**, which provides a list of galleries by *arrondissement*, with links to their websites; and Tri Selectif (**www.triselectif.net**), whose weekly newsletter (Thursdays) lists the best of what's on in the local art world.

and 12th *arrondissements* between Bastille, the Gare de Lyon and Oberkampf, and in the 19th *arrondissement*.

Note that most galleries are closed in August.

MAINSTREAM MUSEUM-GALLERIES

104 `FREE`   Paris's newest mainstream art house (set inside the vast and spooky 19th-century municipal undertakers' building) is a haven for resident artists from all domains, who expose their work in one of four annual festivals. It's taking time for the dust to settle, but 2010 promises extra fun with a restaurant, shops, and more open days, so keep your eyes peeled.

104 Rue d'Aubervilliers, 75019. (©) **01 53 35 50 00.** www.104.fr. Usually free but 3€–5€ for some temporary exhibitions. Sun–Mon 11am–8pm; Tues–Sat 11am–11pm (closed last 2 wks Aug). Metro: Stalingrad, Crimée, or Riquet.

Cité Internationale des Arts `FREE`   Young professional artists and collectives from across the globe giving 'the Paris thang' a spin get

TRAM – A Dirt-Cheap Art Tour

Modern-art institutions aren't confined to central Paris: the Ile-de-France (Greater Paris) is studded with them. But unless you have a set of wheels, or don't mind spending hours riding public transport, they can be fiddly to reach. This is where TRAM steps in—a regional network of no less than 29 contemporary art galleries and museums linked by a minibus called the Taxi-Tram.

One Saturday each month, the Taxi-Tram picks visitors up in central Paris and takes them to a selection of out-of-town art sites, where curators, and sometimes the artists themselves, give you the low-down on the displays. It's a fine way of seeing the spectrum of modern art in the region and a steal at just 5€ for the day, including entry fees (food and drinks at your own cost).

FINE PRINT Apply in advance by email (taxitram@tram-idf.fr).

32 Rue Yves Toudic, 75010. ℂ 01 53 34 64 15. www.tram-idf.fr.

sporadic exposure throughout the year at this international residence. Exhibitions are always free, and the *vernissages* are a fun way to meet the artists.

18 Rue de l'Hôtel de Ville, 75004. ℂ 01 42 78 71 72. www.citedesartsparis.net. Opening dates vary. Metro: Saint-Paul.

Espace Fondation EDF FREE   In a part of the 7th usually associated with high-end shopping, this small exhibition space set up by France's electricity board (EDF) and occupying a 1910 electricity station houses at least two environmentally themed exhibitions each year.

6 Rue Récamier, 75007. No phone. http://fondation.edf.com. Tues–Sun midday–7pm (closed public hols). Metro: Sèvres-Babylone.

Hôtel de Ville FREE   Against all odds, Paris's palatial city hall with its reputation for stuffy admin is proving a dab hand at art, hosting exhibitions on Paris-oriented themes that have previously included photography by Doisneau and Willy Ronis.

29 Rue de Rivoli, 75004. ℂ 01 42 76 40 40. www.paris.fr. Mon–Sat 10am–7pm. Metro: Hôtel de Ville.

★ **Le Grand Palais—Galeries Nationales**   This masterpiece of Belle Epoque architecture with its riot of Art Nouveau ironwork and a vast glass roof (home to some bees whose honey you can buy in the shop) harbours one of France's most important exhibition centres, assembling ever-changing, world-class retrospectives of historically important artists. On the downside, every Parisian and his or her poodle want to see the exhibitions, so get here 20 minutes before opening or buy tickets online. In the Nef area on the other side, look out for annual art fests such as FIAC and Art en Capital (p. 238).

3 Ave. du Général Eisenhower, 75008. ℂ **01 44 13 17 17.** www.rmn.fr. Adm varies but usually 10€, 8€ 13–25s, free under-13s. Open for exhibitions only, 10am–8pm Wed–Mon (until 10pm Wed). Metro: Champs-Elysées—Clemenceau or Franklin Roosevelt. RER: Invalides.

Musée des Arts Derniers `FREE` Contemporary African art (photos, sculpture, video installations and paintings) takes pride of place in this museum-gallery, which aims to distance itself from the 'ethnic labelling' so often associated with art from Africa. Instead, artists' works are displayed without the context of their racial or geographical origins.

28 Rue Saint-Gilles, 75003. ℂ **01 44 49 95 70.** www.art-z.net. Tues–Sat 11am–7pm. Metro: Chemin Vert.

★ **Musée du Luxembourg** The Palais de Luxembourg (today's French Senate) and its gardens were built for Marie de Médicis (widow of Henri IV) to remind her of her native Florence. Before the Revolution, in 1750, a small wing of the palace became France's first public gallery and today, in line with tradition, regular art exhibitions—usually impressive one-offs on some of the world's most famous artists—are held here. Reserve in advance (either online, or at a Fnac or Virgin Megastore). `FINE PRINT` Pay an extra euro and book a 'coupe-file' (queue-jumping) ticket online.

19 Rue de Vaugirard, 75006. ℂ **01 42 34 25 95.** Adm varies but is usually 11€, 9€ 10–25s, free under-10s. Mon, Fri–Sat 10:30am–10pm. Tues–Thurs 10:30–7pm, Sun 9am–7pm (during school hols from 9am daily). Metro: Saint-Sulpice.

★ **Palais de Tokyo** This daring contemporary arts museum houses a succession of small but avant-garde temporary exhibitions that frequently make it look as if a bomb has hit the place. But while the stuff on the floor, walls, and ceilings may appear higgledy piggledy (in fact, some installations don't even look like art at all), they've been chosen to help visitors break away from traditions and perceive contemporary creations in a whole new light.

13 Ave. du Président Wilson, 75016. ℂ **01 47 23 54 01.** www.palaisdetokyo.com. Adm: 6€, 4.50€ 19–26s, free under-18s. Open Tues–Sun midday–midnight (until 6pm 24 and 31 Dec); closed 1 Jan, 1 May, 25 Dec. Metro: Alma-Marceau or Iéna. RER: Pont d'Alma.

★ **Pinacothèque** A relative newcomer, this classy picture gallery is carving itself a fine reputation as one of Paris's best international museum-galleries, with big shows of works by artists such as Rembrandt, Utrillo, and Pollock. FINE PRINT A 'coupe-file' (queue-jumping) ticket is 1.50€ extra booked online.

28 Place de la Madeleine, 75008. ℂ **01 42 68 02 01.** www.pinacotheque.com. Adm: 9€, 7€ 12–25s, free under-12s. Daily 10.30am–6pm (from 2pm 1 May and 14 July; until 9pm 1st Wed of month). Metro: Madeleine.

GALLERIES FOR GRATIS BEAUBOURG & MARAIS

Basia Embiricos FREE Basia Embiricos knows her stuff: The contemporary photography in her gallery frequently features talents on the French and international scene, including rising star Julia Fullerton-Batten whose works explore the coming-of-age of teenage girls.

4 Rue des Jardins Saint-Paul, 75004. ℂ **01 48 87 00 63.** www.galeriebasia embiricos.com. 1–6:30pm Wed–Sun. Metro: Saint-Paul.

Galerie Charlotte Norberg FREE Part of a dynamic new generation of galleries in the Marais, this space is devoted to vibrant, young painters whose works have an obvious 'soul'.

74 Rue Charlot, 75003. ℂ **01 43 26 46 70.** www.galeriecharlottenorberg.com. Tues–Sat 2:30–7pm. Metro: République or Filles du Calvaire.

★ **Arty Club**

Whether you're an artist, an art fan or just art-curious, World Art Lounge (set up by contemporary art-lover Gilles Berthet) is the network to join. Just 20€ a month (30€ for two people) gives you access to organised trips around 10 or more of Paris's hottest contemporary art galleries (far less daunting than turning up by yourself), entry to private artists' studios, specialist art consulting for budding collectors, and invitations to arty dinner parties and brunches. It's a fine way for Parisians to meet like-minded folk and keep a finger on the pulse of the city's complex art scene. Non-members can also join some tours. Look out for Art Tours on Segways (**http://www.walounge. com/Segway.html**) and join their Twitter site at **http:// twitter.com/artyclub**, check out www.walounge.com/artyclub. html, or call Gilles. ℂ **06 99 55 75 75** or **06 71 28 11 45** (cellphone number, so more expensive).

Galerie Chez Valentin `FREE` This place is experimental, thoroughly conceptual and lots of fun, featuring radical artists such as video-maker Laurent Grasso and Prix Duchamp winner Mathieu Mercier.

9 Rue Saint Gilles, 75003. © **01 48 87 42 55.** www.galeriechezvalentin.com. Tues–Sat 11am–1pm, 2–7pm. Metro: Chemin Vert.

★ **Galerie Daniel Templon** `FREE` Templon's been around since the 1960s and is a fave with the art establishment and private collectors, with big names such as Philippe Cognée, Jean-Michel Alberola, and German Expressionist Jonathan Meese featuring in the catalogue.

30 Rue Beaubourg, 75004. © **01 42 72 14 10.** www.danieltemplon.com. Mon–Sat 10am–7pm. Metro: Rambuteau.

Galerie DIX9 `FREE` Founded by Michèle Zakin (head of photos at Condé Nast for 30 years) and contemporary art specialist Hélène Lacharmoise, DIX9 plays a precious role in promoting the photography, installations, and paintings of up-and-coming international artists.

19 Rue des Filles du Calvaire, 75003. © **01 42 78 91 77.** www.galeriedix9.com. Tues–Fri 1–7pm, Sat 11am–7pm. Metro: Filles du Calvaire.

★ **Galerie Emmanuel Perrotin** `FREE` Emmanuel Perrotin was one of the first to promote Damien Hirst in France. Today his gallery is *the* place to see works by big-name French contemporary artists such as Sophie Calle and Prix Marcel Duchamp winner Tatiana Trouvé, and Japanese celebs Takashi Murakami and Mariko Mori.

There's a spacious new annex with yet more biggies at 10 Impasse Saint Claude, 75003.

76 Rue de Turenne, 75003. © **01 42 16 79 79.** www.galerieperrotin.com. Tues–Sat 11am–7pm. Metro: Saint-Sébastien—Froissart.

Galerie Estace and Délidart `FREE` In the burgeoning Haut Marais (the parts of the Marais in the 3rd *arrondissement*, on the border of the 11th), this is both a 'standard' gallery and an art publisher, Délidart (www.delidart.com), offering limited digital editions (5–30 copies) of selected works by the cutting-edge artists on show.

74 Rue Charlot, 75003. © **01 42 71 31 40.** www.estace.fr and www.delidart.com. Tues–Sat 2–7pm. Metro: Filles du Calvaire.

Galerie Jean-Luc & Takako Richard `FREE` This dynamic gallery specialising in emerging and mid-career international artists hosts two exhibitions at a time. Among the regulars are Beverly Fishman, known for her colourful diagrams of scientific codes, and quirky German–British landscape-painting duo Alice Stepanek and Steven Maslin.

74 Rue de Turenne/3 Impasse Saint Claude, 75003. ☎ **01 43 25 27 22.** www.galerie richard.com. Tues–Sat 11am–7pm. Metro: Saint-Sébastien—Froissart.

Galerie Kernot Art FREE This fresh gallery offers up works by intriguing emerging artists such as Gayle Chong Kwan, who uses photography, video, and performance to reflect rituals of exchange (such as food or trade) and Korean artist Argentinelee, known for her photographic interpretations of the human body.

14 Rue Saint Claude, 75003. ☎ **01 43 06 58 72.** www.kernotart.com. Tues–Fri 11am–7pm, Sat 2–7pm. Metro: Saint-Sébastien—Froissart.

★ **Galerie Marian Goodman** FREE Over the last 30 years, Marian Goodman has made it her job to introduce European artists to American audiences and vice versa. Her Paris base—a lovely 17th-century mansion—exhibits an impressive register of artists that has included Brit Steve McQueen, William Kentridge, and Lawrence Weiner.

79 Rue du Temple, 75003. ☎ **01 48 04 70 52.** www.mariangoodman.com. 11am–7pm Tues–Sat. Metro: Rambuteau.

Galerie Polaris FREE Inside an old gym, Polaris shows mainly photo and video artists along the lines of Xavier Zimmerman, who uses mirrors to create surreal urban scenes, and Stéphane Courtier, known for his impressive flattened perspectives of multi-storey buildings.

15 Rue des Arquebusiers, 75003. ☎ **01 42 72 21 27.** www.galeriepolaris.com. Tues–Fri 1–7pm, Sat 11am–1pm and 2–7pm. Metro: Saint-Sébastien—Froissart.

Galerie Taiss FREE It may be the newest kid on the gallery block, but Taiss is already one of the major players on the Parisian contemporary art scene, with a fresh selection of artists such as Szajner, specialising in installation work and oversized models.

5 Rue Debelleyme, 75003. ☎ **01 42 71 18 85.** www.taissgalerie.com. Tues–Sat 11am–9pm. Metro: Saint-Sébastien—Froissart.

★ **Galerie Thaddaeus Ropac** FREE A spin-off of Ropac's Salzburg base, this chic gallery has a museum quality about it, hosting American Pop artists such as Tom Sachs and Alex Katz and big-time Brits Gilbert & George.

7 Rue Debelleyme, 75003. ☎ **01 42 72 99 00.** www.ropac.net. Tues–Sat 2–7pm. Metro: Filles du Calvaire.

Free Home Inspiration FREE

Before trekking off to IKEA for home-décor ideas, get on the French design trail around Saint-Germain-des-Prés, where interior-design galleries have been popping up like *champignons* over the last five years or so. **Jousse Entreprise** (18 Rue de Seine. ✆ **01 53 82 13 60.** www.jousse-entreprise.com) has a startling collection of furniture by architects such as Jean Prouvé and Le Corbusier, cut metal lamps signed Serge Mouille and weird photographic art to decorate your walls. There's a sister site in the 13th; p. 236. Further up the road, François Laffanour (one of the city's most respected dealers) runs the **Galerie Downtown** (33 Rue de Seine. ✆ **01 46 33 82 41.** www.galeriedowntown.com), a slick modern space filled with chairs, tables and shelving by leading designers Charlotte Perriand, George Nakashima, and Carlo Mollino.

Galerie Kréo (31 Rue Dauphine. ✆ **01 53 10 23 00.** www.galerie kreo.com) is a 'research laboratory' exploring the common ground between function and art via limited-edition pieces by Ronan & Erwan Bouroullec, Pierre Charpin, and Martin Szekely. And last but not least, **Perimeter Editions** (47 Rue St-André-des-Arts. ✆ **01 55 42 01 22.** www.perimeter-editions.com) uses a stunning 17th-century interior as a backdrop to its extraordinary limited-edition collection of modern multifunctional and vintage offerings. What better way to get the creative juices flowing?

Galerie Xippas FREE   Anything from photography and painting to light and furniture installations makes its way into this risk-taking gallery, one of the most interesting multidisciplinary spaces in the Marais.

108 Rue Vieille du Temple, 75003. ✆ **01 40 27 07 16.** www.xippas.com. Tues–Sat 10am–1pm, 2–7pm. Metro: Saint-Sébastien—Froissart.

Sitdown FREE   Another new Haut Marais (northern Marais, bordering on the 11th *arrondissement*) arrival, the Sitdown gallery promotes cutting-edge home décor art, including unique contemporary furniture and photography.

4 Rue Sainte-Anastase, 75003. ✆ **01 42 78 08 07.** www.sitdown.fr. Tues–Sat 2–7pm. Metro: Saint-Paul or Chemin Vert.

SAINT-GERMAIN-DES-PRES

Galerie Alfa   Everything on show in this Left-Bank gallery (specialising in 19th- and 20th-century drawings) is the real deal. Drawings by Klimt, Picasso, Kandinsky, Giacometti, and Vuillard make it a veritable sweet shop for wealthy art collectors and those wishing to see lesser-known works by masters.

12 Rue de l'Echaudé, 75006. ✆ **01 43 26 33 56.** www.galeriealfa.com. Mon–Sat 10:30am–1pm and 2–7pm. Metro: Mabillon.

Galerie Georges-Philippe & Nathalie Vallois   Turner prize-winner Keith Tyson and American rebel Paul McCarthy are some of the artists represented by this multidisciplinary institution, a must if you're into intangible art.

36 Rue de Seine, 75006. ✆ **01 46 34 61 07.** www.galerie-vallois.com. Mon–Sat 10.30am–1pm and 2–7pm. Metro: Mabillon or Odéon.

Galerie Marion Meyer   A place to keep coming back to, Meyer's conceptualist choices—everything from sculpture and light installations to painting and photography by emerging French artists—rarely disappoint.

15 Rue Guégenaud, 75006. ✆ **01 46 33 04 38.** www.galeriemarionmeyer.com. Tues–Sat 2–7pm. Metro: Pont Neuf or Mabillon.

8TH

Espace Paul Ricard FREE   One of the best places in town to see on-the-uppers, this artistic foundation introduces emerging French artists to the public via eight exhibitions a year and an annual award, given at the FIAC contemporary art fair (p. 238).

12 Rue Boissy d'Anglas, 75008. ✆ **01 53 30 88 00.** http://fondation-entreprise-ricard.com. Tues–Sat 11am–7pm. Metro: Concorde.

Galerie Jérôme de Noirmont FREE   Jeff Koons, Bettina Rheims, and larger-than-life personalities such as Eva and Adèle are just some of the art-world stars whose works are frequently displayed here, making the *vernissages* particularly fun to attend.

38 Ave. Matignon, 75008. ✆ **01 42 89 89 00.** www.denoirmont.com. Mon–Sat 11am–7pm. Metro: Miromesnil.

Galerie Lelong   Lelong has built its reputation on bankable post-war internationals, biggies, so this may be your last chance to see works by names such as Miró, Bacon, and Tàpies, before they end up in someone's private collection.

Watching the Auction Action at Drouot

Leave your twitching at the door, unless you suddenly want to find yourself the unexpected owner of a 200,000€ Van Gogh etching from Paris's Drouot auction house. In any case, soaking up the electric vibes of the auctions and treating the upcoming lots as museum exhibits can be just as fun, plus there's the chance you'll actually find a bargain.

Drouot is the oldest auction house in the world and a magnet for both high-end and lower-end art-dealers, with 21 sales rooms spread over four sites. **Drouot Richelieu** (9 Rue Drouot, 75009. ℭ **01 48 00 20 20**) is the top house, with 16 rooms devoted to paintings, furniture and knick knacks. The **Montaigne site** (15 Ave. Montaigne, 75008. ℭ **01 48 00 20 80**) is where prestigious art treasures exchange hands. **Drouot Montmartre** (64 Rue Doudeauville, 75018. ℭ **01 48 00 20 99**) deals in everyday objects and furniture. **Drouot-Véhicules** (17 Rue de la Montjoie, 93210 La Plaine Saint-Denis. ℭ **01 48 20 20 81**) auctions anything with two or four wheels.

Fancy a bid? Just raise your hand while the price is right. And don't worry: Despite what I said above, it is the auctioneer's job to recognise a real bid from a twitch, so feel free to scratch and sneeze the day away. See www.drouot.com for auction times and opening hours.

13 Rue Téhéran, 75008. ℭ **01 45 63 13 19.** www.galerie-lelong.com. Tues–Fri 11am–6pm, Sat 10am–4pm. Metro: Miromesnil.

LOUISE WEISS & THE REST OF THE 13TH

Air de Paris FREE   This is one of the hippest galleries to get your work shown in, and one of the hippest to visit, taking neo-conceptualism to an extreme. FINE PRINT Displays continue in the 'Random Gallery', the shop window between Air de Paris and its next-door neighbour.

32 Rue Louise Weiss, 75013. ℭ **01 44 23 02 77.** www.airdeparis.com. Tues–Sat 11am–7pm. Metro: Chevaleret.

★ **Art:Concept** FREE   Artists with a sense of humour (such as Michel Blazy, who uses shaving foam and dog biscuits in his installations) get floor space at this small avant-garde gallery, prized by those who enjoy breaking free from institutionalised art.

Getting Arty in Foreign Cultural Centres `FREE`

Not only do Paris's foreign *centres culturels* tend to occupy lovely buildings, they allow us to open our cultural horizons by visiting their regular art exhibitions (usually by the *crème* of their home-grown artists), and provide free wine and nibbles on opening nights. Here's my list of winners:

★ **Centre Culturel Suédois**   A superb 16th-century mansion setting coupled with quality, experimental exhibitions and the occasional film night. 11 Rue Payenne, 75003. ℂ **01 44 78 80 20.** www.ccs.si.se.

Maison de la Culture du Japon à Paris   One of the most active centres in town, with films, exhibitions, and conferences. 101 Bis Quai Branly, 75015. ℂ **01 44 37 95 00.** www.mcjp.asso.fr.

★ **Maison de l'Amérique Latine**   This mainly hosts retrospectives on major Latin American artists and regular music concerts. 217 Blvd. Saint-Germain, 75007. ℂ **01 49 54 75 00.** http://culturel.mal217.org.

Espace Culturel Inuit   A space with a permanent exhibition on Inuit art and culture, plus frequent temporary exhibitions on related subjects. Centre Culturel Canadien, 5 Rue de Constantine, 75007. No phone. http://espace.inuit.free.fr.

16 Rue Duchefdelaville, 75013. ℂ **01 53 60 90 30.** www.galerieartconcept.com. Tues–Sat 11am–7pm. Metro: Bibliothèque.

gb agency `FREE`   As well as launching emerging artists (Jiri Kovanda and Elina Brotherus are protégés), gb likes to organise group shows. Look out for the theatrical, set-like installations of Welshman Mac Adams and video art by Omer Fast.

20 Rue Louise Weiss, 75013. ℂ **01 53 79 07 13.** www.gbagency.fr. Tues–Sat 11am–7pm. Metro: Chevaleret.

Jousse Entreprise `FREE`   Philippe Jousse's second address (see Free Home Inspirations, p. 233) presents yet more avant-garde furniture, ceramics by Georges Jouve, plus daring contemporary art.

24–34 Rue Louise Weiss, 75013. ℂ **01 53 82 10 18.** www.jousse-entreprise.com. Tues–Sat 11am–7pm. Metro: Chevaleret.

NORTHEAST

Galerie Van der Stegen FREE   This small gallery near the bohemian haunts of the Canal Saint-Martin promotes interesting young artists such as Melissa Steckbauer, whose neo-mythological copulating beast paintings won't leave you indifferent.

1 Rue Gustave Goublier, 75010. ℂ **01 42 59 41 81.** www.vanderstegen.com. Wed–Sat 2–7pm. Metro: Strasbourg—Saint-Denis, Jacques Bonsergent, or Château d'Eau.

Le Plateau FREE   To echo the enormous diversity of today's creativity, freelance curators are invited to present three exhibitions per year at this venue, to wacky but generally stimulating effect.

Angle of Rue des Alouettes and Rue Carducci, 75019. ℂ **01 53 19 84 10.** www.fracidf-leplateau.com. Adm for some events 4€. Wed–Fri 2–7pm, Sat–Sun midday–8pm (closed 24–31 Dec, 1 Jan, 1 May). Metro: Jourdain or Buttes-Chaumont.

Legal Art Squats

We all grow up—even rebellious, art-squatting artists. After colonising rundown factories and warehouses across the city, three squats got smart and convinced the authorities that their collectives were the pillars of modern French creation and not playgrounds of delinquency. As a result, they not only got to rent the buildings, they got funding. Les Mains d'Oeuvres in Saint-Ouen, its sister site Le Point Ephemère on the Canal Saint-Martin, and Les Frigos in the 13th are currently the capital's hottest multidisciplinary art centres, providing exhibition space and residencies for artists working in painting, sculpture, video, light, sound, and movement. All have regular open studios and performances so check websites for details. Les Mains d'Oeuvres and Le Point Ephemère also have decent restaurants.

Le Point Ephemère   Quai de Valmy, 75010. ℂ **01 40 34 02 48.** www.pointephemere.org. Metro: Jaurès.

Les Frigos   19 Rue Frigos, 75013. No phone. http://les-frigos.com. Metro: Bibliothèque.

Les Mains d'Oeuvres   1 Rue Charles Garnier, 93400, Saint-Ouen. ℂ **01 40 11 25 25.** www.mainsdoeuvres.org. Metro: Garibaldi.

Naço Gallery FREE This tiny gallery is run by a hip architecture bureau and hosts photo exhibitions on themes that are usually linked to the building industry. Openings typically end with free booze in the architect's office.

38 Rue de Cîteaux, 75012. ℭ **01 40 09 17 69.** www.naco.net. Opening times vary; check website. Metro: Gare de Lyon or Ledru-Rollin.

4 Art Fests

With the exception of Rue Louise Weiss, which organises communal *vernissages* every two months or so (p. 235) and random open days held at former squats such as Les Frigos and Les Mains d'Oeuvres (p. 237), open studios are increasingly rare. Taking their place are large-scale, international art festivals held in spring and autumn. Sure, the thrill of walking into someone's raw studio isn't there, and yes, you have to pay an entry fee, but the edginess remains, delivered to you under one big roof, so you don't have to traipse around the city looking for it.

★ **Art en Capital** Along with the FIAC (see below) this is the city's pre-eminent arts fest—five festivals rolled into one, and a point of convergence for emerging artists, curious professionals, and the culture-hungry public. The assembly features the following: The Salon des Artistes Français, a throwback to Louis XIV's era representing today's painters, sculptors, engravers, photographers, and architects; the Salon des Indépendants, a body founded by Seurat, Pissarro, Cézanne, Odilon Redon, Gauguin, and Lautrec in 1884 and dedicated to up-and-comers; and the Salon Comparaisons, a modernist festival for new talent that compares different forms of art. Art en Capital is also the primary showroom of the Salon du Dessin et de la Peinture à l'Eau (watercolour and drawing festival) and the Société National des Beaux-Arts (national fine arts society). In short, if you're looking to see those who made it and those who might, the Grand Palais is *the* place to be in November.

Le Grand Palais, Ave. Winston Churchill, 75008. ℭ **01 43 59 52 49.** http://aec.artistes-francais.com. Adm: 10€; 6€ 12–18s, students and over-60s; free under-12s. One weekend in Nov; check website for details. Metro: Champs-Elysées—Clemenceau.

★ **FIAC** Showing what is probably the best art crop in town, this two-site art fair (at the Grand Palais and the Louvre's Cour Carrée) has hundreds of stands by major French and international galleries, plus spin-off events across town—in the Musée d'Orsay (p. 193), MAC/VAL (p. 196), Versailles, the Centre Pompidou (p. 190), the Louvre (p. 193), the Fondation Cartier (p. 210), and the Jeu de Paume (p. 211).

The Espace Pierre Cardin (p. 210) also chips in with its own contemporary art festival, Show Off (www.showoffparis.fr), with the emphasis on video art. And the newly opened 104 (p. 227) has its own version, Slick Paris (www.slick-paris.com), with works by resident artists and guest galleries. FINE PRINT Ironically, during such a busy period you'll have trouble getting into vernissages without an invitation. Your best bet is to consult the FIAC website to find out which galleries are showing, then sign up to their newsletters and ask directly if you can be included on the invitation list.

Le Grand Palais, Ave. Winston Churchill, 75008. Metro: Champs-Elysées—Clemenceau. Cour Carrée du Louvre, 75001. Metro: Louvre Rivoli. ℂ **01 47 56 64 21.** Adm: 28€; 15€ art-school students. Five days in Oct; check website for details. Open midday–8pm.

Pavillon des Arts et du Design   Held inside the Jardin de Tuileries, this annual spring design fest into its 14th year unites so many ancient and contemporary art treasures (from furniture and paintings to jewellery and Primitive Arts) that it calls itself an 'ephemeral museum'. Mostly art professionals attend the trade fair, but members of Paris's culture-frenzied public are increasingly drawn in.

Esplanade des Feuillants, Les Tuileries (opposite 234 Rue de Rivoli), 75001. ℂ **01 53 30 85 20.** www.pad-paris.com. 25–28 March 2010. 11am–8pm (until 11pm on 25 Mar). Metro: Tuileries.

★ **Salon de Dessin Contemporain**   For its fourth edition (in 2010), this nomadic fest is bringing more than 60 galleries to the Louvre, where they'll be presenting a vast and varied collection of contemporary drawings, from standard works on paper to unusual video and digital works and wall-drawings. For art amateurs it demonstrates just how strongly drawing is inscribed in today's world, especially in the fields of architecture, fashion and design. Every year, the fair includes a private collection of drawings—last year's were from the agnès b collection.

Carrousel du Louvre, 99 Rue de Rivoli, 75001. No phone. www.salondudessin contemporain.com. Adm: usually 12€; 6€ students and artists; free under-18s. 25–28 March 2010. 11am–8pm. Metro: Palais-Royal—Musée du Louvre.

5 Tours

Paris pays the price of being the world's most visited city with a network of tours for tourists. But what do we do when we don't want to join Monsieur and Madame Everybody on open-top buses or river rides on Bateaux-Mouches?

Between the Paris we see on the street and the secrets hidden behind the façades, there's a whole world, and the best way to discover it is on foot or by bike, adventuring down narrow streets and nipping behind closed doors at every opportunity. This section lists the best of a limited bunch of intimate tours, while Chapter 8 suggests DIY walking tours around some of the city's most interesting areas and Chapter 5 lists collective rollerblading and bike rambles.

ALWAYS FREE

Les Panamées `FREE`   On the third Thursday of most months, Paris's regional ramblers' association (FFR Comité Départemental) rolls out the red carpet for around 300 Paris-loving regulars with commentated, themed walks around town. Don't expect a restful evening; the walk takes three hours (7–10pm) and covers at least 6km. But it is tremendous fun and rather informative, covering themes such as street art, stately squares and the Canal Saint-Denis. `FINE PRINT` The starting point changes according to the theme, so consult the website beforehand for precise instructions.

35 Rue Piat, 75020. ℂ **01 46 36 95 70.** www.rando-paris.org.

★ **Parisien d'un Jour** `FREE`   Sign up three weeks in advance (online) to become a 'Parisian for a day' in the hands of this volunteers' association made up of students, workers, and retirees helplessly in love with Paris and willing to share historical tit-bits and tips on where to go. Walks take place in the volunteers' own neighbourhoods, taking you to 'insider' places. There's a maximum of six people per group, but separately registered people can do the same walk if there is a common language. `FINE PRINT` Donations are not obligatory but are the association's sole resource.

www.parisiendunjour.fr

WORTH THE SPLURGE

Classic Walks   For Paris virgins, Classic Walks (partnered with American-owned Fat Tire Bike and Segway Tours; p. 242) offer six intimate themed walks around town: The Classic, the Montmartre, the Da Vinci Code, the Latin Quarter, the Second World War, and the Revolution. All do as their names suggest, taking you past the city's major monuments and dispensing interesting bits of info as you go. Tours last 2–3½ hours and run between March and October. Reservations are vital. FINE PRINT The company's headquarters double as an unofficial tourist office, with Internet access, clean loos, and drinks and snacks.

24 Rue Edgar Faure, 75015. ℂ **01 56 58 10 54.** http://classicwalksparis.com. Adm: 20€ (Classic, Da Vinci Code), 12€ (Montmartre, Latin Quarter, Second World War, Revolution). Metro: Dupleix.

> ### Les Balades du Patrimoine—Self-Guided Tours through Paris's Heritage FREE
>
> The Mairie de Paris offers 27 downloadable heritage tours (in French) on themes that include Art & the Tramway, Paris's Fashion Monuments, Myths & Reality, and Atlases and Caryatides on Façades. Just pick the theme, print the map and commentaries, and set off on foot or by bike. ℂ **39 75.** www.paris.fr.

Fat Tire Bike Tours Despite sticking to touristy routes, Fat Tire's tours attract Paris rookies and veterans alike. The 4-hour day tour takes you past the big monuments; the 4-hour night tour is better value, allowing you to see the Eiffel Tower twinkle and including a free boat trip along the Seine and a complimentary glass of wine. (In fact, most people who sign up for the day trip end up buying a combined day and night ticket.) If there's still some pedal-power left in you, Fat Tire also runs bike trips to Monet's garden in Giverny (p. 217) and to Versailles. FINE PRINT Paris tours leave from the Pilier Sud (south leg) of the Eiffel Tower.

24 Rue Edgar Faure, 75015. ℂ **01 56 58 10 54.** http://classicwalksparis.com. Adm: 26€, 24€ student (day); 28€, 26€ student (night); 40€, 38€ student (combined day and night); 65€ Versailles or Monet's garden. Metro: Dupleix.

★ **Paris Walks** Chocoholics rejoice—Paris Walks' latest addition takes you to a selection of Paris's best chocolatiers and provides ample tasting opportunities. For tours where you burn rather than consume calories, check the monthly programme online. Walks tend to be history-orientated and focus on areas such as the Latin Quarter, the Marais, the Ile de la Cité, and Père-Lachaise cemetery, but there are also themed tours such as Art Nouveau Paris, the Saint-Denis

★ Going it Alone on a Segway

Segways are futuristic, self-balancing, personal transportation devices that look like Space Age children's scooters and operate in a pedestrian environment, with a motor entirely operated by your body weight. You want to move forwards? Lean forwards. You want to slow down? Lean backwards. It's fun and different—and trust me, after 10min you'll feel like you've ridden one all your life. You can rent one by the hour for a half day or full day with Moveus by the Eiffel Tower. You're free to go where you like, but my advice is to stick to the wide Haussman-era quarters of the Eiffel Tower, Madeleine, and Champs-Elysées, as Paris's older districts have narrow, uneven pavements that could tip you off balance.
14 Rue Dupleix, 75015. ☏ **01 56 58 15 38.** http://moveus.fr. Prices: 15€ hour; 40€ half-day (45€ weekends and public hols); 65€ day (75€ weekends and public hols). Metro: Dupleix.

Basilica (p. 225), and Jefferson's or Hemingway's Paris. You don't need to book in advance for standard walks (they run every day), but specialist tours (chocolate and so on) won't run if there aren't sufficient bookings. Bring a brolly—Paris Walkers are come-rain-or-shiners. FINE PRINT Walks all have different starting points so check online or when you book.

12 Passage Meunier, 93200 Saint-Denis. ☏ 01 48 09 21 40. www.paris-walks.com. Adm: 25€ chocolate walk and special tours; 12€ other walks.

WORTH THE EXTRA SPLURGE

★ **Edible Paris** Ever dreamed of having a foodie friend in Paris? Your wish is food expert Rosa Jackson's command. This chef, food critic, and *gastronome extraordinaire* will craft you a Paris food itinerary to match your tastes, whether you're a bread junkie, pastry fiend, cheese'o-holic, chocoholic, or an intimate bistro lover, or all of the above (prices range from 100€ for half a day to 350€ for two days, per group up to six). She can also match you with a food guru whose knowledge of food shops and restaurants makes you feel like a local *gourmand*. It's not cheap (prices per person: 100€ group of 4–6; 150€ group of 2–3; 300€ individual tour), but having one of Paris's leading food experts at your side is absolutely priceless—and hey, with the money you're saving by using the tips elsewhere in this book, why not treat yourself? www.edible-paris.com.

6 Green Peace: Gardens

Most Parisians live in stamp-sized, gardenless apartments, so the city's squares and parks become an essential part of life here—vital respites from the urban jungle and a means of keeping in touch with nature. Gardens are also a source of national pride—the French may have chopped the heads off their royals, but the art of landscaping *jardins* fit for a king is still very much alive. The downside is that certain parks won't allow people on the grass (including the Jardin des Tuileries and the Jardin de Luxembourg), acting more as elegant thoroughfares than 'spread-yourself-out-on-the-lawn' sorts of spaces. But others, listed below, are fine spots in which to while away a sunny afternoon and inhale some fresh air for free. Time your visit right, and you might also catch an open-air music performance.

★ **Bois de Boulogne** FREE   Paris's 865-hectare lung—a throwback from the days when kings went hunting—is spectacular all year round, with its Longchamp and Auteuil horse-racing grounds, woodlands, picnic areas, children's mini theme-park (Jardin d'Acclimatation; see p. 95) and museum (Musée en Herbe), and boating lakes. During the warmer months, don't miss the Parc de Bagatelle, the beautiful result of a bet between Marie-Antoinette and the Comte d'Artois, famed for the splendour of its roses, lilies and daffodils, and boasting an orangery used by the Chopin Society for concerts. Between May and September, the Jardin de Shakespeare (a Shakespeare-themed garden) comes alive with the Bard's plays, performed in French and English, and music performances. FINE PRINT There are entry charges for the Jardin d'Acclimatation, Musée en Herbe, Shakespearean plays and, during temporary exhibitions, the Jardin de Bagatelle; everything else is free. The Bois is best avoided at night, when it becomes a showground for transsexual prostitutes and swingers.

75016. Metro: Porte Maillot, Les Sablons, or Porte Dauphine.

★ **Bois de Vincennes** FREE   Even bigger than the Bois de Boulogne, this eastern park (another former hunting forest) was landscaped for

Cemeteries FREE

Some of Paris's leafiest and most peaceful oases are its cemeteries—the resting spots of the great and good, or anyone rich enough to buy a plot, and good hunting grounds for those wishing to pay homage to defunct celebrities. **Père-Lachaise** (Blvd. de Ménilmontant, 75020. Metro: Père-Lachaise) is a veritable hall of fame, with the graves of Oscar Wilde, Molière, Balzac, and Doors singer Jim Morrison, among a great many others. The **Cimetière du Montparnasse** (35 Blvd. Edgar Quinet, 75014. Metro: Edgar Quinet or Raspail) is a close second, harbouring a large proportion of Paris's literary set (Beckett, Baudelaire, Sartre, De Beauvoir, Ionesco, and Maupassant, to name just a few), plus artists including Brancusi and Man Ray and the singer Serge Gainsbourg.

Offthebeaten track, the **Cimetière de Picpus** (35 Rue de Picpus, 75012. Metro: Nation or Picpus) is the final resting place of thousands of victims guillotined at Nation (today's Place de la Réunion) after the Revolution. The grave is communal, but inside the chapel you can see the names and occupations of those slaughtered. Further north, the **Cimetière de Montmartre** (20 Ave. Rachel, 75018. Metro: Blanche or Place de Clichy) is the final resting place of Truffaut, Nijinsky, Degas, Offenbach, and the consumption-riddled courtesan Alphonsine (or Marie) Plessis, who inspired Verdi's *La Traviata*.

Paris's graveyards are open Monday–Friday 8am–6pm; Saturday 8:30am–6pm; Sunday 9am–6pm (or 5:30pm November–early March).

Haussmann in the 19th century and contains boating lakes, a beautiful Buddhist temple, a racetrack, restaurants, a small farm (La Ferme de Paris, p. 248), a zoo, and the Cartoucherie de Vincennes (Route du Champ de Manoeuvre, 75012. www.theatre-du-soleil.fr), an old munitions factory transformed into five avant-garde theatres. This is also where you'll find the 35-hectare Parc Floral (Esplanade du Château de Vincennes, 94330, Metro Château de Vincennes. ☎ **01 48 08 13 00.** www.parcfloraldeparis.com)—a cross between a botanical garden and an amusement park, with plants galore, woodland, and a kids' adventure playground. It also hosts Paris's summer jazz festival (p. 22). FINE PRINT The Bois is free, but activities (such as boating, the farm, the races, the theatres) cost extra. The Parc Floral is also free except Wednesdays, Saturdays and Sundays June–September, when there are frequent summer music performances (5€, 2.50€ for 7–26s, under-7s free).

75012. Metro: Château de Vincennes or Porte Dorée.

Jardin des Plantes `FREE`   It may not look like it at first glance, but this is actually Paris's botanical garden, containing more than 10,000 species of flora, including a false acacia planted in 1636 and a cedar from 1734, a tropical greenhouse (in the pharmacy faculty, 4 Rue de l'Observatoire, 75006), formal gardens, a rose, winter and alpine garden (in the Ecole Botanique), and a little zoo (see Ménagerie, p. 249). The site began as Louis XIII's doctor's medicinal garden in 1626, and the botanically curious can educate themselves by downloading themed guides from the website (a general guide, a tree guide, and an oriental plant guide). `FINE PRINT` The gardens are free except for the Jardin Alpin, which charges a symbolic 1€ (0.50€ children) at weekends.

Rue Cuvier, Rue Buffon, Rue Geoffroy-Saint-Hilaire, Place Valhubert, 75005. ✆ **01 40 79 56 01.** www.mnhn.fr. Main park 7:30am–7:30pm (other opening times vary so consult website). Metro: Gare d'Austerlitz, Censier—Daubenton or Jussieu.

Parc de Belleville `FREE`   Rues Piat and des Envierges with their lovely views over the city lead to this lofty, modern park that was once covered in vines (and still grows a few for good measure). Here you'll find a waterfall, a children's games area, grassy slopes, great views, and the Maison de l'Air—an educational centre that looks at the relationship between

Serres d'Auteuil `FREE`

Imagine a mini version of the Grand Palais's glass roof, colonised by banana trees, orchids, and cacti, and you'll come close to the appearance of the Auteuil greenhouses. Marvellous examples of Belle Epoque technology, they were one of the first places in Paris to be lit by gas and electricity, and the first place in the world to grow plants in artificial light. Nowadays you can admire more than 5,000 species of tropical and sub-tropical beauties in an atmosphere that averages 64°F (18°C) and 60–80% humidity. 1 Ave. Gordon Bennett, 75016. ✆ **01 40 71 74 00.** www.paris.fr. Daily (hours depend on the hours of daylight). Metro: Porte d'Auteuil.

the air we breathe and life in the capital. It's a perfect spot for a quick getaway without leaving the city.

47 Rue des Couronnes, 75020. Metro: Couronnes, Pyrénées, or Belleville.

Parc de Bercy `FREE`   Visions of the old wine-trading village of Bercy don't conjure up modern lawns with contemporary sculptures, gardens laid out to represent the four seasons, or a patchwork of rose, herb, and vegetable plots. Nor do you expect to see rows of narrow vine trestles. But that's exactly what this modern park has got going for it. That, and a prime location between two of Paris's most up-and-coming areas—Bibliothèque, where party boats line the water's edge, and Bercy Village, where former wine warehouses have been converted into shops, restaurants, and a multi-screen cinema.

Rue de Bercy, 75012. Metro: Bercy or Cour Saint-Emilion.

★ **Parc de la Villette** `FREE`   Possibly Paris's most happening park, this feast of postmodern architecture is jam-packed with activities all year round, drawing on the crowds who come for Le Zenith concert hall, the Cité des Sciences (p. 93), the Grande Halle (a conference centre, theatre, and concert hall), the Cité de la Musique (p. 209), and the Canal de l'Ourcq (p. 276). The park was designed by Swiss architect Bernard and is dotted with bright red follies that serve as lookout points, a first-aid post, a café, and a children's art centre. The lawns are a favourite with picnickers (especially in July and August during Paris's Open Air film festival; p. 23) and there are 10 themed gardens, one of which is seized by tam-tam drummers on warm Sunday afternoons, infusing the surroundings with rhythm.

Ave. Corentin-Cariou/Ave. Jean-Jaurès, 75019. ℭ **01 40 03 75 75.** www.villette.com. Metro: Porte de la Villette or Porte de Pantin.

★ **Parc des Buttes-Chaumont** `FREE`   Some of the city's most gorgeous man-made acreage is found on the slopes of this park sculpted in the 19th century to hide a former gypsum quarry, and now boasting waterfalls, caves, and a tall rocky island in the middle of a lake, topped by the mini Temple de la Sybille—the old entrance to the quarry. Locals come here to jog, practise martial arts, eat, drink, and generally be lazy.

Rue Botzaris, Rue Manin, Rue de Crimée, 75019. Metro: Buttes-Chaumont.

Parc Georges Brassens `FREE`   This little-known park named after the singer-poet and set on the site of former abattoirs is an oasis in a residential area of the 15th. Several of Paris's 300 beehives are found here (guided visits can be organised. ℗ **01 45 42 29 08**), while plant fans get their kicks from the aromatic and medicinal plant sections. You can also see remnants of the abattoirs and the bell-tower that was the central point of the meat market and the Halles aux Chevaux, where horses were paraded before being sold for slaughter.

2 Place Jacques Marette, 75015. Metro: Porte de Vanves. T3: Georges Brassens.

Parc Montsouris FREE A sad story marked the opening of this pleasant park—part of Baron Haussmann's urban planning—in 1878: On the opening day, the artificial lake mysteriously emptied itself and the engineer responsible committed suicide. Since then, things have got substantially better, and today Montsouris is one of the city's live- liest parks, with sweeping lawns, gentle slopes and, in true Hauss- mann style, lovely waterfalls.

Blvd. Jourdan, 75014. RER: Cité Universitaire.

7 Zoos & Aquariums

There's more to Paris's animal life than preened poodles and King Charles spaniels, but you have to pay to see it. Animals are high- maintenance attractions, so zoos and aquariums charge high entry fees. The only exceptions are the Ferme de Paris, in the Bois de Vin- cennes, where farmyard animals can be cooed at for free, and the lit- tle aquarium within the Cité des Sciences. Note that the Zoo de Vincennes is closed for renovations until 2013.

Aquarium de la Cité des Sciences et l'Industrie FREE La Villette's futuristic science museum hides this quaint little aquarium two floors below ground level, with 200 species of fish, crustaceans, molluscs, and vegetation from the Mediterranean coast flourishing alongside stingrays, eels, sharks, starfish, and sea urchins.

30 Ave. Corentin-Cariou, 75019. ℗ **01 40 05 80 00.** www.cite-sciences.fr. Tues–Sun 10am–6pm (until 7pm Sun). Metro: Porte de la Villette.

★ **Ciné Aqua** Paris's state-of-the-art aquarium plunges us deep into the heart of ocean life, thanks to huge tanks (the biggest in France) full of shimmering fish, eels, seahorses, lobsters, and other creatures, including 30 fearsome-looking sharks. The best part is the *bassins caresses* (touch pools) where the koi carp and sturgeons come up to nibble your fingers. The tanks are interspersed with cinema screens

★ Day-Tripping with the Beasts at Thoiry

If you're looking for real exotica, grab a set of wheels and head 40km west of Paris to the Parc de Thoiry in Les Yvelines, where big cats thrive alongside elephants and giraffes in the land around a sumptuous 16th-century château. It looks expensive on paper, but you get a whole day out for your money, and a rare chance to observe African animals such as lions, ostriches, rhinos, giraffes, hippos, and elephants from the safety of your car window. On the zoo promenade, see Siberian lynxes, gibbons and Tonkean macaques—all immensely well looked after. Four komodo dragons were conceived and born here in 2006, while 2009 was a baby boom for the zebras, antelopes, gnus, wallabies, kangaroos, and tortoises. The château has a stunning garden designed by Le Nôtre's successor, and a vast maze prized by kids. Thoiry-en-Yvelines, 78770. ℃ **01 34 87 40 67.** www.thoiry.tm.fr. Adm: 25€; 18€ 3–14s; 22€ students and over-60s; free under-3s. Daily 10am–6pm (château closes for lunch 12:45–1:30pm; open from 11am in winter). Accessible by car only: Take A13 from Paris (dir. Rouen or Versailles), then A12 (dir. Rambouillet), followed by the N12 (dir. Dreux), D912, and D11.

showing animal documentaries and cartoons. FINE PRINT Arrive between 10am and midday and get 20% off your admission price.

2 Ave. des Nations Unies, 75016. ℃ **01 40 69 23 23.** www.cineaqua.com. Adm: 19.50€; 15.50€ 13–17s; 12€ 3–12s; free under-3s. Daily 10am–8pm. Metro: Trocadéro or Iéna.

★ **La Ferme de Paris** FREE Somewhat anachronistic but wholly educational and beloved of many Parisian families, this mini-farm in the middle of the Bois de Vincennes (p. 243) is home to cows, sheep, geese, rabbits, hens, and carthorses. At 4pm you can milk the cows, and in the spring you can watch the sheep being sheared or see newborn lambs. The farm even has small fields of wheat and beetroot plus a vegetable plot—a real slice of the countryside on the doorstep. FINE PRINT The farm is reserved for school trips during the week and open to the public on weekends.

1 Route du Pesage, 75012. ⓒ **01 43 28 47 63** or **08 92 68 30 00.** www.paris.fr. Sat–Sun 1:30–5pm (until 5:30pm Oct and Mar, 6:30pm Apr–Sept and 6pm during Easter and summer hols). Metro: Château de Vincennes, then bus 112 and 15min walk. RER: Joinville-le-Pont, then 20min walk.

Ménagerie de Jardin des Plantes   When heads rolled in the aftermath of the Revolution, the exotic fauna collected by the defunct aristocrats needed a new home, and this 5-hectare menagerie (the world's oldest zoo) was the unlikely solution. Small animals take pride of place: More than 190 species in total, including kangaroos, antelopes, wallabies, black pigs, camels, llamas, the famous Przewalski horse (so rare it disappeared from the wild 40 years ago), and a couple of panthers in the *fauverie*. Lizard and snake fans can see boas, anacondas, geckos, and pythons in the reptile house, while for those less daring there are cute monkeys and two gorgeous red pandas.

3 Quai Saint-Bernard or 57 Rue Cuvier, 75005. ⓒ **01 40 79 37 94.** www.mnhn.fr. Daily 9am–6pm Apr–Oct, until 5pm Nov–Mar. Adm: 8€, 6€ 4–13s, free under-4s. See Musée d'Histoire Naturelle for info on combined tickets, p. 216. Metro: Gare d'Austerlitz or Jussieu.

EXPLORING RIGHT BANK NORTH EAST

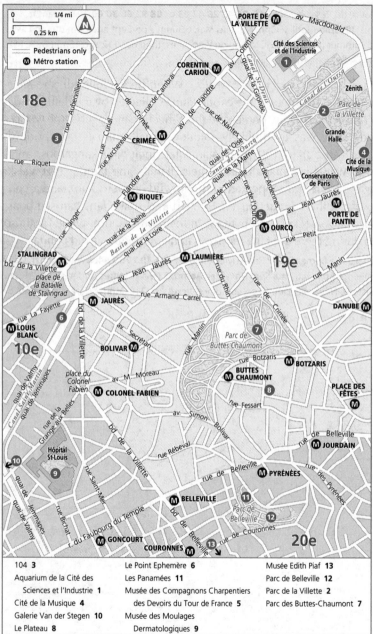

0   1/4 mi
0   0.25 km

Pedestrians only
Ⓜ Métro station

PORTE DE
LA VILLETTE Ⓜ   av. Macdonald

Cité des Sciences
et de l'Industrie
①

Canal St-Denis
quai de la Gironde

CORENTIN
CARIOU Ⓜ   quai de la Charente

18e

Canal de l'Ourcq

Zénith

②

Parc de
la Villette

rue de Cambrai

rue de Crimée

rue de Flandre

rue de Nantes

av. de Flandre

rue de l'Aubervilliers

rue du Canal

rue Archereau

CRIMÉE Ⓜ

Grande
Halle

Cité de la
Musique
④

rue Riquet

quai de l'Oise
Canal de l'Ourcq
quai de la Marne

quai de Thionville

rue des Ardennes

Conservatoire
de Paris

rue Tanger

av. de Flandre

Ⓜ RIQUET

quai de la Seine

rue de l'Ourcq

rue de Thionville

av. Jean Jaurès

PORTE DE
PANTIN

STALINGRAD Ⓜ
bd. de la Villette

place de
la Bataille
de Stalingrad

Bassin de la Villette

quai de la Loire

⑤
Ⓜ OURCQ

rue Petit

19e

rue Manin

rue La Fayette

Ⓜ JAURÈS
⑥

Ⓜ av. Jean Jaurès LAUMIÈRE

rue Armand Carrel

rue du Rhin

rue de Crimée

DANUBE Ⓜ

bd. de la Villette

av. Secrétan

LOUIS
BLANC Ⓜ

10e

BOLIVAR Ⓜ

⑦
Parc de
Buttes Chaumont

rue Manin

rue Botzaris

BOTZARIS Ⓜ

Canal Saint-Martin
quai de Valmy
quai de Jemmapes

place du
Colonel
Fabien

av. M. Moreau

Ⓜ COLONEL FABIEN

BUTTES
CHAUMONT Ⓜ
⑧

rue Fessart

PLACE DES
FÊTES

Ⓜ

rue de la
Grange-aux-Belles

av. Simon Bolivar

rue Rébeval

de Belleville

rue

Ⓜ JOURDAIN

Hôpital
St-Louis

⑩

⑨

rue Saint-Maur

bd. de la Villette

rue des Pyrénées

quai de Jemmapes
quai de Valmy

rue Bichat

rue de Belleville

Ⓜ PYRÉNÉES

Ⓜ BELLEVILLE

⑪
Parc de
Belleville
⑫

20e

r. du Faubourg du Temple

Ⓜ GONCOURT

bd. de Belleville

rue de Couronnes

COURONNES Ⓜ
⑬

104 **3**

Aquarium de la Cité des
   Sciences et l'Industrie **1**

Cité de la Musique **4**

Galerie Van der Stegen **10**

Le Plateau **8**

Le Point Ephemère **6**

Les Panamées **11**

Musée des Compagnons Charpentiers
   des Devoirs du Tour de France **5**

Musée des Moulages
   Dermatologiques **9**

Musée Edith Piaf **13**

Parc de Belleville **12**

Parc de la Villette **2**

Parc des Buttes-Chaumont **7**

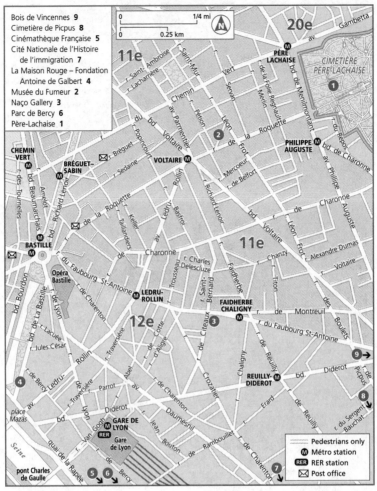

Bois de Vincennes **9**
Cimetière de Picpus **8**
Cinémathèque Française **5**
Cité Nationale de l'Histoire
   de l'immigration **7**
La Maison Rouge – Fondation
   Antoine de Galbert **4**
Musée du Fumeur **2**
Naço Gallery **3**
Parc de Bercy **6**
Père-Lachaise **1**

0   1/4 mi
0   0.25 km

Pedestrians only
Ⓜ Métro station
ⓇⒺⓇ RER station
✉ Post office

EXPLORING RIGHT BANK MARAIS

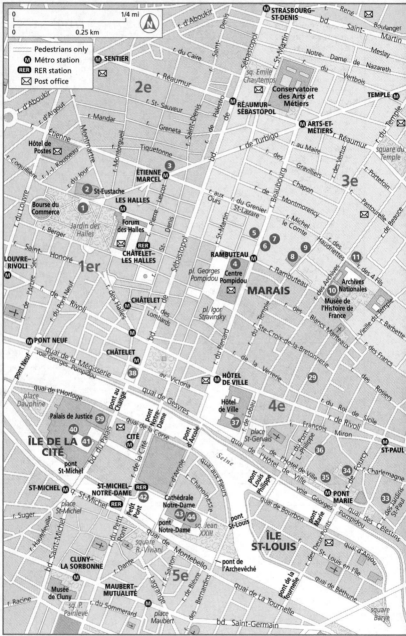

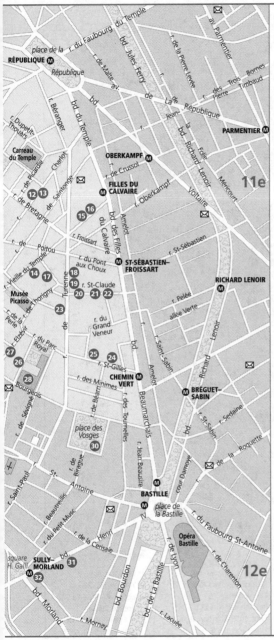

EXPLORING RIGHT BANK CENTRE

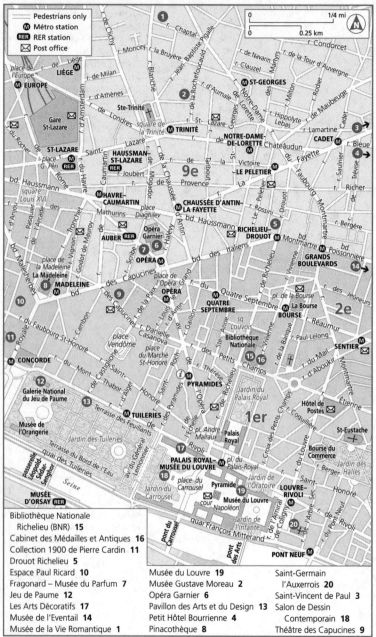

Bibliothèque Nationale
  Richelieu (BNR) **15**
Cabinet des Médailles et Antiques **16**
Collection 1900 de Pierre Cardin **11**
Drouot Richelieu **5**
Espace Paul Ricard **10**
Fragonard – Musée du Parfum **7**
Jeu de Paume **12**
Les Arts Décoratifs **17**
Musée de l'Eventail **14**
Musée de la Vie Romantique **1**

Musée du Louvre **19**
Musée Gustave Moreau **2**
Opéra Garnier **6**
Pavillon des Arts et du Design **13**
Petit Hôtel Bourrienne **4**
Pinacothèque **8**

Saint-Germain
  l'Auxerrois **20**
Saint-Vincent de Paul **3**
Salon de Dessin
  Contemporain **18**
Théâtre des Capucines **9**

EXPLORING RIGHT BANK WEST (A)

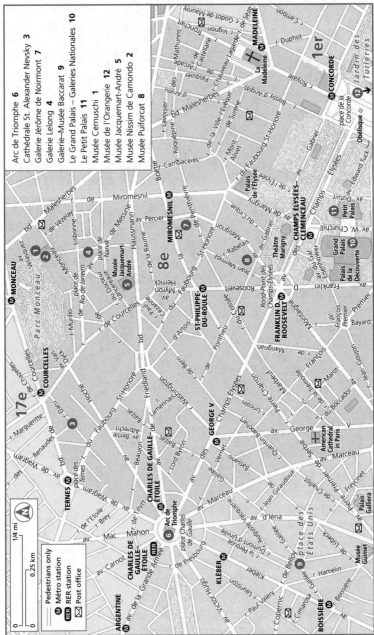

Arc de Triomphe **6**
Cathédrale St. Alexander Nevsky **3**
Galerie Jérôme de Noirmont **7**
Galerie Lelong **4**
Galerie–Musée Baccarat **9**
Le Grand Palais – Galeries Nationales **10**
Le Petit Palais **11**
Musée Cernuschi **1**
Musée de l'Orangerie **12**
Musée Jacquemart-André **5**
Musée Nissim de Camondo **2**
Musée Puiforcat **8**

Pedestrians only
Ⓜ Métro station
RER RER station
⊠ Post office

0   0.25 km
0   1/4 mi

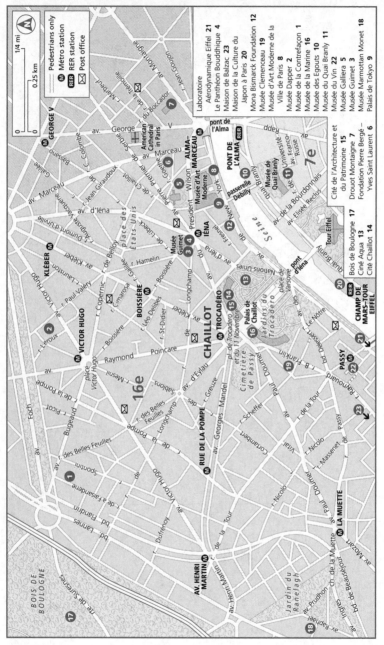

Aérodynamique Eiffel **21**
Le Panthéon Bouddhique **4**
Maison de Balzac **23**
Maison de la Culture du Japon à Paris **20**
Mona Bismarck Foundation **12**
Musée Clemenceau **19**
Musée d'Art Moderne de la Ville de Paris **8**
Musée Dapper **2**
Musée de la Contrefaçon **1**
Musée de la Marine **16**
Musée des Egouts **10**
Musée du Quai Branly **11**
Musée du Vin **22**
Musée Galliera **5**
Musée Guimet **3**
Musée Marmottan Monet **18**
Palais de Tokyo **9**

Cité de l'Architecture et du Patrimoine **15**
Drouot Montaigne **7**
Fondation Pierre Bergé – Yves Saint Laurent **6**

Bois de Boulogne **17**
Ciné Aqua **13**
Cité Chaillot **14**

Pedestrians only
Métro station
RER station
Post office

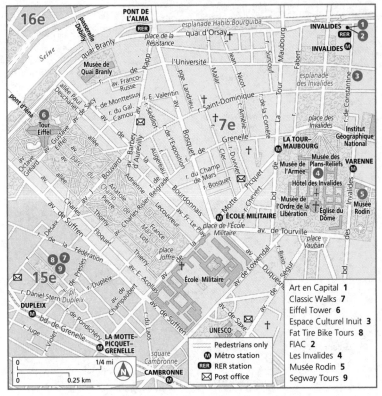

16e

PONT DE
L'ALMA

Passerelle Debilly

Seine

Quai Branly

esplanade Habib Bourguiba

quai d'Orsay

place de la
Résistance

l'Université

av. Franco-
Russe

r. de Monttessuy

r. E. Valentin

Saint-Dominique

r. du Gal.
Camou

allée Paul
Deschanel

pont d'Iéna

Tour
Eiffel

6

av. Gustave
Eiffel

av. de Sacy

r. Sédillot

de l'Exposition

Grenelle

7e

r. Amélie

r. de la Comète

INVALIDES

1

RER

2

INVALIDES

esplanade
des Invalides

3

Institut
Géographique
National

Musée de
Quai Branly

de Rapp

Jean Nicot

r. Surcouf

av. de Tour

Maubourg

Fabert

de Constantine

place des
Invalides

LA TOUR–
MAUBOURG

Musée des
Plans-Reliefs

VARENNE

Octave
Gréard

av. Octave

av. du parc du

Bouvard

Adrienne

av. Charles Risler

France
Mars

Loti

Champ

Anatole

r. Augereau

de Mars

Belgrade

r. Cler

r. Duvivier

Motte

Picquet

r. du Champ
de Mars

r. Bosquet

Musée de
l'Armée

4

Hôtel des Invalides

Musée de
l'Ordre de la
Libération

Église du
Dôme

Invalides

5

Musée
Rodin

Charles

Thomy

Floquet

de Suffren

av. Charles

Pierre

Lecouvreur

av. Fr. Le Play

ÉCOLE MILITAIRE

place de l'École
Militaire

av. de Tourville

place
Vauban

8 7

9

15e

r. de la Fédération

r. de presles

r. Dupleix

pl.
Dupleix

av. E. Acollas

place
Joffre

École Militaire

av. de Lowendal

r. Bixio

av. Duquesne

bd. des Ségur

r. Daniel Stern

DUPLEIX

de Pondichéry

bd. de Grenelle

r. Juge

LA MOTTE–
PICQUET–
GRENELLE

av. de Champaubert

av. de Suffren

r. du Laos

UNESCO

av. de Saxe

av. de Suffren

square
Cambronne

CAMBRONNE

0   1/4 mi

0   0.25 km

N

Pedestrians only

Métro station

RER RER station

Post office

Art en Capital **1**
Classic Walks **7**
Eiffel Tower **6**
Espace Culturel Inuit **3**
Fat Tire Bike Tours **8**
FIAC **2**
Les Invalides **4**
Musée Rodin **5**
Segway Tours **9**

EXPLORING LEFT BANK CENTRE

EXPLORING LEFT BANK EAST

	Pedestrians only
M	Métro station
RER	RER station
✉	Post office

Air de Paris **16**
Art:Concept **19**
Bibliothèque Nationale
  François Mitterrand (BFM) **21**
Collection de Minéralogie de Jussieu **8**
gb agency **17**
Institut du Monde Arabe **7**
Jardin des Plantes **13**
Jousse Entreprise **18**
Le Panthéon **10**
Les Frigos **20**
Manufacture des Gobelins **15**
Ménagerie de Jardin des Plantes **12**
Musée Curie **11**
Musée d'Histoire Naturelle **14**
Musée de l'Assistance Publique **6**
Musée de l'Historie de la Médecine **2**

Musée de la Préfecture de Police **5**
Musée Dupuytren **3**
Musée National du
  Moyen Age (Cluny) **4**
Musée National du Sport **22**
Musée Sainte-Anne **23**
Perimeter Editions **1**
Saint-Etienne du Mont **9**

EXPLORING MONTMARTRE

Cimetière de Montmartre **1**
Drouot Montmartre **7**
Espace Dalí **4**
Halle Saint Pierre **8**
Musée de l'Erotisme **3**
Musée de Montmartre **5**
Musée Maçonnique **2**
Sacré-Coeur **6**

LAMARCK–
CAULAINCOURT

r. Lamarck
r. Caulaincourt
r. des Saules
Francoeur
Lamarck
Custine
Mont Cenis
r. Paul Féval
Becquerel
Cimetière
St-Vincent
Saint-
Vincent
Parc
de la
Turlure
r. de la Bonne
Lamarck
de la Barre
r. S. Dereure
Girardon
de l'Abreuvoir
des Saules
Musée de
Montmartre
5
Cortot
de
Chevalier
de la Barre
sq. S.
Buisson
av. Junot
r. Toutlaque
18e
r. Norvins
r. St-Rustique
Basilique du
Sacré-Coeur
6
Paul Albert
r. Lepic
Cimetière de
Montmartre
1
r. Caulaincourt
MONTMARTRE
Lepic
d'Orchampt
pl. J.B.
Clément
4
Poulbot
r. de
St-Pierre-de-
Montmartre
7
r. J. de Maistre
2
Tholozé
Durantin
Burq
place E.
Goudeau
Berthe
r. du Card.
Dubois
Ch. Nodier
r. des Abbesses
Ravignan
des
r. Drevet
Gabrielle
André
Barsacq
sq. Nadar
FUNICULAR
Foyatier
Ronsard
Moulin
Rouge
r. Lepic
Planquette
Veron
sq.
J. Rictus
place des
Abbesses
r. de La
Vieuville
Trois
Chappe
sq.
Willette
8
Ch. Nodier
place
Blanche
3
r. Puget
Coustou
BLANCHE
Germain Pilon
ABBESSES
r. Yvonne le Tac
r. des
Abbesses
Tardieu
pl. S.
Valadon
pl. St-Pierre
d'Orsel
r. de Steinkerque
Houdon
r. d'Orsel
place
Ch. Dullin
Darcion
d'Orsel
Séveste
Briquet
ANVERS
bd. de Clichy
9e
PIGALLE
place
Pigalle
Martyrs
des

	Steps
	Funicular
Ⓜ	Métro station

0   200 yds
0   200 m

N

An artist at work at the Place du Tertre.

FREE & DIRT CHEAP DAYS

Paris has no qualms about enticing visitors to *spend, spend, spend*, but you can still explore chunks of the city for zilch. Once you've exhausted our free museums (see chapter 7) the city's tightly packed *arrondissements* provide enough cultural and historical fodder for numerous day-long adventures. Most sites can also be covered on foot.

This chapter suggests three special-interest itineraries and two mini-itineraries that either take you off the beaten track or shed new light on prominent areas; all can be walked, cycled or 'metroed'. But if you're fed up with city life, *pas de problème*—Paris is within an hour's ride of several superb sites that even the world's most frugal day-tripper can afford (see Out of Town, p. 291).

Itinerary 1: Paris's Forgotten Villages and their Churches, from Charonne to Les Batignolles

Where to Start	Place St Blaise, 75020. Metro: Alexandre Dumas.
The Time it Takes	4 to 5 hours should do it (depending on how fast you walk or cycle). Plus extra time for obligatory pit-stops in cafés.
Best Time to Go	Morning or afternoon (when shops and cafés are open), preferably on a sunny day, as you'll be spending most of your time outside.
Tip	The itinerary can also be reversed, starting at Sainte-Marie des Batignolles.

Paris is so perfectly contained within its ring-road (*la Périphérique*) that it's easy to forget that the city hasn't always been the size it is today. Just before the Revolution, its borders were marked by the *Enceinte des Fermiers généraux*, a non-defensive tax barrier (roughly corresponding to today's boulevards de Montparnasse, Courcelles, Batignolles, Charonne, Clichy, Ménilmontant, and Belleville), beyond which several villages developed, including Charonne, La Chapelle, Montmartre, and Les Batignolles.

In 1840, King Louis-Philippe created the *Enceinte de Thiers*—fortifications that extended beyond the Fermiers généraux barrier to today's *Périphérique*, protecting Paris and the villages from Prussian invasions (although the Prussians finally assaulted in 1870). Under Napoléon III, Paris absorbed its rural communes in 1860, turning them into the peripheral *arrondissements* you're about to explore. While the crops and vines that once grew on their bucolic slopes have disappeared (except in Montmartre), and 19th- and 20th-century urbanisation has altered the skyline forever, certain streets retain a village-feel. This is true especially around their modest churches, the charming focal points of this itinerary and witnesses of a time that Paris has largely forgotten.

① Rue de Bagnolet

Prepare yourself for some hidden treasures. The route up Rue de Bagnolet from the Alexandre Dumas metro station is, at first sight, far from the "cheerful prairies" Jean-Jacques Rousseau describes in his 1782 novel, *Les Rêveries du Promeneur Solitaire*: Kebab and Chinese takeaways, supermarkets, and cheap shops jostle for space on both sides of the street. But look at the locals and you'll notice a distinct arty vibe to them. Then you'll remark on the spattering of hip bars, and by the time you've had a coffee at the **Piston Pélican** you'll be ready for the bucolic, unkempt charm of adjacent streets such as Rue de Lesseps, which harbours a pocket-sized **Jardin Naturel** where wild flowers and boisterous frogs have free reign and

ITINERARY 1: CHARONNE TO LES BATIGNOLLES

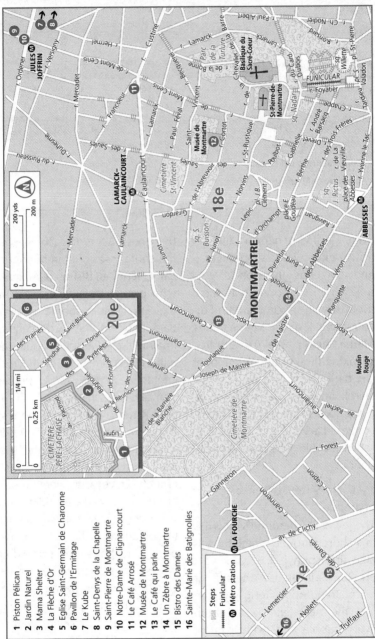

1 Piston Pélican
2 Jardin Naturel
3 Mama Shelter
4 La Flèche d'Or
5 Eglise Saint-Germain de Charonne
6 Pavillon de l'Ermitage
7 Le Kube
8 Saint-Denys de la Chapelle
9 Saint-Pierre de Montmartre
10 Notre-Dame de Clignancourt
11 Le Café Arrosé
12 Musée de Montmartre
13 Le Café qui parle
14 Un Zèbre à Montmartre
15 Bistro des Dames
16 Sainte-Marie des Batignolles

▦▦▦ Steps
〰〰〰 Funicular
Ⓜ Métro station

Costs

Free	
Historic walk, parks	0€
Dirt Cheap	
Transport, coffee, picnic	4€–5.50€
Pavillon de l'Ermitage	3€
Add-ons for Spendthrifts	
Musée de Montmartre	8€ (free under-12s)
Lunch at Bistro des Dames	+/– 15€
Lunch at Café Arrosé	+/– 14€
Lunch at Le Café qui parle	+/– 12.50€

Villa Godin, a narrow alley of flower-clad workers' cottages—and gorgeous throwback to a time when Charonne was rural. (Both streets are on the left.) Further along, look out for the trendy **Mama Shelter** hotel (p. 128) in a spanking new structure (a former car park) decorated by Philippe Starck, and opposite it, one of the city's coolest but cheapest music venues, **La Flèche d'Or** (p. 27), set in the old Charonne railway station.

❷ Eglise Saint-Germain de Charonne

The jewel in Charonne's crown is this church around which the village first sprawled. If you walk up Rue Saint-Blaise (the former main street) opposite it, you can feel the nostalgia oozing from every cobble and, with a bit of imagination, fantasise about how it would have looked surrounded by vines. According to legend, the church was built in honour of Saint Germain, Bishop of Auxerre, who passed through the area in the 5th century. Some sections date back to the 12th century (mainly the tower pillars), but the majority is from the 15th and 16th centuries. What most people don't know is that it is one of the only Parisian churches to possess its own cemetery (Saint-Pierre de Montmartre, p. 269 is the second). In the 18th century, Paris's church graveyards were insalubrious and disease-ridden and were soon made illegal (hence the creation of the Catacombes, p. 212, to house the protruding bones from inner-city graveyards). However, because it was a separate entity until 1860 (like Montmartre), Charonne retained its necropolis, and it indisputably contributes to the area's quaintness today.

③ Pavillon de l'Ermitage

Carry on up Rue de Bagnolet (keeping to the right-hand pavement) for more historic leftovers. The early-18th-century **Pavillon de l'Ermitage** and its park (on the corner of Rue des Balkans) are all that remains of the Château de Bagnolet, the estate of the Duchess of Orléan (Louis XIV's legitimate daughter), which once lay in the shadow of Charonne village. The only Regency-style folly in Paris, it has a small permanent exhibition about the décor of the era (open Friday and Saturday 2–5pm) and surprisingly peaceful gardens.

From here, take the metro from Porte de Bagnolet and change at Père Lachaise for line 2 to La Chapelle (or change at Pigalle for line 12 and get off at Marx Dormoy). If you get off at La Chapelle, walk up Rue Marx Dormoy.

④ La Chapelle

In stark contrast to Charonne, La Chapelle, primarily an African and Arab neighbourhood, bustles with spice shops, Afro-hairdressers, and gaudy fabric boutiques. It's also one of the poorest areas in the city—a status light-years from its pastoral roots as a village in the valley between Montmartre and Belleville, on the old Roman road connecting Lutèce to the north. The area has kept its role as a thoroughfare, though: Hundreds of cars pass through every day on their way out to the Péripherique at Porte de la Chapelle, towards Saint-Denis. It's a petrol-fumed reminder of the days when the villagers of the old La Chapelle would watch royal cortèges to and fro between Paris and the Saint-Denis Basilica (p. 225), resting place of the kings of France.

Tip: Party animals should watch out for the Passage Ruelle on the left as you walk up from La Chapelle metro—it's the unlikely location of one of Paris's trendiest hotels, **Le Kube,** set in a lovely former *hôtel particulier* (mansion) and known for its Grey Goose vodka ice-bar (the only one in Paris).

⑤ Saint-Denys de la Chapelle

The centrepiece of the village is the near-invisible Saint-Denys de la Chapelle church. Today its official entrance is at 16 Rue de la Chapelle, but the oldest part is hidden from the main road, nestled behind trees and a busy food market (Tuesday–Saturday 8am–1pm, 4–7:30pm) on Place de Torcy. It was here that local Christians, at an unknown date, built an oratory on the spot supposed to have contained the tomb of Saint Denis, upon which Sainte Geneviève (patron saint of Paris) prayed. Later, the oratory was replaced by a chapel, around which the village grew, and in

1204 a church was built, the remains of which are still visible. The whole building was revamped in 1670 and then in 1856, hence its mish-mash of styles. On the northern side, there's even a basilica dedicated to Joan of Arc, who allegedly visited the village at least once during her short life.

Go back to Rue Marx Dormoy, then cross the road and take Rue Ordener westwards over the somewhat unsightly railway lines behind the Gare du Nord. Fork left onto Rue Marcadet, which despite its Haussmannian architecture has a wholly African feel. Watch the demography change as you walk towards Rue Simart (on the right), leading to trendy Place Jules Joffrin.

6 Notre-Dame de Clignancourt

A perfect example of a 19th-century religious edifice before the area's annexation to Paris, Notre-Dame de Clignancourt was built for La Chapelle's overspill (when the industrial revolution gripped northeast Paris, the village's population grew from 2,000 to 11,000 inhabitants between 1830 and 1860). Montmartre, too, was getting bigger, and these increases justified the construction of a large church. Paul-Eugène Lequeux, the architect in charge of the *arrondissements* of St-Denis, was the man for the job, designing the building with simple lines that reflect the rationality of the era's town planning. Particularly interesting is how in 1893, after Paris's appropriation of its villages, the city wanted to give this area a village feel and thus built the town hall (the Mairie du 18ème) opposite the church, creating a fake village square. This square is topographically wrong in relation to Montmartre's steep slopes yet is wholly successful, giving today's neighbourhood some sought-after housing.

You now have a choice. Either head directly up Rue du Mont Cenis's sheer slopes (right of the Mairie) straight to Saint-Pierre de Montmartre, or go part of the way up and turn right down Rue Caulaincourt, then left up Rue des Saules. As soon as you hit the cobbles, you're in the heart of the old village of Montmartre, with its cottages (now belonging to the very wealthy), its vineyard, and its postcard-perfect squares and buildings that make this neighbourhood the tourist centre of northern Paris.

7 Mealtime

Options for really cheap food and snacks around Montmartre are limited, but you'll find several *boulangeries* for sandwiches and plenty of cafés offering *omelette frites* (around 10€), salads (12€) and reasonably priced lunchtime menus on Rues Lepic and des Abbesses. **Un Zèbre à Montmartre** is reliably consistent for its tasty *croque-monsieurs* (8.90€) and 15€ lunch menus.

If you don't want to fight the hordes, stop off beforehand on Rue Caulaincourt (A and B), or hold on and eat in Les Batignolles district (C). You could also pack a picnic and eat it on the steps up to the Sacré-Coeur, overwhelmed by tourists but with unbeatable views. Also check out 'Mealtimes' in Itinerary 3 (p. 288).

A **Le Café Arrosé** is one of my faves, with red banquettes, chalkboard menus, a 1930s tiled floor, a traditional zinc bar, smiley staff, and good food such as confit of duck with garlicky potatoes and hamburger au foie-gras, for 9€–14€ a main.

B **Le Café qui parle** is known for its colossal 17.50€ Sunday brunches, but its 12.50€ lunch menu (two courses) also makes this a hot pit-stop. Choices range from homemade quiches and salad to full-blown *steak tartare* and *frites*. A cake trolley tempts the sweet-toothed, and there are take-away coffees should you want to get on with your walk ASAP.

C The **Bistro des Dames'** shady courtyard, old-fashioned décor, and cheap prices lure a young,

arty crowd to this hotel-restaurant. Expect hearty plats du jour, including fish dishes (around 13€), Caesar salad (15€), cheese platters 7€, and chicken breast with chorizo (14€).

⑧ Saint-Pierre de Montmartre

Once you've huffed and puffed your way uphill, past the masses of tourists on Place du Tertre (the former village square) or around the Sacré-Coeur, you'll find Saint-Pierre de Montmartre refreshingly authentic. Its role in the development of Montmartre is central. Saint Denis, the evangelising saint of the 3rd century, became a martyr on this very hill (hence the village's name: *Mont des Martyrs*), sacralising the *Butte* forever more. First a Merovingian chapel and necropolis were built in Denis's honour, around which a small hamlet developed. Then, in 1133, Louis VI and his wife Adélaide replaced the chapel with a Benedictine monastery, which like most mediaeval monasteries became involved in wine production. In the 16th century, the first windmills appeared (only two of which remain, off Rue Lepic), which were used to press Montmartre's grapes and grind the grain produced by the surrounding villages.

St-Pierre-de-Montmartre is the only remaining part of the monastery, which was razed during the Revolution. The village is very much intact. If you fancy getting to grips with more of Montmartre's history, including its time as Paris's artistic capital, splurge on entry to the **Musée de Montmartre** (p. 216) or follow the Montmartre Virgin itinerary on p. 283.

Meander through the Butte's narrow streets (the most direct routes being Rue Lepic and Rue des Abbesses) down to Boulevard de Clichy (the former *Fermiers généraux* barrier) and then head right towards Place de Clichy. Before you get to the Place, where the boulevard curves sharply, take Rue Forest on the right (by the Castorama store). It turns into Rue Cavallotti, which is probably one of the only streets worth visiting when the shops are actually closed, thanks to its lovely painted security screens bearing copies of works by Modigliani, Toulouse-Lautrec, Vermeer, and Gauguin. Turn left down Rue Ganneron, which becomes the Rue des Dames on the other side of Avenue de Clichy (where you can eat at the Bistro des Dames; p. 55) and joins Rue des Batignolles, where you should turn right.

⑨ Sainte-Marie des Batignolles

Until the early 19th century Les Batignolles consisted mainly of uncultivated fields, speckled by the occasional farm and cluster of houses. Unlike in Paris's other villages, urbanisation really took off here under the First Empire, when entrepreneurs acquired the land and purposely created an infrastructure with a town hall, theatre, and church. Sainte-Marie des Batignolles was built in 1826 on what had been designated the town square. Private donors, including the Duchess of Angoulême, funded the build, but the money collected wasn't enough to build more than a nave. However, as the population increased, the commune required a bigger parish, and eventually (between 1839 and 1851), Paul-Eugène Lequeux created the Greek-style building you see today—a toned-down, simplistic version of his grandiose Parisian structure Notre-Dame de Bonne-Nouvelle. Dwarfed by its Haussmannian neighbours, Sainte-Marie looks a little out of place, but the Place remains wholly village-like.

Special Events

● A riot of kilts, sporrans, whisky, and bagpipes awaits those who celebrate the Six Nations Rugby match between Scotland and France at Montmartre's biannual **L'Ecosse à Montmartre** festival (next in February 2011). www.ecosse-montmartre.com.

- Join Montmartre's boozy street bash in honour of its annual grape harvest, **La Fête des Vendanges,** on the 2nd weekend of October. The Butte's Gamay wine, Le Clos de Montmartre (around 300 litres), is auctioned off, with overindulgence the name of the game.

- The Goutte d'Or district sandwiched between La Chapelle and Montmartre celebrates its ethnic diversity with concerts, plays, and street parties in **La Goutte d'Or en Fête** every June. www.gouttedorenfete.org.

- **Le Festival Utinérant des Arènes de Montmartre** showcases Comedia dell'Arte in Montmartre's little-known Roman amphitheatre for the first 10 days of September. ℭ **01 48 40 62 49.** www.mysterebouffe.com.

Itinerary 1 Index

Bistro des Dames   18 Rue des Dames, 75017. ℭ **01 45 22 35 21.** www. eldoradohotel.fr. Mon–Fri midday–3pm, 7pm–2am; Sat–Sun 12:30pm– 2am. Metro: Place de Clichy.

Kube   5 Passage Ruelle, 75018. ℭ **01 42 05 20 00.** www.kubehotel.com. Metro: La Chapelle.

Jardin Naturel   Bottom of Rue de Lesseps or 112 Rue de la Réunion, 75020. 8am to sundown (roughly 5:30pm winter, 8pm summer). Metro: Alexandre Dumas.

Le Café Arrosé   123 Rue Caulaincourt, 75018. ℭ **01 42 57 14 30.** Mon– Sat 8am–2am, Sun 8am–7pm. Metro: Lamarck-Caulaincourt.

Le Café qui parle   24 Rue Caulaincourt, 75018. ℭ **01 46 06 06 88.** Mon– Tues, Thurs–Fri 8:30am–11pm; Sat 7:30pm–11pm; Sun 10am–4pm. Metro: Lamarck-Caulaincourt.

Mama Shelter   109 Rue de Bagnolet, 75020. ℭ **01 43 48 48 48.** www. mamashelter.com. Metro: Alexandre Dumas or Porte de Bagnolet.

Musée de Montmartre   12 Rue Cortot, 75018. ℭ **01 49 25 89 37.** www. museedemontmartre.fr. Tues–Sun 11am–6pm. Metro: Anvers (then the *funiculaire*) or Lamarck-Caulaincourt.

Notre-Dame de Clignancourt 2 place Jules Joffrin, 75018. ✆ 01 44 92 70 21. http://ndclignancourt.org. Daily 9–12:30pm, 2–7:30pm (from 5:30pm Sun). Metro: Jules Joffrin.

Pavillon de l'Ermitage 148 Rue de Bagnolet, 75020. ✆ 01 40 24 15 95. www.pavillondelermitage.com. Fri–Sat 2–5pm. Metro: Porte de Bagnolet.

Piston Pélican 15 Rue de Bagnolet, 75020. ✆ 01 43 71 15 76. www.pistonpelican.com. Mon–Sat 10am–2am. Metro: Alexandre Dumas.

Saint-Denys de la Chapelle 54 Rue de Torcy, 75018. ✆ 01 46 07 35 52. www.stdenysdelachapelle.org. Daily 8am–7pm (from 9am Sun). Metro: Marx Dormoy.

Saint-Germain de Charonne 4 place St Blaise, 75020. ✆ 01 43 71 42 04. http://par.stgch.free.fr/. Daily 8am–7pm. Metro: Alexandre Dumas or Porte de Bagnolet.

Sainte-Marie des Batignolles Place du Docteur Félix Lobligeois, 75017. ✆ 01 46 27 57 67. www.ste-marie-batignolles.com. Metro: La Fourche or Rome.

Saint-Pierre de Montmartre 2 Rue du Mont Cenis, 75018. ✆ 01 46 06 57 63. www.sacre-coeur-montmartre.com. Opening times vary. Metro: Anvers (the *funiculaire*).

Un Zèbre à Montmartre 38 Rue Lepic, 75018. ✆ 01 42 23 97 80. Daily 11:30am–11:30pm. Metro: Abbesses.

Itinerary 2: Bobo Waterways, from the Canal Saint-Martin to the Canal de l'Ourcq

Where to Start	Place de la République, 75011. Metro: République (exit Blvd. Saint-Martin or Blvd. de Magenta).
The Time it Takes	1½ to 3 hours depending on how fast you walk or cycle and how much time you spend in shops and cafés and attractions.
Best Time to Go	Whenever takes your fancy. The atmosphere changes throughout the day—on a balmy summer evening the canal banks attract picnickers and a party atmosphere reigns.
Tip	If you don't want to spend on food, pack a picnic beforehand then choose your spot on the water's edge. The walk can also be done in reverse.

If you're not already with it, you need to learn the lingo: *Bobo* means 'Bohemian–Bourgeois', two little worlds that co'Ourcq (19th). Both scruffy and cosmopolitan, these waterways slice IIide in Paris's Canal Saint-Martin (10th) and Canal de I through some of the most happening parts of town, taking you past legacies of early-20th-century industrialised Paris—tree-lined quays, iron footbridges, old factories and warehouses that are relics of the days when Edith Piaf lifted the nation's spirits with *La Vie en Rose* (1946) and animals were brought to be slaughtered here on the city's north-eastern edge.

① Canal Saint-Martin

Walk up Rue du Faubourg du Temple past the ethnic grocers and discount stores and turn left onto Quai de Valmy, where Canal Saint-Martin, built between 1805 and 1825, resurfaces after dipping below ground on its course beginning at the Seine.

From the Quai de Valmy as far as Jaurès is the prettiest stretch of the canal, lined with chestnut trees and iron footbridges. If you saw the film *Amélie*, know that it was here that the heroine skimmed stones.

② Hôpital Saint-Louis

You have to cross the little bridge opposite Rue de Lancry to get to the Saint-Louis hospital on the Rue de la Grange Aux Belles. Founded by Henri IV in 1607 to house plague victims away from the city centre, it was built using the same brickwork as the Place des Vosges in the Marais—Henri even laid the first stone himself. You enter and exit past the chapel on Rue de la Grange Aux Belles, which is sometimes used for classical music concerts (© **01 42 49 49 49** for information). It was near this spot that the infamous Montfaucon gibbet—a multi-storey contraption used for hanging more than 50 victims at once—stood in 1233. Another gory (yet strangely appealing) point of interest is the hospital's **Musée des moulages dermatologiques**—a skin disease museum filled with gruesome wax mouldings (visits are by appointment only; see p. 206). Remember that this is still a working hospital so you shouldn't stray inside any of the buildings.

Over on Quai de Jemmapes have a gander (and perhaps a *café*) at the **Hôtel du Nord,** made famous in director Marcel Carné's 1938 film of the same name. I sang in a *dîner-cabaret* here for three years, but it has since changed owners and is now a mid-price *bobo* bistro par excellence (costing around 30€ for three courses).

ITINERARY 2: CANAL SAINT-MARTIN TO CANAL DE L'OURCQ

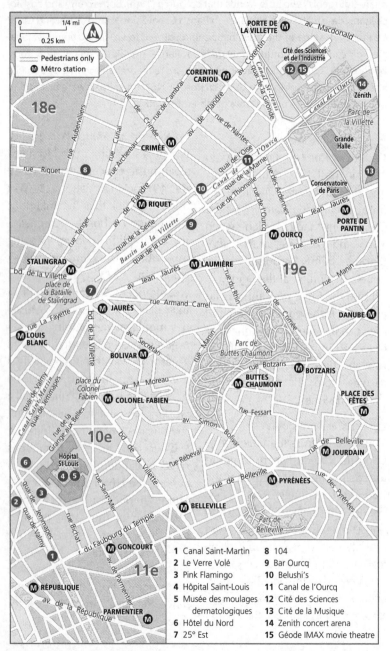

1 Canal Saint-Martin
2 Le Verre Volé
3 Pink Flamingo
4 Hôpital Saint-Louis
5 Musée des moulages dermatologiques
6 Hôtel du Nord
7 25° Est
8 104
9 Bar Ourcq
10 Belushi's
11 Canal de l'Ourcq
12 Cité des Sciences
13 Cité de la Musique
14 Zenith concert arena
15 Géode IMAX movie theatre

Costs

Free	
Relaxing walk, 'Kodak' moments	
Retro-futuristic park setting	0€
Dirt Cheap	
Transport, coffee, picnic	4€–8€
Beer or wine at Belushi's	2.60€
Drink and *pétanques* at Bar Ourcq	2.80€
Musée des moulages dermatologiques	4€ (2€ students)
Joinville market	as much as you want to spend
Add-ons for Spendthrifts	
Cité des Sciences/Géode IMAX	10€–17.50€ (free under-12s)
Pink Flamingo pizza	10€–15€
Wine from Le Verre Volé	8€
Food at 25 Est	9.50€–14€

Cross back over the canal onto Quai de Valmy and walk northwards.

3 Window shopping only, please! New boutiques seem to appear every time you walk along this stretch of canal. The best are Dupleks (N° 83. ✆ **01 42 06 15 08.** www.dupleks.fr), a womenswear shop with a conscience, selling unusual, feminine items made from environmentally friendly and Fair Trade materials; Artazart (also N° 83. ✆ **01 40 40 24 00.** www.artazart.com), a cutting-edge bookshop stocking glossy publications on fashion, art and design; and further up, girly designer offerings at Stella Cadente (N° 93. ✆ **01 42 09 27 00.** www.stella-cadente.com) and brightly coloured outfits and household items by Antoine & Lili (N° 95. ✆ **01 40 37 41 55.** www.antoineetlili.com). All are expensive but great spots for a bit of *lêche-vitrine* (literally, window-licking).

4 Bassin de la Villette
At the Jaurès station at the top of the Canal Saint-Martin, a quick stroll below the *métro aerien* (metro bridge) takes you to the circular Barrière de la Villette, one of the few remaining 18th-century toll houses designed by Nicolas Ledoux and part of the *Enceinte des Fermiers généraux* mentioned in Itinerary 1. The modernist fountains in front channel your view up the Canal de l'Ourcq, past the MK2 art-

house complex of two cinemas linked by a small boat. This wonderful part of town is a perfect example of urban renewal—ten years ago no one set foot here unless they had to. It's increasingly *bobo*, with bars, restaurants and picnic spots galore. Also worth the detour is the nearby **104** art centre (see p. 227) in the former city undertakers on Rue Curial; its resident artists are all rather cutting-edge.

5 Canal de l'Ourcq

Created in 1813 by Napoléon to provide drinking water and haulage, this stretch is dominated by the retro hue of 1960s and 70s tower blocks and the unusual 1885 hydraulic lifting bridge that separates it from the Bassin de la Villette. Fishermen are a regular sight too, and while I've never seen anyone catch anything other than a bloated rat, they assure me that pike-perches and carp are regulars.

If you're food shopping, it doesn't get any cheaper than the Marché de Joinville (place de Joinville, 75019. Thursday & Sunday 7:30am–2:30pm. Metro: Crimée) on the left after the bridge.

6 Quick Pick-me-ups

Maybe it's the gentle lapping of water that makes us hanker after a glass of wine? Or perhaps it's the cheap prices? Either way, there is something about the canals that are synonymous with relaxing, drink in hand. For such moments, these are my favourites:

- Cheap drinks (around 3€) make the **Bar Ourcq** popular with residents, especially on a hot day when *boules* can be hired at the bar for a game of *pétanque* on the sand in front of the door. Be daring and challenge someone to a game.

- **Belushi's,** the bar of trendy new youth hostel St Christopher's Inn, is possibly the cheapest in town (drinks cost 2.50€–3€). It's also good for striking up a chat with other guests, watching sport and, if you're a man, peeing into the giant female lips that make up Paris's funkiest urinals!

7 Parc de la Villette

The city's former abattoir district is now a vast retro-futurist park with spacious lawns and play areas for children. Onsite is also the excellent **Cité des Sciences** (p. 93) with its Cité des Enfants section for kids (p. 93), the **Cité de la Musique** music museum and concert hall (p. 209), the **Zenith concert arena** (www.le-zenith.com), where international bands play, and the **Geode IMAX movie theatre,** whose silver dome sparkles in the sunlight. If you've not unpacked your picnic yet, this is as fine a spot as anywhere.

⑧ Mealtimes

Eating opportunities jump out at you all along the canals. Most are pretty good, but the following are tried, tested and make the grade.

A For warm evenings when you're sans picnic but want to eat on the canal's edge, the **Pink Flamingo** can't be beat. This organic pizzeria (using 100% organic flour and organic toppings where possible) offers lots of unusual combinations (La Poulidor, with smoked duck, goat's cheese and apple or L'Almodovar, a paella pizza) and will even deliver your pizza to your chosen spot along the canal. You take a pink balloon (your beacon) and wait for the delivery cyclist to suss you out. Ask for some plastic cups to enjoy some reasonably priced, quality vino from **Le Verre Volé** (B) wine bar (and excellent restaurant) on the other side of the canal, which will open any bottle you buy but won't provide glasses.

C Très en vogue with money-saving bobos, **25 Est's** lunchtime menu offers a dish of the day or two or three courses for 8.50€, 11.80€ or 14.80€ respectively. Expect delights such as cucumber tartare, caramelised pork spare ribs with coriander rice, and raspberry and pistachio tart. There are no set menus in the evening; salads cost around 12€ and mains 15€. In summer the roof terrace becomes a suntrap and a beer-drinking parlour.

Special Events

● In early July the canals come alive with brocantes, outdoor concerts, street theatre and general merriment during the **Canal en Fête** free celebrations.

● In August the Parc de la Villette is transformed into a great outdoor cinema boasting Europe's biggest inflatable screen, for the **Cinéma en plein air** festival. Showings are a steal at 1€. Ave Corentin-Cariou, 75019. ℂ **01 40 03 75 75.** www.villette. com. Metro: Porte de la Villette or Porte de Pantin. See p. 23.

● Paris's urban beach project (Paris Plages) comes to the Canal de l'Ourcq and extends beyond towards Pantin, bringing fake palms, kayaking on the canal and family attractions from mid-July to mid-August. www.paris.fr.

Itinerary 2 Index

104   104 Rue d'Aubervilliers, 75019. © **01 53 35 50 00**. www.104.fr. Adm usually free but fee for some temporary exhibitions 3€–5€. Sun, Mon 11am–8pm; Tues–Sat 11am–11pm. Closed last 2wks Aug. Metro: Stalingrad, Crimée or Riquet.

25 Est   10 Place de la Bataille de Stalingrad, 75019. © **01 42 09 66 74**. www.25est.com. 11am–2am Tues–Sun.

Bar Ourcq   68 Quai de la Loire, 75019. © **01 42 40 12 26**. http://barourcq. free.fr/. Wed–Sat 3pm–midnight (until 2am Fri–Sat and eve of public holidays), Sun 3–10pm. Metro: Laumière.

Belushi's   159 Rue Crimée, 75019 (inside St Christopher's Inn). © **01 40 34 34 40**. www.belushis.com. Daily 7am–1am.

Cité de la Musique   221 Ave. Jean Jaurès, 75019. © **01 44 84 44 84**. www.cite-musique.fr. Metro: Porte de Pantin. See p. 209.

Cité des Sciences & Géode   30 Ave. Corentin-Cariou, 75019. © **01 40 05 70 00**. www.cite-sciences.fr. Tues–Sat 10am–6pm, Sun 10am–7pm. Metro: Porte de la Villette. See p. 93.

Hôpital Saint-Louis   1 Ave. Claude-Vellefaux, 75010. © **01 42 49 49 49**. www.chu-stlouis.fr. Metro: Colonel Fabien.

Hôtel du Nord   102 Quai de Jemmapes, 75010. © **01 40 40 78 78**. www. hoteldunord.org. Daily 9:30am–1:30am. Metro: Jacques Bonsergent or République.

Le Verre Volé   67 Rue de Lancry, 75010. © **01 48 03 17 34**. www.leverre vole.fr. Daily midday–2:30pm, 8–11pm. Metro: Jacques Bonsergent.

Musée des moulages dermatologiques   1 Ave. Claude-Vellefaux, 75010. © **01 42 49 99 15**. www.bium.univ-paris5.fr/sfhd. Adm: 4€, 2€ students. Metro: Colonel Fabien.

Pink Flamingo   67 Rue Bichat, 75010. © **01 42 02 31 70**. www.pink flamingopizza.com. Tues–Sat midday–3pm, 7:30–11pm; Sun 1–11pm. Metro: Goncourt or Jacques Bonsergent.

Mini-Tour: The Malls of Yesteryear

Start	Metro Quatre-Septembre, Passage Choiseul, 75002.
Finish	Passage Brady, Metro Strasbourg-St Denis, 75010.

For charm and tantric browsing, I love Paris's covered passageways (www.passagesetgaleries.org)—olde-worlde equivalents of modern shopping malls with a thousand times more intrigue and atmosphere. Despite recent investment, many of them still look rough around the edges, with a fetching shabby-chic style that adds to the authenticity of the experience.

Dating back to a time (the 18th and 19th centuries) when the streets were full of mud and other unnameable deposits (the ubiquitous *merde* isn't a modern phenomenon), the passages with their stone floors took away any worries about what your gaskins might land in. They were also the only streets in town to be fully lit with electric or gas lighting and to offer protection from the rain. Not surprisingly, they caught on, and during the Restoration period more than 24 of them graced Paris. Nowadays around 20 still exist to offer offbeat sightseeing opportunities. Here are some of my favourites.

2nd arrondissement

A Passage Choiseul Of all the passages, this looks the most like a street with a roof on it. It's also a busy lunchtime spot for local workers. Created in 1925, it's not particularly picturesque, but the eclectic range of shops within gives it a bazaar-like appeal—cheap prêt-à-porter shops sit beside vintage clothes boutiques, an art gallery, sandwich bars, Chinese takeaways and, at N° 82, a bookshop selling recent editions at a discount. 40 Rue des Petits-Champs and 23 Rue Saint-Augustin, 75002. Monday–Saturday 7am–9pm. Metro: Quatre-Septembre.

B Galerie Vivienne If it's good enough for Jean-Paul Gaultier (who has set up shop just at the entrance), this Second Empire passage is good enough for us! Possibly the most gracious of the galleries, with ochre paintwork, mythological themed mosaics and a bright glass roof, it is home to shops selling everything from antiques and books to wine and silk flowers, to an elegant tea-shop (A Priori Thé, N° 35) and even a chic turn-of-the-century eatery, the Brasserie Vivienne (Rue des Petits-Champs entrance. ✆ **01 49 27 00 50**). 4 Rue des Petits-Champs, 5 Rue de la Banque and 6 Rue Vivienne, 75002. www.galerie-vivienne.com. Daily 8:30am–8:30pm. Metro: Bourse.

C Passage des Panoramas Built in 1800, this was the first public area to have gas lighting (in 1817). The Passage is actually just one wing, forming a square with the rather dark and unappealing Galerie Feydeau, the Galerie des Variétés (with its theatre, stage door and restaurants) and the Galerie Saint-Marc, the charm of which has been slightly diminished by its mediocre eateries but that is still worth a look for its stampsellers and old printers, including Stern (N° 47), the oldest printers in town, dating from 1840. 11–13 Blvd. Montmartre and 151 Rue Montmartre, 75002. Daily 6am–midnight. Metro: Richelieu-Drouot or Grands Boulevards.

9th arrondissement

D Passage Jouffroy and Passage Verdeau Just across the boulevard from the Passage des Panoramas lie my favourite passages. Passage Jouffroy (built in 1847) is the most atmospheric of all. It looks like something out of a Sherlock Holmes novel and indeed there is something quite 'Holmesesque' about its history: it was known for its women of ill repute and its criminal activity as well as its restaurants and for being home to the waxwork Musée Grevin (see p. 94). Between the two parts of the passage, you'll also find the old-fashioned Hôtel Chopin, where Sherlock and Watson still wouldn't look out of place. Tacked onto Passage Jouffroy, Passage Verdeau is, if you like old relics, good for a rummage, with fabulous antique shops that sell everything from musical instruments to stamps, cameras, jewellery and furniture. Passage Jouffroy: 10–12 boulevard Montmartre and 9 Rue de la Grange-Batelière, 75009. Daily 7am–9:30pm. Metro: Grands Boulevards. Passage Verdeau: 6 Rue de la Grange-Batelière and 31 Bis Rue du Faubourg Montmartre, 75009. Monday–Friday 7.30am–9pm; Saturday–Sunday 7:30am–9:30pm. Metro: Grands Boulevards.

10th arrondissement

E Passage Brady Further east, off Rue du Faubourg Saint-Denis, Passage Brady is for multi-taskers: it's the only place in Paris where you can go for an inexpensive vindaloo (one side is lined with dirt-cheap if not first-rate curry houses), hire a giant chicken costume from one of several fancy-dress shops, and risk a cheap short-back-and-sides at one of the barbers. The *passage* was created in 1828 by a shopkeeper called Brady but cut in half in 1854 to let the Boulevard de Strasbourg through the middle. 33 Boulevard de Strasbourg and 46 Rue du Faubourg Saint-Denis, 75010. Daily 24/7. Metro: Saint-Denis or Château d'Eau.

Food-fix

You might have to queue behind old-faithfuls, students and tourists to get into the institution that is **Chartier**, famed for its authentic 19th-century décor and low-priced French cuisine, but it's well worth it. Eating à la carte rarely costs more than 15€, and the 16 waiters, who serve some 1,200 people each day, perform veritable choreographies between tables. 7 Rue du Faubourg Montmartre, 75009. ℂ **01 47 70 86 29.** www.gerard-joulie.com. Daily 11:30am–10pm. Metro: Grands Boulevards.

Itinerary 3: The Montmartre Virgin Tour

Where to Start	Place des Abbesses, 75018. Metro: Abbesses.
The Time it Takes	1½ to 3 hours depending on how fast your legs will carry you and how often you stop off.
Best Time to Go	For peace and quiet, early in the morning. To experience the hustle and bustle of Montmartre, early afternoon. Or make a night of it and head out before dinner.

No, Madonna hasn't just bought a pad in Montmartre (although plenty of French stars do live here). This Virgin tour is for those of us who have never really taken the time (or had the opportunity) to dip into Montmartre's splendiferous nooks and crannies. You'd be surprised at how many Parisians fall into that category. The area around the Sacré-Coeur (the part most associated with the name Montmartre) is probably the most tourist-clogged in the capital, and the thought of rubbing shoulders with ice-cream-dripping foreigners is too much for most Parisians to handle. They venture happily into the trendy Rues des Abbesses, Lepic, and Caulaincourt but break into panic-stricken sweats at the idea of any other part of it.

Yet the cobbled streets, corner cafés, arty boutiques, and apartments of the artists and writers who made the village famous (Matisse, Picasso, Dalí, Utrillo, Max Jacob, Apollinaire, and Braque, to name but a few) are magical places in which to lose your Montmartre cherry. Whilst sometimes touristy, they have become such an intrinsic part of our psyche that you really have to see them at least once.

Costs

Free	
Walking through the cobbled streets	
The panoramic views, the Sacré-Coeur	
Saint-Pierre de Montmartre	0€
Dirt Cheap	
Transport, coffee	3€–5€
Add-ons for Spendthrifts	
Lunch at La Gazelle	11.50€–14.50€
Lunch at Dan Bau	10€
Food at Le Saint Jean	9€–17€
Musée de Montmartre	4€–8€
Espace Dalí	6€–10€ (free under-7s)

① Place des Abbesses

As you ride up in the lift from Abbesses metro to the surface, think about the fact that over the centuries the *Butte* was mined for its gypsum (plaster of Paris is from here), with the result that it's now as hollow as a Swiss cheese. While measures have been taken to prevent it from caving in, you can never be 100% sure!

Emerge from the deepest metro in the city, at 35m below street level—with one of the two remaining Art Nouveau station entrances designed by Hector Guimard at the beginning of the 20th century. Another turn-of-the-century treasure awaits you opposite—the red-brick **Saint-Jean l'Evangéliste** church. While most locals enjoy it from the outside (erected in 1904, it was the first church built of reinforced concrete and has beautiful, slender pillars, and graceful modern arches), few venture in, yet it has an imposingly beautiful interior complete with Art Nouveau floral designs and stained-glass windows, inspired by 16th-century German paintings, that fuse in solemn elegance.

② Georges Seurat's Death Place

Leave the church and descend the stairs on your left. At the foot of Rue André Antoine, **No. 39** is the three-storey white house where neo-Impressionist painter Georges Seurat died suddenly from diphtheria in 1891, aged just 31. This house is where he painted *Le Chahut*, which depicts a lively dance from a Montmartre music hall (on display in the Kröller-Müller Museum in the Hoge Veluwe National Park in the Netherlands).

ITINERARY 3: THE MONTMARTRE VIRGIN TOUR

1 Saint-Jean l'Evangéliste church	**6** Moulin de la Galette	**11** Musée de Montmartre
2 No. 39 rue André Antoine	**7** Ciné 13	**12** La Bonne Franquette
3 Studio 28	**8** Avenue Junot	**13** Espace Dalí
4 Café des 2 Moulins	**9** Château des Brouillards	**14** Saint-Pierre de Montmartre
5 Moulin Rouge	**10** Place Dalida	**15** Basilique du Sacré-Coeur
		16 Dan Bau
		17 Le Saint Jean
		18 La Gazelle

🄷 Rue Tholozé

Go back up the stairs and walk left down Rue des Abbesses, where trendy designer clothes shops have begun to homogenise the street. You'll pass Rue Tholozé on your right, at the top of which you can see part of the adorable Blute-Fin windmill (see N° 7). Halfway up is **Studio 28,** the city's first proper art-house cinema, named after the year it opened. When it showed Luis Buñuel's *L'Age d'Or* in 1930, outraged locals ripped the screen from the wall. This is still a cool venue for arty flicks.

🄸 For *Amélie* Fans

Just past the Rue Tholozé, Rue des Abbesses branches off into Rue Lepic. It's a cliché, but if you're a fan of Jean-Pierre Jeunet's film *Amélie Poulain* (the quirky, 2001 international hit that saw Audrey Tautou and Mathieu Kassovitz gallivant around Montmartre falling in love), bear left and follow Rue Lepic south. On your right, the **Café des 2 Moulins** (on the corner with Rue Cauchois) is where Amélie worked as a waitress. The new owner nixed the

283

cigarette stand that was featured in the film to make more table space, but a 1950s feel still reigns, and if you're hungry, this is as good a spot as any to eat (lunch menu 14.90€). It also has a popular Happy Hour with drinks at 3.90€.

5 A Chocolate-box Treasure

Go down Rue Cauchois and turn right onto Rue Constance then immediately left into the Impasse Marie Blanche. The sumptuous 19th-century folly at the bottom of the road, the Maison de l'Escalopier, built in a heavy, Gothic style by the Comte de l'Escalopier, is proof that Montmartre holds architectural treasures most of us don't always know about (even veteran guide-book writers!). It's only open to the public in July, August, and during the Journées du Patrimoine (National Heritage days; p. 198); the rest of the year its wooden carvings, intricate window frames, and heavy panelling can be admired from the outside (unless you're lucky enough to catch a resident or someone from Viapresse, the media company snuggled into the lower west wing, who might show you round).

6 Vincent VanGogh's House

Carry on up Rue Constance, then turn right towards Rue des Abbesses before taking a sharp turn left up Rue Lepic. On your right, **No. 54** is where Vincent Van Gogh and his brother, Théo, lived from 1886 to 1888, on the third floor. Théo helped support Vincent, both financially and emotionally, throughout his life. The gardens and windmills of Montmartre inspired a number of Van Gogh paintings and he became friendly with the painters Toulouse-Lautrec, Gauguin, and Signac, brightening his palette under Signac's influence.

7 Windmills

Further along Rue Lepic are the last two windmills of Montmartre, the Blute-Fin, hidden at the top of a slope behind trees (with a friendly sign informing you that it's under electronic surveillance and is protected by radars and guard dogs) and the Moulin du Radet. The latter is now a restaurant confusingly called the **Moulin de la Galette**, after the famous *bal populaire* (dance hall) that was once formed by both windmills and immortalised by Toulouse-Lautrec, Van Gogh, Utrillo, and Renoir (who's version is in the Musée d'Orsay; p. 193).

Before the dance hall was created, it was the scene of a horrifying event during the 1814 Prussian invasion of Paris. The windmills belonged to flour millers, the Debray family. Three Debray brothers were killed defending their hill from the Prussians, while the fourth and his son hid in the Blute-Fin. When discovered, the father killed an enemy officer, and in retaliation the Prussians cut him into four pieces, attaching each piece to the sails of his windmill. His widow and son collected his remains and buried them in a tomb topped with a statue of a windmill, painted red to signify the bloodshed.

The surviving son turned the windmills into the Moulin de la Galette dance hall in memory of his family. Later, in 1889, the tomb of the red windmill inspired entrepreneurs Odler and Zidler to create the **Moulin Rouge** ('red windmill') cabaret, which celebrated its 150th birthday in 2009.

8 Ciné 13

Take a left on Rue Girardon. At the intersection with Avenue Junot is **Ciné 13,** a tiny art-house theatre owned by the film director Claude Lelouch and run by his daughter Salomé. It's a fine spot for eyeing-up local actors as the stage is often given over to emerging talents, especially during the annual *Mise-en-Capsules* festival, when a parade of 20min plays provides a whole evening of entertainment.

Next-door, on the right, is the gated entrance to a private compound where, to keep their names private, residents (several of whom are French stars) have given the names of famous artists as their aliases on the intercom, so that the panel of names reads like a *Who's Who* of French art, including Degas, Matisse, Utrillo, Toulouse-Lautrec, and Seurat.

9 The Man Who Walked Through Walls

On the northeast corner of the crossroads is Place Marcel Aymé, named after the writer who lived in the building here until his death in 1967. The surreal sculpture of a man emerging from the wall was inspired by Aymé's short story *Le Passe-Muraille* or 'The Man Who Could Walk Through Walls', about a petty bureaucrat who used his super-hero talent to make mischief. One night, after much hullabaloo, he got trapped inside a wall, where he has remained ever since. It's said that on certain restless nights, you can still hear his sad wails echoing through Montmartre. The story went on to become a movie and a hit musical.

10 Avenue Junot

Take a left and walk up **Avenue Junot,** a chic, curving street planted with linden trees and replete with artistic history and urban mythology.

- Maurice Utrillo lived in an artists' hamlet at **No. 11** from 1926 to 1937.

● **No. 13** was the studio of Francisque Poulbot, a designer whose distinctive illustrations of street urchins were so widely copied that they gave rise to the term *petits poulbots* (little street urchins). You can see several of his designs decorating the top of the building.

● **No. 15** is forever linked to the Dadaist movement thanks to the Romanian-born French poet Tristan Tzara, who lived there. Tzara and his contemporary André Breton collaborated briefly before Breton broke with the Dadaists to start the Surrealist movement.

● At **No. 23** is the romantic, leafy *Passage de la Sorcière* (Witch's Passage), where a giant rock sits at the top of a set of stairs leading down to Rue Lepic. The rock is known as *le rocher de la sorcière* or 'witch's rock' and used to be a natural fountain. Authorities are threatening to make the *passage* private (despite local uproar), so hurry to see it.

● At **No. 25** is the Villa Léandre, a cul-de-sac of houses so English (in brick, surrounded by creeping vines and tiny gardens) that some say they were magically transported here from London in 1926. Harry Potter eat your heart out!

11 Château des Brouillards

Back on Avenue Junot, walk down the hill, turn right at Rue Simon Dereure past the entrance to the pretty Square Suzanne Buisson, which used to be the grounds of a white country manor known as the **Château des Brouillards,** or Fog Castle. Built in 1772 for a lawyer in the Parisian parliament, this romantic dwelling most likely got its name from the mist that crept up from a nearby spring when the water met the cold morning air. The mansion fell into disrepair in the late 19th century and became a sort of shelter for homeless and impoverished artists around 1890. It's now a private home.

The stairs on the left lead you to the allée des Brouillards—a tranquil path with houses to die for, set back in large gardens, most of them at least partially shielded from prying eyes by tall fences. No. 6 was the studio and family home of Pierre-Auguste Renoir from 1890 to 1897. His son, Jean Renoir, born here in 1894, became a director of classic French films such as *Rules of the Game* and *The Grand Illusion*.

12 Place Dalida

This pilgrimage site for lovers of French pop is a square graced by a bust of one of Montmartre's best-loved residents, Yolanda

Gigliotti, aka Dalida. This Egyptian-born singer of Italian ancestry was one of France's biggest stars and is still a gay icon. Her personal life was less successful: Three of her ex-lovers killed themselves over two decades. After at least one previous attempt of her own, Dalida committed suicide in 1987. Her statue looks out on one of the most gorgeous views of Montmartre: A cobbled lane leading up a hill with the Sacré-Coeur in the background.

⑬ Touristy Montmartre

If you can't stand the heat, get out of the kitchen—but bear in mind that you might miss some gems. I recommend bracing the crowds and ticking off this list.

- Rue de l'Abreuvoir was a country lane used by horses and cattle on their way to the *abreuvoir* or watering trough. The Café de l'Abreuvoir, a former artists' hangout, was at No. 14. Impressionist painter Camille Pissarro rented No. 12 as a *pied-à-terre*. No. 4 belonged to Henry Lachouque, the noted historian of Napoléon, whose symbol was an eagle; and the café at No. 2, La Maison Rose, was made famous by Utrillo in one of his first successful paintings.

- Rue Cortot is home to the **Musée de Montmartre** (p. 216),

set inside a 17th-century building converted into artists' studios in 1875. Renoir rented a studio in the left wing in 1886 (where he put the finishing touches on the painting *Le Moulin de la Galette*), and in 1896 the artist Suzanne Valadon moved into the first floor with her painter son, Maurice Utrillo. At No. 6, composer Erik Satie (nicknamed 'Esoteric Satie' because of his enthusiasm for matters supernatural) lived in a tiny room he called his 'closet'.

- Turn left on Rue du Mont Cenis and left again down Rue Saint-Vincent to the Vignes de Montmartre, the only remaining vineyards in Paris (see Itinerary 1).

- On your right is Au Lapin Agile, the original Cabaret des Assassins. Legend has it that the cabaret got its name because a band of assassins broke in and killed the owner's son. It was renamed in 1880, after artist André Gill painted a picture of a rabbit in a bow tie. People began saying that it was the 'Lapin à Gill' (Gill's Rabbit). Picasso, Verlaine, Renoir, Utrillo, and Apollinaire were some of the young upstarts who used to show up for wine, women, and song.

- Up Rue des Saules, at the corner of Rue Saint-Rustique, is the restaurant **La Bonne Franquette,** another watering hole for the Impressionists as well as for the writer Emile Zola. Van Gogh painted its garden in 1886; the resulting painting, *La Guinguette,* is in the Musée d'Orsay (p. 193).

- If you haven't already done so, get your pointy elbows out and walk past the hoards to Rue Norvins and turn right on Rue Poulbot to reach the **Espace Dalí,** the only permanent Dalí collection in France and one worth a visit if you like his Surrealist art (also see p. 210).

- When you come out of the museum, turn left and walk to the Place du Calvaire for a panoramic view of northern Paris. Then turn left and brace yourself for Place du Tertre, the old village square, whose charm has disappeared behind layers of tourist tat. Walk tall to show the artists begging to relieve you of 20€ for a caricature that you're not a tourist, and head to the 12th-century **Saint-Pierre de Montmartre** (p. 269), the authentic focal point of the old village and the last remnant of a Benedictine abbey that held sway in Montmartre up until the Revolution.

14 Sacré-Coeur

Unmissable beside Saint-Pierre is the **Basilique du Sacré-Coeur**— as much a part of Paris's skyline as the Eiffel Tower. Of course you've seen it and you've probably been inside, but it's the sort of place worth coming back to, for the breathtaking views over the whole city.

Construction began in 1876, and the basilica was consecrated in 1919. It holds the distinction of being a self-whitening church, being made from a white stone that secretes calcium when it rains. The dome rises 78m, and its bell is one of the heaviest in the world, weighing in at 19 tons.

15 Mealtimes

- Theatregoers' fave **La Gazelle** brings a North African flavour to the *Butte* with its tasty couscous and tajines (from 11.50€). If there's a few of you, the boss's tender stuffed lamb is a pure delight. Lunch menus are excellent value at 14.50€ for three courses; in the evening expect to pay around 25€.

- The bamboo-clad **Dan Bau** (run by a young journalist from Hanoi) serves scrumptious Vietnamese food at low prices; the 10€ lunch menu is a hit with locals and tourists alike.

The signature dish is the Dan Bau salad, served on green papaya and banana leaves.

- For a quick chicken and chips or a croque-monsieur on the run, you can't go wrong at **Le Saint Jean,** the local cheapskates' HQ and a fine spot for people-watching.

Itinerary 3 Index

Café des 2 Moulins   15 Rue Lepic, 75018. ✆ **01 42 54 90 50.** Open daily 7am–2am.

Ciné 13   1 Ave. Junot, 75018. ✆ **01 42 54 15 12.** www.cine13-theatre. com. Open for shows most evenings and some matinées. Metro: Abbesses or Lamarck-Caulaincourt.

Dan Bau   18 Rue des Trois-Frères, 75018. ✆ **01 42 62 45 69.** Fri–Mon midday–2pm, 7–11pm; Tues–Thurs 7–11pm. Metro: Abbesses.

Espace Dalí   11 Rue Poulbot, 75018. ✆ **01 42 64 40 10.** www.daliparis. com. Adm: 10€, 6€ 8–26s, free under-8s, 7€ over-60s. Daily 10am–6pm. Metro: Anvers or Abbesses then *funiculaire*.

La Gazelle   15 Rue des Trois-Frères, 75018. ✆ **01 42 54 05 95.** Daily midday–5pm, 6:30pm–midnight (except Mon lunch). Metro: Abbesses or Anvers.

Le Saint Jean   23 Rue des Abbesses, 75018. ✆ **01 46 06 13 78.** Daily 8am–midnight. Metro: Abbesses.

Moulin de la Galette   83 Rue Lepic, 75018. ✆ **01 46 06 84 77.** www. lemoulindelagalette.eu. Daily midday–11pm. Metro: Abbesses.

Moulin Rouge   82 Boulevard de Clichy, 75018. ✆ **01 53 09 82 82.** www. moulinrouge.fr.

Sacré-Coeur   ✆ **01 53 41 89 00.** www.sacre-coeur-montmartre.com. Free admission to basilica. Open daily 9am–6pm. Metro: Anvers or Abbesses then *funiculaire*.

Saint-Pierre de Montmartre   2 Rue du Mont Cenis, 75018. ✆ **01 46 06 57 63.** www.sacre-coeur-montmartre.com. Opening times vary. Metro: Anvers then *funiculaire*.

Mini-Tour: Another Village & Some Cheap Pho Noodles

Start	Place d'Italie. Metro: Place d'Italie.
End	Porte d'Ivry, Porte de Choisy or Porte de Gentilly. Metro: Porte d'Ivry, Porte de Choisy or Tramway Porte de Gentilly.

Who'd have thought that a *place* named after the Mighty Boot (Place d'Italie) would actually act as a gateway between Olde France and the Orient? Yet the 13th *arrondissement*'s main roundabout has on one side of it the villagey **Butte aux Cailles**—a funky area of cobbled streets, hip (and dirt-cheap) bars, and old houses between boulevard Auguste-Blanqui and Rue Bobillot—and on the other, the city's main **Chinatown**, which runs along Avenue d'Ivry and Avenue de Choisy. Both are cheap and fun to walk around when you're looking for a change of scenery.

① Butte aux Cailles

Like Montmartre, the Butte aux Cailles was a village separate from Paris and, during the Paris *commune,* one of the first places to fight. The village still harbours a defiant, *soixante-huitard* streak, which has paid off in that it has prevented commercial developers from wiping it off the map in favour of high-rises like those in Chinatown below. The mock-*Alsacien* cottages built around a central garden on Rue Daviel were one of Paris's first public-housing schemes. And nearby, in Rue Bobillot, you can still swim in the Art Déco-style Piscine Butte-aux-Cailles (5 Place Paul Verlaine, 75013. ☏ **01 45 89 60 05**). The *Butte* is also a magnet for nighthawks, with relaxed bistros and low-priced bars concentrated on Rues Butte aux Cailles and des Cinq Diamants (p. 72).

② Mealtimes

Run as a cooperative, Chez Gladines is always overrun and won't accept reservations, packing in its punters like sardines at rustic wooden tables. You may as well make friends with your neighbours as you'll be spending the next hour and a half sharing elbow room, and tuck into hearty salads (8€–12.50€) covered in crunchy fried potatoes, lardons, poached egg, and lashings of vinaigrette. 30 Rue des Cinq Diamants, 75013. ☏ **01 45 80 70 10**. Daily midday–3pm, 7pm–midnight. Metro: Place d'Italie.

③ Chinatown Walk down Avenue de Choisy from Place d'Italie and everything below Rue Tolbiac suddenly takes on a Chinese or Vietnamese slant: *Pho* noodle bars sit among Chinese hairdressers, patisseries, and grocers as well as the great Tang brothers' supermarket, *Tang Frères* (48 Ave. d'Ivry, 75013. ℂ **01 45 70 80 00**), which sells a host of exotic wares and marinated meats. Even the McDonald's has been festooned with a Chinese-style interior, and there's a Buddhist temple within the car park of the tallest tower on Avenue d'Ivry (opposite Rue Frères d'Astier de la Vigerie)!

Concentrated on Avenues d'Ivry, and de Choisy, and most of the unsightly tower blocks in between, Paris's main Chinatown (there's another one in Belleville in the northeast) purveys a strange East meets West atmosphere, with the East parts winning most people over through the smell of spices wafting along the streets. One of the best times to visit is Chinese New Year, when dragon and lion dancing and martial arts demonstrations fill the streets (p. 17).

④ A food fix

Among the host of exotic eateries in Chinatown, **Pho 14** stands out for its *pho* noodle soups (from 6.50€) served with fresh herbs, soya shoots, and meatballs—in my opinion, some of the best in the 13th. Don't look at the shabby décor and don't expect smiley waiters—just piping hot Vietnamese dishes wolfed down by locals, and a lunchtime business crowd. 129 Ave. de Choisy, 75013. ℂ **01 45 83 61 15.** Daily 9am–11pm. Metro: Tolbiac.

⑤ While

you're there   Rue Vandrezanne (just off Place Paul Verlaine) leads you towards the Square des Peupliers, Rue des Peupliers and Rue Dieulafoy, where the little houses and their gardens create a country feel, and further south (towards Porte de Gentilly, along Rue Bobillot to Place de Rungis) the flower-named streets (Orchidées, Mimosas, and Iris) of the Cité Florale.

Mini-Tour: Heading Out of Town

Fortunately for culture-craving Parisians, the world doesn't end at the *Péripherique*. Whilst many of us wouldn't dream of living in the *Banlieue* (although with ever-increasing house prices, despite the credit crunch, the cheaper suburbs are attracting young families), destinations on the suburban RER lines are still high on the list of cheap escapes.

Paris's outer reaches were once the playground of royalty and aristocracy, and their opulent legacies can still be admired in a handful of chateaux and parks. The most famous are Versailles and Fontainebleau, but by the time you've paid the train fare and entry fees, neither can be classed as 'dirt cheap', so you won't find them listed here (if you really want to go, check out www.chateau versailles.fr and www.musee-chateau-fontainebleau.fr).

Instead, I recommend Rueil-Malmaison and Saint-Germain-en-Laye. Both can be reached on the RER in under an hour from central Paris and cost less than 15€ (for transport and one site; less if you skip the chateaux and just hang around the parks and forests). They are perfect picnic destinations too, so save a few extra euros by bringing your own nosh.

1 Rueil-Malmaison

This semi-rural retreat was favoured by both Cardinal Richelieu and Napoléon Bonaparte—two grand characters who liked leaving big legacies. No surprise, then, that this bourgeois suburb on the banks of the Seine (favoured by painters Manet and Renoir) has several grandiose buildings and an attractive chunk of old hunting forest for you to chill out in.

● The star of the show is the Château de Malmaison, Cardinal Richelieu's former home, acquired by Bonaparte upon his return from Egypt and used, between 1800 and 1802, as the seat of government. Today it contains the fascinating ★ **Musée National des Châteaux de Malmaison,** evoking the different periods in Bonaparte's life, especially his marriage to Joséphine, to whom he granted the house after their divorce.

● The Empress Joséphine's influence is especially felt in the palatial **Petite Malmaison** (once part of the estate), which was built to house her greenhouses—an architectural feat in the early 19th century. It was finally finished in 1805, greenhouses and all, and is still utterly gorgeous, arousing pangs of jealousy when you learn that it is privately owned (hence the fact that it's mostly only open in the summer).

● Also part of the old estate is the house and gardens of Père Joseph, Cardinal Richelieu's advisor, who died here in December 1638. After falling into disrepair, the house was converted into a cultural centre called L'Ermitage (the cultural activities on offer can be consulted on www.mairie-rueilmalmaison.fr). But the real attraction is the lush **Parc du Père Joseph**—9,000m2 of chestnut-tree-clad parkland (the house's former gardens), forming a perfect spot for a picnic and a hit with local families.

Costs

Free	
Fôret de Malmaison	0€
Musée d'Histoire Locale	0€
Maison et Parc du Père Joseph	0€
Dirt Cheap	
Transport	6€
Château de la Petite Malmaison	5€ (3€ under-18s, free under-12s)
Musée National des Châteaux de Malmaison	6€–8€ (under-18s and under-25s from EU free)

- If wilder greenery is your forte, head to the château's former **Fôret de Malmaison,** where walking routes and cycle paths are clearly marked. There are numerous opportunities for bird-watching and picnicking.

- History fans should pop into the town's red-brick Second Empire-style Mairie (a copy of the Mairie de Fontainebleau), which contains the free **Musée d'Histoire Locale.** A lot of history has played out within the boundaries of this small town, and this little museum retraces all the main events via helpful exhibits such as a 1,600-strong collection of figurines that represent Napoléon's Grande Armée.

Rueil-Malmaison Itinerary Index

Château de la Petite Malmaison 229 Bis Ave. Napoléon Bonaparte, 92500 Rueil-Malmaison. ✆ 01 47 32 02 02. www.chateaupetitemalmaison. com. Adm: 5€; 3€ 12–18s; free under-12s. July–October Sunday 3–6pm and Monday 11am–4pm (once a month rest of the year). RER: A to Grande Arche de la Défense then bus 258 to Le Parc.

Fôret de Malmaison Ave. de Versailles (parking Forestier). Note that the *route forestière* is closed on weekends and during school holidays but access is still possible on foot or by bike. www.mairie-rueilmalmaison.fr. RER: A to Rueil-Malmaison then bus 467 to Saint-Cucufa.

Parc du Père Joseph 34 Blvd. Richelieu, 92500 Rueil-Malmaison. Park October–March daily 9:30am–6pm; April–September daily 9:30am–8pm.

Costs

Free	
Fôret Domaniale de Saint-Germain-en-Laye	0€

Dirt Cheap	
Transport	6€
Musée des Antiquités Nationales	3€–4.50€

Musée d'Histoire Locale `FREE` Ancienne Mairie de Rueil, Place du 11 Novembre 1918, 92500 Rueil-Malmaison. ✆ **01 47 32 66 50.** Monday–Saturday 2:30–6pm.

Musée National des Châteaux de Malmaison   Ave. du Château de Malmaison, 92500 Rueil-Malmaison. ✆ **01 41 29 05 55.** www.chateau-malmaison.fr. Adm: 6€; 4.50€ 18–25s from outside EU; free under-25s from EU. Wednesday–Monday 10am–12.30pm, 1:30–5:15pm (until 5:45pm weekends October–March and 6:15pm weekends April–September). RER: A to Grande Arche de la Défense then bus 258 to Le Château.

★ **2 Saint-Germain-en-Laye**   As you take the RER A beyond La Défense, you will see Saint-Germain-en-Laye's outline appear on a rocky crag above rows of cream-coloured houses. Once you get there, you'll find a smart suburb bursting with royal history and views to die for (from the château gardens) over the Yvelines and onto the futuristic skyline of La Défense beyond. The town itself is like a miniature Neuilly-sur-Seine (i.e. chic as hell) dripping in expensive shops; avoid them like the plague and head for its imposing castle, with its cool prehistory museum, landscaped gardens, and vast forest.

● As you leave the RER, you can't miss the Château de Saint-Germain-en-Laye with its heavy, almost austere elegance. Henri II was born here in 1518. Scotland's very own Mary Queen of Scots also spent time here, as did James II and Louis XIV, who was also born in the castle and left for Versailles in 1682. Today it houses the excellent **Musée des Antiquités Nationales** tracing France's archaeological heritage, with displays including statue-menhirs, female fertility figures, Bronze Age jewellery, and huge antlers from prehistoric deer. The bookshop has a fantastic range of coffee-table books on all subjects, not just French prehistory—look out for the spooky France section, which includes literature on the château's links with the infamous *Affaire des Poisons*—a series of scandalous poisonings under Louis XVI, which some say were linked to devil worship.

● The **Fôret Domaniale de Saint-Germain-en-Laye** is the second biggest forest in the Ile de France region after Rambouillet, and for hyperactives looking to burn off some energy it makes for a fabulous day out, with several tracks to follow. One of the best for those moving on foot or by bike is the *sentier des Oratoires*, marked by blue crosses. It's 18km long and takes 5–6 hours, taking you past intriguing old statue-filled oratories hidden in the forest (leave from the swimming-pool car park at L'Etoile des Neuf Routes). Another good route for nature-lovers is the *sentier de découverte du Val*, a 13-point walk that lets you discover the forest flora through a series of panels.

Saint-Germain-en-Laye Itinerary Index

Fôret Domaniale   Call tourist office for more information.

Maison Claude Debussy   38 Rue au Pain, 78105 Saint-Germain-en-Laye. © 01 34 51 05 12. www.ot-saintgermainenlaye.fr.

Musée des Antiquités Nationales   Château de Saint-Germain, Place Charles de Gaulle, 78105 Saint-Germain-en-Laye. © 01 39 10 13 00. www.musee-antiquitesnationales.fr. Admission 3€–4.50€; free 1st Sunday of the month. Wednesday–Monday 10am–5:15pm. RER: A to Saint-Germain-en-Laye.

Tourists at Trocadero consulting a map of Paris.

PARIS
BASICS

1 Information Centres

If you're not a fully fledged Parisian, France's official tourist board, the **Maison de la France**, has an excellent website (www.franceguide.com) with online services that include a travel shop with booking for accommodation and events. Each country also has its own Maison de la France headquarters open to the public:

UK Lincoln House, 300 High Holborn, WC1V 7JH, London. ✆ **090 68 244 123** (60p/min).

USA 825 Third Avenue, 29th floor (entrance on 50th S), NY 100 22. ✆ **01 514 288-1904**.

France 23 Place de Catalogne, 75014. ✆ **01 42 96 70 00**.
Paris runs seven permanent information centres with free maps and brochures as well as discount coupons for touristy attractions. ✆ **08 92 68 30 00** (0.34€/min).

Current Events

The city does a decent job of providing us with info about what's going on around town.

Websites for tourism and events in Paris and in the Ile de France (its suburbs) are www.parisinfo.com (L'Office de Tourisme de Paris) and www. nouveau-paris-ile-de-france.fr (Paris—Ile de France's regional tourist board). The Mairie de Paris (town hall) also gives a good list of goings-on at www. paris.fr.

Anvers   72 Blvd. Rochechouart, 75018. Daily 10am–6pm (except 25th Dec, 1st Jan, and 1st May). Metro: Anvers.

Gare de l'Est Place du 11 Novembre 1918, 75010 (TGV arrivals, exit Cour d'Alsace). Mon–Sat 7am–8pm (except 25th Dec, 1st Jan, and 1st May). Metro: Gare de l'Est.

Gare de Lyon   20 Blvd. Diderot, 75012.   Mon–Sat   8am–6pm. Metro/RER: Gare de Lyon.

Gare du Nord 18 Rue de Dunkerque, 75010. Daily 8am–6pm (except 25th Dec, 1st Jan, and 1st May). Metro/RER: Gare du Nord.

Montmartre   21 Place du Tertre, 75018. Daily 10am–7pm. Metro: Abbesses or Anvers (then *funiculaire*).

Pyramides   25 Rue des Pyramides, 75001. 1st Nov–31st May: Mon–Sat 10am–7pm; Sun and public hols 11am–7pm. 1st Jun–31st Oct: Daily 9am–7pm. Metro: Pyramides. RER: Auber.

Porte de Versailles   1 Place de la Porte de Versailles, 75015. 11am–7pm during Trade Fairs. Metro: Porte de Versailles.

Other peak-season (May–Sept) offices are found at Bastille, Hôtel de Ville, Notre Dame, Champs-Elysées—Clemenceau, and Trocadéro.

2 Transportation

BY PLANE

Paris is an international hub with both low-cost and major airlines flying to its two main airports: **Aéroport Roissy CDG** (Charles de Gaulle) 23km north of the city (℗ **39 50** within France or ℗ **+33 1 70 36 39 50** from abroad. www.aeroportsdeparis.fr) and the **Aéroport d'Orly**, 14km to the south (℗ **39 50** within France or ℗ **+33 1 70 36 39 50** from abroad. www.aeroportsdeparis.fr). A third airport, the **Aéroport de Beauvais** (℗ **08 92 68 20 66.** www.aeroportbeauvais.com), a 1hr

15min drive (80km) north of Paris, is used by the low-cost airlines Ryanair and Blue Islands.

GETTING TO & FROM THE AIRPORTS (CHEAPLY)

Roissy CDG Air France runs coaches between central Paris and Roissy CDG, but you pay for the luxury (around 14€ one-way. www. airfrance.fr). Taking the **RER B** to CDG airport can be cumbersome if you have a lot of luggage, but it's fast (usually under 45min), is usually a smooth ride and costs 8.50€ one-way. It connects the terminals with a free shuttle bus (*navette*) and new monorail. There are two RER terminals: CDG T1 for Terminals 1 and 3 (you can walk to T3) and CDG T2 for terminals 2A through to 2G. ✆ **32 46** (0.34€/min), www. ratp.fr.

Another cheap option is to take the **Roissy Bus**, a shuttle that runs from Opéra (corner of Rue Scribe and Rue Auber) every 15–20min from 6am to 11pm to Roissy CDG (all 3 terminals). The cost for the 50min ride is 9.10€. ✆ **32 46** (0.34€/min), www.ratp.fr.

Orly The **RER B** also links the centre to Orly's two terminals: Orly Sud (south) for international flights and Orly Ouest (west) for domestic flights. Again, this is one of the fastest and cheapest ways to get to the airport. The 25min ride costs 9.80€. Once there, the Orly Val monorail takes you from RER Anthony to your required terminal. ✆ **32 46** (0.34€/min), www.ratp.fr.

But by far the cheapest option for ORLY is the **Orlybus**, a shuttle bus that runs from Denfert-Rochereau every 15–20min (roughly 5:30am–11pm) and costs just 6.40€ for the 25min ride. ✆ **32 46** (0.34€/min), www.ratp.fr.

Beauvais Beauvais runs a shuttle service from Porte Maillot (75017. Metro: Porte Maillot, at the bus park on Blvd. Pershing near the James Joyce pub). Show up at least 3¼ hours before your flight. A one-way ticket costs 13€ and the journey takes just over an hour. ✆ **08 92 68 20 64.** www.paris-beauvais.fr. www.aeroportbeauvais.com.

BY CAR

Driving to Paris from the UK inevitably means getting a ferry or the Eurotunnel. Prices vary for both means, but as a general rule the best deals are found online, and off-season and mid-week travel is always cheaper.

FERRIES

Ferry prices vary widely according to whether you travel by day or night, the standard of accommodation you choose (it's obligatory on overnight sailings), the number of passengers, the size of your car, and more.

P&O Ferries   (UK ℂ **08716 645 645**/France ℂ **08 25 12 01 56.** www.poferries.com) sail from Dover to Calais in just over an hour.

Seafrance   (UK ℂ **0871 423 7119**/France ℂ **03 21 17 70 33.** www. seafrance.com) also offers reasonable prices for the hour-long sail.

Brittany Ferries   (UK ℂ **0871 244 0744**/France ℂ **08 25 82 88 28.** www.brittany-ferries.co.uk) sail from Poole to Cherbourg and from Portsmouth to Caen, Cherbourg, and Saint-Malo and may be more convenient for holidaymakers from the southwest of England. Bear in mind that these are mostly overnight crossings. The distances you'll need to drive to Paris are: 360km from Cherbourg, 400km from Saint-Malo, and 240km from Caen.

It is often possible to save money by booking ferries (and Eurotunnel) through a 'one-stop-shop' site such as www.ferrysavers.co.uk, which also shows price comparisons between the different carriers.

EUROTUNNEL

This shuttle train taking cars through the Channel Tunnel (UK ℂ **08705 353535**/France ℂ **08 10 63 03 04.** www.eurotunnel.com) between Folkestone and Calais is the least painful crossing option, since the journey takes just 35min and you don't even need to get out of your car.

The major *autoroutes* into Paris are the A1 from the north (United Kingdom and Benelux); A13 from Rouen, Normandy, and northwest France; A10 from Bordeaux, the Pyrénées, France's southwest, and Spain; A6 from Lyon, the French Alps, the Riviera, and Italy; and A4 from Metz, Nancy, and Strasbourg in eastern France.

BY TRAIN

Eurostar   Eurostar fares vary according to how far in advance you book and the degree of flexibility you require regarding exchanges or refunds. From London (St Pancras International), Ashford International, and Ebbsfleet International in Kent (where there's extra parking space) to Paris they can be as low as £109 for a return ticket in standard class. If you're travelling from the French side towards the UK, prices are even lower (sometimes just 77€ return). (Eurostar UK ✆ **0870 530 0003**/France ✆ **08 92 35 35 39.** www.eurostar.com).

SNCF   If you're travelling by train from elsewhere in France, Paris has six major train stations:

Gare d'Austerlitz, 55 Quai d'Austerlitz, 75013 (the southwest, with trains from the Loire Valley, the Bordeaux region, and the Pyrénées).

Gare de Bercy, 48 Blvd. de Bercy, 75012 (overspill from the Gare de Lyon below, plus passenger and 'auto-trains' (car carrying trains) from Italy).

Gare de l'Est, Place du 11 Novembre 1918, 75010 (the east, with trains from Strasbourg, Nancy, Reims, and beyond—Zurich, Basel, Luxembourg and Austria).

Gare de Lyon, 20 Blvd. Diderot, 75012 (the southeast, with trains from the Côte d'Azur and Provence, Geneva, Lausanne, and Italy).

Gare Montparnasse, 17 Blvd. Vaugirard, 75015 (the west, with trains from Nantes and Brittany).

Gare du Nord, 18 Rue de Dunkerque, 75010 (the north, with trains from Holland, Denmark, and Germany, as well as Eurostar trains from the UK and Thalys trains from Belgium).

Gare Saint-Lazare, 13 Rue d'Amsterdam, 75008 (the northwest, with trains from Normandy).

For general train information and to make reservations, call ✆ **36 35** (special number).

GETTING AROUND TOWN

The RATP (Paris transport provider) puts the prices up a little every year but generally speaking (and compared with other capitals), getting around town won't break the bank.

METRO, RER & BUS

Getting the best deal on the metro, bus and RER (underground suburban train lines) all depends on how you plan to use the network. Tickets can be used on both the underground system (including RER) and buses, and the city is split into price zones: 1–2 is the centre and therefore the cheapest, 5 is the airports and Disneyland Paris.

If you're into pedal power or live right in the centre, the chances are you'll use public transport sporadically, in which case a 11.60€ pack of 10 tickets will probably suffice for a week. Single tickets cost 1.60€ for the metro and 1.70€ on the bus.

If you're a resident who rides the metro a lot, the **Pass Navigo** (a digitalised version of the old Carte Orange; www.navigo.fr) will be up your alley. You'll need ID, a passport photo, and a Parisian address in order to enrol. Paperwork can be filled in at Pass Navigo spots around the city, but a handy address is: Les Halles, Le Club RATP, Salle d'échanges, exit Place Carré, 75001. Mon–Sat 7am–6.30pm. Metro: Les Halles. Prices range from 56.60€/month for zones 1–2 to 123.60€/ month for zones 1–5.

For visitors, **Paris Visite** pass (© **32 46.** www.parisvisite.com; available from all RATP desks in the metro and from tourist offices) may be worthwhile. You get unlimited rides for 1, 2, 3 or 5 days for access to zones 1 to 3, which includes central Paris and its nearby suburbs, or zones 1 to 6, which includes Disneyland (zone 5), Versailles (zone 4) and the CDG (zone 5) and Orly (zone 4) airports. It is valid only from the first time you use it so you can buy it in advance. Remember to fill in your name as well as the series number on the card and the date of its first use. Prices: from 8.80€ for 1 day to 48.40€ for 5 days.

Another discount pass is **Carte Mobilis**, which allows unlimited travel on bus, subway, and RER lines for one day for 5.90€ to 16.70€, depending on the zone. Ask for it at any metro station (you'll need a passport photo).

BY BIKE

For information on where to hire a bike or how to use Paris's self-service bike system Vélib, see chapter 5. Bear in mind that your Pass Navigo can be charged with credit for Vélibs by applying online; it takes up to three weeks to come through.

3 Free & Dirt Cheap Resources

Disability General information can be found on the **Secretaire d'Etat aux Personnes Handicapées** website: www.handicap.gouv.fr (© **08 20 03 33 33**). The **Association des Paralysées de France** (13 Place Rungis, 75013. © **01 53 80 92 98.** www.apf.asso.fr. Metro: Place d'Italie) publishes a cultural guide to Paris for the disabled; and the **Fédération APAJH** (185 Bureaux de la Colline, 92213 Saint-Cloud. © **01 55 39 56 00.** www.apajh.org. Metro: Marcel Sembat) offers advice for disabled people living in France.

Embassies

British Consulate   18 bis Rue d'Anjou, 75008. 🕾 **01 44 51 31 02.** http://ukinfrance.fco.gov.uk. Metro: Concorde or Madeleine.

US Embassy in France   2 av Gabriel, 75008. 🕾 **01 43 12 22 22.** http://france.usembassy.gov. Metro: Concorde.

Embassy of Canada   35 av Montaigne, 75008. 🕾 **01 44 43 29 00.** www.international.gc.ca. Metro: Franklin D. Roosevelt or Alma—Marceau.

Embassy of Australia   4 Rue Jean Rey, 75015. 🕾 **01 40 59 33 00.** www.france.embassy.gov.au. Metro: Bir-Hakeim.

Embassy of New Zealand   7 ter Rue Léonard de Vinci, 75016. 🕾 **01 45 01 43 43.** www.nzembassy.com. Metro: Victor Hugo.

Emergencies

Ambulance   (🕾 **15**) You will be expected to pay for the ambulance service (if you're being admitted or discharged from hospital—emergencies are free) and claim reimbursement from your insurer, so adequate health or travel insurance is essential.

Fire Brigade   (🕾 **18**).

Police   (🕾 **17**; 🕾 **112** from a mobile).

GDF Gas Leaks   (🕾 **08 10 80 08 01.** www.gazdefrance.fr).

EDF Electricity   (🕾 **08 10 33 39** + the number of the *arrondissement*: **01 20**).

SOS Help   (🕾 **01 46 21 46 46**, an English-speaking helpline. www.soshelpline.org).

Centre Anti-Poison   (🕾 **01 40 05 48 48.** www.centres-antipoison.net).

Gay & Lesbian resources

The **Centre Gai & Lesbien** (63 Rue Beaubourg, 75003. 🕾 **01 43 57 21 47.** www.cglparis.org. Metro: Arts et Métiers) in the Marais provides a wealth of info on gay rights, biomedical research, and HIV treatment and hosts regular support-group meetings. The **Inter LG BT** (c/o Maisons des Associations du 3ème, Boîte 8, 5 Rue Perrée, 75003. 🕾 **01 72 70 39 22.** www.inter-lgbt.org) is the meeting-place for more than 50 gay and lesbian associations and the brainchild behind the annual Gay Pride march (p. 21).

Good places to look for events are the magazines **Têtu** (www.tetu.com) and **Préf** (www.prefmag.com), which report of happenings in gay life and include some sections in English. You can also pick up several

WiFi Wave: Wireless Access

I'm always amazed at how few cybercafés there are in Paris. **Milk** tends to be the most reliable, with a café, **Les Grands Moulins** (41 Quai Levassor, 75013. Metro: Bibliothèque) open 24/7. WiFi, on the other hand, is a little too rife. Over 400 free points across the city fry our brains in public parks and outside monuments (www.paris.fr lists the spots).

Most cafés also provide free access nowadays—see www.cafes-wifi.com for a list—and so do many hotels.

free bi-monthly mags in gay bookshops, bars and clubs; the most useful are **2 X-Paris** (www.2xparis.fr) for boys and **Barbi(e)turix** (www.myspace.com/barbieturix) for girls.

Two excellent websites are www.paris-gay.com and www.gayvox.com.

Libraries Every *arrondissement* has its own free public library. To get a library card you'll need proof of address in Paris and ID. For a full list of general and specialised libraries visit www.paris.fr.

Postal Service The main *Poste* at 52 Rue du Louvre, 75001 (Metro: Louvre—Rivoli) is open 24/7.

Telephone Services The main cellphone providers in France are **SFR** (www.sfr.fr), **Bouygues** (www.ideo.bouyguestelecom.fr) and **Orange** (www.orange.fr); and subscription (*abonnement*) will usually entitle you to a free mobile if you sign up for at least a year. As each company tries to out-do the other, special offers are a regular occurrence; as a general rule, however, expect to pay a hefty 35€ for two hours of calls per month—the French get stung with some of the highest prices in Europe.

INDEX